TIGER

The Ultimate Guide

TIGER
The Ultimate Guide

Valmik Thapar

CDS Books

in association with

Two Brothers Press

Published by CDS Books in association with Two Brothers Press

Orders, inquiries, and correspondence should be addressed to:
CDS Books
425 Madison Avenue
New York, NY 10017
Tel: (212) 223-2969   Fax: (212) 223-1504
www.cdsbooks.com

Printed in the United States of America on acid-free paper

First edition, June 2004

10 9 8 7 6 5 4 3 2 1

ISBN 1-59315-024-5

Book designed by Jeremy Eberts

Contents

INTRODUCTION   THE TAIL OF THE TIGER   ix

CHAPTER ONE   THE ORIGINS OF THE TIGER   1
Why On the Origin of Species *Barely Mentions Tigers* by Ruth Padel   10
How Many Tiger Subspecies? by Andrew Kitchener   18

CHAPTER TWO   THE ANATOMY OF A SUPREME HUNTER   23
Listening to the Tiger by Edward J. Walsh   34

CHAPTER THREE   THE LIFE OF THE TIGER   41
Territorial Changeover: A Mystery by Raghu S. Chundawat   46
Orphans and Tiger Territories by Fateh Singh Rathore   79
The Noble Tiger by Billy Arjan Singh   80
Tigers of the Dry Forest by Raghu S. Chundawat and Joanna Van Gruisen   85
Living on the Edge by Dale Miquelle   88
Mysterious Tigers of the Sundarbans by M. Monirul H. Khan   94
The Magic of the Tiger by John Goodrich   108
Counting Tigers in the Wild by K. Ullas Karanth   114
Sloth Bear, Crocodile, and Tiger Conflict by Fateh Singh Rathore   142
Tigers and Leopards by K. Ullas Karanth   144

CHAPTER FOUR   THE CULT OF THE TIGER   151
In Times Past by Romila Thapar   153

CHAPTER FIVE   TIGER AND MAN   169
The Tiger in the Ancient World by Paola Manfredi   170
Filming Tigers by Mike Birkhead   208

CHAPTER SIX   THE TIGER IN ART   217
The Tiger in Ancient Mosaics by Paola Manfredi   219
The Tiger in Miniature Painting by Archana Verma   229
The Tiger As Inspiration by Rose Corcoran   248

CHAPTER SEVEN   THE TIGER IN WESTERN LITERATURE   261

Emblem, Prisoner, Fiction by Ruth Padel   261

CHAPTER EIGHT   THE FUTURE OF THE TIGER   273

Massacre by Geoffrey C. Ward   284

Vladimir by Dale Miquelle   292

Poaching and the Illegal Trade in Tiger Parts by Belinda Wright   301

Tackling the Tiger Takers and Traders by John M. Sellar   304

The Future of the Tiger by George B. Schaller   312

Acknowledgments   317

Notes   319

Bibliography   321

About the Author   329

Contributors   330

Conservation Organizations Focused on Protecting Wild Tigers   332

Illustration Credits   333

Index   336

for Sanjna and Hamir

The Tail of the Tiger

One could say that the tiger lives in my bloodstream. Tigers h[...] since I first saw one at the age of eight. I was sitting on top of an [...] grasslands of one of India's first national parks, Corbett National Park, named after the legendary hunter of man-eating tigers, Jim Corbett. Suddenly, the grass in front of the elephant parted, and a roaring tigress with her two six-month-old cubs rushed past. The sight stunned me.

By the time I was twenty-four, I was following them in a tiny northern Indian forest called Ranthambhore, in the state of Rajasthan. For ten to twenty days each month, I tracked tigers in order to understand every detail of their lives. I also photographed them and sometimes filmed them. From dawn to dusk, I followed the tail of the tiger, though the first years were tough. Tigers were evasive and difficult to observe. My life changed over that time, and I have spent nearly thirty years absorbing every nuance of the tiger's life, from its natural history to its cultural history. The tiger commands a deep involvement from those who pursue it.

For the last thirteen years, I have been fighting to ensure the survival of the tiger by forcing government policy to adapt to the tigers' needs and by networking both nationally and internationally in the interest of the tiger so that more and more people engage in the battle to save it. I have served on the National Board for Wildlife and the steering committee of Project Tiger for nearly a decade. At the moment, I serve on the Central Empowered Committee, which has been charged by the Supreme Court of India with looking at all issues that concern the forests of India. While doing all this, I was able to create Tiger Link, a way of bringing together nongovernmental organizations and individuals from around the world. Over the past thirteen years I have written ten books on various issues relating to the tiger. This book—addressing all the different facets of the tiger—collects a great breadth of information in one volume.

I have in the last decade presented or been part of more than twelve films, primarily in association with Mike Birkhead. My relation with Mike started when the tigers in India were in a severe crisis and both poaching and habitat loss were devastating their homes. Mike put together a film called *Tiger Crisis*, and I played a role in presenting part of it. Since then, we haven't looked back, continuing our efforts through books and films to increase the world's awareness of the tiger, its life, and its plight.

This book was born out of the passion of people. Film director Jean-Jacques Annaud has always wanted to make a film involving the tiger. One of his friends and financiers was an old family friend of mine, Jérôme Seydoux. Through him, a circle was completed. Jean-Jacques had read several of my books, and he contacted me in 1998 with the aim of gaining an understanding of the behavior of wild tigers. We talked from different continents until eventually he visited me in Ranthambhore for a week to observe two brother tigers in the wild. His feature film *Two Brothers* came to fruition, and with it there was a request for Mike Birkhead and I to make a related documentary film on tigers. When I met producer Jake Eberts in December 2002, I suggested that we add a book to the project. Jake is a deeply committed man, and he immediately agreed to this. And subsequently, I was with Jake when he saw his first wild tiger! So within months, a feature film, a documentary, and a book all raced to completion. I focused on the book, Mike Birkhead on the documentary film, and we worked as a team to celebrate the tiger as never before. We have put everything we could into the creation of this book. For me, it is a dream come true, made possible by the total commitment of men like Jean-Jacques Annaud, Jake Eberts, and Jérôme Seydoux.

A research budget made it possible for us to explore and discover new insights into the natural and cultural history of the tiger, whether in ancient Rome, India, or Siberia. We also approached a broad cross-section of experts—zoologists, historians, anthropologists, writers, artists—to contribute short pieces outlining their research, their encounters, and the myriad ways in which the tiger has become their passion.

It is our hope that this book will engage people with the tiger and increase their awareness and appreciation of this magnificent animal. In this way, we can continue to strive together to ensure its survival.

VALMIK THAPAR
New Delhi
March 2004

Do not cut down the forest with its tigers and do not banish the tigers from the forest.
The tiger perishes without the forest, and the forest perishes without its tigers. Therefore
the tiger should stand guard over the forest and the forest should protect all its tigers.

From the *Mahabharata*, Udyogaparvan, 29, 47–48.
Composed circa 400 B.C.E.

Genus *Panthera*

Tiger *(Panthera tigris)*

Lion *(Panthera leo)*

Leopard *(Panthera pardus)*

Jaguar *(Panthera onca)*

CHAPTER 1

The Origins of the Tiger

No single animal has influenced art, literature, legend, religious cults, attitudes and ideas more than the tiger. His image of power and malevolence, magnificence and nobility is second to none. His presence has always fascinated man.... Before the advent of Western man with his gun, the tiger had few natural enemies and was free to roam in huge numbers from the Hindu Kush to Siberia, from the Mediterranean Sea to the Pacific Ocean.
—from *The Tiger: Symbol of Freedom* by Nicholas Courtney

Zoologists and other animal experts call the majestic striped big cat commonly known as the tiger, *Panthera tigris. Panthera* is the name given to the genus (group) of the four big cats in the world that have the ability to roar with spine-chilling effect: the tiger, lion, leopard, and jaguar, although technically tigers do not roar in the same way lions and leopards do. The snow leopard has sometimes been classed as *Panthera*, although nowadays it is placed in its own genus, *Uncia*, and is believed to have diverged from *Pan*... ...years ago. Roaring is made p... ...f thickened vocal folds just be... ...e larynx. Snow leopards have ... ...folds and are thus not qui... ...e smaller cats, which can only ... ...arrow vocal folds. *Tigris*—the species name that differenti... ...ther members of the genus, *Panthera leo* (lion), *Panthera p*... ...*era onca* (jaguar)—is classical Greek for "arrow," from whicl... ...st-flowing river Tigris and the speedy tiger get their names.

Snow leopard
(*Uncia uncia*)

THE TIGER FIFTY MILLION YEARS AGO

The origins of the tiger trace back some fifty million years, long before anything recognizable as today's big cats existed. Fossils provide most of the evidence scientists and researchers have used to piece together our understanding of the emergence of the tiger. Because fossils are created under very specific conditions—requiring a combination of chance, time, and place that ensures that the body does not decompose completely—they are relatively scarce. Rapid burial—in volcanic lava, for example—is one of the best means of ensuring preservation. In this circumstance, fleshy tissue quickly decays, but bones may become saturated by groundwaters and gradually replaced by dissolved minerals from the rocks and sediments above; the bones quite literally turn to stone.

Miacids are an extinct group of carnivores that gave rise to dogs, bears, skunks, mongooses, cats, and hyenas.

The age of a fossil can be determined largely by looking at the layer of rock in which the fossil is found, since deposits accumulate in layers on top of one another, the top being the most recent. Radioactive carbon dating can provide more precise information, but it only works for fossils no older than forty thousand years, as beyond that time the results are unreliable. A variety of other dating techniques yield more or less certain information about when a fossil's original body was wandering the planet.

The oldest tiger ancestors were mammals called miacids, the first true carnivores, which crept around in the treetops. They were not spectacular to look at, just small, long tree-climbers, a bit like pine martens today. Miacids appeared fifty million years ago, a mere fifteen million years after the mass extinction of dinosaurs and flying and swimming reptiles—in evolutionary terms, a very short time. This extinction allowed mammals to spread out and take over the world.

Twenty Million Years Ago

The Pseudaelurines, a group of cats that first appear in the fossil record about this time, are thought to be the direct ancestors of today's thirty-seven species of cat, including the tiger. The oldest cat, *Proailurus*, came from what we now call France about thirty million years ago. It was about the same size as and probably had an arboreal lifestyle similar to that of the fossa of Madagascar, which is closely related to mongooses, but in isolation and in the absence of competing cats it evolved a catlike morphology. Proailurus had eight more teeth than today's cats.

Two to Three Million Years Ago

It is thought that more than two million years ago the common ancestor to the *Panthera* cats was fairly similar to the modern leopard in looks. Today's clouded leopard (*Neofelis nebulosa*), however, diverged from the common ancestor of all the pantherine cats about seven million years ago, making it a more distant relative of the tiger than the lion, leopard, or jaguar. Using molecular techniques to compare the genetic similarities among the modern-day members of the *Panthera* genus, zoologists have determined that the tiger diverged first from the common *Panthera* ancestor and that the lion, leopard, and jaguar evolved much later. The tiger's stripes may have evolved later as well, although this cannot be proved, as no skins have survived from this time period. Thus, the other big cats have more in common genetically with one another than with the tiger.

Clouded leopard
(*Neofelis nebulosa*)

1.6 Million Years Ago to Ten Thousand Years Ago

Although popularly termed the ice age because of the glaciers that covered as much as 30 percent of the Earth's surface, this period was actually a succession of ninety or more protracted cold cycles interspersed with warm spells. About two million years ago, our ancestor, *Homo habilis*, began to evolve into *Homo erectus* and eventually dispersed out of Africa and migrated as far as China. They made stone hand axes and

SABER-TOOTHED CATS

Despite their name, the famous saber-toothed cats are probably not ancestors of today's tigers at all. They are distant relatives who used terrifyingly long and specialized "saber" teeth to kill their prey.

The most famous of the saber-toothed cats is *Smilodon*, well-known because of the huge number of fossils found in the Rancho La Brea tar pits in Hollywood, California. We know that it lived from about 1.5 million years ago to 120,000 years ago and was an awesome predator about 1.2 meters (four feet) long (similar in size to an African lion), with a bobbed tail. It was *Smilodon*'s jaws that made it stand out in the crowd; they were huge, opening to an angle of more than ninety degrees (today's lions can open their jaws only to sixty-five degrees), which made it easy to sink their eighteen-centimeter (seven-inch) canine teeth into prey. Surprisingly, these sabers were quite delicate—any contact with bone would shatter them, so they could be used only in the soft parts of the prey such as the underbelly and throat. *Smilodon* therefore needed strong front legs to hold its victim still and very sharp claws to help it hang on during hunting.

Saber-toothed predators have evolved at least four times, in different animal groups, not just the "cat" family, suggesting that the saber tooth was a pretty good adaptation. In fact meat-eating beasts with large, curved, and often serrated saber teeth were around over a very long period, from about forty million years ago to only ten thousand years ago, when they shared the planet with both humans and the tiger.

The saber-toothed cats died out probably in large part because of their lack of adaptability in hunting techniques, although hunting pressure from early humans and competition from pantherine species such as the lion may also have contributed to their demise.

Discovered in a tomb dating back more than 6,000 years, to the Yangshao culture, this skeleton—flanked by a tiger and a dragon made of clam shells—is the only one of its kind found in China.

wooden spears and containers, built huts, and helped one another to hunt game and gather food. *Homo sapiens*, the species to which all modern humans belong, did not appear until about four hundred thousand years ago.

That tigers existed at this time cannot be definitively proved by the distribution of tiger fossils. Tigers and lions look very similar when stripped of their stripes and manes, and incomplete, badly weathered skeletons have made the job of identification exceedingly difficult. Moreover, tigers tend to live in dense forests with lots of moisture, heat, and mud about—conditions that don't help fossil formation. With only a few, fragmented fossils of uncertain age scattered across the huge continent of Asia, we can begin to understand why, even in our highly technological era, experts are unwilling to state the exact evolutionary path and distribution of the tiger.

Early tiger fossils (one to two million years old) have been found in China, Java, and Sumatra. The earliest in Russia are only seven hundred thousand years old, and those in India are only ten thousand years old. Interestingly, a few fossils have recently been found in Beringia, the land bridge that connected Asia to North America during the ice ages, but there is no evidence yet that tigers entered North America. Recent fossil and other evidence suggests that tigers existed in Borneo, perhaps even as recently as a few hundred years ago.

A cave painting from central India, dating back 5,000 years. The picture is thought to illustrate a pun, something like: once you mount a tiger you cannot dismount. Such sayings were common in classical and tribal fables of the period.

From this scant fossil evidence, scientists have come up with two alternative theories. The most accepted version, the Asian theory, asserts that more than two million years ago, when early man had yet to venture out of Africa, tigers separated from their big-cat cousins in East Asia, with the South China form being the original template. These tigers dispersed two million years ago in two directions, one group traveling north to Russia while the second spread southeast to the Indonesian islands and southwest to India. Some scientists debate the notion that there was a single point of origin in China, as natural selection acting on an isolated but geographically widespread population could also result in its simultaneous evolution elsewhere.

Around twelve thousand years ago (or ten thousand radiocarbon years), mastodons, mammoths, woolly rhinoceroses, and other megafauna became extinct, and the last major ice age, which had covered Britain in ice as far south as Oxford, ended. During that time, people and animals had been able to walk from continental Europe to Britain and across to Ireland, until the ice at the poles melted, making the North and Irish seas and the English Channel too deep to cross. As the land became warmer, trees

grew, creating forests across Britain. European lions, which had been common for nine hundred thousand years, became extinct. The Sahara had higher rainfall and became habitable. Mehrgarh, one of the oldest cities in the world, was founded about this time in the Indus Valley. In North America, saber-toothed cats and the American lion were nearing the end of their lengthy carnivorous reigns and were going extinct. Fossils discovered at Karnool cave deposits in Andhra Pradesh tell us that this is the period when tigers first entered India.

FIVE THOUSAND YEARS AGO

In South America, people had begun to domesticate plants and animals, including cotton, potatoes, cavies (guinea pigs), and guanacos (relatives of the llama). In Britain, people of the late Neolithic period and their ancestors built Stonehenge, and the giant ox became extinct.

A few of the rock paintings discovered in cave sites in India date back to this period, and others are still being discovered today. There are paintings of men and various animals, including the tiger, either resting or running, and many hunting scenes featuring tigers. The peoples of the Indus Valley civilization of Harappa and Mohenjo Daro (part of modern Pakistan) were the first to use the tiger as an important symbol in their cultures, engraved on seals that are believed to have marked ownership of property and were worn as amulets.

TWO THOUSAND TO ONE THOUSAND YEARS AGO

The Roman Empire was at its peak at the start of this period. Use of Caspian tigers in the games and slaughters in amphitheaters introduced the first significant threat to the tiger's existence. One thousand years ago, Europe entered the Dark Ages, and Asia (excluding Japan) accounted for two thirds of world gross domestic product. In Cambodia, the Hindu King Jayavarman II founded the complex of carved stone buildings and temples called Angkor Wat. In global economic terms, western Europe was in its infancy.

The earth as a whole was warmer, and wild boars, beavers, and wolves still roamed the diminishing forests of Britain. Not much is known about the tiger in this period; the few skeletons that have been unearthed do not vary much from today's specimens and maintain the wide distribution that the tigers enjoyed before the invention of the gun. With people far less numerous and lethal than they are now, tiger populations maintained an equilibrium.

A woman grapples with a pair of standing tigers in this Harappa seal dating to 2,500 B.C.E.

7

Hunting for sport drastically reduced tiger populations across their range. Between 1800 and 1950, more than 160,000 tigers were killed.

Two Hundred to One Hundred Years Ago

The tiger population suffered unprecedented decimation when the proliferation of firearms and cars facilitated hunting for sport or purely medicinal purposes. People also hunted the tiger's prey, leaving tigers with less and less to eat. Humankind encroached upon the tiger's natural habitats, converting them to agricultural lands.

In the fifty years between 1875 and 1925, eighty thousand tigers were killed in India alone. Probably an equal number were injured and died later of their wounds. Based on these and other figures, it is conservatively estimated that at the dawn of the twentieth century one hundred thousand tigers inhabited the range from eastern Turkey across the Asian continent to the Russian Far East and the islands of Indonesia.

Given the relatively sizable population of tigers at the time, it is interesting to note that Charles Darwin mentions them only briefly in *On the Origin of Species by Means of Natural Selection, or The Preservation of Favoured Races in the Struggle for Life*, first published in 1859. The following essay by Ruth Padel, his great-great-granddaughter, eloquently addresses the question of why this was.

The number of tigers killed every year increased with the arrival of the automobile, which made the forests more and more accessible. Tiger hunting was not banned in India until 1970.

Why *On the Origin of Species* Barely Mentions Tigers

Ruth Padel

Watercolor of Charles Darwin by George Richmond, 1840.

"I Felt Most Sublime in the Forests"

One evening in the 1870s, George Romanes was talking to Charles Darwin about "the sublime." Darwin said he had felt it most on the summit of the Cordillera, looking at "the magnificent prospect all around." They talked of other things and went to bed. Romanes, a devoted Darwin disciple, fell comfortably asleep. But at one in the morning the great man, a fairly elderly great man by now, put on dressing gown and slippers and gently opened his friend's door.

"I have been thinking over our conversation," he said. "It has occurred to me I was wrong in telling you I felt most sublime on top of the Cordillera. I am quite sure I felt it even more in the forests of Brazil. I am sure now, that I felt most sublime in the forests."

But in the *Origin of Species*, this man who felt most sublime in the forests does not mention their sublimest inhabitant, save for a passing reference on predation and numbers in chapter 3: "The amount of food for each species of course gives the extreme limit to which each can increase; but very frequently it is not the obtaining food, but the serving as prey to other animals, which determines the average numbers of a species. . . . In some cases, as with the elephant and rhinoceros, none are destroyed by beasts of prey: even the tiger in India rarely dares to attack a young elephant protected by its dam."

The reasons why Darwin did not dwell on tigers speak to important aspects of his thought and his work—to his particular pathways of mind and historical accidents of his life, but also the kind of inquiry his work was, in which he laid out his insights on evolution and biodiversity.

Von Humboldt, South America, and "Tangle"

The obvious reason is that he was focused on the wrong continent. His starting point was the *Beagle*'s voyage to

South America, 1831–1836. Even in his last year at Cambridge, Darwin had an imagination that was passionately imprinted with the South American jungle. He read *Personal Narrative* by Alexander von Humboldt (1769–1859), one of the greatest of the "romantic" scientists—imaginative, committed, subjective—who wrote vividly and very personally about extraordinary experiences. This book, along with J. Herschel's *Introduction to the Study of Natural History*, stirred up in the young Darwin "a burning zeal to make even the most humble contribution to the noble structure of Natural Science." He was especially fired by Humboldt's description of Tenerife. In 1831, before setting foot on the *Beagle*, he wrote to his sister Caroline, "My head is running about the Tropics. In the morning I go and gaze at palm trees in the hothouse and come home and read Humboldt. My enthusiasm is so great that I can hardly sit still in my chair. Sandy dazzling plains and gloomy, silent forests are alternately uppermost in my mind."

He found tropical vegetation even better in the leaf than on the page. When he met it on the Cape Verde Islands he wrote in his journal: "Here I first saw the glory of tropical vegetation. Tamarinds, bananas and palms were flourishing at my feet. I expected a good deal, for I had read Humboldt's descriptions and I was afraid of disappointments. How utterly vain such fear is, none can tell but those who have experienced what I today have, . . . treading on volcanic rocks, hearing the notes of unknown birds, seeing new insects fluttering about still newer flowers."

Tellingly, in this entry describing his first contact with tropical vegetation, he records both the external data and his own response to it. This combination was the wellspring of his work. "It is not only the gracefulness of their forms," he wrote, "or the novel richness of their colors, it is the numberless and confusing associations that rush together on the mind. It has been for me a glorious day, like giving to a blind man eyes." Or like, you could say, that moment when a poet or painter finds his or her true subject. For Darwin's deepest subject was the thrill of interaction between his own mind and the natural world outside. "During the five years of my voyage," he wrote later to his fiancée, "which may be said to be the commencement of my real life, the whole of my pleasure was derived from what passed in my mind whilst admiring views by myself, traveling across wild deserts or glorious forests, or pacing the deck of the poor little *Beagle* at night." His mind responding to those forests was, he said, "a chaos of delight."

For the next twenty years he worked out the fruits of that chaos and delight in a quiet Kent meadow, but the wild tropical original was always there, the basis of his vision into biodiversity and the intense pleasure he took in it. A word he often used for it was "tangle." "Walked along a brook flowing between huge granite blocks," he says, exploring a Brazilian forest in June 1832. "No art could depict so stupendous a scene. The decaying trunks of enormous trees scattered about formed in many places natural bridges; beneath and around them the damp shade favored the growth of fern and palm trees. . . . Even by creeping, I could not penetrate the entangled mass of the living and dead vegetation."

By "tangle" he meant the whole mixed-up self-perpetuating wildness of plants and animals interacting with one another—the tangle on which tigers depend, without which no wild tiger can live.

This tangle dominates the final paragraph of the *Origin of Species*, where Darwin's jungle insight is projected onto modest British woodland: "It is interesting to contemplate an entangled bank, clothed with many plants of many kinds, with birds singing on the bushes, with various insects flitting about, and with worms crawling through the damp earth, and to reflect that these elaborately constructed forms, so different from each other, and dependent upon each other in so complex a manner, have all been produced by laws acting around us." But, though Darwin always had this intricate tangle in mind, his business was with origin, cause, and process; namely, how this tangle came to be.

Origin, Process, and the Apparently Insignificant

Here is another reason for not much mentioning tigers: tigers are very much the end result of a process. Darwin would not have called them the end result but the latest result: he always insisted that evolution was continuing and might go any direction in the future. Still, as I understand it, though there is dispute about whether the *Panthera* genus is the absolute latest of feline developments, it does come pretty far along the road, whereas Darwin focused on smaller, humbler wonders that suggested to him insights into origin or long process. Earthworms, plankton, barnacles, bumblebees, the insect-eating sundew (*Drosera*), and finches' beaks: he built his theories on the intricacies of these apparently insignificant things, as well as on their relations to "higher" things and on the universal laws these relationships suggested. You could never call a tiger insignificant.

On the *Beagle*, Darwin thrilled to great scenic visions. He may have felt most sublime in the forests, but on the Andean Cordillera he marveled at "the profound valleys, wild broken forms, heaps of ruins piled up during the lapse of ages, the bright colored rocks contrasted with the quiet mountains of Snow, which together produced a scene I never could have imagined." And yet, while collecting and making notes, he also thrilled to the minutest details of individual organisms. He brought the same strenuous wonder to a forest as to the hair on a single plant. His characteristic mental move was from the physically tiny to the universal. Walking near Socego in Brazil, he commented, "If the eye is turned from the world of foliage above, to the ground, it is attracted by the extreme elegance of the leaves of numberless species of ferns and mimosas. . . . Wonder, astonishment and sublime devotion fill and elevate the mind."

Twenty years later, out for a walk near the end of writing the *Origin of Species* and anxious to discuss the way red ants enslaved black ones, he met a trail of red ants migrating from one nest to another, carrying black ants. After experiments in prizing their burdens off them, he settled down to watch one particular ant. A tramp came along; Darwin paid him a shilling to watch another ant. The two of them squatted, shuffled, and kept pace with their ants. They heard a carriage trotting up, slowing to a walk as the coachman saw them in the road. "You mustn't look up," Darwin told the tramp. They stayed squatting, watching, but Darwin's ant reached a bare place just as the carriage passed him. He glanced up a second and saw a coach full of people gazing at him and the tramp with open mouths. Then he went back to his ant.

He pondered not only the behavior of minuscule creatures but their effects. On Keeling Island, in the Indian Ocean, he saw surf battering the windward coast. "The ocean throwing its waters over the broad reef," he said,

appears an invincible, all-powerful enemy, yet we see it resisted and even conquered by means which at first seem most weak and inefficient. It is not that the ocean spares the rock of coral; the great fragments scattered over the reef, and accumulated on the beach, plainly bespeak the unrelenting power of its waves. . . . Yet these low, insignificant coral islets stand and are victorious: for here another power, as antagonist to the former, takes part in the contest. The organic forces separate the atoms of carbonate of lime one by one from the foaming breakers, and unite them into a symmetrical structure. Let the hurricane tear up its thousand huge fragments; what will this tell against the accumulated labor of myriads of architects at work night and day, month after month?

After the description comes, as always, the moral: "Thus do we see the soft and gelatinous body of a polypus, through the agency of the vital laws, conquering the great mechanical power of the waves of an ocean, which neither the art of man, nor the inanimate works of nature could successfully resist."

He gloried in rain forest but saw rainbow beauties in plankton, too: "I am quite tired having worked all day at the produce of my net. The number of animals that the net collects is very great. . . . Many of these creatures so low in the scale of nature are most exquisite in their forms and rich colors. It creates a feeling of wonder that so much beauty should be apparently created for so little purpose." In the East Falkland Islands, he commented on the "immense quantity and number of kinds of organic beings intimately connected with the kelp. . . . I can only compare these great forests to terrestrial ones in the most teeming part of the tropics; yet if the latter in any country were to be destroyed, I do not believe *nearly* the same number of animals would perish in them as would happen in the case of kelp. (I refer to numbers of individuals as well as kinds.) All the fishing quadrupeds and birds (and man) haunt the beds, attracted by the infinite number of small fish which live amongst the leaves."

He uses his tangle image for watery as well as land forests: "On shaking the great entangled roots, it is curious to see the heap of fish, shells, crabs, sea-eggs, cuttle-fish, star fish, Planariae, Nereidae, which fall out. . . . One single plant form is an immense and most interesting menagerie. If this Fucus were to cease living, with it would go many: the seals, cormorants and certainly the small fish, and then sooner or later the Fuegian man must follow."

If, unlike Darwin, you *started* from the most beautiful and significant of higher animals, where on earth (or out of it) would you end? The tiger was, as it were, the summit that Darwin was working toward.

Personal Observation

A third reason why Darwin barely mentioned tigers is that he never studied them. Inspired by Humboldt's *Personal Narrative* and honoring the "personal" of Humboldt's title, he worked from close personal observation. He was not at all against the higher mammals. At home, his dogs and babies were always under the spotlight, foci of his scrutiny, questioning, and theory. Despite the constant glide of his own mind into theory, he believed no one had the right to examine the question of species who had not minutely described many himself, and he did this constantly in later life all over the house and garden. His son Horace helped with the study of earthworms; his daughter Etty wrote labels for shells on the backs of his barnacle notes.

Barnacles were so pervasive in the house for a time that one small son was overheard asking a friend, "What does your father do to his barnacles?"

But it was on the *Beagle* that Darwin trained himself to study and think with what he saw around him. He wrote in his journal every day, taking "much pains in describing carefully and vividly all I had seen." He learned to observe among plankton and rock, acquiring a "habit of energetic industry and of concentrated attention to whatever I was engaged in. Everything about which I thought or read was made to bear directly on what I had seen or was likely to see. This habit of mind was continued during the five years of the voyage. I feel sure that it was this training which has enabled me to do whatever I have done in science."

There were not many tigers on board—but he would have been thrilled to observe them. A remark in one of his Metaphysical Notebooks gives some idea what he felt about them. He is considering the pleasures of imagination, how trains of thought in response to landscape vary from person to person. "My pleasure in Kensington Gardens," he writes in August 1838, "has often been greatly excited by looking at trees [as] great compound animals united by wonderful & mysterious manner. There is much imagination in every view. If one were admiring one in India & a tiger stalked across the plains, how ones [*sic*] feelings would be excited, & how the scenery would rise." He wrote this while living in London, in Great Marlborough Street, working out his first sketch of evolutionary theory, consciously tackling what he called the "mystery of mysteries." He then kept this sketch in a drawer, for many years.

During that London period, he often visited the Zoological Gardens, where there was, by then, a captive tiger. A tigress, the first tiger representative exhibited at the London Zoo, was presented to it on June 8, 1829, and tigers have been shown there continuously ever since. But Darwin could not observe them in the wild, and his insights came from what he studied—though, according to his son Francis, he also said no one could be a good observer unless he was an active theorizer, too. "It naturally happened," said Francis, "that many untenable theories occurred to him." But he always tested them. "He was willing to test what would seem to most people not at all worth testing. These rather wild trials he called 'fool's experiments,' and enjoyed extremely." These experiments included stringing his children through the grass to plot the flight path of bumblebees and asking Francis to play the bassoon to earthworms to see if they could hear. Many experiments went no further; but many others did prove their theories. Etty helped her father breed ninety-three varieties of pigeon that he skeletonized in the kitchen to prove they all descended from the African rock pigeon. The resultant passage in chapter 1 is the only part of the *Origin of Species* of which the publisher's first reader approved. Everyone loves pigeons, he said. Keep that bit, and throw the rest away. (Luckily, John Murray ignored his reader and went with evolution.)

The historical accidents of Darwin's life meant that he spent five years on a voyage and the following twenty very retiringly, mainly in Kent. So though tropical tangle was his image of interrelatedness, he worked out the insights gained from it in a very different setting. The famous pollination example in the *Origin of Species,* from which modern understanding of biodiversity evolved, came from observing long grass in his garden. He saw that the only bees to visit red clover were bumblebees: others could not reach the nectar. So, he suggested, if bumblebees became extinct in England, red clover would become rare or disappear. But the number of bumblebees depends on that of field mice, who destroy their nests; and *their* numbers depend on the number of cats. So the numbers of cats in a neighborhood may well determine the wildflowers that grow in it.

Grandeur Is in the Mind

In 1958, to celebrate the hundred years since the theory of evolution was announced, two of Darwin's granddaughters—my grandmother Nora Barlow and her cousin Margaret Keynes—decided to restore the garden where Darwin worked out his tropics-won ideas. My cousin Randal Keynes, Margaret's grandson, is helping English Heritage grow the garden back. From photographs, they have identified specific climbers draggling round the veranda; from records, they have restored Darwin's greenhouses. They have grown back the "Sandwalk," where Darwin solved problems on his constitutional saunters, grading his intellectual workings-out as one-stone, two-stone, or three-stone problems, adding a stone to a cairn after every lap.

But one thing is hard for English Heritage to replicate: a fact about Darwin that touches on my last reason why he did not much mention tigers. Darwin was instinctively ungrand, and you cannot get much grander, zoologically, than a tiger. The house and garden are on show now but were very much *not* a showplace then. They were pretty untidy—something English Heritage is reluctant to be Darwinian about. Lawn and drawing room were strewn with children's paraphernalia, picnic rugs, and earthworm experiments. The local flower society gave up on Darwin. Unlike most Kent gentry, he had greenhouses because he worked in them, not because he wanted to win prizes. He did not want to show plants but to study them and then move on to the next thing. For to Darwin, grandeur came not so much from outward structure but from inner vision. He felt sublime in forests, but the grandeur lay not only in their physical impressiveness but in the imagination's response to it, the intellect's leap from small ferny details to understanding the universal processes that made the whole. He once said that his deepest pleasure in the Galápagos had been observing and then understanding. It lay in the insight, "the discovery of the singular relations of the animals and plants inhabiting the several islands." What was grand was not the writhing interrelated vegetation itself but one's own intuitive grasp of that interrelatedness and how it came to be.

As he began developing his theory of evolution after the voyage, he wrote lyrically, in Notebook D, of the grandeur in understanding cause: "What a magnificent view one can take of the world. Astronomical causes, modified by unknown ones, cause changes in geography and changes in climate superadded to change of climate from physical causes. [These superinduce changes in form in the organic world, as adaptation, and these changes affect each other. Their bodies, by certain laws of harmony, keep perfect in themselves.] Instincts alter, reason is formed, and the world peopled with myriads of distinct forms from a period short of eternity to the present time, to the future." This view of nature, he says, is "far grander" than the defenses against the chronological implications of fossils, mounted by the religion of the day: "the idea from cramped imagination that God (warring against those very laws he established in all organic nature) created the rhinoceros of Java and Sumatra, that since the time of the Silurian he has made a long succession of vile molluscous animals."

Darwin always had a vivid sense of nature's beauty. But to him, grandeur lay in realizing how ruthlessly it came into being and will go on changing, via survival of the fittest: "You can understand the true conditions of life only if you use your imagination to hold on to a sense of the ruthlessness of the natural forces that could waste the bright surface." This is Darwin's paradox: the beauty and the brightness are bound to the cruelty that created them.

Behind all this is a ruthlessly intellectual notion of the grand. "Grand" lies in the causes of tangle and in apprehending the complexities of action and reaction behind those causes. "When we look at the plants and bushes clothing an entangled bank," Darwin said, "we are tempted to attribute their proportional numbers and kind to what we call chance. But how false a view is this! Everyone has heard that when an American forest is cut down, a very different vegetation springs up; but it has been observed that the trees now growing on the ancient Indian mounds in the Southern United States, display the same beautiful diversity and proportion of kinds as in the surrounding virgin forests."

So Darwin does not care about the difference between pristine and secondary forest. What he is gunning for is the process by which both are made: "What a struggle between the several kinds of trees must here have gone on during long centuries, each annually scattering its seeds by the thousand; what war between insect and insect—between insects, snails and other animals with birds and beasts of prey—all striving to increase, and all feeding on each other or on trees or their seeds and seedlings, or on the other plants which first clothed the ground and thus checked the growth of the trees!" Intricacy, complexity: he wonders at them over and over. He did not, of course, envisage a world of genetically engineered simplicity, where complexity itself might be dangerously lost: "Throw up a handful of feathers, and all must fall to the ground according to definite laws; but how simple is this problem compared to the action and reaction of the innumerable plants and animals which have determined, in the course of centuries, the proportional numbers and kinds of trees now growing on the old Indian ruins!"

At the end of the *Origin of Species* he returns to the "entangled bank": to how the richness of the natural world, this beautiful tangle, is the outcome of the struggle for existence. The "bright surface" and "tangle" were created

by laws acting around us: growth with reproduction; inheritance which is also implied by reproduction; variability from the indirect and direct action of the external conditions of life, and from use and disuse; a ratio of increase so high as to lead to a struggle for life, and as a consequence to natural selection, entailing divergence of character and the extinction of less-improved forms. Thus, from the war of nature, from famine and death, the most exalted object which we are capable of conceiving, namely, the production of the higher animals, directly follows.

Grandeur crops up again when he draws the conclusion: "There is a grandeur in this view of life, with its several powers, having been originally breathed into a few forms or into one; and that, whilst this planet has gone cycling on according to the fixed law of gravity, from so simple a beginning endless forms most beautiful and most wonderful have been, and are being, evolved."

"Forms the most beautiful and wonderful"

Tigers, at the top of every bright surface and forest tangle on their continent, were among the highest of such forms and are the perfect goal for Darwin's key insights of the *Origin of Species* (for tigers came out on top, or have done until now, in survival of the fittest), and of biodiversity, since tigers and their forests depend completely on the intricate interrelatedness of which Darwin wrote with such wonder. Charles Darwin did not need to write explicitly about tigers in the *Origin of Species*. In a sense, he was writing about them all the time. They are the evolved paradigm of what he was working toward. Tigers are what Darwin wanted to explain.

RUTH PADEL is an award-winning British poet, and a Fellow of the Royal Society of Literature. She is also the great-great-granddaughter of Charles Darwin and a Fellow of the Zoological Society of London. Her book about wild tigers and where they live will be published by Little, Brown in 2005.

The author is very grateful to Randal Keynes for insights on Darwin in his book Annie's Box, *in unpublished material from his forthcoming book about Darwin's garden, and in personal discussion on journeys to Down House and Kew.*

TIGERS TODAY

Today there are an estimated five thousand to seven thousand tigers living in the wild, spanning eighteen countries, from the snowy Russian Far East to the sweltering dense jungles of Sumatra. Tigers are incredibly versatile animals, living in temperatures that range from −33°C (−28°F) in the northern extreme of their range to 50°C (122°F) in the southern parts, and altitudes ranging from sea level to more than three thousand meters (ten thousand feet). Not only do temperature and altitude vary greatly, so, of course, does vegetation, from the tropical evergreen and deciduous forests of southern Asia to the coniferous, scrub oak, and birch woodlands of Siberia. Tigers also thrive in the mangrove swamps of the Sundarbans, the dry thorn forests of northwestern India, and the tall grass jungles at the foot of Himalayas. They need only dense vegetative cover, sufficient large ungulate prey, and access to water to survive.

TIGER SUBSPECIES

Within any given subspecies, there is variation in size and coloring from individual to individual, and there is often overlap in morphology between subspecies, but the tiger has adapted to cope with the different habitats, climates, and available prey. The most northerly animals are generally larger, paler, and have thick, shaggy coats to cope with the cold, while the southern animals, which live in dense jungle and intense heat, are smaller, darker, and have shorter fur.

Until recently, tigers were divided into eight subspecies, often with country-specific names. Andrew Kitchener pioneered the research that led to the reduction in the number of tiger subspecies from eight to three.

How Many Tiger Subspecies?

Andrew Kitchener

Many animals have very wide geographical distributions. Not surprisingly, as climate and habitats vary throughout their ranges, the local populations of a species may express this variation in several ways. Sometimes a species's morphology changes gradually over its geographic distribution so that at the extremes of their range animals may look completely different. This is known as a cline, and even though individuals on the opposite ends of a cline may look very different, it is inappropriate to regard them as belonging to different subspecies. There is always gene flow throughout the geographic range, albeit tempered by natural selection for particular morphotypes or perhaps reflecting a pattern of broad hybridization between two populations that differentiated previously in isolation. Sometimes local populations are separated from one another by geographical barriers, such as a river or a mountain range, and they differ in their appearance such that at least 75 percent of one population can be distinguished from 100 percent of the other. In such a case, it is possible to recognize two distinct subspecies or geographical races, which can be given different scientific names. Finally, in many cases, local populations of morphologically different animals may meet but have a narrow hybrid zone between the two, where animals of mixed appearance occur. Therefore, there is always some limited gene flow between most subspecies. Again, these can be classified as separate subspecies if they conform to the 75 percent rule. In these last two cases, although local populations have been isolated or may continue to be isolated from one another, there has been insufficient differentiation between the populations for a new species to have evolved. However, reality is often not that simple.

Although each animal species and subspecies has its own scientific name, science was often not involved in determining their distinctiveness. Many scientific names date back to between the late eighteenth and early twentieth centuries and are often based on a single or a few specimens. For example, Coenraad Temminck described the Amur and Javan tigers as distinct species in 1844, based on the length of the fur on a handful of specimens. Of course, he could not have known how tigers varied in between (or even if there were any), as no samples were available to him. However, the two tigers he had from the extremes of their geographic range were so different that he decided they must be different species.

Despite the tens, if not hundreds, of thousands of tigers that have been killed during the last two hundred years, sadly very few are preserved in the world's natural-history museums. This means that some local populations of tigers are barely available for mammalogists to study—for example, there are fewer than ten Bali and possibly only thirty to forty Javan tigers. Moreover, we do not have a good geographical spread of specimens, so that it may be difficult to decide where one supposed tiger subspecies ends and another begins. In the north of China, there is even a historical gap in the tiger's distribution between the so-called South China and Amur tigers, which probably reflects a local extinction caused by the early development of civilization in this region and its demand for tigers for use in traditional Chinese medicine.

By applying modern molecular and morphological studies to the specimens we have available, it is possible to gain some insight into the variation throughout the tiger's range. A preliminary morphological study suggested that the ground color of the fur and the number of flank stripes were more variable within supposed subspecies than between them. There was also a clinal variation in the size of the skull in male tigers, with those of northern tigers in Russia and India the largest and those on the equator in Sumatra the smallest. Interestingly, male Javan tigers were significantly bigger than Sumatran males; this size variation probably reflects either the effects of temperature on body size (i.e., Bergmann's rule, where bigger bodies retain heat better than smaller ones and so are found further north where it is cooler, and vice versa) or the productivity of the environment, allowing for different potentials for body growth or adaptation to different-sized prey. Females on the mainland did not vary in size, although those on the Sunda islands (which include Sumatra and Java) were smaller. A molecular study also suggested little difference between supposed tiger subspecies, although a later study suggested that Sumatran tigers should be recognized as a distinct species; this study, however, relied heavily on zoo-bred tigers, which were closely related to one another and likely to be genetically similar.

The problem with all modern studies of tiger taxonomy is that the sample sizes are likely to be small and do not reflect the former widespread distribution of the species, so it may be difficult to arrive at unambiguous conclusions. Therefore, it may be more appropriate to carry out biogeographical studies, which provide insight into how a species was distributed before human interference and how this has changed over time as climate and habitats varied, as in the ice ages. By correlating known tiger distribution records with environmental factors that are thought to be important to tigers, such as habitat, precipitation, snow depth, and temperature, it is possible to create a model of the tiger's original distribution. This indicates that all mainland populations were once contiguous with one another during warm climatic periods, such as the one we are in now. Looking back in time to the coldest period of the last ice age, about twenty thousand years ago, we see that tigers were pushed south by colder global temperatures and a southward shift in their key habitats, but again mainland populations were contiguous, except for the Caspian tiger, which was isolated in perhaps two areas. The ice ages resulted in a fall in sea levels, which allowed mainland and Sunda Island tigers to meet each other, encouraging gene flow between populations. In theory, Sumatran tigers ought

to be hybrids between the mainland and Sunda Island forms, except that a volcano in northern Sumatra intervened seventy thousand years ago (which is another story). So whether the world is hot or cold, there has always been some potential for considerable gene flow between so-called tiger subspecies. However, Caspian and Sunda Island tigers did experience periods of isolation during the ninety or so glacial cycles (as these climatic oscillations are known) in the last two million years, and they are morphologically distinct enough to be recognized as subspecies. So we can conclude that it is most likely that there were originally three tiger subspecies: the Asian tiger, *Panthera tigris tigris*, which occurred from India through Indochina and China as far north as the Russian Far East; the Sunda Island tiger, *Panthera tigris sondaica*, which was originally found on Sumatra, Java, Bali, and Borneo; and the Caspian tiger, *Panthera tigris virgata*, which occurred in western Asia. However, this is unlikely to be the last word on the subject, as new methods and approaches are applied to the little we have left of living and museum tigers.

ANDREW KITCHENER, Curator of Mammals and Birds at the National Museums of Scotland, conducted recent research that has led to the reclassification of tiger subspecies. He is also involved in long-term research into the effects of captivity on the morphology of cats and other mammals. He is a member of the Cat Specialist Group of IUCN, the World Conservation Union.

Tiger range, circa 1900

Current range or potential habitat

EXTINCT TIGERS

The world's current total population of tigers represents five of the original eight subspecies into which the tiger was divided: the Amur (*Panthera tigris altaica*), the Bengal (*Panthera tigris tigris*), the Indo-Chinese (*Panthera tigris corbetti*), the South China (*Panthera tigris amoyensis*) and the Sumatran (*Panthera tigris sumatrae*) tigers. The first four are now classified as the Asian tiger (*Panthera tigris tigris*), the last as the Sunda Island tiger (*Panthera tigris sondaica*). In fact, no South China tigers have been seen in the wild since the 1980s, although there are records of pugmarks and of prey killed by tigers. They may already be extinct, or a few may still be roaming the forests.

Of the original eight subspecies, at least three are now extinct. Little is known of these populations beyond a handful of rare photographs and museum specimens left in existence today. The Caspian, also known locally as the Hyrcanian or Turan tiger, once roamed across Turkey, Iran, Iraq, Afghanistan, Mongolia, and the central Asiatic area of Russia. Much of this habitat was quite arid and therefore unique to this tiger subspecies. The Caspian also differed from other tigers in that it followed prey, such as boars, on their migrations instead of holding territories all year round as the other tigers do. (Having said this, there is some evidence that some Amur tigers also followed prey migrations, until these were disrupted by overhunting.) The demise of the Caspian tigers began in the early twentieth century, when the Russian government ordered its army to kill them in order to free up land for cultivation. The soldiers soon pushed the last remaining tigers into the mountain forests, where they found life more difficult. The last certain sighting of a Caspian tiger was in the 1950s. Although it is now extinct, it is still regarded as one of the three subspecies—the West Asian tiger—according to the new classification.

> ### TIGER SUBSPECIES
>
> **Asian *Panthera tigris tigris***
> Mainland Asia, from India through Indochina, China and as far north as the Russian Far East
>
> **Sunda Island *Panthera tigris sondaica***
> Sumatra, Java, Bali, and Borneo
>
> **Caspian *Panthera tigris virgata***
> Western Asia

The Balinese tiger, from the island of Bali in Indonesia, was the smallest subspecies, being only half the size of the Amur or Siberian tiger. It was dark with many thin stripes, much like the Sumatran and Javan tigers. As it was confined to a tiny island and suffered from speedily increasing human populations, the Balinese tiger was the first to go extinct. It had vanished by the early 1930s.

The Javan tiger was, as the name suggests, found solely on the island of Java, which at 132,000 square kilometers (51,500 square miles) is just over one quarter the size of Sumatra. The Javan looked very much like the Sunda Island tiger of today, with thin dark stripes, which were often double-looped. Another distinctive feature was its long cheek whiskers. Until the early nineteenth century, Javan tigers were common, but like the Caspian they were exterminated as people continued to expand their agricultural lands. As Java became exceptionally densely populated, the Javan tiger, not surprisingly, became the most recent known extinction, sometime in the 1970s. Both the Javan and the Balinese tigers are regarded as a part of the Sunda Island subspecies in the new classification.

There are sporadic reports of all three of these extinct tigers being spotted in the wild, but none has been professionally validated or backed up with photographic or other hard evidence. It is assumed that most of these possible sightings were of leopards or other big cats.

Tiger Skeleton, Lateral View Finished Study for Table IV
by George Stubbs

CHAPTER 2

Anatomy of a Supreme Hunter

The tiger, whose proper nutrition depends upon consuming one deer-sized animal a week, has evolved into a supreme hunter. Its sensory organs help it to locate elusive animals in the densest of undergrowth or on the blackest of nights, and its striped fur allows it to blend in with the surroundings. The tiger's padded paws permit a stealthy and silent approach when stalking a potential kill, and its skeleton and muscles provide the strength and speed necessary to catch prey as big as an elephant or as small as a grasshopper. A strong jaw and razor-sharp teeth can deliver a quick death, tearing tough hide and slicing through raw meat.

THE SKELETON

Even experts have difficulty distinguishing between the skeleton of a tiger and that of a lion; the two cats are so similar in size and shape that without the telltale fur they are hard to tell apart.

The flexibility of the tiger's skeleton allows it to jump to heights of up to ten to twelve feet.

An understanding of the tiger's hunting habits and daily behavior illuminates the particularly striking features of its skeleton—one that enables it to endure the vastly different rigors of both speed and strength.

Tigers have longer hind legs than forelegs and can therefore spring forward 10 meters (32.5 feet), while the reduced size of their clavicle (collarbone) allows for greater stride length. Their solid forelimb bones, which can support large muscles, give their forelegs incredible power, enabling them to bring down large prey. In addition, the bones of a tiger's feet are closely bound by ligaments to make them strong enough to survive the impact of landing, an important factor in the tiger's ability to sprint at high speeds.

The skull makes the hard-core engineering behind the business end of the tiger possible. By looking more closely at the shapes of the various skull pieces we can see

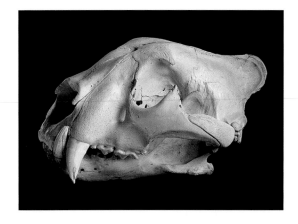

how evolution has created a structure that is perfectly shaped for the job at hand. A short, rounded skull provides more power behind the jaws than can the kind of long skull found in herbivores such as sheep. The perfectly adapted teeth are thus strongly supported in the final act of dispatching prey. Because smell is less important to tigers than sight, the nose need not be long, and the brain-cavity space for the olfactory area can be compact.

Several other features of the skull contribute to its strength. The tiger's bony septum, which separates the cerebrum from the cerebellum, and which in humans and many other creatures consists of only a membrane, increases skull strength. The jaw joints do not allow side-to-side movement, making the bite stronger and firmer. The jaw muscles, which are attached to a special extra bony ridge on the top of the skull called the sagittal crest, react quickly and clamp down with crushing force.

A tiger can run at speeds of up to sixty miles an hour.

Since they lack molars, tigers cannot chew, so they have to swallow lumps of meat whole. Like those of most animals, tigers' glistening white teeth turn a creamy yellow with age.

Tigers have thirty teeth, fewer than other carnivores (dogs and bears have forty-two) but no less dangerous, because of their specialization.

The tiger has the largest canines of all the big cats, at 6.4 to 7.6 centimeters (2.5 to 3 inches) long. Moreover, these canines are rich in pressure-sensitive nerves, enabling the tiger to make an accurate and deadly stab between a victim's neck bones to severe the spinal cord. The back teeth, called carnassials, act as shearing blades, with which tigers are able to slice the meat off their prey. The incisors (small front teeth) are positioned in a straight line, enabling them to efficiently pluck feathers and clean meat off the bone. Because of a huge gap between the canines and carnassials, the tiger can dig its teeth deep into its prey for the kill. One tiger in six has a broken canine as the result of an attack. Some old tigers, having lost as many as three canines, have become man-eaters because they are unable to kill their traditional prey.

Pads, Paws, and Claws

Tigers walk on their toes, which have big, soft pads to help them tread almost silently through the undergrowth. These sensitive pads can be a disadvantage: if a tiger treads on something sharp, the pads will bleed profusely; if it tries to cross hot ground its feet will burn and blister easily. These common injuries do heal quickly, with lots of licking and care.

A tiger's padded paws allow it to move silently, and help make it a superior stalker in the jungles of Asia.

A tiger's claws can take the face off a human in one swipe, and deer lucky enough to escape a confrontation with a tiger often bear the scars of the encounter on their hides. Claws play a critical role in the tiger's hunting abilities, helping it to grab and hold prey still until its teeth can inflict the final blow. The claws can be a fearsome ten centimeters (four inches) long. A tiger has four of these deadly weapons on each paw, with an extra dewclaw on the front ones. Dewclaws are set back a little and do not touch the ground when the tiger is walking; they are used like thumbs in gripping prey and in climbing.

The tiger keeps its claws retracted when not in use, in order to stalk silently and ensure that they remain sharp and ready for action. This is in fact the relaxed position, as ligaments hold them in their protective skin sheath and no muscular effort is needed. When necessary, other ligaments pull the claws out and straighten the toes. Curved claws allow tigers to climb trees head first, but to come down they must crawl backward or jump. This disadvantage, coupled with their size and weight, makes tigers inferior climbers compared with other big cats.

STOMACH AND DIGESTION

Meat can be digested far more efficiently than grass. It requires a far less complicated gut to convert meat to protein than it does to convert grass to protein. Thus tigers have shortened guts (four times their body length, as compared with five times in an omnivorous fox) and comparatively small and light abdomens, a factor that contributes to the tiger's ability to accelerate quickly when in pursuit of prey.

Recently, scientists have been observing how many animals self-medicate—that is, treat themselves when they are ill. Tigers, like other cats, eat grass to help with digestion or with bringing up furballs. But when looking at the scats of emaciated tigers who were riddled with parasites, zoologist George Schaller noted the presence of both grass and tapeworms, suggesting that tigers ate grass in attempts to cleanse their intestines of the parasites. Other studies of tiger scats show that their stomachs can cope with everything from porcupine quills to bear claws.

HAIR, COAT, OR PELAGE

Hair, coat, or pelage—the magnificent striping, so characteristic of the tiger—provides a perfect camouflage, but it functions primarily to keep the tiger warm and protect its skin. Fur traps air, which is a poor conductor of heat, thus insulating the tiger's body to keep it at a temperature of 37°C (99°F). The longer and denser the fur, the better the heat retention. This fact explains why tigers that live in warmer southern latitudes have shorter fur (7 to 20 millimeters on the back and 15 to 35 millimeters on the stomach) than those that live in the colder northern habitats (40 to 60 millimeters on the back and 70 to 105 millimeters on the stomach, with as many as 3,000 to 3,300 hairs per square centimeter). Males also have prominent ruffs.

Grooming is an essential activity for keeping a tiger's coat in condition.

A tiger's fur is made up of two types of hair: the outer guard hairs, which are longer and stronger, for physical protection; and the underfur, which is shorter and denser and is the fluffy heat retainer.

Like many other mammals, tigers shed their hair once or twice per year, having a longer winter coat and a shorter summer coat. And, just like domestic cats, tigers spend time grooming. As part of this, they use their tongues to spread the oils from their sebaceous glands over their coats, keeping them in condition.

Tigers are very clean animals, using their rasping tongues like combs to remove loose hairs and dirt, just like domestic cats. And like domestic cats, they lick their paws and then wash their heads. (They also carefully lick any injuries, coating them with

The tiger's striped coat makes excellent camouflage, rendering the tiger all but invisible to its prey.

antiseptic saliva from the tongue. This helps prevent infection from entering a wound. Observers in the wild have noted that wounds that the tongue has been able to reach and lick have healed, whereas those that are inaccessible have not.)

While all tigers share basic similarities, there are of course several distinct types. The orange color ranges from a pale yellow in the northern extreme of the tiger's range to a deep reddish-ocher in the south of Sumatra. However, the huge color range within each subspecies means that color differences cannot be regarded as definitive. In all subspecies, the tiger's stripes are also found on the skin underneath, while the stomach, cheeks, chin, and the area around the eyes are whitish.

Exceptions, such as white tigers, exist, albeit rarely in the wild because they would be at an obvious disadvantage when hunting and so would seldom survive to pass on their white genes. White tigers are not actually albinos, which would be totally white with red eyes. Instead, they are described as leucocystic, meaning that they have a recessive trait that causes a lack of dark pigments, which produces a white coat, gray to brown stripes, and stunning blue eyes. For some reason, they also seem to grow faster and bigger than their yellow relatives.

White tigers were first observed in India around the turn of the nineteenth century, and may have surfaced due to inbreeding in overhunted and fragmented populations. They are common nowadays because of the large zoo population, most of which stems from a white _____ zal tiger cub named Mohan, the last known wild whi_____ was caught and set to breeding by the maharaj_____

A few black tigers _____ ut the only evidence for their exi_____ head and back (but stripes at the _____ graph of tigers with only a few _____ ack leopards and jaguars, this is _____ stic form, just a darker version of the _____

We are even less certain of the _____ e blue tiger, supposed to have a bluish coat with dar_____ stripes. A handful of sightings, often from reliable source_, is the only proof. However, blue lynx and bobcats occur in the wild, so we cannot rule out the possibility of blue tigers. There are also reports of some white and black tigers having no stripes at all.

The stripes themselves differ greatly in color and thickness, depending on the subspecies, but are also quite distinctive to each individual as well as to each side of the body. If you look at the top of a tiger's head, the stripes make a pattern that looks like the Chinese character of "wang," meaning "king."

A tiger cools itself with a flick of the tail. Summer temperatures in India can soar to 45°C (113°F) or more.

THE TIGER'S TAIL

The tiger's tail is surprisingly important in catching prey. A meter or more long, it gathers a lot of momentum when swung from side to side, helping the tiger balance when it has to turn suddenly during a chase. It also plays a part in tiger communication. A relaxed tiger has a droopy tail. A tiger meeting a friend waves a raised tail slowly. A tiger's tail swishing madly from side to side or held low with just the occasional twitch indicates aggression.

THE SENSE OF TOUCH

Sensitive whiskers and padded feet give tigers the ability to feel their way silently—even in pitch darkness, through dense cover—to approach unwary prey.

Tigers have specialized hairs on their heads known as whiskers, or vibrissae, which serve a sensory function. About twice as thick as the outer guard hairs of the coat, they are rooted more deeply in the skin, in a capsule of blood. When the whisker brushes against something, its root moves the blood, thus amplifying the movement. Nerves pick up on the movement and send signals to the brain.

Sensitive to the slightest stimulation, a tiger's whiskers provide precise sensory information.

Whiskers are grouped in four different positions. The most important and well-developed are the mystacial group on the muzzle. Typically these are extended, at right angles to the jaws, when the tiger is resting. When sniffing, tigers retract these whiskers against the side of the face. As they advance, they bring them forward in the direction of the mouth like a circular net. The net of whiskers senses a prey's attempts to escape and provides crucial information about where to inflict the fatal bite. We now know that the whiskers and eyes function together, complementing each other.

The mystacial whiskers also help the tiger to find its way in the dark when the pupils, which are fully dilated, have difficulty focusing on nearby objects. It is now believed that there is a link between the tiger's sensory and visual inputs and that a degree of parallel processing takes place within the brain. For example, touching the end of the whiskers on a domestic cat triggers an automatic blink response in the cat, which serves to protect the eyes from injury.

The entire area of the tiger's face is well-endowed for sensory input: the skin between the whiskers has separate receptors which are very sensitive to pressure. It may not even be necessary for the whiskers to come into direct contact with an object, since they can detect the slight disturbance of air pressure when passing close by it.

Additional whiskers, known as the superciliary whiskers, are located above the eyes. This group may have a protective function, augmenting those on the side of the face. A third group, known as the genal or cheek whiskers, occurs farther back on the sides of the face than the mystacial whiskers and is probably less significant. There are other hairs on the body, notably at the back of the forelegs; these, sometimes called carpal hairs, are very responsive to touch. Body whiskers, or tylotrichs, are slightly longer single hairs spread apparently randomly across a cat's coat. These operate in the same way as facial whiskers to deliver sensory information.

A tiger's facial whiskers can be about fifteen centimeters (six inches) long, with those of males longer and heavier than those of females. Of all tigers, the Sunda Island subspecies *Panthera tigris sondaica* possesses the most generous number of whiskers.

THE SENSE OF SIGHT

The beautiful golden glint of a tiger's eye suggests its complexity and precision. Tigers' eyes also have several special features to increase their ability to see in the dark: large lenses and pupils receive more light; specially sensitive cells absorb the light; and reflective layers at the back of the retina (the light-sensitive cells at the back of the eye) give light more than one chance at stimulating light-receptor cells. The retina contains two different types of light-receptor cell, which connect via the optic nerve to the tiger's brain. These cells are known as rods and cones; rods are more responsive in low levels of light, while cones are sensitive to high levels of light and are used in color vision. Tigers, like many other animals, have traded in many cones and in return acquired more rods, so they have increased night vision, which is useful for hunting, at the expense of color vision. Finally, the eyes work together to create a 3-D image (a phenomenon known as binocular vision)—a quality that is of huge importance in calculating how far away the prey is and then striking with accuracy.

Cats have a broad horizontal streak (the visual streak) near the center of the eye, where a high concentration of nerve cells leads to the optic nerve. This increases their visual acuity horizontally, making them better than humans at spotting movement and fleeing prey moving across this plane. In comparison, our visual streak is symmetrically round and so allows us to spot movement in all fields but not in any specialized plane.

Tigers also have a tapetum lucidum ("bright carpet"), meaning a reflective retinal layer. This layer causes their eyes to glow at night and increases their ability to see in the dark. The tapetum lucidum is a highly evolved layered structure that reflects light

A reflective retinal layer increases a tiger's ability to see at night at the expense of color vision.

back to the retina, stimulating the light receptors again and so creating a brighter image. Research on domestic cats has shown that they require only one sixth of the light that humans need in order to see effectively.

The upper and lower eyelids of cats, like those of humans, sheathe the eyeballs. For further protection, all cats have an opaque, white third eyelid, called the nictitating membrane, between the lower lid and inside corner of the eye. This layer helps moisten the eye and clear dust from the surface of the cornea. Many other animals, including dogs, horses, and birds, also have a nictitating membrane.

THE SENSE OF SOUND

All tigers have noticeable white spots on the backs of their ears. The evolutionary purpose of these spots has not yet been determined. It has been suggested that the spots look like false eyes or "predator spots" to anything approaching from behind, making the tiger seem bigger and watchful to the rear, so putting off an attacker. This seems a plausible explanation, as many other species, including some caterpillars and butterflies, use this technique for self-preservation.

A second possibility is that the spots are used in aggressive communication. When one tiger threatens another, it twists its ears so that the backs face forward, prominently displaying the white markings. It is probable that both ideas have an element of truth in them and are not mutually exclusive.

Whatever the purpose of these spots, a tiger's hearing is its most highly developed sense, far more important to its success as a hunter than either sight or smell. With large pinnae—external ear flaps—rotating like radar dishes, a tiger can catch many sounds and with experience determine precisely where they originated. The ear picks up the high-frequency sounds made by prey rustling in the undergrowth and also low-frequency contact calls, neither of which humans can hear. The tiger's sensitive hearing alerts it not only to prey but also to the footsteps of people, making it one of the most elusive of animals. In the days when tiger hunting was a common pastime, tigers quickly learned to make their escapes when they heard the distant noise of a gun being loaded.

The tiger's ability to communicate by infrasound, a sound wave with a frequency below the range of normally audible sound (twenty hertz), has opened a new and exciting area of research. Many animals, such as elephants and whales, communicate at this low-pitched level. Infrasound is fantastically useful for communicating over long distances or through dense vegetation because it literally passes straight through objects ranging from leaves to trees to mountains. It is the perfect tool with which a solitary animal like the tiger can communicate with rivals and mates who are distributed widely in dense jungles. Edward J. Walsh and his team in Omaha, Nebraska, are now working with captive tigers in an effort to learn more about tiger sounds and, in particular, to discover whether different tigers can be identified by their infrasound roars. If so, conservationists would be able to count tigers more easily and accurately in the future. Here are Walsh's views on "listening to the tiger."

The white spots on the ears of this tigress are visible as she drinks at a quiet pool.

Listening to the Tiger

Edward J. Walsh

Snarl *by Rose Corcoran*

THE FULL RANGE OF *Panthera tigris* communication calls is less clearly understood and less formally documented than that of many other species of cat. This is due in part, no doubt, to the fact that tigers are generally taciturn, shy animals, living much of their lives in isolation and hunting quietly over relatively expansive territories. Accordingly, our understanding of tiger vocalization is derived largely from anecdotal reports filed by naturalists working in the field and close encounters between scientists and captive animals. As a consequence, the acoustical properties of a subset of utterances produced by tigers and communicated in close quarters are rather precisely characterized. On the other hand, the acoustic properties of many calls commonly uttered in the wild—for example, those intended to communicate over large distances as in territory-staking roars—have not been quantified, although they have been described anecdotally.

Close-encounter calls produced by an agitated tiger clearly convey the message that an attack is imminent; these calls include growling, snarling, barking, snorting, grunting, and roaring sounds, most of which form a spectral continuum with relatively clear features that are unique to a given category. While roars and barks are intense utterances, reaching levels in the range of 120 dB SPL (decibels sound pressure level, the standard unit for measuring sound) at distances close to the source, other close-encounter calls, most prominently represented by snarls, grunts, and growls, are relatively low-level ways of conveying the same basic message: an attack should be expected. The roar of a tiger contains sound energy spanning a relatively broad frequency range, although most of the acoustic power falls in the low-frequency portion of the spectrum, peaking in a relatively narrow frequency band centered at approximately three hundred hertz. At least occasionally, some tigers produce significant amounts of energy in the infrasonic band. The portion of the spectrogram representing growls reveals that the telltale difference between a growl and a roar is basically the absence of the three-hundred-hertz peak and associated harmonics.

The low-frequency character of utterances typically produced by tigers reflects their large vocal tract and the mass of their vocal folds in particular. As in essentially all vocal productions generated by forcing air over the vocal folds, the spectral signature of an individual is registered, in part at least, in the form of narrow, concentrated bands of acoustic energy known as formants, which are themselves determined by the volume of the vocal tract and the actions of articulators that modulate the frequency of an utterance. A snarling tiger illustrates the fact that utterances intended to intimidate are associated with dramatic visual displays—squinting eyes, flattened pinnae, furled muzzle, and glaring canines. Add a 120 dB SPL roar, and you have the ultimate package of intimidation.

Another relatively well-characterized close-encounter, low-intensity vocal production that is more sociable in

nature and sends an equally clear message of camaraderie to those who happen to wander into eye- and earshot is known as prusten, or chuffing. By forcing small bursts of air through the nasal cavity, a tiger in an agreeable mood greets a neighbor with a fluttering sound that gives an impression as much of a neighing horse as of a sociable tiger.

While most cats are widely known for their capacity to purr, the question of whether tigers are able to purr is unresolved. The debate pivots on the question of the anatomy of the hyoid bone, a structure lying at the back of the throat to which the musculature of both the tongue and larynx is attached. The structure is partially cartilaginous in tigers and other roaring cats but in most other felids it is completely bony, a feature that makes it less flexible. One school of thought suggests that purring is to the inflexible, bony hyoid apparatus as roaring is to the more flexible, cartilaginous version. Others disagree.

Efforts to determine precisely what tigers are capable of hearing are currently under way, and it appears that individuals representing all surviving subspecies are capable of sensing sounds in a relatively broad frequency band that extends into the ultrasonic range. Although the low-frequency limit of hearing remains untested, it is clear that individuals respond preferentially to low-frequency sounds, especially those carrying acoustic energy in the range of three hundred hertz, the precise frequency band that carries most of the sound energy associated with close-encounter roars.

EDWARD J. WALSH is the Director of the Developmental Auditory Physiology Laboratory at the Boys Town National Research Hospital in Omaha, Nebraska. He also holds appointments in the School of Medicine and in the Department of Special Education and Communication Disorders at the University of Nebraska.

THE SENSE OF SMELL

Like other cats, tigers do not rely heavily on scent to find prey. The nose of a tiger is much shorter than that of most dogs (except of course for such breeds as pugs and Pekinese, whose noses have been deliberately shortened through selective breeding).

A flehmen display, which is the result of encountering the scent of another tiger.

Tigers have fewer olfactory or smell-sensing cells than do dogs, and they have a correspondingly small smell-receiving area, called the olfactory bulb, in the brain. In cats, however, the cells are much more densely packed, making their odor-detecting ability equal to nearly half that of dogs and appreciably more than that of humans. Tigers can detect a scent another tiger left on a tree days earlier as a strong smell from which they can glean a good deal of information.

Scent may not be the most important sense in hunting, but it is extremely important for the purposes of communication. Cats, like other carnivores, have a pouchlike structure in the roof of the mouth known as the Jacobson's organ. Lined with receptor cells, it is positioned just behind the front incisors. Two tiny openings in the palate allow the scented air to reach this organ as the cat inhales. Nerves then carry a message to the olfactory part of the brain, where the scent is analyzed and identified.

This sniffing behavior is known as flehmen. The tiger curls back its upper lip, wrinkles its nose, and raises its head. To the uninitiated, it looks rather like a silent growl. Because adult tigers lead largely solitary lives, this form of communication is useful for finding out what is going on in their world—whether a female is in estrus, say, or a rival male has been encroaching on another's territory. Scent marking communicates a territorial boundary without the need for aggression, helps an individual find a mate at the right moment, and enables a female to keep in close contact with her cubs without making a sound.

Both males and females leave scented messages around the boundaries of their territories, in several different forms. Both sexes particularly favor spraying urine, since it is not costly in terms of energy and has a very strong, pungent odor. They choose prominent sites such as the bases of trees for this purpose. The positioning of the male's retractable penis enables him to spray urine effectively in various directions, so that it can be left where it is most likely to be detected by other tigers. Tigers spray-

Tigers mark their territory in a variety of ways. They identify the territories of others by sniffing the scented "messages."

mark more frequently after rain has washed away their previous marks and when they feel threatened. Amazingly, they can spray-mark every minute if necessary.

Spraying may be reinforced by visual signals in the form of scratching on the ground to leave a distinct impression called a scrape. Tigers then often mark their scrapes—mostly with urine (54 percent), sometimes with feces (17 percent). They sometimes leave a claw marking on specific soft trees as a visual signal. Tigers nearly always stand on their hind legs to scratch high up a tree trunk, usually at favorite spots around their territory, so these trees are covered in scratches.

They also leave behind a distinctive odor—on an object, on another tiger, or rubbed into patches of grass—produced by one of their scent glands. As a day-to-day example of this, when a domestic cat brushes itself around your legs or rubs against a chair leg, it intends to leave a scent. There are four main sites for scent glands on a cat's body:

OPPOSITE: *A tiger rakes its claws on a tree, leaving a territorial signal of its presence.*

- Glands between the toes can produce secretions that are left on scratching posts. This is why a tiger usually sniffs at a spot first, presumably to see if any of its scent remains from the previous visit. Cubs follow their mother by sniffing her scent left in her pugmarks.
- Glands around the anus leave their especially pungent mark on fecal deposits.
- Sebaceous glands on the cat's head, chin, lips, cheeks, and facial whiskers are often used to mark objects. Those on the cheeks are also used when a tigress and cub or a courting pair communicate by face rubbing.
- The tail gland acts as a means of communication between cats or between a domestic cat and its owner.

Researchers investigating tiger pheromone have discovered that it contains the same aroma as certain fragrant rice. Yet each tiger's smell is so individual that scientists in Russia are teaching highly trained dogs to learn these different scents, to help them count the number of tigers in the wild.

The Sense of Taste

Tigers taste salt, bitter, and acid flavors but are not as sensitive to sugar as other carnivores, such as dogs. A large number of minute, sharp, backward-pointing projections known as papillae cover their tongues, giving them rough surfaces, which are used in conjunction with the teeth to remove feathers or fur from prey and to scrape particles of meat off bones when licking them.

Everything about the tiger's anatomy contributes to making it a supreme hunter stationed at the top of the food chain.

CHAPTER 3

The I___ __e Tiger

Throughout the centur_____ _____, and other rulers of the land went after the tiger with spear_____ _____ants, and hundreds of people in efforts to kill this "striped devil," there was always a minority eager to keep forest habitats and wildlife alive. In the twentieth century, a few people began to take an interest in dis-covering something about the way the tiger lived, rather than focusing exclusively on how to kill it. In India, Major Jim Corbett, a legendary tiger hunter, and Frederick W. Champion, a forest officer, tried to photograph tigers with both still and movie cameras in an effort to understand more about them. In the 1920s and 1930s, little was known about the tiger save that it was solitary and evasive. Studying an elusive animal whose habits are unknown is difficult. Corbett may never have given up hunting, but he spent more and more time photographing tigers: he bought his first camera in the 1920s and filmed for

more than twenty years. His major achievement was his ability to get the provincial government in the foothills of the western Himalayas to create Hailey National Park in 1935, today a paradise for tigers called Corbett National Park.

The first serious information on tiger behavior did not emerge until 1965, with the conclusion of a research project undertaken in central India by American zoologist George Schaller, who had already opened the eyes of the world to the behavior of lions in the Serengeti. Now, for the first time, with the advent of some real "tiger science," we began to understand facets of territorial behavior and family life as never before.

On elephant and horseback, maharajahs hunted tigers with spears.

41

By 1970, there was a complete ban on tiger shooting in India, and more and more areas were protected from development so that the tiger could live its life without fear of encroachment by mankind.

Until that time, tiger hunting had continued, with the result that tigers avoided people wherever they could, becoming nocturnal and never appearing unless attracted to bait—Schaller had relied heavily on the use of tethered buffalo to attract tigers to areas where they could be observed. While most of the world still believed that tigers were basically man-eaters and generally evil in nature, Schaller's groundbreaking study provided momentum that the conservation movement in Asia had never had before. The deep concern expressed by political leaders such as Indira Gandhi and Rajiv Gandhi about the fate of the tiger made an enormous difference to policy and to its implementation on the grassroots level.

With the ban on hunting, the tiger enjoyed some kind of protection for the first time in centuries. By 1980, a small national park called Ranthambhore, in the state of Rajasthan in northwestern India, became a tiger haven, and over the next decade it and places like it reshaped the natural history of the tiger, thanks to the lack of human disturbance. In the 1980s, there were no hunters or people cutting wood and grass in Ranthambhore. Cubs born in these circumstances grew up free of the fear of people and produced cubs that were similarly unconcerned about human observers. It was one of the best periods in our history to watch tigers in the wild—a time that may never come again.

Ranthambhore became so important in part because the park consists largely of dry deciduous forest with excellent visibility. When the tigers lost their fear of the daylight in this protected habitat and ceased to hide their activities under cover of darkness, it gave us a fantastic opportunity to observe them. Even today, in denser habitat or where populations are more widely dispersed, tigers are rarely seen, and many scientists can track them only through radio-collaring.

Ranthambhore National Park covers an area of four hundred square kilometers (155 square miles), and at its core are a medieval fort, a rest house known as Jogi Mahal, and three lakes, Padam Talao, Rajbagh, and the seasonal Malik Talao, around which much tiger activity is centered. Ranthambhore's forests are situated at the meeting point of two hill ranges, the Aravallies and the Vindhyans, at the extreme western end of the tiger's Indian territory.

What follows is the story of the life of the tiger as I was able to observe it in Ranthambhore in the 1980s and early 1990s, with examples and additional information from scientists and conservationists around the world. Many secrets revealed during this time about the life of the tiger helped to combat the idea of the tiger being the most fearful and dreaded beast of the jungle. Observations at Ranthambhore were and continue to be crucial to our understanding of tiger behavior.

A tiger walks along the edge of a lake in Ranthambhore National Park. The Ranthambhore fort—nearly one thousand years old—crests the hill in the background.

Tiny cubs not even a few weeks old, cuddled up in their den.
At this stage of their growth they are especially vulnerable
and totally dependent on their mother.

BIRTH

Gestation varies from 93 to 110 days, with records of captive tigers indicating that 103 days (about three and a half months) is the norm. Cubs may be born at any time of the year—there seems to be no significant seasonal variation, even in harsh climates such as Siberia.

It is difficult to spot a pregnant tigress in the wild, as the bulge of her belly is visible only during the last ten to twelve days of pregnancy. However, she is heavy and may struggle to find sufficient food as hunting becomes more difficult. In his book *Tiger Trails in Assam* (1961), a tea planter named Patrick Hanley describes finding a heavily pregnant tigress lying in tall elephant grass at the edge of a tea estate. For two weeks, a male tiger brought her portions of kills, and when he arrived he would call out to her with a strange cry as if asking her to come out and start eating. This was an unusual incident—for the most part, the expectant mother is on her own.

In the last ten to fifteen days of her pregnancy, a tigress tends to become preoccupied with finding a safe place in which to give birth. This may be in a cave, under a rock overhang, or within a patch of thick bush with dense cover all around. As the time of delivery approaches, she will spend most of her time in the vicinity of the den, familiarizing herself with every corner of the terrain, including details of water supply and the movements of other animals. Her chosen spot not only must have sufficient prey within easy striking range but also must be able to conceal her cubs from predators on the ground and in the sky.

Zoo records indicate that a litter of cubs can be born within one hour, but sometimes the birth takes as long as twenty-four hours, during which time the tigress gets some nourishment from eating the placentas and embryonic sacs. The cubs are born blind and helpless, weighing between 785 and 1610 grams (1.75 to 3.5 pounds). It takes anywhere from three to fourteen days for their eyes to open, though full vision is not acquired until some weeks later. There may be as many as six or seven cubs in a litter, though in Ranthambhore the norm is three. The average recorded in zoos and in Chitwan National Park in Nepal is just under three, and in the harsher conditions of the Russian Far East it is between 1.2 and 1.9. The ratio of the sexes at birth is one to one. The tigress now becomes a committed, caring, and ruthlessly protective mother.

I have tried desperately to record this period of mystery, but I have never yet seen a tigress giving birth in the wild. Nor, so far as I know, has anyone else. However, Raghu S. Chundawat, one of India's finest scientists, has had the unique opportunity to watch the first days in a cub's life. His observation is the only one of which I am aware. He filmed a mother and newly born cubs from one hundred meters away as they lay together in a cave. This period is all about cuddling and suckling. On film, the cubs are like wriggling balls of fur, rolling all over their mother and drinking her nutritious milk. Chundawat's description reveals much about the birth and nurturing of tiger cubs.

TERRITORIAL CHANGEOVER: A MYSTERY

Raghu S. Chundawat

Biologist Raghu S. Chundawat attaches a radio collar on a tranquilized tiger as veterinarian Pradeep Malik and a forest guard look on.

EVERY TIGER SIGHTING IN THE WILD brings great excitement, and I, like many others, never grow tired of watching them. Tracking them with the help of radio telemetry and being able to observe them is an elating experience.

We were back in the field after a monsoon break in November. I was expecting a second litter of cubs from the collared tigress we called "120." According to our telemetry monitoring, 120's cubs would be about three months old; two sets of tiny pugmarks on the road were the first evidence of their existence. No one had seen the tigress while we were away, but now the signal from her collar indicated that she was nearby. We soon caught up with her. Her nipples were enlarged and red, a sure sign that she had cubs suckling. But it seemed they were not with her. We made several attempts to see the cubs but failed every time. We also found that her movements and behavior were unusual, and she always looked nervous and alert, very unlike her normal self. Moreover, she was not visiting her favorite places as regularly as she used to. We wondered what had caused this change in her. There were signs of her cubs coming to kills and feeding, and we spent hours hoping that she would bring them out. But she never did. We also set up a remote video monitor, but that did not reveal much either.

Her movements continued to be irregular; she started spending more time away from her core area and was calling frequently. During this time, we also noticed the presence of a new male in the area. If he had taken over the territory, he may have been a threat to the young cubs and the cause of 120's uneasiness. We had one glimpse of the cubs over a cattle kill on December 26. Things shortly settled down and 120 returned to her old haunts, but we never saw the cubs again. We suspected infanticide, a common occurrence when a new male usurps a territory, and were hoping that by early June or July 120 would have cubs by the new territorial male.

Her movements became localized in a gorge much earlier than we expected. It was about three months since we had last seen her with cubs, only six months since she had given birth to them, much too early to expect a new litter from her. But we went to look and after some hours saw her come out of thick undergrowth and walk away, trying to hide herself among the rocks at the base of a huge escarpment. We were relieved that she was all right but were still not sure why she had stayed in this place for so long. Looking through the binoculars on the second day, we could make out that her breasts were large and hanging. This was certainly a surprise. How could she have new cubs, when we had seen her previous offspring only ninety-five days before? Had she conceived when her cubs were still with her? If so, how did she come to be receptive? It remains a physiological mystery to us. Did constant association with the new male induce her? We don't know, and there are not many examples and explanations for this extraordinary event. Her irregular movements early on do indicate that she was unsettled, so perhaps she was being pushed around by the new male. Going through such a phase is very stressful for a tigress, but at least she might now have a set of cubs with the new male; as long as he was around she should have no worries.

On the seventh day, we found her signals coming from a different location. Finding a small ledge from which we could look down into the gorge from the cover of a bush, we tried to pinpoint the exact source. As the sun moved down the slope opposite, 120 suddenly came into view at the entrance of a cave. She lay down in the sun at the opening. Moments later, we spotted a movement to one side, and two tiny cubs tumbled their way to her belly. It was an exhilarating experience. Watching the family over several days was the most memorable time I have ever spent with tigers.

It is rare to see cubs as young as these, and this was one of the most unusual opportunities I ever had. We particularly noticed how conscientious 120 was about cleanliness. Not only did she keep her babies clean, she would also always lick her nipples clean after the cubs had suckled, thus minimizing the infections to which these tiny creatures are vulnerable. She also moved the cubs frequently until they were able to walk with her. For the cubs she was like a milk bar—they drank frequently and often went to sleep attached to their mother's nipples.

She, however, went without a meal for seven to eight days before going out of the gorge to find food. Once she made a kill, she fed quickly and returned to the cubs as fast and as directly as possible. We observed that if the kill was too far from the den and her cubs, she rarely went back to it. Twice she made a kill far from the den, then returned to her cubs without even feeding on the carcass and never returned to it. This shows how concerned these mothers are when they are away from their cubs. When her kill was nearby, she made several short visits to it.

When cubs are ten to twenty days old, the mother spends, on average, fourteen to sixteen hours per day either with them or nearby, keeping a constant watch. It is only when the cubs are three to four weeks old that she is able to spend a substantial amount of time away from them. On one occasion, 120 was away from her cubs for more than fourteen hours. She had killed a nilgai (a great Indian antelope) about six kilometers (3.6 miles) away, fed on it a little, and hurried back to the den. When the cubs are more than two months old, they start moving with their mother, and it is at this stage that they are very rarely seen. By the time they are two and half months old they are able to move long distances with her and she will bring them to a kill. 120 returned to her favorite areas with her new cubs. She was back to her old self—cool and trusting—and she brought her cubs to the kill in our presence, as she had with her first litter. The cubs were also open and bold, and we saw them frequently in their mother's usual territory.

RAGHU S. CHUNDAWAT is one of India's foremost wildlife biologists. He did his doctorate on the snow leopard and has spent the last eight years studying the behavior of wild tigers in Panna National Park in central India.

THE FIRST MONTHS

The youngest cubs I have seen in Ranthambhore were about ten weeks old. This was in March 2002, when Mike Birkhead, a film producer with whom I was associated, and I found four cubs with their mother and were able to watch and film them for long periods. Surprisingly, the tigress was walking her little cubs down the middle of a road and seemed perfectly comfortable in the presence of human observers. Tiger mothers are very individualistic in their behavior when they have cubs. But whether they are shy and elusive or relaxed and confident, finding sufficient food is vital, as the tigress must keep herself well fed in order to provide enough milk to nourish her family.

These early hunting forays must be nerve-racking times for the tigress, with half her mind always on the safety of her cubs. If disturbed, she will be aggressive and may even charge to kill, whether the disturbance comes from other predators, scavengers, or human intruders. In *Man-eaters and Jungle Killers* (1957), a memoir of his experience hunting tigers in Madras, Kenneth Anderson, a legendary slayer of man-eating tigers, described an encounter with a tiger family that was denning under "a shelving rock which met the rising ground at an angle of perhaps thirty degrees, forming a shallow recess rather than a real cave":

> Two large balls of russet brown, striped with black, white underneath, were tumbling over one another in a vigorous game of "catch-as-catch-can." They were two tiger cubs, and they were playing. I stopped in my tracks, the only movement being an imperceptible cocking of the rifle, with the faintest of clicks. But it was enough. They stopped playing, disentangled themselves, and looked at me in alarm. One with a look of innocent surprise and the other with its features wrinkled to emit a hiss of consternation.
>
> That hiss was the signal for all hell to break loose, for it awoke the tigress, who was sleeping. With a series of shattering roars she dashed out of the cavern, vaulted over the cubs and came straight at me. The distance may have been twenty yards. I covered her between the eyes as she advanced. Then, five yards away, she stopped. She crouched with her belly to the ground, eyes blazing, while her roars and snarls shook the very ground on which I stood.
>
> Wonder of wonders, she had not charged home. Her courage had failed her at the last moment. She was telling me, in the simplest language, "Get out quickly, and don't harm my cubs or I will kill you." Step by step I retreated backwards, while never removing my eyes from her, never allowing the rifle sights to waver in the slightest, my forefinger still on the trigger. And she remained where she was. It was as if she understood that I was going.

I know of three occasions in the last five years when a patrolling party in Ranthambhore has had a fleeting glimpse of a tigress with tiny cubs tucked away in

OPPOSITE: *Mother and cub in their den, only days after the cub was born. This picture, taken in Panna National Park in central India, is one of the earliest of a wild cub and its mother.*

thick bush surrounded by high grass. In each case, they were charged by the furious mother and escaped by the skins of their teeth.

A tigress treats any intrusion into the area where she has hidden her cubs with great suspicion, and if sufficiently disturbed she is likely to abandon the den. She moves her helpless cubs one by one, holding each by the scruff of the neck as it hangs from her mouth and whimpers, and leaving it in the safety of the new den before returning for the next cub. I have witnessed such a scene, and it is amazing to see this supreme predator holding her cubs so gently with those fearsome teeth. A solo parent, the tigress is alone in providing this protection and security, doing the job efficiently and with great care.

Tiger cubs are vulnerable in their first few months, with mortality as high as 50 percent, sometimes more. They may fall victim to attacks by wild dogs, leopards, snakes, or other tigers, so all their mother's attention goes into keeping them alive and healthy. She spends endless time licking and cleaning them to promote better circulation and bowel movements. She also eats their feces, which may make it more difficult for potential predators to pick up their smell.

ABOVE: *A two-month-old cub approaches the photographer. Young cubs are curious and eager to explore their environment.*

OPPOSITE: *In the first month, the intensely protective mother might change dens if she feels threatened or disturbed. Here, a tigress is shown gently carrying her cub to a new den.*

ABOVE: *A tigress just moments after killing an adult spotted deer stag. She is dragging it to her cubs in a nearby shelter. Mothers can drag the carcasses of animals several kilometers to waiting cubs.*

OPPOSITE: *A tigress leads her four-month-old cubs out of a pool of water on a hot summer's day. Cooling off is an essential activity when temperatures soar.*

As the days roll by and the cubs grow, they become frisky, starting limited exploratory ventures around their den and playing with leaves, branches, and anything else that takes their fancy. By the time they are six to eight weeks old, their mother is carrying meat back to the den for them, and I once followed the drag marks of a chital (the Indian spotted deer, and along with the sambar deer—the largest deer in India, standing five feet at the shoulders and weighing 320 kilograms (704 pounds) or more—a favorite prey of tigers in Ranthambhore) nearly 1.5 kilometers (one mile) from where it was killed before I lost it in a thick gorge. Unlike a lion, a tigress will open up a kill for her cubs, but she rarely eats first unless her cubs are very young.

FAMILY LIFE

In March 1985, after nine years of watching tigers, I had my first real insight into family life when I discovered a tigress named Laxmi with a brood of three small cubs. On the day I encountered her, I was driving in my jeep. In the distance, two sambar hinds moved gingerly away, tails half raised. A chital, motionless, looked sharply toward the forest. I was unable to pick out anything. The shrill alarm of a peacock broke the silence, then another peacock picked up the call. After a few seconds, the alarm call of the chital pierced my ears. Frenzied and frequent calling surrounded me. Quietly, I watched the forest. It sounded as if the tigers must be walking toward the vehicle track.

Suddenly, shades of tan and black emerge from the dull yellow of the forest. Laxmi appeared with three tiny cubs, one of which jumped across the road. It looked about two and a half to three months old. It was my first glimpse ever of cubs this size. Laxmi settled down on the track for a few minutes. Her cubs looked at me furtively from the cover of a bush. She soon rose and paced leisurely into the forest, followed by the three scampering cubs. They moved toward a network of ravines and disappeared from sight. I rushed back to base, my heart pounding with excitement.

The next morning, I found Laxmi sitting in a patch of grass ten to fifteen meters (eleven to sixteen yards) from the forest track. Her three cubs surrounded her. One nuzzled her face, another rested against her back, the third watched us curiously, moving tentatively toward us before rushing back to the security of its mother. The cubs turned their attention on one another, leaping into the air and knocking into one another. Then they dashed toward Laxmi. She licked one of them thoroughly, then laid down on her side to suckle them. All three soon found the right teat and fed, stimulating the flow of milk with their tiny paws. For fifteen minutes I watched this remarkable spectacle. I have never seen such a display of love and warmth, such evidence of the strong bond between a tigress and her cubs.

There is a close physical bond between mother and cubs. Here three four-month-old cubs surround a tigress as they watch the photographer. At this age nuzzling, cuddling, licking, and rubbing is a part of daily life for the cubs.

All this activity seems to continue without the presence of a father, as the male is said to leave the female immediately after mating. Most of the time while her cubs are young, the tigress must protect them from adult males. Infanticide is common when a new male takes over a territory, and as long ago as 1892 a forest officer named J. Inglis reported in the *Journal of the Bombay Natural History Society* an instance of a mauled cub being found at the site of a fight between a male and female. However, Sainthill Eardley-Wilmot, also a forest officer, took another view in his book *Forest Life and Sport in India* (1910): "The male tiger does not seem to be addicted to infanticide, though when they are in confinement this crime is reported as not uncommon: in fact I have seen him in company with cubs of all ages and it is probably the difficulty of finding food for many voracious mouths that ultimately enforces separation." Eardley-Wilmot's view was not widely accepted—for three quarters of a century after his book was published almost everyone believed that adult male tigers killed cubs. But in the spring of 1986 I observed behavior at a pool of water in Ranthambhore Park that supported Eardley-Wilmot's assertion. At four in the afternoon Kublai (the resident male) ambled toward the pool and slid into the water, hind legs first, soaking himself completely and leaving just his head visible. (Tigers don't like water splashing in their eyes and most of them enter the water backward.)

Cubs are suckled by their mother for several months. These four-month-olds subsist on a diet of both milk and meat.

A rare photograph of a tiger family cooling off in a water hole. It is uncommon for a resident male (in front) to be observed with a tigress and her cubs.

About twenty minutes later Nalghati (a resident female) followed and they both lazed around in the water. Minutes later her male cub walked quite nonchalantly toward the pool, not a flicker of surprise or fear on his face, circled the two adults, and entered the water near where Kublai was stretched out. Soon, following her brother, a female cub walked to the pool, entering the water to sit on her mother's paw. Nalghati licked her face. One big happy family: Nalghati, Kublai, and two five-month-old cubs were all in close proximity, soaking themselves in this rather small pool of water.

A half hour later the male cub rose, quickly nuzzled Kublai, and left the pool. The female cub followed him and they played, leaping at each other, slowly drifting toward a tree, clambering up the branches under the protective eye of Kublai. At dusk, Kublai heaved himself out of the water and moved toward the cubs. The cubs rushed up to him and he licked one of them.

When I left, Kublai was sitting a meter or so from the two cubs. I had witnessed what must be one of the most closely kept secrets of a tiger's life and now have the first photographic record in the world of a resident male associating with a tigress and her cubs in his range.

That same month, I saw exactly the same thing happening in another part of the forest. Just at the edge of Semli, in the gorge of Bakaula, we found the Bakaula male and Laxmi sitting on the vehicle track facing each other. Thick groves of jamun trees, cool, lush, and green, lined both sides of the track. There were pools of water of various sizes nearby. Laxmi rose briefly and nuzzled the Bakaula male before moving a little way ahead to lie down on her side.

The tranquil scene was disturbed by the distant sound of a rolling pebble. Both tigers became alert. Laxmi moved stealthily toward the sound. The Bakaula male sat up expectantly. A sambar walked carefully down an incline. Laxmi was too far away to attack, but the sambar's path was taking it unknowingly toward the Bakaula male, who crouched, muscles tense. The sambar approached the vehicle track. The tiger took off like a bullet. Six bounds and he leapt onto the back of the sambar, bringing it crashing down. He quickly transferred his grip to the sambar's throat. At the same instant a group of noisy tourists arrived and disturbed the male, who walked off behind a bush, leaving the sambar injured but not quite dead.

Laxmi arrived. Comfortable in the presence of jeeps, she gripped the sambar's throat for a couple of minutes, ensuring that there was no life left in it, and started the tedious process of dragging the 180-kilogram carcass away, a few meters at a time, into thick cover. The Bakaula male watched her carefully. The carcass was now some fifteen meters inside the jamun grove, at the edge of a small clearing. The male moved toward it.

A resident male with a fourteen-month-old cub. This unique picture provides startling insights into the secret world of tigers. The role of the male as a father has only been recorded on film in the last twenty years.

An amusing scene now confronted us: the male tiger, with his forepaws on the sambar's rump, had a firm grip on one of the hind legs; Laxmi had a firm grip on the throat. The carcass was stretched between the two tigers. A tug-of-war ensued as each tried to pull the carcass a little toward itself. Both tigers emitted low-pitched growls, interspersed with Herculean tugs at the carcass. Then, with a sudden burst of energy and strength, Laxmi yanked the carcass some four meters away with the Bakaula male astride its rump: a remarkable feat, as sambar and tiger together must weigh about 450 kilograms. But the effort exhausted her and she let go of the sambar's throat. The male quickly pulled the carcass out of sight.

Laxmi strode off. Entering a dry streambed that led to her den, she started to call loudly and was greeted by birdlike squeaks from her cubs. In minutes Laxmi returned to the site of the struggle with the cubs running around her in circles. They seemed quite relaxed, as if this wasn't the first occasion on which they were going to share a feast with the Bakaula male. Soon they all disappeared out of sight to where the Bakaula male and the carcass lay. Twice I had seen a remarkable facet of the family life of tigers—the resident male playing the role of father.

This was, needless to say, one of the most extraordinary encounters I had ever had with tigers.

Mother Protection

In March 2003, in the Bandhavgarh National Park in central India, a resident male tiger in his prime was frequently found spending time in the company of a tigress and her four seven-month-old cubs. The relationships between all the tigers seemed familiar and comfortable. A colleague visited the area at that time and was told that the female, who was suckling her cubs, had even suckled the male.

From these observations it became clear that a resident male fulfilled a paternal role for all the litters in his territory. Contrary to many earlier reports, we saw adult males sharing kills with their cubs, spending time with them, and protecting the area from other tigers so that the youngsters had a secure environment in which to grow up.

In Ranthambhore, it is rare to hear of a fatal interaction between tigers, especially between a male and a female. If these do occur the natural cycle of a forest destroys the evidence, burying it in the earth. In all the years I have been following tigers, I know of only one example of mortal combat, and it demonstrates how fiercely a tigress will defend her cubs when she encounters a transient male. From traces I discovered the next morning, I was able to reconstruct what must have happened.

There was a full moon on the night of November 10, 1981, when a tigress with two cubs was apparently walking down the Lahpur valley, nearly twenty kilometers (twelve miles) from Jogi Mahal, the rest house in the park. She must have spotted an adult male tiger walking in the opposite direction. There were signs that the cubs had

scampered away. The tigress seems to have continued toward the tiger, and there were marks where both had sat down in the middle of the road. They must then have risen and gone to sit in the sandy part of a nearby streambed, perhaps an attempt on the part of the tigress to show affection and thus pacify the male and then bid him a rapid farewell before there was any possibility of contact between him and the cubs. Apparently, the cubs attempted to scamper back to their mother, probably finding the insecurity of separation too much to take.

The havoc this caused was heard at a guard post some two kilometers away. The male must have moved in a flash toward the cubs, forcing the mother to take lightning action. With a leap and a bound she attacked the male from the rear, clawing his right foreleg before sinking in her canines and killing him. Likely caught completely by surprise, he quickly succumbed. Later, the tigress proceeded to open his rump and eat off his left hind leg. (In this instance, and in most cases of tiger cannibalism, a part of the defeated animal is eaten to prove domination.) This was a rare example of tiger eating tiger and a graphic demonstration of the complete devotion of the mother to the safety of her cubs.

W. D. Ritchie, a British forest officer who stayed in India after independence, recorded a similar fight in Assam in 1950, when a tigress killed a big male, presumably also to protect her cubs. She, too, ate a chunk of meat from his carcass.

FAMILY AND THE COMPETITION FOR FOOD

By the time they are six months old, the cubs are weaned and roam around more freely. They are now the size of large dogs, and the tigress moves them greater distances, her hunting range expanding considerably as the youngsters familiarize themselves with various landmarks; observe the habits of prey and the way their mother stalks, kills, and eats it; explore waterholes; and generally learn about the forest. The tigress now has two major concerns: training her cubs to hunt and to fend for themselves, and procuring enough food for them all. The cubs are growing fast, their increased appetites demanding a constant supply of food. They are not mature enough to help their mother hunt; indeed, they are more likely to get in her way and spoil her chances of making a kill. It is during this period that she instills discipline with the occasional slap and sharp growl, and through a complex series of sounds the cubs are trained to avoid danger and to remain quiet when their mother hunts. In fact, on her instruction they can remain rooted to a spot for hours on end.

OPPOSITE: *At twelve months old, cubs frequently run, stalk, and leap. The play between cubs will determine their hunting abilities in the future.*

By the time the cubs are eight to ten months old, mother and youngsters are beginning to hunt together. Hunting is now a full-time obsession—a tigress with two cubs has to kill seventy to seventy-five deer-sized animals in a year, about 45 percent more than her solo requirement, to ensure that there is enough food to go around.

On a memorable morning in 1987, I was watching Noon, one of the females I was able to study most closely during that time. I had stopped near Rajbagh, but the barking of a langur monkey from the side of the lake spurred me on. The sun was just rising over a hill. Amid a cacophony of chital, sambar, and langur calls, I turned a corner to find Noon walking nonchalantly with a chital fawn swinging in her mouth. As she walked along the shore of the lake, a few peahens took flight. She headed for a bank of high grass, startling two peacocks. The male cub, in the lead, grabbed the fawn from Noon's jaws and darted back to a clump of grass. Noon licked her female cub, and they both reclined at the edge of the grass. The male polished off most of the carcass, but toward the end Noon interrupted him. He snarled at her, but she ignored him and picked up the remnants.

The female joined her mother, and they chewed on the bits and pieces the male left behind. An hour went by, and then mother and cubs left the grass, walking along the edge of the lake toward Padam Talao. The cubs jumped and chased each other as they walked around the lake. One charged into Noon, and she snarled in annoyance. All three reached the edge of the first lake. The cubs turned a corner and disappeared.

Noon walked in front of us on the vehicle track. Two sambar alarm calls blasted the silence. The cubs had been seen. Noon was now completely alert and darted forward on the track, realizing that the sambar was caught between the track and her cubs. The cubs assisted her unintentionally. There was a thud of hooves and a noise in the undergrowth. Noon settled down on her belly, frozen to the ground at a point where a narrow animal path led out from the edge of the lake. She judged the exit point exactly. A large rock hid her. In a flash, she leaped into the forest and was out of sight. I heard a grunt.

Driving a little farther, I saw Noon a few meters off the track, in the process of killing a sambar hind. She had a perfect grip on the throat. The sambar's legs twisted in vain; her hold was firm. The cubs approached cautiously and watched their mother intently. The male cub moved to the carcass, but a flicker from the sambar's hind leg forced it to retreat. In minutes, the sambar was dead. The cub rested his forepaw on the rump, while Noon held her grip and the female cub stood near her mother. Noon dragged the carcass away to where a thick bush made visibility difficult. The cubs jumped all over the sambar and their mother. A kill of this size fed mother and cubs for three days.

One of the largest litters I ever had the privilege of observing numbered five cubs, born to the tigress Padmini in 1977. A litter of this size is rare, the only other example I have found being recorded by another forest officer, R. C. Morris, in 1925.

As the month following my encounter with Padmini and her cubs went by, sightings of the cubs became more frequent, and I found that there were three males and two females. One of the females was in poor condition and lagged behind. She was obviously getting the smallest share of the meat. Padmini's task was enormous: to hunt and kill for such a large brood, now needing at least twenty to thirty kilograms (forty-four to sixty-six pounds) of meat per day. By the following month, there was no sign of the small female, and I felt sure that nature must have taken its course. Survival is only of the fittest, and feeding five cubs is no easy task. This age of six to eight months can be very tough to survive.

THREATS TO CUBS

Until the age of about fourteen to fifteen months, the cubs spend much of their time playing either with one another or with their mother. Bouts of play can be long and tiring as the cubs charge and swat at one another and even race up and down trees, something they continue to do until they become too heavy—it also provides a haven if they are threatened by wild dogs or other tigers. Adult tigers do not climb trees under normal circumstances, but when cornered by hunters they have been known to take refuge in surprisingly high branches. In the *Journal of the Bombay Natural History Society* in 1923, a government officer named G. E. R. Cooper reported an incident of a tiger climbing eleven meters (thirty-five feet) up toward a machan (the raised platform used by tiger hunters).

During the floods of 1969 in the Sundarbans delta in northeastern India, tigers climbed up trees ten meters high to escape drowning. But these were exceptional

Until they are about sixteen months old, cubs routinely explore the branches of trees, and they are light enough to clamber up and down. In a way, this is playtime.

circumstances. In Ranthambhore I have seen tigers on trees about ten times, and only once was it an adult tigress, who was sitting on the lowest branches. On all the other occasions it was cubs, whether in play or to escape from danger.

In 2001–2002, a resident tigress named Machli was rearing two male cubs, who spent endless time charging back and forth on the edge of the lake, splashing water at each other and playing hide-and-seek in the tall grass. They would snarl and hiss at sunbathing crocodiles, which would turn on them, sending them scampering back to cover. All these activities strengthen the cubs' muscles and flex their limbs for what lies ahead.

Nevertheless, the mother has to be alert to any kind of danger. In the first few months, the resident male who had fathered Machli's litter kept a protective eye on them, but suddenly he vanished, and within a couple of months younger male tigers were vying for the area and the tigress's attentions. When new males kill cubs it brings the female back into estrus, enabling a newcomer to mate with her and sire cubs of his own. Given the chance, he will kill small cubs of both sexes; however, once they are about a year old he seems to tolerate the females, perhaps viewing them as future

reproductive partners, whereas he will kill the males, whom he presumably sees as potential rivals.

Machli had enormous difficulty keeping her cubs safe from the new males. Along with a colleague, I watched her over a two-week period during which she roared constantly, asserting her territorial rights to the area and demonstrating her aggression toward the intruders. She even fought one of them off, clawing his paw and forcing him to limp away. Her whole nature had changed—she was much more watchful and tense, buying time so that the cubs could reach subadulthood unscathed. She even seduced one of the new males, briefly allowing him to mate with her. This was the first time I had noticed something like this, although a similar incident occurred in Panna National Park, in Chundawat's study area. These are the only examples I know of a tigress giving temporary "conjugal rights" to a new male and thereby protecting her cubs from infanticide.

Machli succeeded in raising her cubs and quickly conceived again once they matured and left her to carve out their own territories elsewhere. By this time, her mate had established himself as the new resident of the area, and everything was much calmer. Machli's actions prove that a tigress can protect her cubs till adulthood even when the male who fathered the litter is gone, though only with difficulty.

Avoiding danger may be even more challenging when the threat comes from people. In September 2002, as part of an organized protest, hundreds of people armed with long sticks, muzzle-loading guns, and swords led thousands of head of livestock into Ranthambhore National Park to graze illegally. The place where they camped was the heart of the territory of a superb tigress who had four nine-month-old cubs. It was a traumatic day. No one now knows exactly what happened, but the tigress was probably poisoned along with two of her cubs. The other two survived and were found roaming a patch of forest in a starved condition. In the absence of their mother, cubs of that age normally die, since they have no idea how to hunt. In addition, the monsoon of 2002 was virtually nonexistent, so Ranthambhore was in the grip of the severest drought in decades. In an attempt to keep the cubs alive and see whether they could learn to fend for themselves, the park authorities fed these two orphaned cubs goats, but the cubs had a tough year ahead of them nonetheless. In March 2003 they were both alive, their permanent teeth had replaced their milk teeth—a key factor in a young tiger's ability to fend for itself—and the male cub was able to kill small chital. The female still needed goats. She had also started to focus her attention on the fringe of the forest in her search for food, where there was a danger that she would start taking livestock and come into conflict with the forest communities. When this happens, local grazers may deliberately poison carcasses in revenge. Monitoring the female became essential. The incident was a tragic reminder of how easy it is for people to destroy an entire tiger family.

LEARNING ADULT SKILLS

It is the mother's skill in training her cubs that ensures their survival. Until the age of eighteen months, cubs are dependent on their mother's hunting abilities. Our observations of Padmini's large litter made clear the trouble a tigress takes to show her offspring how to hunt for themselves.

Padmini spent a lot of time trying to prevent us from seeing her cubs. In fact, twice she led us off in pursuit, allowing the cubs to evade us. Nevertheless, I had a marvelous opportunity to observe the growing-up process. The cub known as Akbar was the most confident of the four and always came closest to us, followed by Babar and Hamir, and finally the only female, Laxmi.

Late one evening, I spotted the family by the side of a road. Akbar was sitting boldly in front, with Padmini and Laxmi sleeping behind him. Our presence heralded some interaction, with Laxmi getting up and nuzzling her mother, and Padmini returning her gesture with a few licks. Babar and Hamir played in the distance, circling each other and mock pawing. Akbar rose suddenly and, in a few bounds, leaped toward his brothers. Hamir rose in anticipation and they greeted each other—both rising on their hind feet and boxing each other gently with their forepaws.

We wanted to observe the behavior of the family around a kill. The park director brought a buffalo and turned it loose close by the tigers. Padmini moved in a flash, but instead of killing it she chose to incapacitate it with a blow to its hindquarters. She then withdrew and sat a little distance away. The injured buffalo limped around in front of the cubs. Very cautiously, Akbar and Hamir approached it, but the buffalo charged them clumsily, and they rushed away into high grass. Again they emerged, with Babar and Laxmi following, taking up four positions to encircle the prey, but whenever they tried to go in close the buffalo charged. This little scene lasted thirty minutes while Padmini looked on. Suddenly, Akbar leaped toward the buffalo, landing on its hindquarters and bringing it down. After several clumsy movements he sank his canines into the animal's neck. Hamir now entered the fray and sat on the rump. Soon they started eating, but after some twenty minutes Padmini rose and moved them off, walking toward Babar and Laxmi and nudging them as if to say, "Come on, it's your turn." Being shier than their brothers, they did not get up and feed until Akbar and Hamir had eaten their fill. Padmini then started feeding herself. She was not only allowing the cubs to learn how to kill but also ensuring the equal sharing of food.

This method of training the young has been recorded by many observers, among them forest officer Frederick C. Hicks, who wrote in *Forty Years Among the Wild Animals of India* (1910): "If cubs are present, the hind leg of the kill will frequently be found to be broken, the idea being to disable the animal and then to play with it alive for the edification of the cubs, while the nose, ears and eyes will invariably be found much gnawed and torn by the cubs." George Schaller witnessed a tigress teaching her

three-year-old cubs to kill a tethered buffalo, which kept them at bay for two and a half hours—the tigress twice had to throw the prey to the ground to assist the cubs' endeavors.

Until the cubs are about fourteen or fifteen months, the tigress tends, in my experience, to give way to them on a kill, allowing them to eat first, but in the last months that the cubs are with her she becomes much more aggressive and will eat first if she chooses. As the cubs grow, they actively assist their mother in the hunt, even though they are still clumsy and sometimes get in the way.

The strong bonds that persist between members of a tiger family are remarkable. Some ten years after the incident described above, I was watching Laxmi, now with three cubs of her own, two females and a male. One warm afternoon in March 1987, I arrived at a water hole to find Laxmi's cubs resting in the cool of the undergrowth. One of the females moved toward us, in her normal way, walking very close to the jeep. There was no sign of Laxmi. The cubs lazed around for nearly an hour, but at four o'clock one of them suddenly became alert. It darted off to the far side of the water hole, followed by its siblings. The forest exploded with the sound of purring as the cubs exhaled great bursts of what sounded like joy. I followed to find the cubs rubbing their flanks against Laxmi. All four tigers purred incessantly, as if orchestrated, as the cubs licked, nuzzled, and cuddled their mother. The sounds echoed and resounded

with great intensity. Although they are capable of a wide range of sounds, tigers are basically silent animals, and vocalization is rare. In all my years of tiger watching in Ranthambhore I have never heard purring the way I did on this occasion.

The purring continued for nearly ten minutes, as all four tigers walked toward us. The cubs rubbed their bodies against Laxmi, expressing their delight at seeing her. They moved to the water hole and quenched their thirst, then Laxmi moved some twenty meters away to rest in the shade of a tree. The cubs returned to their original positions.

It was nearly five when I decided to watch from a distance, hoping that some deer would come to the water hole to quench their thirst. At six o'clock, a group of fourteen chital emerged from the cover of the forest and cautiously approached the water. Laxmi was suddenly alert, watching intensely. The deer had not seen her or the cubs. The cubs froze, knowing that the slightest movement would give them away. Most of the deer had their tails up, a sign that they at least sensed the tigers' presence. They stood between the mother and her cubs, a perfect situation for Laxmi. She crouched, then moved forward some three meters on her belly as if gliding along the ground. A chital alarm call pierced the evening.

Laxmi moved in a flash. Her cubs sprinted from the far side, and in the panic and confusion of the moment a fawn became separated from the group and fled toward the tigress, who pinioned it between her paws and grabbed the back of its neck. The fawn squealed and died. A stork-billed kingfisher flew away from its perch, its blue wings glinting in the evening light. Picking up the fawn, Laxmi carried it away.

Her cubs moved in, hoping to feast on a few morsels. Laxmi dropped the fawn to the ground and settled on it, covering the tiny carcass with her paws. She turned and snarled viciously at the approaching cubs. One of the females moved off, but the other two settled down a meter away to face their mother. Both emitted low-pitched moaning sounds, which I had never heard before. The noises soon turned into wails, as if the cubs were begging for the carcass. Laxmi snarled and coughed sharply at them. The male cub rose and moved toward her, but she growled, picking up the carcass and lying down again some three meters away, the fawn between her paws.

All three cubs now settled around her, moaning. She snarled in response, and this continued for fifteen minutes. Suddenly, two of the cubs cannonballed into her, and all three tigers rolled over in a flurry of activity; then the male cub snatched the carcass expertly and rushed away with it, followed by one of his sisters. Laxmi sat unconcerned and began to groom herself. The male would not tolerate his sisters on the carcass, so they returned to their mother. They watched their brother eating, waiting patiently for forty-five minutes until the fawn had been consumed. Then they all moved on. When the prey is tiny, the dominant cub asserts his right to eat most of it. He shares only when the kill is large.

THE BREAKUP OF THE FAMILY

By the age of sixteen months, young tigers have grown the permanent teeth that enable them to kill prey effectively. At this time, the hierarchical order among cubs becomes clearly defined: the dominant one has the pick of everything and will always eat first. Although this is most frequently a male, I have seen two litters in which the dominant cub was a female who totally tyrannized her brother. Whatever its sex, the dominant cub is now more confident, aggressive, and even able to push its mother around. Eating on a carcass may follow a strict "pecking order," and if the cubs are three or four in number and the prey small, the least dominant one rarely gets a chance to eat.

OPPOSITE: *A rare picture of a father (right) and a mother with their ten-month-old cub. The cuddling that takes place between cub and parents fosters a vital bond that cubs frequently reassert.*

Within a few months, the dominant cub will leave the family unit, followed in due course by his or her siblings. Up to the age of twenty-two months and sometimes even later, subadults will still join their mother on kills, even though they are spending most of the rest of the time away from her. In this way, they are assured of a supply of food while they continue to polish their own hunting skills.

In 2003, when Machli's two male cubs were nearly eighteen months old and ready to leave her, I witnessed an encounter that revealed the intense bonds that exist between mother and cubs, even at this age. Although both cubs were now the same size as their mother, she nevertheless allowed them to suckle for ten minutes. Not that she had any milk—it was more like a farewell gesture, with the young tigers tasting the intimacy of their mother's devotion for the last time. A remarkable scene.

I often wonder what exactly happens as family groups break up. After watching wild tigers for decades, I remain convinced that you cannot generalize about this or anything else to do with their behavior. At the same time as Machli's eighteen-month-old cubs were leaving her to lead their own lives, the Lahpur family in another part of the park was still together, though the youngsters were twenty-four months old. In fact, the two male cubs tended to roam around together while the female and her mother kept together, and they would all meet up to feed on a kill, irrespective of who had made it. I had an amazing opportunity to witness this in January 2003, when the Lahpur female killed an enormous sambar stag and all four tigers gathered around the kill. Feeding was controlled by the mother, amid a diversity of snarling, growling, low-pitched sounds and much submission among the cubs. The young female inched her way forward to partake in the feast and succeeded. This was in itself an amazing sight, as she squirmed and squeezed her way in, forcing her two big brothers to give way. The next morning, the mother was gone, but all three cubs—subadults, really—were chewing at the bones. Because they had eaten they were much more relaxed than they had been the evening before.

So, family links and associations, especially over food, can continue even after the age of two years. In April 2003, when the Lahpur cubs were nearly twenty-seven months, the two brothers were still hunting together and feeding on the same kills.

I saw both of them just after the smaller male had killed a female nilgai. I watched him as he squatted right on top of the carcass, telling the world that he owned it. Then he slipped away. Late in the evening, I had a glimpse of both brothers. Throughout the day they had not eaten a morsel—perhaps they were too nervous in our presence. When I returned the next morning, I saw them both in the distance. Somehow, they had managed to drag a two-hundred-kilogram antelope at least four hundred meters away so that they could eat in private.

RANGE AND TERRITORY

OPPOSITE: A two-year-old tiger explores the forest in search of a new range to live in. It may take another year for this animal to find his own territory.

Usually, when tigers reach the age of eighteen to twenty-four months, their mother, ready to mate again, forces them out of the family unit. In Ranthambhore, males tend to spend their first independent years around the fringes of the forest, transecting the ranges of one or more dominant males. Sometimes brothers will remain together for a few months. But this movement outward is temporary; in a year or two, they will move back into the heart of the forest, ready to usurp the resident males, take control of important hunting grounds, and mate with the females who live there. This continuous process of assertion results in much shifting and adjusting. Levels of mortality can be very high—as much as 35 percent—as the young males come into conflict with territory holders and have to fight to establish themselves. Until that happens, they are like drifters looking for a bed each night. They may continue to float around in this way till they are four to four and a half years old, struggling to keep alive but at the same time maturing and building up their strength.

It is believed that tigers can walk up to thirty kilometers in one night. During its period of transition, a young male may range over an area of up to two hundred square kilometers.

A female of twenty-four to thirty-six months has a much easier time of it than her brothers—her cohort's mortality rate is only about 5 percent. She tends to remain in her mother's range, which slowly shrinks to accommodate her. I know that this happened with Machli and one of her daughters, Broken Tail, who stayed very close to the area where she was born and whose range overlapped that of her mother. It is not unusual to find a number of adjacent areas serving as homes to related tigresses, with a lot of overlap. My experience reveals that overlap is not altogether uncommon with males, too.

On the following pages, Fateh Singh Rathore, former director of Ranthambhore National Park, recounts an unusual instance of territorial negotiation. Billy Arjan Singh, perhaps India's most renowned contemporary tiger conservationist, describes an attempt to introduce a zoo-born tiger to the wild in the Dudhwa region.

*A young tiger patrols his area. Tigers will walk as many as
thirty kilometers in a single night across their home range in
their perpetual quest to defend their areas.*

ORPHANS AND TIGER TERRITORIES

Fateh Singh Rathore

IN NOVEMBER 2001, one of the Ranthambhore tigresses was seen with four cubs aged about four months. She was relaxed in our presence, but the cubs were shy and ran away. Later on, they became more tolerant of human observers, and we were able to photograph them until they were a year old, when the grass became too high and the undergrowth too dense. But although we could no longer see them, we could tell from their pugmarks that they were still in the area.

At the end of August 2002, I found the tigress lying on the ground, obviously unwell and with a porcupine quill stuck in her upper lip. She died three days later, and her body was brought to the range headquarters at Sawai Madhopur for examination. Her intestine was found to be completely porous, with lots of ruptures and holes, although there was no specific sign that she had eaten a porcupine, and the doctors were unable to say anything about the cause of death.

I was worried about the cubs, who would now be about fourteen months old—not mature enough to hunt successfully for themselves. A week or so after the mother died, I got a message that one of them had been found and that I should check on it and do something to help.

The cub was a female, too weak and hungry to run. I asked the staff to bring a goat, which we threw to her so that she could grab it and kill it. The next time we did this, a male cub appeared and joined his sister. We provided goats on several more occasions, but before long the cubs were able to kill for themselves. When it is a matter of life and death, young tigers learn quickly. Sadly, we heard that the other two cubs had been stoned to death when cattle grazers entered the park.

An interesting feature of this episode is that, while it is generally believed that when a territory becomes vacant through the death of an adult tiger an interloper will

Porcupine quills can cause serious injury to tigers and have been known to force tigers to pursue more vulnerable prey, including man.

appear, kill any cubs, and take over the area, surprisingly no other tiger entered this area, and the two surviving cubs have grown up beautifully. The last time we saw them they were twenty-two months old, healthy, and occupying the same territory as their mother had.

FATEH SINGH RATHORE has observed wild tigers in Ranthambhore National Park for the past forty years.

THE NOBLE TIGER

Billy Arjan Singh

Billy Arjan Singh, now in his mid-eighties, has spent a lifetime defending the tigers of Dudhwa in northern India. He is a great inspiration to tiger watchers worldwide.

THE SHADES OF EVENING WERE DRAWING in when across the immensity of space a deep, rumbling call echoed from the direction of Mutana Tal, west of Tiger Haven, perhaps named by some humorist who had urinated in the lake. ("Mutana" means "piss"!) This extensive stretch of water was the headquarters of the largest herd of barasingha, or swamp deer, in Uttar Pradesh. The next morning revealed the deeply indented pugmarks of a tiger we eventually named Old Crooked Foot because three of the toes of his right paw were grotesquely distorted.

Tiger history was made when Tara was born in Twycross Zoo in England on May 5, 1976, of supposedly Indian antecedents. She was then presented to Indira Gandhi, prime minister of India, by Dr. Bernhard Grzimek, famous as the author of *Serengeti Shall Not Die* (1961), as part of a pilot experiment to establish that superpredators could be hand-reared and returned to a wild existence.

On January 16, 1978, Tara left the security of Tiger Haven in the company of a young male tiger I called Tara's male. His "deep rumbling call" was a probe, presaging the entry of a strange tiger into the Tiger Haven range. Gradually, the calls increased in frequency and intensity as he extended his probe, until he spanned the entire range of the younger tigers; this amounted to a full-scale takeover but indicated a familial relationship, which accorded precedence to Old Crooked Foot. It appears that tiger protocol permits coexistence among relatives.

The baiting to establish Tara's wild identity revealed aspects of tiger ethology that showed the old cliché "cruel as a tiger" to be nothing more than a defamatory canard. As the visits of different tigers increased, it became obvious that the animals communicated in undertones, inaudible to human hearing. I set up a machan, or raised platform, with activated camera equipment overlooking the kill site, to observe the entire gamut of tiger protocol in action.

After the initial takeover, Tara's male had feeding priority, with approach-spacing calls functioning on a hierarchical basis, preventing crowding at the kill site, which could otherwise trigger offensive action.

By 1981 Tara was well into her fifth year and sexually mature, but she had not mated. Though she rolled in the company of Old Crooked Foot, was the age gap perhaps too great? But the shadows were closing in. The old tiger now limped, and his spacing calls had a hesitation in them. One night, he killed an old chital hind and devoured it completely. The next night, he came to the entrance to Tiger Haven in search of bait, which had not been put out. The next night, he killed bait at Tiger Haven and fed once before vanishing forever, as Tara's male took over. Shrouded in his regal past, Old Crooked Foot, like old soldiers who never die, just faded away.

Old Crooked Foot had reigned for two years, but it was only after his disappearance that Tara mated with the young male, who had then established his complete dominance. DNA testing of Tara's offspring has revealed Indo-Siberian genes, and later scientific research confirms that the two subspecies are liable to breed true — so perhaps extinction may not be forever.

BILLY ARJAN SINGH, who was born in 1917, is the oldest tiger conservationist in contemporary India. He resides in Tiger Haven, his farm adjacent to the Dudhwa tiger reserve in Uttar Pradesh, India. He has successfully reared a few panthers and a tigress, and reintroduced them to the wild. The author of many books on tigers, Singh addresses the fragmentation of tiger habitat and poaching that have devastated tiger populations across the world.

THE SIZE OF A TERRITORY

Those who study tigers are keenly interested in the size of a tiger's range or territory. (These terms are used fairly loosely: the area where a female lives is usually described as her home range, while a male patrols a larger area generally called a territory, which may encompass the range of as many as five or, as in one exceptional case in Nepal, seven females.) It seems that the presence of females, rather than availability of prey, is what makes a territory attractive to a male, whereas a female, probably instinctively aware that she will have cubs to rear, is more interested in resources. So when a male takes over a territory, he is likely to acquire both females and resources. In Ranthambhore, a male's territory may vary from 5 to 150 square kilometers, while in Panna one is known to have covered 280 square kilometers and included the range of three females. In the icy cold of Siberia, where prey populations are much less concentrated, males can have territories of 800 to 1,200 square kilometers. By contrast, females in Ranthambhore have occupied 5 to 25 square kilometers, in Panna 30 to 50 square kilometers, and in the Russian Far East

ABOVE AND OPPOSITE:

The size of a tiger's territory depends on the prey density in the area. Tigers will continuously patrol their areas to ensure and assert their control over them.

200 to 500 square kilometers. In other words, there is tremendous variation from place to place.

To a large extent, the size of a territory depends on the density of prey and can vary seasonally because of monsoon, drought, or any other event that affects the availability of food. At one time, twelve tigers shared the area around the lakes in Ranthambhore. At another time, there was only one. So there have been tremendous fluctuations even in the same place. But at any given moment one tiger or tigress reigns supreme in any one spot, and no other is tolerated. If another appears, one or the other will submit by rolling on its back, or else there will be a fierce fight.

In Chitwan National Park it has been established that females move on average 9.7 kilometers (six miles) from their natal range, while males move thirty-three kilometers (20.5 miles). In Ranthambhore, males move fewer than fifteen kilometers, but this may be because Ranthambhore is an "island" of forest surrounded by a large area that is inhospitable to tigers. Under these circumstances, there is likely to be even more conflict than usual between males, and a lot of youngsters probably perish because there is nowhere for them to go. A large area of connected habitat is vital if subadults are going to disperse evenly and survive. Some scientists working in areas that have healthy densities of tigers consider that most dispersing cubs could end up as part of a "doomed surplus" that has little chance of finding a range or territory in which to

function. These young floaters are bound to perish as forest areas become more and more fragmented.

What is particularly interesting is the number of changes and shifts that occur during the monsoon. Soon afterward, during October, when it is possible to go out looking for tigers after a lull of several weeks, I often find that new animals have arrived.

Two ongoing scientific studies at opposite ends of the tiger's world examine space and ranges occupied by tigers. Raghu S. Chundawat and Joanna Van Gruisen are studying tigers in central India; Dale Miquelle is conducting similar research in the Russian Far East and nearby northeast China. Their studies have contributed a great deal to our understanding of tiger behavior.

TIGERS OF THE DRY FOREST:
DO THEY HAVE ENOUGH SPACE TO SURVIVE?

Raghu S. Chundawat and Joanna Van Gruisen

THE TIGER OCCUPIES DIVERSE HABITATS—at one extreme it is found in the cold Arctic forests of Siberia, where temperatures can plummet to –40°C (–40°F), and at the other in the dry tropical forests of the Indian subcontinent, where temperatures can touch 50°C (122°F). It is in these two extreme ecological environments that the tiger struggles to survive.

On the Indian subcontinent, dry forests form the largest tiger habitat, and past trends indicate that tiger populations are most vulnerable in these areas. I started my research in an attempt to understand why tigers are disappearing in this habitat. I chose the dry forest of Panna Tiger Reserve, which covers an area of 540 square kilometers (208 square miles). During the first few years of my study I estimated a density of two to three tigers per hundred square kilometers (nearly forty square miles). Five years later, this had increased to 6.92 tigers in the same space, with a prey density of thirty-two animals per square kilometer. This ratio included 9.16 sambar, 10.6 chital, 6.2 nilgai, 4.03 four-horned antelope, and 0.92 chinkara. These figures do not include the large populations of livestock that also graze in the area.

I found parallels between the two extreme tiger environments of Siberia and Panna. In Panna, home ranges (at 210 to 280 square kilometers [81 to 108 square miles] for males and 30 to 60 square kilometers [12 to 23 square miles] for females) are two to three times larger than those known in other tropical populations. This was unexpected and has serious conservation implications. We know from studies of other species that, for various demographic and genetic reasons, populations with large home ranges are more vulnerable to extinction. This trend also applies to tigers.

In addition, if we explore the current status of tiger habitats, it is shocking to note that the average size of a protected area is smallest in dry forests (less than 350 square kilometers [135 square miles]). Most of these protected areas contain only fifteen tigers or fewer.

Larger ranges mean smaller populations, and when this is associated with isolation the result can be catastrophic for the tiger. Despite the size of their territories and their timid nature, males rarely escape conflict—they live very precarious lives and suffer a high rate of mortality. A frequent changeover of territorial males is not good for tiger society. It disrupts the peace and causes an enormous amount of stress, the end result of which is lower reproductive success. Young tigers need the territorial male who sired them to live an optimal life so as to be able to protect them as they grow up. The male needs to hold on to his territory long enough to ensure that his offspring survive to maturity and thus pass on his genes. So males play an important role in the viability of the population. But they use larger spaces, and because they frequent uncongenial environments they often live at the very edge of hostilities. This is a syndrome from which most of the tiger populations in dry forest suffer and one that adds to their vulnerability.

Male tigers travel more than do females. In Panna, they patrol large areas and frequently move beyond the reserve boundary. They come into contact with humans more often and prey mainly on cattle. Our observations of the movements of radio-collared males have helped us learn about their response to human disturbance and how they try to minimize conflict. Unlike females, male tigers are relatively timid and rarely defend a kill when any wandering humans come across them. Females in a similar situation will stay until the very last moment and often show aggression before escaping. They may even mock charge the intruder. One of the radio-collared males in my study area developed the habit of eating a substantial amount from a cattle kill only once; he would rarely return to the same carcass a second time. He also stayed far away from the kill.

But are tigers safe in larger protected ares? Our study says no, not entirely. The Panna Tiger Reserve is a relatively large protected area of dry forest. But even here the ranges of all the radio-collared breeding females extend beyond the reserve boundaries. These tigers are well protected inside the reserve, but once outside they are exposed to a more hostile environment. Just across the boundary, conflict rules, and it is there that most of the mortalities occur. The death of two radio-collared tigresses in Panna highlights the vulnerability of tigers even in well-protected areas. One of them moved with her two young cubs into an area near a village at the periphery, where she was caught in a snare and choked to death. Though the trap was set to catch deer for meat and was not targeted at the tiger, the result was fatal for this tigress and her two cubs.

The reality that the tiger faces is tough. There is simply not enough space for the tiger, and the average size of a protected population is small. Most of the dry-forest tiger population suffers from such problems. If urgent measures are not taken, India will lose a large percentage of its wild tigers.

RAGHU S. CHUNDAWAT is one of India's leading wildlife biologists. He earned his doctorate in wildlife biology, focusing on the snow leopard. He now studies the behavior of wild tigers in Panna National Park in central India. His wife, JOANNA VAN GRUISEN, is a wildlife photographer who has produced a book on India's wildlife.

OPPOSITE: *A tiger quenches its thirst.*

BELOW: *In the summer months, a tiger will find a patch of shade and sleep for most of the day to conserve energy.*

LIVING ON THE EDGE:
TIGERS AT THE NORTHERN LIMITS OF THEIR RANGE

Dale Miquelle

MOST OF US, when asked to conjure up an image of the tiger, imagine a magnificent predator skulking through the steamy jungles of southern Asia, more often than not somewhere on the Indian subcontinent. Despite this stereotype, the tiger is in fact at home in a great variety of environments across a surprisingly wide range of latitudes. Our studies of the tiger living on the very edge of its range in the Russian Far East have emphatically demonstrated how elastic tiger behavior is and how capable it is of adapting to environmental variation.

It is surprising how "at home" Amur tigers appear in the snowy forests of Russia. The orange background with black stripes, assumed to provide camouflage in tropical forests and grasslands, also conceals these animals in masterly fashion in oak forests (where the leaf litter is a dingy orange) and temperate forest thickets (where vertical striping can make the animal "disappear" before your very eyes). A thick winter coat, absent in animals from other populations, provides adequate protection against winter temperatures that can drop to −40°C (−40°F). Despite repeated claims in popular literature that members of the Amur population are the largest of all tigers, our measurements on more than fifty captured individuals suggest that their body size is similar to that of Bengal tigers.

As with all predators, the population density of Amur tigers is ultimately limited by prey availability. As elsewhere across their range, Amur tigers prey on medium-sized and large cervids (deer) and wild boar, although wild cattle, an important component of their diet in some areas, are absent in the north. Amur tigers make kills at a similar rate as in the south, despite slightly higher energy requirements associated with the cold temperatures. Rapid decay of carcasses in the tropics prevents tigers from fully utilizing meat from large kills, whereas in the north 90 percent of meat is normally consumed. However, because plant productivity declines with latitude, ungulate carrying capacity in northern temperate forests is reduced by an order of magnitude in comparison to southern areas. Prey-biomass estimates in high-quality habitats in India range from 2,000 to nearly 7,500 kilograms per square kilometer (5 to 18.5 tons per square mile), whereas in the Russian Far East high-quality habitat can support a prey biomass of less than two hundred kilograms per kilometer (about half a ton per square mile). Amur tigers must traverse home ranges that are dramatically larger to find sufficient food: tigresses in prime habitat in India use home ranges of only twenty square kilometers (eight square miles), while tigresses in Russia maintain home ranges that on average are twenty-two times as large. As a result, tiger densities at the northern limits of their range rarely exceed one animal per hundred square kilometers, whereas some parts of India can boast of more than sixteen animals in a similar-sized area.

The conservation implications of these ecological differences are vast. While India is attempting to conserve its tigers in small, isolated islands of habitat (tiger reserves), such a tactic would be impossible in the north. The largest protected area in Russia within tiger range (Sikhote-Alin Reserve), which covers four thousand square kilometers (nearly 1,600 square miles), harbors fewer than thirty animals, at least half of which regularly use areas outside the boundaries of the reserve. Because Amur tigers require such vast home ranges, no single protected area can retain a viable population of tigers. Conservation in Russia will therefore depend upon development of a core network of protected areas interspersed with multiple-use lands that integrate tiger conservation with sustainable use of natural resources by humans.

Despite the dramatic differences in the scale at which tigers use the landscape across their ranges, their social structure is similar in India and Russia. In both areas, females generally occupy exclusive home ranges, and

males attempt to secure exclusive access to females by retaining territories that overlap with those of one or more females but exclude other males. Surprisingly, despite the low densities of prey, the reproductive rate of Amur tigers appears to be similar to that of Bengal tigers. Contrary to some theories, our data suggest that tigers are not particularly resilient in the face of human poaching and that relatively low levels of human-caused mortality can result in dramatic decreases in population size.

Although India still retains the largest number of tigers in the world, its burgeoning human population has fragmented remaining tigers into small subpopulations isolated from one another. Because the remaining habitat is so productive, tigers there require only small home ranges, and reasonably large numbers of tigers can be retained in these protected areas. At least in the short term, this tactic is working to retain tigers in the Indian landscape. In contrast, although Amur tigers require vast home ranges, Russia retains the largest existent single population of tigers in the world in a single, unbroken forest tract that exceeds 180,000 square kilometers (70,000 square miles). Although future development and timber harvest are unavoidable, a decreasing human population there provides hope that this landscape may not undergo serious fragmentation in the near future. If suitable management regimes can be developed on existing forest tracts to provide minimum requirements for tigers, and if incentives can be found for local people to benefit from—or at least tolerate the presence of—tigers, the future of tigers in the Russian Far East is bright.

DALE MIQUELLE received a B.S. at Yale University, an M.S. from University of Minnesota, and a Ph.D. from University of Idaho. He worked on the Smithsonian Tiger Ecology Project in Chitwan National Park before joining the Hornocker Wildlife Institute's Siberian Tiger Project. Miquelle is now country coordinator for the Wildlife Conservation Society's Russia Program.

RANGE AND MOBILITY

Until October 1982, the area around the three lakes in Ranthambhore was occupied by two transient males, one of whom was probably Genghis, who became the dominant male and was one of the most remarkable tigers I have ever watched—we shall hear more of him later in this chapter. There were also Padmini and her three nearly adult cubs; and two other females, Nick Ear, who was Padmini's daughter from a previous litter, and Nasty, so named because of her aggressive nature. She was quite the fiercest tigress I have encountered in my years of tiger watching.

Padmini's daughter Laxmi, then about five years old, was also occasionally seen at the edges of the third lake with three cubs of her own. These tigresses' ranges overlapped for several months, but by the end of 1982 there were few signs of Padmini and her latest family, except for one memorable occasion described later. She shifted her range to the far side of the forest, leaving her former range completely and never returning. Her cubs survived to maturity, but I lost track of them after they separated from their mother.

So at this time some twelve tigers of varying ages lived in the limited area of the three to four square kilometers around the lakes. For a year after Padmini moved away, most of our sightings were of Nick Ear, one other female, and the two males. I saw very little of Nasty after the middle of 1983, but Nick Ear could be found around the lakes nearly every day. Then, for no apparent reason, she, too, disappeared.

By October 1984, Genghis had moved out, and the area was frequented by another large male, named Kublai. Initially very elusive, he slowly became more confident, spending a lot of time marking and asserting his presence. He was totally different from Genghis in his general behavior, though he used the same paths, niches, and water holes. I kept a detailed record through March and April 1985, and from March 16 to April 15 Kublai's pugmarks were always somewhere in the vicinity of the lakes.

These movements and appearances and disappearances are extremely complex, and the reasons underlying them are often far from clear. I know of one instance when a female wounded in a clash with another tiger moved twelve kilometers away from her home range to a completely new area. But why did Nick Ear leave when Genghis arrived? Why did Genghis disappear when Kublai arrived? Did Kublai kill Genghis? These remain difficult questions, apparently without answers.

The lakes support large concentrations of deer and are therefore prime hunting grounds for the tiger. This may also be a factor in the changes that occur every year as new tigers take over from old ones—there are always going to be newcomers competing for control in the most desirable areas.

I believe that male tigers have nonaggressive contact with other males in their area, but only rarely. As with so many aspects of their behavior, tigers seem very individualistic in their attitudes toward range and territory and especially toward the

A tigress in full stride—the grace and elegance of the chase.

A tigress rests at the edge of a lake in Ranthambhore. The spotted deer in the background are aware that she is not hunting.

sharing of it. In 1923, A. A. Dunbar Brander, another forest officer working in India, observed three adult males hunting together, and both George Schaller and Billy Arjan Singh have recorded cordial associations between resident and transient male tigers. I have only once seen two adult males strolling together and then stalking off in search of prey. I have also seen two male siblings clash just after breaking away from the family, but before things could become vicious one of the males submitted, rolling on his back twice, and peace descended. Males in a given area probably establish a rank order, which is then accepted by all, though I know that Genghis never tolerated another male in the area for the year that he ruled the Ranthambhore lakes. When territorial conflict does take place, evidence suggests that it is ferocious and blood-curdling, and Ranthambhore must have seen huge battles between male tigers, but I have never observed them with my own eyes, nor do I know anyone who has.

Mobility among tigers is an ever-changing phenomenon, affected by seasonal variations, prey movement, and the availability of water. Tigers seem to move around more in the winter than in the intense summer heat, probably because of the cooler temperatures and plentiful water, a process that disperses the prey species otherwise found around the numerous water holes. Tigers are powerful swimmers and can cross lakes and rivers with ease—water seems to be no obstacle to them. Their ranges can encompass lakes and small islands, as in the mangrove swamps of the Sundarbans. According to some observers, the tiger can swim more than fifteen kilometers (nine miles)—a truly amazing feat if it is true. A government officer named R. K. M. Battye described the tiger's swimming ability in the *Journal of the Bombay Natural History Society* in 1942:

> During several years of shooting in the Sunderbunds [*sic*] forests, I discovered that tigers readily take to water, and in some instances swim considerable distances (three or four miles), and in a tidal river with a four to five knot tide running during spring tides, but what struck me most, however, was the intelligence displayed by tigers in choosing their time for swimming, which was invariably at or about high water, when they were able to "take off" and land on hard ground, and anyone who has had experience in the Sunderbunds will appreciate what this means! — At all other states of the tide one has to flounder up several yards of bank through more than knee-deep mud, which would prove very embarrassing to a heavy animal like a tiger.

On March 2, 1858, the crew of the steamer *Aden* killed a tiger that was swimming roughly eleven kilometers (seven miles) from Mumbai. Tigers have been spotted eight kilometers (five miles) out to sea near the islands around Singapore and were once known to swim between the islands of Java and Bali—for some of them, the Selat Bali Strait, which is four kilometers (2.5 miles) wide at its narrowest point, must simply have run through part of their territory.

The dense mangrove swamps of the Sundarbans have produced some of the most unusual tiger behavior ever recorded. M. Monirul H. Khan, a wildlife biologist, explores how these tigers cope with vast waterways, and how their interaction with humans has evolved.

Mysterious Tigers of the Sundarbans

M. Monirul H. Khan

OUT OF FEAR AND RESPECT people call them *Mama* (uncle). Both Muslims and Hindus worship them. They are rarely seen, but they kill many people every year. They are the mysterious tigers of the Sundarbans—the least known to scientists of all the world's tigers, the only ones that live in mangroves, and yet one of the most thriving populations. The Sundarbans are the largest single mass of tidal mangrove forest on Earth, covering an area of about ten thousand square kilometers (nearly four thousand square miles) in the Ganges-Brahmaputra delta of Bangladesh and India. Roughly 60 percent of this forest is in Bangladesh and the rest in India. Here, the tiger is the flagship species and supreme predator.

Mangroves are very different from other tiger habitats. With the rapid decline of the evergreen and deciduous forests in the north, east, and west of the area—and the subsequent diminution of the prey population—tigers find the Sundarbans a relatively safe but challenging place to colonize. They have to adapt to the semiaquatic ecosystem, facing a lot of water and mud, and thus they need to swim much more than any other tiger population. This scarcity of land might explain why the Sundarban tigers are thinner than other populations of the same subspecies.

The tiger is classified by the World Conservation Union (IUCN) as a globally endangered species, but its conservation status in Bangladesh is even more dire: there, it is identified as critically endangered. And yet, the question of how many tigers there are in the Sundarbans is a puzzling one that has yet to be answered confidently. Using Mel Sunquist's crude estimate of one adult tiger in every forty square kilometers (15.4 square miles) in Nepal's Royal Chitwan National Park, John Seidensticker believes that there is room for about 250 adult tigers in the entire Sundarbans. With the use of camera traps in the Indian part of the Sundarbans, Ullas Karanth and James Nichols have estimated the tiger density to be only 0.8 tigers per hundred square kilometers, which would mean there are only about eighty individuals in the entire area. However, based on recent pugmark censuses, the tiger population has been estimated to be 362 in the Bangladesh Sundarbans and 263 in the Indian Sundarbans—a total of 625 tigers. These figures are the ones officially used in the two countries. From them it is clear that pugmark-based estimates are much higher than other estimates, which challenges the validity of the pugmark-based census method, at least in the Sundarbans. While following tiger tracks in the Sundarbans East Wildlife Sanctuary, I observed that pugmarks of the same tiger vary in different soil types. Not only that, some pugmarks produced in the early winter (i.e., after the last rain) remained intact for more than two months. If we imagine the number of intact pugmarks produced by any one tiger during that period (thousands indeed!), it is only natural that any estimates from pugmark studies will be inaccurate, because it is virtually impossible to prove that all the pugmarks in different soil types are actually produced by the same individual. It should be mentioned here that most of the pugmark censuses were conducted in the winter, when it is relatively dry and thus convenient for census work. Unfortunately, the wide availability of the pugmarks apparently gives some the idea that tiger density is extremely high in the Sundarbans, which is not correct.

I have worked on the tiger and its prey in the Sundarbans East WS, where I have estimated the density of sizable prey (spotted deer and wild boar together contribute about 80 percent of the diet of the tiger). The prey density on land was found to be 43 individuals per square kilometer (111 per square mile). Since half of the Sundarbans East Wildlife Sanctuary's 312 square kilometers is deep-water bodies such as rivers and estuaries,

Tigers in the Sundarbans can swim large distances across the waterways of the mangrove swamps.

I estimate a total prey population of around 6,700 individuals. Assuming that tigers crop about 10 percent of the large ungulate population annually, and assuming a kill rate of fifty prey animals per tiger per year, this area might support around thirteen tigers (excluding cubs), i.e., four tigers per hundred square kilometers (eleven tigers per hundred square miles). The presence of some grassland pockets in this area has made it one of the richest parts of the Sundarbans, with perhaps the highest density of tigers and prey. Given this rough estimate in one of the richest areas of the Sundarbans, we can expect a maximum of three hundred tigers in total: two hundred in the Bangladesh part and one hundred in the Indian.

It is very difficult to estimate the actual tiger population in such an inaccessible habitat—a tangle of water, mud, and dense vegetation. However, the exact number is not very important, so long as there is a sufficiently large and viable population. The population trend is rather more important, and this can be easily monitored from tiger signs. Despite all the deadly conflicts with people, it is still relatively stable, thanks to the natural inaccessibility of the habitat and human fear of man-eating tigers. Since the ecosystem is tidal, the land is suitable neither for agriculture nor for human settlement: this is the main reason why such a huge forest remains intact in one of the most densely populated areas in the world. Perhaps the tiger population in the Sundarbans is one of the largest unfragmented populations on Earth. For these reasons, the area offers vital potential for long-term tiger conservation.

Unlike other tigers, those in the Sundarbans have a reputation for eating people. Officially, tigers killed a total of 173 humans (17.3 per year) in the Bangladesh Sundarbans between 1993 and 2002. During the same period, humans killed thirty tigers (3 per year). However, based on field survey it was found that, between September 2001 and February 2003, a total of forty-one humans were killed by tigers while seven tigers were killed by humans, although officially these figures are only five and four respectively. Since the Sundarbans are big and inaccessible, not all the reports of human and tiger deaths reach the forest department. Moreover, since many of the human victims were illegal intruders, their deaths were not officially recorded. On the other hand, a report quoted the deaths of ten humans in eleven months (April 1999 to February 2000) in the Indian Sundarbans. However, the number of humans killed each year is very low in relation to the number working in the Sundarbans (possibly less than 0.05 percent).

In other tiger ranges, man-eating tigers are rare and are usually either old or injured tigers; in the Sundarbans, however, both healthy and unhealthy tigers were found to become man-eaters. There are several theories regarding why this should be: water salinity (some experts think that drinking saline water might make the tiger more aggressive) and availability of human beings as an easy prey are two of a number of suggested causal factors, but neither has any concrete evidence to prove the hypothesis. Hence, it might be better to conclude that the man-eating habit is simply a behavioral character of some tigers in the Sundarbans. It is possible that in the past some tigers of the western Sundarbans might have encountered many dead bodies (perhaps as the outcome of a tidal wave, cyclone, or epidemic disease), which gave them the opportunity to taste human flesh. Once they learned that human beings were "edible," they became man-eaters.

The trend then transferred and spread from generation to generation. It is very likely that if the mother is a man-eater, the cubs will learn to consider humans as part of their normal menu.

Based on interviews with local people, forest department records, and newspaper reports, I found that man-eating tigers mainly hunt middle-aged people (73 percent of their victims are in the thirty-to-fifty age group), perhaps because people of this age are the most available kind (45 percent) in the Sundarbans. Most of the victims (92 percent) were attacked from behind and grabbed by the neck or head.

Human kills were found to have been carried from the spot of attack as little as a few meters or up to eight kilometers (five miles). Of the few who survived tiger attacks, 67 percent did not have a neck or head bite. Most (53 percent) of the people of the Sundarbans rely only on spiritual protection from the tiger. Interestingly, despite many fatal encounters with tigers, 75 percent of the people interviewed said that they wanted the tiger to survive in the Sundarbans, because once it was gone poachers would have nothing to fear and would destroy the area by cutting down trees and killing wild animals, and as a result the local people would lose their livelihood.

I have recorded that individuals isolated from a group are the most vulnerable to man-eating tigers. Working in groups, with everyone carrying a big stick, and keeping a pet dog (which must be chained) with each team might be a useful form of protection. Face masks at the back of the head (in order to confuse the tiger about which is the front and which the back of a human) and electrified dummy humans are used in the western Sundarbans, but it might not be wise to assume that man-eating tigers are stupid enough to be fooled by these devices.

Every year, people in the Sundarbans sacrifice live goats and chickens, releasing them in areas where they are ultimately killed and eaten by the wildlife. Some people of the Muslim community believe that the tiger was born from the menstrual blood of the great mother Fatema, which is why it has a strong odor. People also believe that the man-eating tiger is actually an evil spirit named *Ufari* (which literally means something that comes from above). The Ufari comes from the sky and sits at the top of a tree. Due to the weight of the *Ufari*, the tree starts bending. Once the top of the tree touches the ground, the *Ufari* takes the shape of a tiger that kills people. Whenever people talk about the tiger, they do so very respectfully. They carry sacred beads and threads given to them by spiritual leaders in the belief that these will protect them from man-eating tigers. People also put sacred red flags in the area in which they work so that the tiger cannot approach them. Furthermore, they do not usually go to work in the Sundarbans without a companion of the "same blood"— that is, a close relative such as a brother or son. This is because they believe that if a man-eating tiger attacks someone in the group, everyone other than a close relative will run away to save himself. People always try to work in groups, and many groups have a professional spiritual man, locally known as the *Gunin* or *Guni*, who is believed to have the spiritual power to lock the jaws of the tiger and move it away so that people can work freely. The *Guni* carries a big stick and carefully watches the surroundings while others work. The verses he uses to deter the tiger are considered top secret and are not normally revealed. Three of them, translated, are: "Sunken on the blood, the soul from the blood [tiger], if you look toward my people, [you will have to] tear out your own penis and eat"; "In the name of Ali, in the name of Fatema, hey bastard [tiger], get lost"; and "Mother Fatema, [I have] come to your forest, please keep me in mind."

The growing concern for tiger conservation among government bodies, international organizations, and people in general is affirmative progress on the road to ensuring that the tiger survives. This magnificent creature has lived in the incredible wilderness of the Sundarbans for hundreds of years, intimately intertwined with the history and culture of the region; hence, the tiger is the national animal of both Bangladesh and India. It is the heart of the Sundarbans. As Asir Johnsingh said, "Saving the tiger is a challenge for mankind." We do need to take it as a challenge. We cannot let the tiger become extinct.

M. MONIRUL H. KHAN is a wildlife biologist working on the tiger and other wild animals of Bangladesh. Currently he is at the final stage of his Ph.D. degree at the University of Cambridge, U.K. He conducted his Ph.D. fieldwork on the ecology and conservation of the tiger in the Sundarbans of Bangladesh. He was involved with a number of wildlife projects in Bangladesh, and has written fifteen scientific articles and many popular articles. Mr. Khan is also a keen wildlife photographer.

COMMUNICATION

Not very vocal by nature, tigers use sound far less frequently than, for example, lions. Whenever I hear the roar of a tiger, I feel a surge of excitement and anticipation, because they never vocalize without a specific reason.

The roar is a resonant sound like "aaoom," which reverberates through the forest and is used by a male to assert his territorial right, either by inviting another tiger to possible conflict or by encouraging his hurried departure. While he was in residence around the Ranthambhore lakes, Genghis spent many evenings roaring and was once heard to roar thirty-six times in eighty-four minutes. I know that on three of these occasions there was a tigress in close proximity, and once he repeatedly answered the roar of another tiger a couple of kilometers away.

OPPOSITE: *Tigers use a wide range of sounds to communicate, including snarling and hissing.*

Twice I have heard a female and on several occasions a male roaring in response to a cacophony of alarm calls from sambar, chital, and langur monkeys that had spotted the threat of the tiger's presence. The tiger roared as if in annoyance—presumably its chances of hunting successfully were ruined—and most of the alarms fell silent.

Frederick W. Champion captures some of the power of this sound in his book *With a Camera in Tiger-land* (1927):

> I remember an occasion when I was waiting . . . in a dense jungle just as night was closing in, listening to a roaring tiger coming closer and closer. When it was practically dark the animal came to within twenty yards of where I was waiting, by which time the volume and malignity of the roaring seemed simply appalling. The whole dark forest seemed to vibrate with the very sound and I confess that, accustomed as I am to the roaring of tigers, I began to feel somewhat nervous.

In *The Highlands of Central India* (1872), Captain James Forsyth of the Bengal Staff Corps describes listening to "the most remarkable serenade of tigers" he ever heard:

> A peculiar long wail, like the drawn-out mew of a huge cat, first rose from a river course a few hundred yards below my tent. Presently, from a mile or so higher up the river, came a deep tremendous roar which had scarcely died away ere it was answered from behind my camp by another pitched in yet a deeper tone, startling us from its suddenness and proximity. All three were repeated at short intervals as the three tigers approached each other along the bottom of the deep, dry watercourses between and above which the camp had been pitched. As they drew together the noise ceased for about a quarter of an hour and I was dozing off to sleep again when suddenly arose the most fearful din near to where the tigress had first sounded the love note to her rival lovers, a din like the caterwauling of midnight cats magnified a hundredfold. Intervals of silence broken by the outburst of this infernal shrieking and moaning disturbed our rest

for the next hour, dying away gradually as the tigers retreated along the bed of the river. In the morning I found all the incidents of a three-volume novel in feline life imprinted on the sand, and marks of blood showed how genuine the combat part of the performance had been.

OPPOSITE: *A tigress snarls while protecting the carcass of a great Indian antelope. Tigers protect their food zealously and will attack any intruder that ventures into the immediate vicinity.*

I have heard a tigress moan on several occasions. It is a subdued sound, at a lower pitch than a roar, and is used with great frequency by a female in estrus. The sharp aggressive woof and cough of tigers I have heard only twice. The first time, two males confronted each other in the forest, woofing and leaping and then woofing and coughing, face-to-face at a distance of a few centimeters. It is a very sharp, loud sound, chilling for the listener. On the second occasion, two adult females used much the same sound as they settled to feed on a chital. It is very rare for tigers to feed together, and I imagine that these two were related. As they ate, they also snarled, growled, and hissed. The sounds started off with great ferocity, but after an hour they seemed to fade into a lower key. Champion describes a similar situation: "For the next hour they quarreled violently over their meal, making the most awful growls and snarls as they demolished the carcass, while I, shaking with suppressed excitement, sat pondering upon my foolishness in having allowed my machan to be tied in such an insecure position. Every now and then there would be a terrific outburst of snarling as one of them drove the other away from the kill."

I have heard growling and snarling several times. A tigress annoyed at her subadult cubs emits a low growl that seems to come from deep within her and lingers in the air. Angry tigers mock-charging my jeep make a sharp, aggressive growl-cum-roar as they leap toward me. I have also often been snarled at by tigers I am observing. In this instance, the tiger holds its mouth slightly open, bares its canines, wrinkles its nose, and exhales. I once heard a male who had seized a tigress's kill utter a low, growling snarl whenever she tried to join him; over the space of a couple of hours he drove her farther and farther away. Twice I have heard a strange blowing sound like a continuous puffing, made by a tiger who had settled down to eat after protecting a kill for several hours. Prusten, a puffing sound made by air being pushed out through the nostrils and mouth and audible only at close range, is a part of greeting behavior.

Young cubs squeak like birds to attract their mother, and, although I have never heard it, there are reports of a "pooking" that seems to prevent sudden encounters. Purring, grunting, squeaking, and a low rolling growl all add to the tiger's diverse repertoire. R. C. Morris described the sounds of the tiger in the *Journal of the Bombay Natural History Society* of 1953: "The sound commenced every time, with a perfect imitation of a locomotive suddenly letting off steam, lasting only about four or five seconds, followed by a series of guttural 'chuckles' repeated from sixty to eighty times; not unlike the chuckles emitted by a hyena. At night this sounds extremely eerie."

My most exciting week of tiger sound was with Machli in March 2002. During this week, she roared 226 times in my presence—an extraordinary performance for a normally silent cat. At the time, she had two cubs aged six or seven months, and she was probably roaring to ensure that a new male tiger kept his distance.

MARKING AND MESSAGES

The tiger's ear is many times more sensitive than the human's to both high and low frequencies. On many occasions, tigers have heard animals or humans before I did, although I was watching from only a few feet away. Their ability to pick up high-frequency sound enables them to detect the movements of prey species—the distant thud of a hoof is registered as the ears twitch from side to side, assessing sound much like a rotating radar antenna. Even when the tiger is asleep the ears are continuously receiving sound—as we shall see later in this chapter, this sensitivity is vital to hunting success.

When tigers are able to see one another they communicate through their facial expressions. They use their eyes, the position of their ears, a flick of their tail, and the stretching of their cheeks to express their feelings, whether aggression or affection. The way a tiger moves also reveals its mood.

Tigers also communicate by scent marking. Here a male tiger sprays his scent mark on a tree in his range. The scent can last for more than two weeks.

But more significantly, tigers have devised a way of communicating their movements and establishing their territorial claims through the use of scent. The most important facet of this is spray marking. As an adult tiger of either sex walks along, it will turn its hindquarters toward a tree, bush, or patch of grass, and with tail raised vertically shoot out a spray of fluid, hitting the target at an upward angle. A male's

fluid stream is narrow compared with that of a female, but in both sexes the fluid—a mixture of urine and a secretion from the anal glands—smells musky and strong. The smell can last for up to forty days and is an excellent indication of how recently a tiger has passed by and whether or not the area is occupied. This may discourage or encourage other tigers, depending on the situation. Even human observers can identify the spray of an individual tiger if they know its "marking trees."

After ejecting this spray, a tiger will often sniff it and then hang its tongue out with nose wrinkled, a gesture known as flehmen. Flehmen is also used when sniffing another tiger's scent—it conveys a wealth of information, such as the age and sex of the owner and whether or not a female is in estrus. Cubs can follow their mother through her scent, and the scent of a tigress in estrus will pinpoint her location for the resident male.

Most scent marking is done on elevated spots such as leaning trees or rock overhangs that are easily accessible for other tigers and that shelter the scents from the rain. A patrolling tiger will scent-mark regularly so that the message remains.

The flehmen display as a young male tiger sniffs the scent of a tigress in his immediate vicinity. Scents are a critical part of tigers' communications with one another.

Spraying is not the only means of marking an area with scent. A gland between the toes exudes a scent that enables cubs to follow literally in their mother's footsteps. There are also scent glands in the tail, around the anus, and on the cheeks and chin. Tigers frequently roll in patches of grass in order to leave their scents, and they also rub their cheeks on the bark of trees. All the scent glands are at work to communicate a tiger's presence for territorial and reproductive reasons.

Fresh scent can indicate a danger, especially between males, whereas an old scent may be a signal that the animal can go ahead with care. But whether the scent is stale or fresh, a passing tiger will always sniff at it and spray over it, thereby asserting his or her own claim to the spot. I have on several occasions seen a tigress at the edge of her range, sniffing the scent of another and immediately retracing her steps. Scent marking is at its peak on the fringes of territories, where it helps to prevent direct confrontations and avoid conflict.

Up until 1980, I had never seen a tiger spray-marking. This was partly because the tiger was still primarily nocturnal and partly because the population in Ranthambhore was low enough for encounters between tigers to be infrequent. In the last twenty years, spraying has become normal activity throughout the year, especially after the monsoon, since the rain washes all these carefully placed scents away and a tiger has to mark his or her territory all over again.

Most tigers I have seen in Ranthambhore seem to prefer depositing their feces on the central grass strip that runs down the middle of a road, or at the edge of a road or an animal path. They do not cover their feces, but I have frequently observed scrape marks around the spot, as if the soil and grass have been raked. Sometimes defecation has taken place, in other cases urination, but at times the animal has simply left scrape marks. On five occasions, I have seen just a tiny sample of defecation on a raked patch, as if marking the spot; obviously, this is yet another way in which tigers communicate their presence to others. They also rake their claws on the trunks of trees, which may again act as a territorial signal.

When Genghis was new to the area around Ranthambhore's lakes, he indulged in regular and incessant spray marking, tree clawing, soil scraping, defecation, and vocalization. On one walk around the lakes he covered a distance of two kilometers (1.2 miles) in seventy-five minutes and spray-marked eighteen trees, scraped the soil

ABOVE: *A tiger deposits its feces and scrapes the ground to leave its scent mark on the area.*

OPPOSITE: *A tiger rubs the bark of a tree with its cheeks, leaving its scent behind to assert its rights on the area.*

OPPOSITE: *A tiger claws the bark of a tree to leave a territorial signal for other tigers. These marks and indicators are vital in the world of the tiger.*

BELOW: *A tiger sniffs at the scent left behind by another tiger. The freshness of the scent will determine whether a tiger moves forward or reverses its tracks in order to avoid conflict.*

seven times, defecated once, and raked his claws on the bark of five trees. He also clutched the branches of two trees with his forepaws while standing on his hind legs. He was leaving every signal he could. This activity lessened markedly over the following months as he gained control of the area. When Kublai moved in, he did much the same through November and December but had eased off by March, by which time his presence was established.

Whether clawing, spraying, or scratching, most signals are left on the animal paths, *nallahs* [watercourses], and man-made roads that crisscross the forest in Ranthambhore. This is probably because such belts and paths act as natural boundaries, demarcating ranges, especially for resident males. Specific trees in such areas are regularly sprayed and clawed, more so when a new tiger is asserting his rights.

John Goodrich, field coordinator of the Siberian Tiger Project, had an extraordinary encounter with a tiger while patrolling the icy coastline of the northernmost part of the tiger's range.

THE MAGIC OF THE TIGER

John Goodrich

PICTURE THIS: IT'S LATE DECEMBER and you are in a winter paradise in a faraway place on the coast of the Sea of Japan in the Russian Far East. You are staying in a small cabin on a small bay where Haunta-mi Creek winds its way across a sandy beach to meet the sea. You've just arrived, having hiked down along a trail through a long, marshy meadow where you saw red deer and roe deer and wild boar. You are here with a purpose: to radio-track a 450-pound male Siberian tiger named Zheny. From his signal, you know that he is resting in an oak grove less than a kilometer away; a pair of ravens perched on top of a larch tree marks precisely the place where he lies. Maybe he's on a kill, or maybe the birds are just hanging around, ever hopeful. It's just after 4:00 P.M., and the sun is almost touching the hills across the bay. The sky is a dozen shades of blue and purple, beginning to fade to orange in the southwest. It's cold, with a stiff breeze, so you're in a hurry to split some wood and get the cabin warm. But then a red deer barks in the woods across the meadow, so before you shatter the calm with a swing of the ax, you turn on the radio receiver. Sure enough, he's moving. There's not a chance that he is going to walk out onto the beach in broad daylight—that's just a foolish dream—but, hopeful fool that you are, you climb to the watchtower on top of the cabin to have a look.

You raise your binoculars and immediately, as if your gaze were drawn to the spot by some unseen force, he's there. Big as life, walking through the meadow along the edge of the woods. He's huge, the size of a red deer, and magnificent, thick orange-and-white coat glowing in the setting sun. A tear runs down your face because you never imagined that you might see something so beautiful that was alive and free. He moves with graceful ease. He's in no hurry, walking slowly but not hunting—maybe he's just enjoying a stroll along the coast? Then he ducks back into the woods, gliding through underbrush, but instead of disappearing into the forest he turns and continues along the meadow's edge.

Thinking that he'll never hear you at five hundred meters against the noise of the wind and the waves, you utter a few words of awe. He freezes, snaps his head around, and locks his big yellow eyes on you, white face set off against orange body. You also freeze, hardly breathing, and wait, praying he doesn't bolt. But he's known you were there all along, and, after making sure you are keeping your distance, he continues on his way, as slowly as ever. Suddenly, he turns sharply to his right and crouches as if drinking. Then he stands and does a flehmen, turning his head from side to side several times. After maybe fifteen seconds, he crouches and drinks in the scent again—three sniffs and three flehmen before he continues on his way, having spent about four minutes examining the scent. And now you know his purpose—he's following a female who passed this way sometime earlier. (Tomorrow you will find her tracks and determine that she moved through about a day earlier than Zheny.) Twenty meters ahead, he pauses to scrape and then sprays a bush with urine another fifty meters farther on. He approaches the end of the meadow, turns, and walks down to the beach. As he strolls along the sand you wonder if he finds the activity as peaceful as you do, or if he's just following the path of the tigress before him. After a few hundred meters, he reaches the far side of the bay, where the beach gives way to a steep, rocky shoreline. He continues on, picking his way among the rocks. A red deer spooks and bolts seventy-five meters above him, but he barely takes notice—too busy keeping track of his tigress.

This is truly a dream: a tiger walking along an icy beach flanked by towering snow-covered cliffs, silhouetted by the deep orange of a long since set winter sun. Finally, he reaches a point where the cliffs drop straight into the ocean and, after spraying them twice to mark his passing, he turns up the hill and disappears back into the forest, forty-five minutes after he first appeared.

You are a conservation biologist fighting to save the last of the world's tigers: a difficult and thankless job. But a few times a year, you get an experience like today's, from which you return to the battle with renewed energy, with the hope that your grandchildren will have the opportunity to watch his grandchildren walk the same beach.

JOHN GOODRICH received a Ph.D. in zoology from the University of Wyoming in 1994. In March 1995, he moved to Terney, Russia, and began working as the field coordinator for the Hornocker Wildlife Institute's (HWI) Siberian Tiger Project. HWI later merged with the Wildlife Conservation Society and John is now the field coordinator for Sikhote-Alin research projects, which have included brown bears, Asiatic black bears, Eurasian lynx, wild boar, and red deer, in addition to Amur tigers.

SOLITARY OR NOT?

Tigers have long been thought to be solitary creatures, but twenty years ago two adult groups were very active in Ranthambhore. One of them consisted of two males and three females. One of the males was noticeably larger than the other, but the others were so similar in size that it was difficult to tell them apart. They could have been a family that never split up, although it would have been unusual for a tigress to raise a litter of five cubs to adulthood. Their general behavior when hunting was not unlike that of a pride of lions. Around the meadows of the third lake, they would take different positions and lie in wait. If a deer came into the circle, one tiger would first stalk and then make a dash for it, pushing it toward one of the others, and in this way they would confuse the deer. I occasionally saw two of them, and on one occasion three, feeding together on the same carcass, but this is most unusual behavior. I have seen tigers interacting over a kill only a few times, and Charles McDougal notes in his book *The Face of the Tiger* (1977) that on the fifty-nine occasions on which he observed tigers feeding on bait, he never once encountered two feeding at the same time.

The most exciting feeding behavior I have seen in my life involved the tigress Padmini and her cubs. One chilly November morning, I was driving when in the distance I saw a man on a bicycle gesticulating wildly as he approached. He shouted, "There is a tree full of crows, and I have just seen a tiger feeding on a nilgai by Rajbagh." I rushed to the tree he described, in which indeed fifty crows had perched. Below it sat Padmini with three fourteen-month-old cubs around her. Nearby lay the carcass of a huge bull nilgai, which must have weighed at least 250 kilograms (550 pounds), appreciably more than the tigress herself. It was far too heavy for Padmini to move, and she was nibbling at the rump, a small portion of which had already been eaten. The two cubs sitting behind her got up in an attempt to approach the kill, but she rose, coughed sharply, and slapped one of them across the face. The cub submitted, rolling over on its back, and settled down restlessly near her while the other cub started to eat from the rump. Padmini seemed to be dictating that the prey would be consumed one at a time.

Eventually, Padmini got up, grabbed the carcass by the neck, and tried to drag it away, but its foot got stuck in a forked tree root. She settled down to eat some more, and half an hour later tried again—this time dragging the carcass about eight meters. She then permitted the second cub to eat. A third cub waited some thirty meters away.

Padmini then dragged the carcass about ten meters farther up the rise of a hill. I followed quickly and saw five tigers at different distances around the carcass, Padmini and Laxmi closest to it. Padmini got up, sniffed a tree, spray-marked it, and walked toward her nearest cub, nuzzling it briefly. She then turned around and walked past Laxmi, snarling at her before grabbing the neck of the nilgai and pulling it farther up the hill.

OPPOSITE: *A resident male tiger walks his territory in Ranthambhore National Park.*

A few minutes later, Padmini got up and walked down the slope of the hill toward the lake. Laxmi moved toward the carcass and started to feed. Surprisingly, I saw another adult tigress sitting nearby. It was Nick Ear, Padmini's daughter from her second litter. Padmini reappeared from the rear, marked a tree, and moved toward the kill. She and Laxmi coughed at each other. Padmini sat and snarled at Laxmi, who moved off toward Nick Ear and settled down on her side to sleep. Padmini also dozed off, but with a watchful eye on the crows perched on the branches. Then the dominant cub returned from the lakeside and sat at the kill, nibbling at the fast-diminishing rump while Padmini watched alertly. By the end of the day, Padmini and her cubs, Laxmi, Nasty, Akbar, another of Padmini's offspring, and another tiger I couldn't identify—nine tigers in all—shared the kill.

I have never come across a description of a scene like this one, and I don't think one has been recorded in the wild before or since, anywhere in the world. I was sure that Padmini had made the kill but had decided to share the carcass with eight other tigers, two of whom were, so far as I knew, totally unrelated to her. And she was in complete control of the situation—not once did she permit two tigers to eat together, thereby obviating the conflict that could have arisen.

To find more than two tigers around a kill is a rarity. Nine was simply unbelievable. The fact that seven were related suggests the possibility of strong kinship links among tigers, sustained over long periods of time. I think that individual tigers do recognize one another. A great deal more observation is needed to gather conclusive evidence on kinship links and their role, but this example shows that tigers can congregate without conflict around a kill—and with a female in charge of the feeding process.

From the summer of 1983 to early 1984, another group of tigers, also comprising two males and three females, roamed a similar area. The dominant member was a female who seemed to control the group's movements, and I observed them hunting on a number of occasions. But in February 1984, one of the males and one of the females disappeared. A month later, I found the surviving male and one female together and later discovered the second female with a gash on her rear flank, presumably the result of a conflict within the group.

In both groups, the tigers remained together for varying periods, and their numbers changed due to conflict, which may have been caused by a tigress coming into estrus or by squabbles over food. Past observations of similar adult groups are quite illuminating. Edward B. Baker, a government officer serving in India, wrote in his book *Sport in Bengal* (1886): "This animal is not the unsocial creature it is commonly understood to be. On the contrary, it is fond of consorting with others, and not seldom three or four may be found together; a mother and nearly full grown cubs; both parents and half grown ones, or a charming party of young males and females living and hunting together for a considerable length of time."

One of the most startling descriptions of communal tiger behavior comes from William Bazé in his book *Tiger! Tiger!*, describing his observations in Indochina in the 1950s.

> Before us lay a great jumble of rocks, surmounted by an immense bare plateau. . . . Here and there the rocks were banded together with clay, but for the most part it was a colossal jumble of loose boulders and great yawning chasms. In several places the rock face was hollowed into shallow caves, reached by steep rocky little tracks which could possibly be used by a tiger; one of them, bigger than the rest, looked as though it might be the main entrance to the caves. The earth all round was clear of all grass and had no doubt been worn smooth by the tiger's feet. Twenty or thirty feet higher was a range of smaller caves inaccessible to the tigers; these were the home of a whole tribe of monkeys. Tough plants and tree creepers gave access from the upper caves to the tops of the trees and provided them with a marvellous playground. . . .
>
> Those nearest to us would hang on to the thick creepers and make comic faces at us while they shook them as if they were trying to shake apples down from the trees, and others performed incredible balancing feats for our delight.

Bazé found and killed six tigers who lived in this extraordinary labyrinth of caves. The corners were full of the bones of animals that the tigers must have fed on. There were dark, narrow passages opening out into the "rooms," and in one annex he found a dead tiger cub. He continued: "Actually there was only one complete family living here—the tigress, her cubs, and the big tiger my friend shot. Another tiger—the one I accounted for—lived by himself in a separate apartment, and the last tigress lived in another cul-de-sac with the baby whose body we found. The maze of caverns and passages provided a safe retreat, sheltered from bad weather, and they would sally forth separately at night to scour the countryside, keeping as far as possible out of one another's way." Truly an amazing description of a tiger's "home."

But this sort of temporary association is the exception: it is very rare to find groups of tigers living together like lions. Except when a tigress has cubs, the long-held belief that tigers are basically solitary seems to be true.

Monitoring tiger populations poses enormous challenges to scientists and animal conservationists. K. Ullas Karanth, who has spent twenty years studying tigers in India, describes the complexity of the task.

Counting Tigers in the Wild

K. Ullas Karanth

Wildlife biologist K. Ullas Karanth (crouching at right) at work with his team.

THERE WAS A TIME when people counted only dead tigers. For centuries, local "noblemen" and colonial rulers slaughtered tigers by the thousands all over Asia, as ostensible proof of valor, wealth, or virility, before an admiring public. Although criminals today still clandestinely kill tigers, in the present conservation era focus has shifted to counting living tigers. Because of the tiger's rarity and conservation value, we now devote substantial resources to the enterprise of "saving tigers." Clearly, we can judge

the effectiveness of this enterprise only by knowing how wild tigers are faring. However, counting free-ranging tigers is easier said than done.

Tigers occur at low population densities even in their best habitats. Worse, they are extremely secretive animals that shun human company. It is naïve to assume (as many conservationists seem to) that we can simply go out and take an accurate census of wild tigers. Whether we count sightings of tigers or their photographs or signs such as paw prints, two formidable challenges confront us. First, given that there are more than 1.5 million square kilometers (580,000 square miles) of tiger forests across Asia, it is impossible to search for tigers everywhere. Equally critically, even where we manage to search, we can detect and count only a portion of all the tigers (or their signs) that are out there.

Therefore, any reliable tiger-counting method must have a statistical basis that allows us to estimate what fraction of the total area was surveyed and, within that area, what proportion of tigers was actually counted. Over the past couple of centuries, ecologists, mathematicians, and statisticians have indeed established such reliable counting methods, which allow us to "sample" animal populations. We can make valid inferences from such sample counts about tigers, tortoises, or any other creature that we may care to count.

How such sampling methods are used to estimate tiger numbers is described below.

If money, personnel, and technical resources are not

constraints (as in advanced research projects or well-funded tiger reserves), a method known as "capture-recapture sampling" is useful for estimating tiger numbers. This approach involves "catching" tigers from a wild population on successive "sampling occasions" and identifying each individual in order to build up individual "capture histories." For example, a particular tiger may have a capture history of 01001, indicating that it was caught only on the second and fifth sampling occasions in a five-sample survey. These capture-frequency data are used to estimate the proportion of animals that were "caught," thus allowing us to estimate total number of tigers in the sampled area.

Of course, if we physically had to catch tigers in order to identify them, the capture-recapture method would be almost impossible to put into practice. Fortunately, each tiger has a unique pattern of stripes. By deploying camera traps that automatically photograph all tigers that pass before them, we can obtain capture histories and population estimates from "photographic captures." Biologists are now using camera-trap surveys at dozens of sites across Asia. The best tiger habitats in the world, like the grasslands of the Himalayan foothills or the deciduous forests of peninsular India, can potentially support relatively high densities of fifteen to twenty tigers per hundred square kilometers (about forty square miles). Ecologically poorer habitats, such as the mangroves of the Sundarbans or the temperate forests of Russia, may support tiger densities of only one tenth of that figure.

Capture-recapture sampling can potentially work with methods other than photography. Individual identifications based on DNA extracted from tiger hair or scats, perhaps even scent-based identifications made by trained dogs, may allow us to employ this method in the future.

Because a single tiger requires about five hundred large prey animals for its support, estimating prey abundance is also a good indirect way of estimating potential tiger numbers. Prey animals can be counted using distance sampling, in which observers walk along transect lines that sample the forest. Line-transect surveys need relatively simple field equipment and can thus be employed in most important tiger reserves, if camera traps are not available.

Where field equipment is unavailable and workers lack basic survey skills, we can still try to monitor tiger numbers using relatively unsophisticated indexes. These do not give us tiger numbers but, much like stock-market indexes, they reflect population trends. Generating such indexes requires sample surveys in which observers move along roads, game trails, or streams, simply counting tiger tracks or other visible signs. The results may be stated as the number of tiger tracks (or other signs) seen for every kilometer walked, driven, or traversed in a boat. Even such simple indexes can tell us how a tiger population is faring under our management.

Setting realistic tiger-counting goals and achieving them using an array of scientifically valid methods, which can be employed practically under given field conditions, is the key to counting tigers reliably.

K. ULLAS KARANTH has spent twenty years working with tigers in India and is an expert on the methodology of counting tigers.

Hunting

Cubs start to leave their mother when they are able to hunt successfully for themselves. Hunting is the most vital skill they learn from her; without this ability they have no chance of surviving as adults. Along with the need to reproduce, the search for food is the driving force of a tiger's life. Each tiger needs fifty deer-sized animals to eat each year—pretty much one per week—and of course a tigress with cubs needs more. Every animal killed necessitates a population ten times that in order for the species to remain sustainable. So fifty tigers need to kill a total of 2,500 deer-sized animals per year, and an area that supports fifty tigers requires 25,000 such prey animals if the predators are to survive. In tropical forests like those in India, a carcass will be consumed in one to four days depending on its size, whereas in Siberia a kill may last up to a few weeks, since cold retards decomposition. Even in Siberia, however, there are few records in the wild of tigers coming back to eat their kills after about one week. A sambar deer, which can weigh 225 to 275 kilograms (495 to 605 pounds), will satisfy a large family. In the moist, deciduous forests of southern India, tigers can bring down an Indian ox or gaur weighing 550 kilograms, and a large family will do well on this for more than a week.

One of the most interesting facets of how tigers hunt is that, unlike many other predators, they do not seem to single out the young, the old, or the sick among their prey. George Schaller examined two hundred kills in the course of his study, and none of the prey was ill or suffering from injury. Mel Sunquist, studying tigers in Chitwan, reckons that 80 percent of tiger kills weigh fifty to one hundred kilograms, although adult male sambar are also taken. In Nagarahole National Park in southern India, K. Ullas Karanth noted that the average weight of eighty-three tiger kills was 401 kilograms, but this sample included several enormous gaur. In fact, the Nagarahole study has established the tiger's preference for large prey such as gaur and sambar.

I have watched tigers killing prey more than seventy times, and in my experience their hunting techniques vary tremendously depending on the individual and its mood. Tigers generally spend a fair amount of time patrolling their "beats," mainly on man-made roads, on animal paths, or along streambeds. In between, they do a lot of sitting, watching, or sleeping, all of which conserve precious energy. Grooming is also an important activity, as the rasping tongue of the tiger flicks over every crevice and corner that it finds.

All this resting and grooming is done in a strategically placed day shelter where the tiger's senses will pick up any hint of prey. These shelters are generally in areas where deer graze, congregate, or are moving from one point to another. The tiger is a great observer of all the wildlife around it and a perfect opportunist. At the first suggestion of the presence of prey, the predator tends first to freeze, then to crouch and start a careful, silent, slow-motion movement toward its victim.

OPPOSITE: *A tiger advances silently through the forest, moving ever closer to the intended prey.*

One morning, I encountered a tigress concealed in a patch of tall grass. She sat absolutely motionless, watching the movements of a small group of deer. At one point, she rose on her haunches and peered over the grass, checking her position in relation to the deer. Her stripes made her invisible, blurring any silhouette. They were the perfect camouflage.

The tigress settled again, quite still. Unaware of danger, a sambar moved some five meters toward her. She lifted her head. A quiver ran through her body, and then in a kind of slow motion she stalked forward a couple of meters with her belly touching the ground. The sambar looked up suspiciously, and the tigress dropped her head, completely concealed in the high grass. The sambar was now only ten meters away, but the tigress made no attempt to rush it. The light was low, but a tiger's eyes can detect any movement, as they concentrate available light on the retina, and the curve of the cornea creates wide-angle vision. They also provide binocular and 3-D vision. Tigers require only one sixth of the light human eyes need in order to see.

The tiger moved a few meters with muscles bunched up. Its highly sensitive

ABOVE: *A tigress leaves the shelter of the tall grass and stalks toward a grazing spotted deer stag.*

OPPOSITE: *A tiger's body is completely camouflaged in high grass, making it an ideal location from which to watch prey.*

119

whiskers were nearly fifteen centimeters long, circling the tiger's head and leading the way. Every time they touch an object, the tiger blinks in response and is thus alerted to what lies ahead. The sensitive touch of the padded paws also helps make the approach totally silent—avoiding even a dry leaf. Tigers creep, stalk, and walk on their toes.

Suddenly, the tigress stopped. Her tail twitched. It, too, is highly sensory. Even the hairs on the back of her forelegs are responsive to touch. A crested hawk eagle flew overhead. A couple of partridges scuttled away into a bush. A peacock cried in alarm. Soon, the sambar drifted away, and the chital moved off. The tigress's effort was in vain. She lifted her head for a moment, surveying the situation, then fell asleep in that position, her ears ever alert and responsive to sound. The deer had not spotted her. She stayed in the same patch of grass all day, waiting for the deer to drift close enough for her to launch her attack over a short distance. But they never did, and she had to wait until the next day to kill a young sambar and satisfy her hunger.

A second common hunting strategy is to take up a position near a water hole or grassy meadow and remain concealed, sometimes even asleep, until the unsuspecting deer move in closer. This is more prevalent during the summer, when the deer are forced toward water in large numbers—if a tiger remains undetected it will probably not move from its concealed spot all day.

It is an endless game of patience, with success depending on the wisdom and experience of the tiger. Sometimes one in ten attacks is successful, at other times one in fifteen. I once watched Nick Ear fail over and over again while trying out a new hunting technique.

One day I found her concealed in a bank of grass, carefully watching a sambar about fifty meters away in the water. Shortly afterward, she came right out into the open and in slow motion covered the distance to the edge of the water one step at a time, freezing whenever the sambar glanced up. The confrontation between predator and prey was hypnotic. Just as Nick Ear reached the water's edge, one of the sambar hinds saw her and bellowed in alarm, and Nick Ear charged into the water, splashing and wading with powerful strides and then breaking into a swim. The sambar escaped out of the water, bellowing continuously. Nick Ear repeated this charge the next day at the same time, again unsuccessfully. Her careful stalk in the open, alternating between motion and freezing, was immaculate, and the sambar remained undisturbed until she reached the lakeside. Only her lack of skill in attacking in water prevented her from succeeding.

One of the first natural kills I ever saw was from the balcony of Jogi Mahal, the forest rest house in Ranthambhore that overlooks one of the lakes. At 8:30 A.M., I had just returned from a morning drive. I decided to sit out on the balcony and have a cup of coffee. My gaze drifted to a group of fourteen chital grazing on the lush green grass at the edge of the lake. The coffee arrived, and I took my first sip, watching this serene

A tigress charges through the waters of one of Ranthambhore's lakes to catch a sambar deer. This behavior in water was observed for the first time in Ranthambhore National Park in the early 1980s.

lake and its surroundings. Then, quite unexpectedly, a cacophony of chital alarm calls alerted my attention to a tiger who had charged the herd from the tall grass, startling them into confusion and successfully catching one.

The suddenness of the attack caught me by surprise. The next moment, the tiger gripped the neck of the chital and carried it off into the high grass around the lake. It looked as if it might be a doe.

Three other chital leaped in fright into the lake in an attempted to swim across to the far side. Within seconds, the first one vanished, followed rapidly by the other two—crocodiles having plucked them from under the water to gobble them up like chocolates. One tiger's attack has resulted in the death of four spotted deer.

The tiger's attack mechanisms are remarkable. The long leg bones above the knee joints provide leverage for handling heavy prey, while the extraordinary skeletal structure permits flexing, turning, twisting, and the rapid grasping of prey using the heavily muscled shoulders and forelimbs. This flexibility is particularly useful when dealing with large prey—a tiger learns from experience to avoid hooves, horns, antlers, even tusks if its intended victim is a wild boar. The thirty teeth are vital for killing and eating. The two upper canines can be 5 to 7.5 centimeters (2 to 3 inches) long, the lower two 4 to 5 centimeters (1.6 to 2 inches); combined with the strong jaw muscles, they can deliver a lethal bite. With heavier prey, the aim is to force it down and then strangle it, basically crushing the windpipe. Smaller prey can often be dispatched with a single bite to the nape, which ruptures the neck vertebrae.

Stalking is a vital part of the tiger's hunting technique—the short lower limbs do not permit fast running, so the predator needs to be as close as possible to its prey before it is detected. Very seldom do you see the moment of impact when a tiger actually pounces on its prey. More often, you hear the kill and then come upon the aftermath. For human observers as for the animals themselves, ears are vital in a forest.

One day, while out scouting, I heard frantic chital calls and then a choked squeak. Convinced that it was the death cry of a chital, I move to the spot. Just ahead, a tiger sat on its haunches, panting heavily. As I crossed a patch of grass, I encountered two more tigers. One was sitting with its paws hugging the carcass of a chital doe while the other watched alertly, moving a few steps forward. The first tiger emitted a low growl and then with a loud "woof" charged at the second. Both rose briefly onto their hind feet, "mock boxing" each other, but soon the second one rolled over on its back as if in submission.

The second tigress eventually began to crawl toward the kill. Her head was close to the carcass and near the neck of the first tigress. The latter snarled viciously at her, but it had no effect. Amazingly, they sat like this, without eating, for thirty minutes. The growling, coughing, and snarling rose in a crescendo. I had never heard such a variety of tiger vocalizations before. It was aggression through sound, for at no time did the two animals attempt to injure each other.

Soon afterward, the first tigress relinquished her hold and sat at the rump to start feeding. The second immediately went to the neck and did the same. The dominant one plucked the tail of the carcass and spat it out. (Tigers in Ranthambhore tend to do this before eating from the rump.) The two tigresses ate ferociously from either side of the carcass, the dominant animal keeping up a continuous low growl. I clearly saw her carnassial teeth slicing at the meat while the other molars and premolars gripped it. Her sharp claws were extended for grip and leverage—unsheathed they are a mind-boggling eleven centimeters (4.3 inches) long. Rough projections on the tongue also helped to remove hair and particles of meat. I have rarely seen two adults eating together. If a kill has to be shared, the subordinate tiger will normally wait its turn so that each eats alone.

As they ate, the tigresses' aggression manifested itself in great pulls from side to side, and after forty-five minutes the carcass appeared to be split down the middle, held together only by the skin. Eventually, it broke in two, the rump left with the dominant tigress and the neck, forelegs, and chest with the second. They both crunched on for another thirty minutes; intestines, rumen, and skin were all rapidly consumed.

In the late afternoon, this frantic eating was rudely interrupted by yet another

Two subadult male siblings spar with each other using their powerful forelimbs.

tigress, who rose from a shady spot nearby and charged the two on the kill. To my surprise, the first two quickly dispersed, leaving the remains to the newcomer, who immediately started feeding. I was sure she was the one I saw panting earlier and think it likely that she killed the chital in the first place. However, she had permitted the other two females to eat before taking over. Most tigers in Ranthambhore are related in some way, which might explain this tolerance.

According to Charles McDougal, an adult tiger can consume thirty-five kilograms of meat at a single sitting. Mel Sunquist thinks the figure may be even higher. He argues that the maximum amount a tiger can eat in twenty-four hours is about one fifth of its own body weight, which for a large male translates into forty-five kilograms. I have seen a tiger consume an entire chital—about thirty kilograms of meat—at one meal.

I witnessed the incident described above because I had heard the sounds of the kill. The tiger does much the same thing. It is not only a master opportunist but also a great scavenger. It observes everything, following the alarm calls of sambar and chital or carefully watching vultures circling overhead and falling toward a kill. I have seen a tigress annexing a jackal's kill by tracing the movements of vultures in the sky. Tigers also respond to the sound of crows and magpies, the chatter of which leads them to the kills of other predators or to animals that have died of natural causes. There is a sense of inquiry and investigation in the tiger as it roams its forest. I remember once hearing a distant wailing cry of a sambar. I had been watching a sleeping tigress, who awoke instantly at the sound and shot away like a bullet; within minutes, she was furiously charging some crocodiles that had captured a sambar fawn. On this occasion, she did not succeed in stealing the kill, but her ears had assessed the sound and dictated immediate action. Over the years, the dying shrieks of sambar attacked by crocodiles in Ranthambhore's lakes have often attracted tigers, some of whom have managed to appropriate the kill.

The way in which a tiger kills has long been a controversial subject among sportsmen and naturalists and remains so among observers of the tiger today. This description, by Captain Thomas Williamson in *Oriental Field Sports* (1807), highlights the contempt in which tigers were held by early hunters but also shows that he had studied the tiger's hunting technique:

> I have already observed that the tiger is of all beasts of prey the most cowardly, its treacherous disposition induces it, almost without exception, to conceal itself until its prey may arrive within reach of its spring, be its victim either bulky or diminutive. Size seems to occasion no deviation in the tiger's system of attack, which is founded on the art of surprising. We find, accordingly, that such as happen to keep the opposite side of a road, by which they are somewhat beyond the first spring, often escape injury, the tiger being unwilling to be seen before he is felt. Hence it is rarely that a tiger pursues....

OPPOSITE: *A tigress dragging the carcass of a sambar deer that she has just killed. She will move to a dense area of the forest to eat and guard her kill from hungry scavengers.*

The tiger's forepaw is the invariable engine of destruction. Most persons imagine that if a tiger were deprived of his claws and teeth he would be rendered harmless, but this is a gross error. The weight of the limb is the real cause of the mischief, for the talons are rarely extended when a tiger seizes. The operation is similar to that of a hammer, the tiger raising his paw and bringing it down with such force as not only to stun a common sized bullock, or buffalo, but often crushing the bones of the skull.

Naturalist Richard Perry wrote in *The World of the Tiger* (1964):

> A tiger coming up to deer, which he has heard or winded, halts at the edge of the jungle and surveys the clearing where they are grazing. Then having ascertained their exact position he begins his stalk. With white belly trailing the ground and his great head, with jaw open and ears cocked, held very low he flows along with such stealth, placing each paw with infinite care, that the watcher must keep glancing to and fro between tiger and deer before he can ascertain that the former is in fact closing the distance between them.
>
> A number of observers have likened a stalking tiger to a brilliantly patterned giant snake, as with head extended so that chin and throat touch the ground, and every muscle seemingly strained, he propels himself along with amazing speed and absolutely no motion other than what appears to be a mere quivering of shoulders and hips.

Jim Corbett saw some twenty kills of tigers and leopards in his time. In one of these, a tiger made a head-on attack on a chital doe; otherwise, all the attacks were from the rear or at an angle. On one occasion when a tiger attacked a buffalo, the latter took off at full speed—with the tiger riding on its back. Eventually, the buffalo shook the tiger off and escaped, but not before the tiger had eaten some two kilograms of flesh from its withers and five or six more from its hindquarters. Corbett also recorded a pair of mating tigers who fought and killed a very large elephant tusker, after a battle that lasted most of the night. While one leaped on the elephant's back, the other mauled its head.

Both Champion and Dunbar Brander point out that a tiger sometimes kills by dislocating its victim's neck and sometimes by strangulation. Hamstringing—severing the tendon at the back of the hock—is a technique used against very big prey. Only much later, once such an animal is down, will the tiger attempt to grip it by its neck. Sometimes it is not successful.

George Schaller once found a freshly killed chital doe with a lacerated throat and tooth punctures on the lower back, as if the tiger had tried everything before succeeding in killing it. He also recorded a sambar stag that was apparently straddled by a tiger and severely lacerated before it managed to escape with deep scars on its shoulders, side, and rump.

Traditional observation concludes that the tiger's primary method of killing is through a powerful wrenching grip on the neck that can crush the windpipe or neck vertebrae. Its eyes and whiskers function together, providing crucial information about where to deliver the lethal bite. Even the long canines are rich in pressure-sensitive nerves, enabling the tiger to hit the gaps between the bones of the neck, biting into and sometimes rupturing the spinal cord. But that is a generalization. In practice, the process of killing depends on the specific situation and the experience of the animal.

Special Hunting Techniques

I once had the extraordinary good fortune to encounter a tigress and her prey locked in struggle. For about twenty minutes I watched Noon, a tigress, trying and failing to kill a sambar.

I had returned from a morning drive, in the course of which I had had a brief glimpse of Noon and two cubs moving toward a dense area below the walls of the fort in Ranthambhore Park, presumably to lie up for the day. I was eating breakfast when a sambar alarm called twice. I left everything, grabbed the closest camera, and jumped into my jeep. In the clearing between the two lakes I found the three tigers moving toward Rajbagh. Noon had apparently changed her mind about her day shelter, for the group passed an old ruin that must have once been the entrance to a mosque. Now overgrown by grass and shrubs, it was one of Noon's regular day shelters.

Suddenly one of the largest sambar stags I have ever seen came galloping out of the area into which the tigers had disappeared. It was pursued closely by Noon. Stag and tigress disappeared from sight some thirty meters ahead. After fumbling with the starter of the jeep, I moved ahead, my heart pounding. In a clearing a couple of meters from the vehicle track the stag stood motionless. Noon was clinging to the side of its neck. Her canines had a grip, but they were nowhere near the throat. Tiger and sambar were frozen in this position, staring at each other.

Because Noon's grip was on the side of the neck, she was unable to bring the sambar down or to suffocate it with the characteristic killing bite of the big cats. She was going to have to use every hunting technique she had learned over the years. I took a few quick pictures, not sure how steady my hands were in the excitement of the moment. I decided to change position and moved up to within three meters of them. They, too involved in their own struggle, were not in the least bothered by my presence.

After a few minutes, the sambar, with a great heave of his neck, shrugged the tigress off, but in a flash she attacked his forelegs. He jerked away, and Noon went again for the neck, rising on her haunches with one paw on his shoulder for leverage. The sambar swiveled around, so Noon had the chance to go for the belly and legs. After

much struggling, the sambar found himself in a sitting position, with Noon keeping a firm grip on one of his hind legs. Noon's male cub appeared and stood motionless, observing the encounter. Noon and the sambar were again frozen in their position. The cub inched closer, perhaps sensing victory. Noon yanked at the sambar's hind leg, opening the skin and trying desperately to break a bone. This was the only way she would be able to prevent him from escaping.

Suddenly, the sambar, utilizing every ounce of his strength, shook Noon off, stood up, and ran. The cub fled in fear, and an exhausted Noon tried to chase after her prey. The sambar, with a burst of adrenaline, escaped in the direction from which he had come. Noon loped after him but hadn't the energy to sustain any speed. The sambar gave his alarm call for the first time, a strange, dull, hollow sound, as if his vocal cords had been damaged in the attack. He waded into the lake, leaving Noon and her cubs watching from the shore. He stumbled forward and found himself in a patch of deep water; forced to swim, he nearly drowned, his head bobbing up and down, his limbs moving frantically as he struggled to reach the far bank. The tigers followed along the shore, but Noon soon gave up and lay down, exhausted and panting. Her tongue was cut and bleeding. The cubs jumped around her, but she snarled again; getting the message, they left her alone, moving off to rest in the shade of a nearby bush.

The stag limped toward the shore and stood motionless for many minutes in the shallow water. Noon watched for a bit but then decided against pursuit—perhaps she simply didn't have the energy for another battle. Instead, she walked away into dense cover to shelter, followed by her cubs. The sambar slowly hobbled out of the water and onto a bank of grass. His right foreleg looked twisted and broken; patches of skin showed the raking marks of Noon's claws; and a bloody injury swelled on the side of his neck. He died of his injuries a month later.

ABOVE AND OPPOSITE: *Rare photographs of a tigress's attack on an enormous sambar stag. The tigress Noon tried to topple the animal and then find a killing grip on the throat. She failed and the deer escaped.*

Noon rested for the remainder of the day, recovering from her exertions, but managed to kill a different sambar stag the next day. Predation is a complex art for which tigers evolve their own techniques, which may vary according to seasonal changes and even to the density of the habitat. Tigers commonly stalk prey stealthily for up to forty meters, inching forward and using every available rock, tree, or bush as cover to get as close as possible to their target before the final charge, which could be from three to nine meters. In Ranthambhore, tigers have also used jeeps as cover when stalking, and in the Russian Far East they have used dense fog. Tigers in Ranthambhore's dry and open habitat may develop hunting techniques very different from those who inhabit the mangrove swamps at the edge of the Bay of Bengal. There, the cover is so dense that a tiger is able to creep very close to its prey before pouncing, so the prey has to deal with an almost invisible predator. On the face of it, the Ranthambhore tigers have a more difficult time, but on the other hand prey densities are much greater in Ranthambhore, so the odds are probably the same as anywhere.

I witnessed one of the most fascinating hunting techniques for the first time when Genghis, who had established himself as the resident male, started to attack sambar in the shallow waters of the lakes. To me, Genghis was the great thinking tiger of Ranthambhore. On a typical day in the spring of 1984 I watched as Genghis moved into a patch of long grass after consuming the remains of a wild boar piglet he had killed the evening before. He slept in the shade of the grass until 2:30 P.M., when a group of sambar appeared on the shore and moved toward him. Genghis stood motionless in the tall grass at the lake edge, deciding which of the sambar to target. His eyes settled on one, and he started his charge, rushing diagonally through the grass toward it. The deer saw him, and with tails raised, calling in alarm, they fled farther into the lake. Genghis's diagonal run cut off any chance of the sambar escaping onto the shore, and they were forced into deeper water, confused and panic-stricken.

With a mighty leap, Genghis launched himself into the lake. The sambar frantically tried to flee, but the weight of the water hampered their movements. Crashing through the water amid sheets of spray, Genghis's power and speed were astonishing. He swerved toward his target, a young fawn, in an attempt to cut it off from the rest of the group. Its mother realized and turned in apparent anguish, knowing that her offspring had little hope of survival yet reluctant to desert it.

Genghis closed fast, pounding through the water with powerful strides. The sambar mother rushed away: she gave up, but from a safe distance she watched in distress. The tiger's paw smashed down on the helpless fawn with such force that fawn and tiger both disappeared beneath the water. Only Genghis's tail was visible. Beneath the water, his canines closed in a viselike grip on the fawn's throat.

Genghis waded ashore, carrying the fawn in his mouth, flicking water from his tail as he headed for the cover of the grass thicket to feed in peace. The chase, from his emergence from the thicket to his disappearance back into it, lasted barely two minutes.

Genghis was a unique creature. I have never seen another tiger as powerful or as enterprising as he was. He ruled Ranthambhore's lakes for nine months then suddenly vanished, and I never saw him again. His hunting activity in the water remains unique in the body of tiger literature across the world.

Diet

The feeding behavior of the tiger is also individualistic. Some tigers have been known to feed till the last morsel of meat is gone and to protect a kill with extraordinary ferocity even against crows and magpies. On the other hand, there are those who will eat what they can in their first sitting and then move on, leaving the leftovers to scavengers. I have seen tigers walk away from a kill even when hungry because they were weary of human disturbance. Some will allow humans to observe them at close quarters, while others are aggressive. Some will drag their kill to the thickest part of a forest to feed; others will happily feed in the open. A tiger, which itself weighs 110 to 220 kilograms (242 to 484 pounds), is capable of dragging a carcass weighing 180 to 225 kilograms up to three hundred meters. It yanks the kill in short bursts, either straddling it or pulling it in reverse. In Myanmar, formerly known as Burma, a tiger is said to have dragged a 770-kilogram gaur bull that thirteen men were unable to move even a meter. Lighter carcasses are often moved a few kilometers until a safe place can be found, especially if a tigress is carrying food to her cubs. She holds the prey in her mouth, and the limbs trail along the ground, leaving drag marks. Decades of observation reveal, however, that it is difficult to generalize about this or any aspect of tiger behavior.

A tigress stands guard over her kill of a sambar deer. Not an ounce of meat will be wasted.

SMALLER PREY

It is rare to see a tiger hunting smaller animals—the encounters tend to be quieter, for a start, so you have to be in the right spot at the right time.

Peafowl are well dispersed through the forest and can be found around bushy, grassy, and shrub areas, especially close to water. They play a vital role in helping humans pinpoint concealed tigers, mainly through two kinds of alarm—one when a bird watches a tiger at close quarters and shrieks its warning, the other when it takes flight after a close brush with a tiger. These alarms are also sounded if a peafowl spots a jungle cat, jackal, or bird of prey.

Twice when Laxmi and her family were walking through tall grass, I saw one of the cubs suddenly take off and leap into the grass. On the second occasion, this was followed by the shriek and death rattle of a peacock. I later had a fleeting glimpse of the cub as it bounded away, the peacock dangling from its mouth. I also once watched the amazing sight of a tigress with two cubs racing at full speed after a peacock who was frantically getting ready for flight, and on several occasions I have found the remains of a kill, with the peacock's exotic feathers scattered all over the place. As young tigers grow they chase everything in the bushes from quail to partridge and upward, and they regularly lie in wait for peafowl. For them, it is the first step in learning the art of killing and eating. Even adult tigers will pounce on or swat an unsuspecting peacock on the ground or on a low branch. The body contains two to three kilograms of meat, and tigers likely look on it as a tasty snack.

Tigers also consume a variety of other birds and animals, in addition to the soil and grass that they munch with some regularity. H. R. Caldwell—an extraordinary character who was both a Christian missionary and a keen amateur naturalist working in China in the 1920s—reported tigers eating pangolins (scaly anteaters). This has also been known in Bandhavgarh in central India. In Ranthambhore, I have twice seen remnants of monitor lizard in tiger scats.

George Schaller, in his study in Kanha, once spotted a tigress sitting alertly in tall grass; suddenly, she leaped high into the air to pounce on something, probably a rat or a mouse. Observers over the last century have discovered an enormous range of food items in the tiger's diet, including snakes, turtles, lizards, crocodiles, frogs, fish, and

A tiger's diet varies greatly. Here a tiger has killed a jungle cat.

crabs—Schaller even found remains of winged termites and Sisyphus fruit in the droppings of a tiger. As long ago as 1886 Frank Simpson of the Bengal Civil Service wrote in *Letters on Sport in Eastern Bengal*, "I have proved . . . that [tigers] catch fish, turtles, crocodiles, and large lizards. I believe they will occasionally eat sugar cane and maize; but the most curious thing I ever knew them to eat was grasshoppers. I once killed a tiger whose paunch was crammed full of grasshoppers or locusts."

In addition to larger animals, tigers subsist on a wide variety of smaller prey. Here, a tiger eats a pangolin.

CHALLENGING PREY

The incident with Noon and the sambar is just one illustration of the difficulties entailed in hunting a powerful adversary. The Indian wild boar and especially the nilgai also present enormous challenges for the tiger. I remember late one evening hearing a ruckus in a field just outside the park. I rushed to the spot with a flashlight to find a tiger and wild boar facing each other. Amid snarls, roars, and grunts they charged each other, but in minutes the tiger was forced to flee. Only an experienced tiger or leopard would take on an adult boar. The male in particular, with his heavy body and fearsome tusks, poses a serious challenge.

Historical accounts leave no doubt that the boar is a courageous and daunting adversary for a tiger and that confrontations between the two are bloody and uncompromising affairs. In most encounters, the boar faces the tiger with hair and bristles erect, wheeling around with head lowered. The tiger, ears back and crouched low, circles the boar, then suddenly springs forward, attempting to strike a crippling blow with its paw. But the boar, even though squat and heavy, is very agile. It quickly exploits any weakness on the part of the tiger by charging with all its weight behind it, attempting to drive its tusks into the tiger's side or belly. The tiger tries to tear out chunks of flesh, but unless it is a really skilled hunter the boar is likely to wound or even disembowel it with its flashing tusks. One writer witnessed an incident in which even when dripping with blood and with bits of skin hanging from gaping wounds, the boar would not give up. Tiger and boar, bleeding, wounded, and exhausted, faced each other. The tiger was the first to limp off into thicker forest, followed by the boar. Both later died of their wounds.

On one occasion in Assam in the middle of the twentieth century, Patrick Hanley, the tea planter, observed a tiger preparing to spring on a group of wild boars when suddenly a chital let out its alarm call and the boars spotted the tiger. The adults instantly formed a protective screen behind which the young ones scattered for shelter. The tiger rose slowly, looked at them in disgust, and sauntered off.

The wild buffalo is another formidable adversary. Mike Birkhead and I once filmed an incident in Kaziranga, Assam, in which a buffalo chased a tiger away. Seventy years earlier, Victor Narayan, working in eastern India, witnessed a remarkable encounter between the two species in Cooch Behar in Eastern India which is recorded in *Thirty-Seven Years of Big Game Shooting in Cooch Behar, the Duars, and Assam: A Rough Diary* by the Maharajah of Cooch Behar (1908, reprinted in 1993):

> He [Narayan] moved up to investigate, when to his astonishment he saw a magnificent bull buffalo moving along leisurely with on each side a tiger (probably tiger and tigress). Every now and then one tiger would dash in to try and get a hold, and the buffalo would merely sweep his horns. The tigers were

evidently sparring for an opening. Neither the buffalo nor the tigers took any notice of the elephants which were following. This went on for about half a mile when suddenly one of the tigers got too close, and the buffalo immediately ripped it right up with his horns. The beast died at once. The other tiger bolted and the buffalo carried on unconcernedly.

The tiger is arguably the most powerful predator that walks the earth. The only animal to which it has sometimes fallen prey in the past is the dhole or wild dog. Packs of more than twenty dogs surround a tiger and slowly tear it apart, even if losing several of their number to the tiger's powerful swipes. W. Connell, writing in the *Journal of the Bombay Natural History Society* in 1944, described an occasion on which twenty-two wild dogs attacked a tiger. The tiger killed twelve dogs but died in the process; the ten survivors feasted on him.

Kenneth Anderson, who shot man-eaters during the 1940s and 1950s, witnessed an amazing battle between a pack of wild dogs and a tigress that took place near Mysore in southern India:

> The dogs had spread themselves around the tigress, who was growling ferociously. Every now and again one would then turn to attempt to rend asunder this puny aggressor, when a couple of others would rush in from another direction. In this way she was kept going continually, and I could see she was fast becoming spent. All this time the dogs were making a tremendous noise, the reason for which I soon came to know, when, in a lull in the fray, I heard the whistling cry of the main pack. The tigress must have also heard the sound, for in sudden, renewed fury she charged two of the dogs, one of which she caught a tremendous blow on its back with her paw, cracking its spine with the sharp report of a broken twig. The other just managed to leap out of danger. The tigress then followed up her momentary advantage by bounding away, to be immediately followed by the five remaining dogs. They were just out of sight when the main pack streamed by, in which I counted twenty-three dogs, as they galloped past me without the slightest interest in my presence.

The next day, Anderson's trackers returned with a few fragments of tiger skin. The dogs had cornered the tigress some eight kilometers (five miles) away and torn her apart. Five dogs had been killed in the final fight.

Colonel Kesri Singh was the steward of Ranthambhore at the start of the twentieth century and combined an uncanny ability to satisfy the maharajahs and foreign royalty who came to shoot there with an instinctive understanding that the area must not be overexploited nor the tiger populations depleted. In his book *The Tiger of Rajasthan* (1959), he describes an evening he spent observing a tiger on a sambar carcass in the forest. He was able to watch it feeding for nearly thirty minutes. Suddenly, it looked up. In the distance, the cries of dholes echoed, and they seemed to be approaching. The tiger appeared anxious and uncomfortable but remained with its kill. Soon, the dogs arrived and surrounded the tiger, inching closer with loud cries. The tiger growled viciously, and the dogs whimpered. The tiger rushed at them, striking a couple with its paws, but then decided to flee through the opening it had made in the circle. Sacrificing its kill, it disappeared from sight, and the dogs tore at the carcass.

This description is all the more exciting because the dhole is no longer found in Ranthambhore. Or it wasn't until 1998, when a single animal appeared from nowhere. No one knows where it might have come from. It is a male and is still alive at the time of writing, in 2004. Many people hope that a female will also stray in and that one day a pack will form.

Tigers and dholes tend to keep away from one another. The BBC television series *Land of the Tiger* includes footage shot in Kanha National Park in 1997 of a tigress chasing away a pack of dholes and appropriating their kill. Today, the wild dog is found only in small numbers, and large packs are rare. People, with their guns, are the only other predators the tiger needs to fear.

Interestingly, the tiger is potentially vulnerable to the defenses of one of its smaller prey species, the porcupine. Scattered widely across India in open areas and grasslands, porcupines live in the earth or in rock crevices. They are great excavators, and in Ranthambhore are almost totally nocturnal. I have occasionally seen them rushing across the roads at night but never during the day. Porcupines weigh twelve to sixteen kilograms (twenty-six to thirty-five pounds), can reach lengths of eighty to ninety centimeters (31.5 to 35.4 inches), live mainly on vegetables, fruits, and roots, and seem to have a good sense of smell. They defend themselves by charging backward with their quills erect, often also making a strange grunting sound.

I have on several occasions come across the scattered remnants of quills where a tiger has killed and eaten a porcupine, but I have never witnessed the kill itself. These quills are extremely sharp and can cause painful, sometimes fatal, injuries, so experienced tigers aim to effect a clean kill by striking or biting the porcupine's head, its most vulnerable spot. Amazingly, the tiger's intestine is tough enough to allow bits of porcupine quill to pass through it, but if it gets quills stuck in its paw it will try to pull them out. Often it will be successful and the wound will heal, but if the quills are deeply embedded, or if they are stuck in the neck, mouth, or jaw where they cannot be reached, the wound may turn septic. If this happens, the tiger is in constant pain and its hunting ability is seriously affected. It is forced to look for easier targets than its normal prey and so may turn to cattle being grazed in the marginal parts of the forest. Jim Corbett describes a tigress who was seriously injured in an encounter with a porcupine and turned man-eater, killing twenty-four people before she herself was killed. Dead tigers have been found with quills embedded in their chests, paws, mouths, necks, and throats and even in the back of their heads. Corbett is said to have removed nearly two hundred quills from man-eaters he had shot, and some of these were up to twenty centimeters (almost eight inches) in length. The porcupine is no easy prey, but tigers continue to relish it.

UNUSUAL PREY

Tigers have a remarkably opportunistic diet. From Siberia comes an exceptional story of the tiger's approach to food. A seven-month-old tiger named Roma was captured after he attacked a person at a logging camp. Soon afterward, he was released several hundred kilometers away. Four months later, he was found roaming a forest looking thin and starved. The scientists who found him thought that as he had survived four months on his own he should be released again, but they radio-collared him so that they could keep track of his progress. Less than a month later, he was seen in a seal rookery along the coast, where he had killed and eaten seven seals. Hungry and weak though he was, he had found the seals easy prey. John Goodrich of the Siberian Tiger Project said of this, "He didn't have a mother to teach him that seals are not normal tiger food! The seals, with their thick layer of energy-rich fat, gave Roma what he needed and when sighted by biologists a few months later in early spring, he appeared fat and healthy."

Tigers have very rarely been known to kill langurs. It was my good fortune to witness this rare occurrence. I was watching Noon while she slept. Many hours had passed with little happening when suddenly I noticed a troop of langurs—the black-faced gray monkeys that inhabit much of the Indian subcontinent—behind her, jumping about in the branches of a tree and feeding on fruit. Noon briefly raised her head to watch them but then went back to sleep. After a few minutes, a large langur came out of the undergrowth as if to go toward the lake for water. It was walking through tall grass, and I noticed it was getting very close to the tigress. Sure enough, it passed within five meters of her.

Noon, disturbed by the rustling of the grass, awoke. Instantly, she spotted the langur and from a crouched position took one bound, followed by a flashing leap, and seemed to fall directly onto the defenseless monkey. For a crucial split second the langur was stunned, paralyzed by this leaping apparition. Noon first pinioned it with her forepaws and then took a grip on its rear flank with her canines. The monkey shrieked and struggled furiously. Swiftly, Noon shifted her hold. Her canines closed on the neck, and in seconds the monkey was silenced. She now rose, holding the dead langur firmly by the neck, and stood still for some three minutes before moving off into the long grass to feed.

I had jumped onto the hood of the jeep to get a better angle from which to record this rare sight. Up in the trees, where they spend most of their time, langurs are safe from the tiger, but when they descend to the ground—and particularly when crossing open ground to drink at a water hole—they are very vulnerable. In this instance, the langur had been caught right in the open. As Noon fed, the rest of the langur troop climbed into a tree, gave a few sporadic alarm calls, and then sat in silence, as if uncertain what to do.

I soon left, only to find a large male langur striding down the road in the direction of the troop. My guess is that the dead langur was the dominant male and that this newcomer was from a nearby bachelor group.

The langur monkey is most vulnerable to a tiger's attack when on the ground.

139

In Ranthambhore, we can actually see firsthand what the tiger eats. In addition, researchers can analyze material that tigers vomit—tiny bone splinters that lodge themselves in the stomach or digestive tract—or what they regurgitate for their cubs. In less open areas, observers have to rely on scat analysis, in which bits and pieces of prey and especially hair can provide detailed information.

In other parts of their range, tigers will also take livestock such as donkeys, goats, sheep, and even camels when the opportunity presents itself. Ranthambhore has known several instances of tigers attacking and eating camels around the fringes of the forest. On very rare occasions, tigers have been known to kill young elephants and rhinos and sometimes even bears and leopards. As far as elephants are concerned, probably the most amazing story comes from E. A. Smythies, a forest officer who observed this incident near the Sarda River in Uttar Pradesh, northern India, in 1940:

> Late one evening in the last week of September, three men were fishing with nets in the waters of the Sarda, two or three furlongs from the bungalows on the bluff, when suddenly two tigers and a half-grown cub emerged from one of the grassy islands close by. The men shouted and yelled until the tigers moved off across the dry bed of the river toward the forest on the right bank, a quarter of a mile away upstream from the trumpeting of a wild elephant. Shortly afterwards the fishermen, and the few dozen inhabitants of the bazaar, heard the nerve-shattering roar of a charging tiger, and the fishermen saw a big male tusker elephant come out into the open river bed, being attacked by the two tigers. For three hours the battle between the elephant and the tigers raged up and down the river bed, below the high bluff, in full moonlit view of the bungalows on the cliff. Would that I had been there to see and hear! The bazaar inhabitants were so terrified at the appalling noise and infuriated roars of the tigers close at hand, that they barricaded themselves in their houses and no one, except the petrified fishermen who were cut off, saw this awe-inspiring and unique spectacle. At about 11 P.M. the noise died down, and by next morning the tigers had departed, but the dead elephant was lying at the foot of the bluff, within a stone's throw of a bungalow.

Some records from the early twentieth century contain accounts of tigers killing and eating leopards, especially in battles over kills. Even recently in Corbett National Park a tiger fought and killed a leopard and proceeded to eat it. There have been similar reports from elsewhere in India, which help to explain why leopards keep away from tigers. In Ranthambhore and Kanha national parks tigers have been known to "tree" leopards and keep them there for several hours.

In Chitwan, Charles McDougal recorded five leopards killed by tigers over a period of twenty-one months. In one instance, a female with two cubs was attacked by a tigress who killed and ate the mother, leaving only the head and front paws. The two cubs escaped but returned to the area the next night only to be killed by the tigress, whose own cubs, aged six months, dragged the small corpses around.

Tiger and crocodile were first seen coming into conflict in Genghis's time—even when he wasn't hunting for himself he would charge into the water, snarl ferociously at crocodiles feasting on a sambar carcass, and literally yank it away, splashing at the crocodiles with his huge paws. National Geographic's documentary *Land of the Tiger* has footage of a tiger emerging from a lake with a sambar that he has stolen from a crocodile.

Instances of tigers eating another reptile—the huge India python, which can attain a length of four meters (thirteen feet)—have been recorded in Dudhwa on the India-Nepal border and in Bandhavgarh in central India. If the python happens to be constricting a small deer, the tiger is able to chew on both!

One of the most exciting incidents I have found in the thousands of pages written on tiger hunting in India comes from Colonel F. W. T. Pollok in *Incidents of Foreign Sport and Travel* (1894). He was up a tree on a machan, waiting to shoot a man-eating tiger near the corpse of one of its victims:

> I do not think I could have borne the gruesome sight much longer, when there was a roar, and a brindled mass sprang at something which was invisible to me. Instantaneously a vast speckled body coiled itself round the brindled matter, there was a struggle, bones seemed to be crunched to bits, the tiger gave a feeble roar or two, and then all was still except an occasional convulsive up-heaving.... That long, long night at length terminated, and thankful I was to see the dawn of day and hear the jungle fowls proclaim that sunrise was at hand—losing no time I descended to solve last night's mystery. The sight that met my eyes was marvellous. A huge rock snake, a python, just over twenty-one feet in length, lay coiled round the body of the tiger whose fangs in turn were imbedded in the back of the snake's head, while the reptile's folds, after enveloping the tiger, had got a purchase by lashing its tail round the adjoining sapling, and so assisted the vast muscular power it possessed in crushing the tiger to death.

In the following pages, Fateh Singh Rathore relates his observations of tigers in conflict with both bears and crocodiles in Ranthambhore National Park, and K. Ullas Karanth describes an amazing encounter between tigers and leopards in Nagarahole National Park in India.

Sloth Bear, Crocodile, and Tiger Conflict

Fateh Singh Rathore

I HAVE SEEN SLOTH BEARS MANY TIMES, digging in termite mounds; quite often, a tiger will pass by, and the two creatures will ignore each other. But in April 2001, I saw a tigress, who I knew had young cubs, charging a sloth bear. A few weeks later, the same tigress left her sambar kill to stalk slowly toward a sloth bear that was feeding on the fruits of a nearby tendu tree. The bear came down from the tree and charged her. It was a kind of hide-and-seek for fifteen minutes until the sloth bear left the area. It is possible that the bear was trying to approach the kill and that the tigress was trying to divert it on behalf of her cubs.

In December 2002, I watched a sloth bear approach the Sakari water hole. A young male tiger was also watching from the bushes. After drinking the bear moved toward a Ber tree, which he shook in order to dislodge its fruit. As he fed, the tiger crept up on him, unable to charge because of the long grass. After almost half an hour, the bear turned on the tiger. Both tiger and bear stood on their hind legs and tried to hit each other. This happened three times; then the tiger retreated a few meters, and the bear, unperturbed, wandered off. A few meters away, another tiger, the brother of the first, appeared in front of the bear but did not attack or approach him. The bear simply walked past. The second tiger joined his brother, and the incident was over.

Two months later, on February 13, 2003, a sloth bear and two tigers again came face-to-face. The tigers had killed a sambar near the Sakari water hole. They were both drinking when the sloth bear appeared. They turned on him aggressively, but he seemed indifferent to them. Totally relaxed, he approached the water, drank, and moved off toward the tigers' kill. The tigers also returned to the kill; one of them tried to attack the bear, roaring loudly, but the bear turned on him and charged, also roaring. Once the tiger had retreated, the bear returned to the kill and continued to feed. Only one tiger attempted to attack the bear; the other sat watching. Over the next thirty minutes, the first tiger approached a number of times, but the bear simply ignored him.

In Ranthambhore, tigers do not seem to be interested in killing sloth bears, although the bears often appropriate their kills; perhaps they have never learned from their mothers to kill bears nor seen her doing so. In many other places, there is evidence that tigers have killed sloth bears in the presence of cubs, so the cubs grow up knowing that this is a prey species and not a competitor to be feared. Later, on March 10, I found a drag mark and lots of bear hairs. Looking around, I found tiger pugmarks but no bear carcass. It seems likely that the mother of the two cubs killed the bear, and I have not seen a sloth bear in the area since.

In November 2002, I was driving in the park along the road behind the rest house when I heard a sambar call. I drove fast and found that the resident tigress had killed a sambar in thick bushes and was sitting on its neck. She had to rest for a while, as tigers become breathless after a kill.

Later, she went to fetch her cubs from the other side of Jogi Mahal. On her return, she found a large crocodile feasting on her kill. She was furious and rushed at it, roaring loudly; the croc responded with a loud snapping of its jaws. The tigress tried to topple it off the kill, but every time it regained its normal position and hit out at her, lashing its tail vigorously. Then the tigress managed to straddle the crocodile's neck, struggling to bite the joint between head and shoulder. She bit off a piece of skin before the croc shook itself free and moved off toward the lake; the tigress then dragged the sambar across the road, where the cubs started eating. They had been watching from a safe distance and seemed quite excited while the fight was going on.

Early the next morning, I found that the sambar kill had

been dragged about fifty meters into the ruins of the fort. I could see the tigress's face in the shadows. The crocodile was still lying where I had last seen it, at the side of the lake. I thought it was dead. At 10:30 A.M., three village dogs appeared—they must have thought the croc was dead, too, because they started feeding on it, but then it got up and dragged itself to the water. The dogs were quite taken aback, and after two more attacks they gave up and ran away.

Meanwhile, the tigress had been watching all that was happening. She dashed from cover, grabbed the crocodile by the tail as it struggled toward the comparative safety of the water, and turned it around so that it was facing away from the lake and toward the jungle. It must have been weak and disoriented, because it stayed there all day. The tigress returned to her sambar kill. At about five o'clock she called her cubs, who appeared from the nearby bushes.

One of the only pictures of its kind in the world: a tiger attacking an enormous crocodile, unusual prey for the tiger. It took hours for the crocodile to die, and then the tigress and her two cubs ate part of it.

She left them feeding on the sambar while she went down to the lake to drink. As she passed the crocodile she tried to step on its back, but it shook her off, moving just a little and wagging its tail. On her way back, she ignored the crocodile completely and returned to her cubs, who were waiting in the road.

The next day the crocodile died.

FATEH SINGH RATHORE has observed tigers in Ranthambhore National Park for the past forty years.

143

Tigers and Leopards

K. Ullas Karanth

It was 10:00 a.m. The sun was getting unpleasantly hot in my open jeep parked alongside a game road in southern India's Nagarahole National Park. I had been radio-tracking Sundari, a 145-kilogram beauty of a tigress, since dawn. In fact, I had been studying her for almost exactly three years to that day in 1993. Her inactive radio signals indicated that she was resting in a nearby shady forest patch of dense lantana, bamboo, and scattered trees. Speculating that she was unlikely to stir until late that evening, I drove back to the field camp for a quick breakfast.

When I returned a mere half hour later, Sundari's signals were emerging from across the road. She had moved about two hundred meters, disturbed or attracted by some event. I decided to investigate by calling in my most versatile all-terrain vehicle: a riding elephant named Kalpana, with her mahout, Kariya. Although the thick-skinned beast pushed through thorny bamboos with silky smoothness, riding on her back Kariya and I were clawed relentlessly by them. The signals drew us to the base of a fifteen-meter-tall *lagerstroemia* tree.

As we got closer, an extraordinary sight greeted us: perched precariously on the *lagerstroemia*, looking down and growling hideously in fear, was a big male leopard. We could see Sundari's striped hide. I knew her fearsome canines could snap the sixty-kilogram leopard's neck like a matchstick if she caught him.

As we drew closer, the leopard grew increasingly nervous: he did not like being forced to choose between this lumbering pachyderm and the silent assassin below. Jumping off his perch, he made a sudden dash for safety. Sundari was after him like a rocket. Fierce growls rent the air as the two big cats grappled in a struggle that lasted barely twenty seconds. Evading Sundari's clutches, the leopard raced back up the tree with an agility unimaginable in a creature its size. Sundari charged at the tree, trying to grab him. She missed, and her bulky form slid down the tree trunk. She made one more futile attempt, reaching about five meters high before sliding down. By then, the leopard had reached the top and found a safe perch. He sat there, bobbing and glaring sullenly, at the tigress and at us. Gradually, his growls subsided. In a few minutes, radio signals emerging from the dense cover told me that Sundari, too, had gone to sleep somewhere close by, in case the leopard made a move again. We withdrew some distance away to make sure he did not.

The scorching sun rose in the sky and then slid slowly to the western horizon. I kept up the vigil, with the two big cats frozen in their respective positions. By 6:45 P.M., it was pitch dark and time to head back to camp. Although I could still hear Sundari's signals, I could not see anything.

I returned to the spot at daybreak. Sundari's distant signals told me she was rapidly moving away. I feared the worst for the leopard as a crow flew off from beneath the *lagerstroemia* with a piece of red, raw meat in its mouth. However, a closer look led me to the pitiful remains of a sambar fawn.

The leopard had apparently killed the fawn the previous morning, after I left for breakfast. Attracted by the deer's distress calls, Sundari had come to investigate, forcing the panicky leopard up the tree, just before I returned. Having waited in ambush through the night, the tigress had given up and walked away earlier in the morning. In his hurry to escape, the leopard had even left uneaten what remained of his hard-earned kill. Here was living proof of the social domination that the larger-sized carnivores usually exercise over their smaller cousins.

K. Ullas Karanth has worked with tigers for twenty years.

Courtship and Mating

Adult life for wild tigers is about hunting and reproduction. Real adulthood begins with the ability to reproduce. For females, it is between the ages of twenty-eight and thirty-six months when they first come into estrus and are able to conceive; for males it is later, forty to fifty months, when they are able to father a litter.

The process of courtship and mating starts with the tigress coming into estrus, and on the three occasions on which I have witnessed this stage the behavior pattern has been identical. The tigress becomes restless, vocal, and very mobile. My first encounter proved to be typical. Early one morning, I was listening intently for sounds of alarm in the forest when I heard a long moan, repeated at regular intervals. I followed the sound and found a tigress walking down the road. In the forty-five minutes that I kept pace behind her, she vocalized some thirty times and spray-marked trees or rubbed herself on the bushes some twenty-five times. The forest echoed with her wails—peacocks flew off in alarm, and at one time a group of sambar bellowed at her in panic before fleeing. She was completely unconcerned and walked along briskly, stopping to spray a tree or rub her haunches on patches of grass or bush. Sometimes she would rub her neck high against the trunk of a tree. I was mesmerized by her total obsession with her physical condition. She was using all her energies to call and mark so as to attract any male in the vicinity. Even if one did not pass through the area until later, he would be able to smell her scent and follow her. Eventually, I lost sight of her as she disappeared into a thick ravine.

Sometimes a tigress's intense marking and calling will attract a single male. On other occasions, more than one will appear, and then a vicious fight may break out. Patrick Hanley recorded an instance when he found a tigress calling with great regularity. This soon attracted a male tiger who cautiously started his approach, but before he could reach her another male arrived and promptly attacked the first. The two tigers seem to have wrestled on their hind legs, clawing and attempting to bite each other and roaring viciously. One of them succeeded in tearing the other's neck open with a slash of its claws. The battle was savage, and one of the tigers soon departed from the fray, bleeding and limping badly.

Hanley then observed a third male watching from behind a bush. The victor of the recent fight had a great weal across his ribs where he had been torn by his opponent's claws. He rolled around in a patch of grass, wiping the blood away, and then approached the tigress. As he came to within a few paces of her, the third male sprang toward him. The exhausted victor was no match for the third tiger and was easily chased away. Soon, the tigress and the third male bounded away into the forest. The tigress had sat quietly throughout, observing the aggressive conflict over her.

Fateh Singh Rathore had a once-in-a-lifetime experience observing mating tigers, which he described in detail to me. On a spring morning the sky was dark and stormy.

A sambar carcass was floating in one of the pools, but there were no signs of tigers. Satisfied that Kublai and Noon were not in the immediate area, Fateh drove back to the rest house, content to try again later. At four in the afternoon, a radio message came through, telling of alarm calls in the area of Rajbagh. Fateh rushed back to the lake and to the small pool where the carcass was still lying. By then, a gale was blowing. Covered with a film of dust, Fateh sought the shelter of some trees.

At 5:20 P.M., Noon emerged from a thicket of grass and sat at the edge. She was soon followed by Kublai, who reclined some meters away. Both tigers appeared relaxed. Suddenly, Noon rose and strode rapidly over to Kublai, who raised his head. Noon rubbed her flank against him. He rose, and she quickly settled in front of him, offering him her rear quarters. Immediately, Kublai mounted her, and some fifteen seconds later Noon growled sharply, followed by a few lower-pitched growls, which lasted another ten seconds. Then Kublai jumped off, and Noon, after a sharp grunt, stood up and moved away. They both lay down to rest. Eleven minutes later, Noon rose again and moved quickly toward Kublai, seductively rubbing her head and her right flank against his mouth. She then sat in front of him. Kublai stood again and mounted her. This time, they were partially hidden by the grass thicket. Noon emitted a sharp grunt, and after thirty seconds Kublai jumped off.

Then Kublai moved right out of the grass and slowly walked around the edge of the lake. He paused to stretch himself on the fallen trunk of a palm tree and then walked on the trunk before moving to the edge of the water, close to the sambar carcass. He snarled viciously at a couple of crocodiles attempting to nibble at the carcass and settled down to watch against a backdrop of a red flowering tree, the "flame of the forest," with the flowers scattered around him on the grass. Fateh, watching from the other side of the pool, was astonished at the raw beauty of the scene. Tiger, red flowers, and sambar carcass were all reflected in the water, creating images of poetic intensity.

Noon quickly followed Kublai's path to the edge of the water. With a sharp snarl at a gliding crocodile she encouraged a response from Kublai by nuzzling him, sliding her flank against his, and then sitting receptively at the edge of the water less than a meter in front of him. Kublai rose, seemingly aroused again by Noon's provocative position. He mounted her, sliding his forepaws down her back until they made contact with the ground near her forelegs. His head leaned against the side of her neck, as if they were entwined. His hind legs remained half bent as his forelegs straddled Noon's neck. Her forelegs were fully stretched and the hind legs slightly bent. After fifteen seconds, she again emitted a sharp growl, and Kublai gripped the folds of skin around the nape of her neck. Some seconds later, she threw him off, snarling aggressively. Carefully, they each licked every inch of their rears, especially their genitals. Fifteen minutes later, Noon initiated another session of copulation in much the same way.

OPPOSITE: *A tigress pushes the male away just after copulation. The protection of breeding habitats is vital to her future litters.*

The sun had set and the forest sounds had changed as the crickets took over. Way out in the distance, a brown fishing owl flew off in search of prey, and a pair of golden orioles flitted across the sky, the bright yellow of their chests providing relief against a dull forest green.

Then Noon walked off around the edge of the lake. Kublai followed, but he had gone only a few meters when the crocodiles returned to the carcass, and he decided to retrace his steps. Amid much snarling, he settled down at the edge of the water, looking carefully at the carcass some three to four meters away. Noon was out of sight. After five minutes Kublai rose again as if to follow her, but the crocodile activity again forced him to retrace his steps. He seemed caught between staying around the carcass and being with Noon. The light slowly faded. Minutes later, Noon returned; again she rubbed bodies with Kublai, and they mated.

Kublai's interest in the sambar carcass was much greater than Noon's—she seemed not in the least bothered about food. In the next half hour, the two tigers mated three more times. Their perfect reflections glinted off the water. Night slowly took over. Fateh had watched eight copulations in eighty-eight minutes. It had been his most exciting observation ever of tiger behavior. Awed by the power and beauty of the scene, he drove slowly back to Jogi Mahal.

The next day, there was no trace of the tigers. The saga was over. Thirty-five days of regular interaction had finally culminated in the mating of Kublai and Noon.

Observations of mating are rare and very seldom recorded. Tigers obviously prefer privacy, free from the disturbance of humans, but we know that mating couples may spend two to four days together. A tigress who conceives may not come into estrus again for eighteen to twenty-two months, though there are exceptions to this. Very little information is available on the tiger estrus cycle in the wild, but zoo records show that tigresses who do not conceive—or who lose their litters for some reason—will come into estrus again anywhere from one to three months later. Like other cats, tigers are induced ovulators—the female releases an egg only once mating has begun. This helps to ensure that a female in estrus finds a male before she is actually ready to conceive, increasing the chances of her becoming pregnant when she mates. The penis bone (in the male tiger, an actual bone) stimulates the tigress, inducing ovulation.

A male tiger may be capable of mating and fathering cubs before he reaches the age of four to five years, but he seldom gets the chance. By that age, he is in his prime, strong enough to have taken over a territory and protect the females that go with it. Yet his active reproductive life will probably last only a few years before he is ousted by a younger male. The reign of one male tiger in Chitwan lasted only four years, but he had seven females in his territory and succeeded in siring twenty-seven cubs in that time. In zoos, a tiger may survive to the age of twenty-six, and age twenty is not uncommon. A captive female has been known at give birth at seventeen. But in the

wild, a female does well to live and breed until the age of fourteen or fifteen. Most male tigers fare rather worse, dying by the age of ten or even younger because of the frequent territorial struggles they must endure. But much remains to be discovered on this subject, as the body of a dead tiger is rarely found in the wild—the tiger is as evasive in death as it often is in life.

It is very clear that undisturbed breeding habitats are essential to the tiger's future. Tigers can breed well and rapidly, but the areas in which they bring up their cubs must be free of disturbance or intrusion. Most of the tiger's natural habitats fall far short of this ideal, whether they are in Siberia, China, Indonesia, or India. There are enormous problems of illegal felling, grazing, poaching, and industrial encroachment. We still need to maintain inviolate tracts so that wild tigers can breed peacefully.

The tiger is one of the world's most mesmerizing creatures. The secrets of its life have only started to be revealed in the last twenty years. Conservationists hope that with countless people watching tigers in zoos each year, man's appreciation and awareness of this magnificent predator will ensure the preservation of its breeding habitats and its safety in the future. For many reasons, not least the haunting attraction of man to tiger, we must keep the tiger alive in the fragments of wilderness where it still exists.

Eighteen-month-old subadults playing on a fallen tree in Kanha National Park in central India.

150

CHAPTER 4

The Cult of the Tiger

Indian and South Asian ancient history was full of tigers, of course, but an enormous cult of the tiger arose across the rest of Asia, including even parts of Siberia. Across its entire range, the tiger became an integral part of the life of the traditional communities, and its influence on religious cults and legends, on art and literature, and on a widespread way of life was unmatched by any other nondomesticated animal. Wherever it existed, it left its impression on the psyche of the people. The Warli tribal peoples of India believed that the tiger was the greatest of all gods and that all other gods existed because of him. Phallus-shaped wooden and stone images of the tiger, often daubed in red to indicate their extreme sanctity, were placed everywhere as symbols of fertility, not just for crops but also for marriage and the birth of children. There were festivals to the tiger god all across India, and there were frequent ritualistic dances in which dancers painted themselves with tiger stripes and then propitiated the tiger god. The tiger commanded great fear and respect across different religions. A legend of the compassionate prince giving his body to save the life of a starving tigress and her cubs is found in several sacred Buddhist texts.

Thousands of miles away in Siberia, the Udege tribal peoples also honored the tiger as their god. To the Udege, the tiger is the spirit of the taiga (evergreen forests) and guardian of the trees and mountains, a divine force of nature. Similarly, many Koreans still believe that their land is blessed by the blue dragon and the white tiger and that the image of the tiger repels evil spirits and protect people's fortunes. Much the same was felt in China. Many believe that the tiger first originated in China and then spread across Asia. At one time, most Chinese believed that the breath of the tiger created wind. Edward Schafer in his book *The Vermilion Bird* (1967) states, "Chinese literature from the earliest times is full of tiger stories—man-eating tigers, were-tigers, symbolic tigers, anti-tiger spells, tiger hunts—tigers in China are like mice in a cheese factory." Three thousand years ago, during the Shang Dynasty, people in the Shaanxi province believed that the tiger symbolized regeneration. A bride would receive two dough tigers when she first arrived at her husband's house (a tradition that continues to this day). In Chinese medicine, the body of the tiger was believed to hold miraculous cures.

OPPOSITE: *A seventeenth-century ritualistic Tantric painting of Varahi, the boar incarnation of the great god Vishnu. Ten-armed and sow-headed, Varahi sits on a magnificent tiger, symbolizing his power to defeat evil.*

Nearly any kind of disease could be overcome by "eating the tiger." Tribal communities believed that the white tiger was a part of the Milky Way and from there he protected the Earth. Just as the goddess Durga rides a tiger in her attempt to defeat evil, the Taoist leader in China is shown riding a tiger in his search for a dragon-tiger elixir for eternal life. Indeed, the parallels in tiger belief between China and India are extraordinary.

Tigers were also a symbol of power in China, and their image conferred both strength and courage. The male tiger, as god of war, was responsible for fighting demons. Chinese soldiers dressed in imitation tiger skins with tails for protection. The tiger was the guardian of China, the protector against evil, and the protector of the living and the dead. Tiger-striped pillows still keep away nightmares, and children don tiger-patterned hats, collars, and shoes to keep away evil. The richness of tiger symbolism in China has no equivalent in the belief systems of Christian Europe.

Wherever the tiger lived, its cult enveloped people. In the forests of Vietnam, Laos, and Cambodia, the tribal Mnong believed that the tiger was first among animals and had intense supernatural powers, including the ability to transform into a human being. The Mnong, much like the Warlis in India, connected the worship of the tiger to the worship of grain, and they believed this resulted in rich harvests from fertile soil. All across Malaysia and Indonesia, people believed in the tiger shaman who could evoke the tiger and then perform miraculous cures on any patient's body in order to repel sickness and disease. They also believed in "were-tigers," who are spirit people that can change into tigers and then back into humans. Were-tigers were protective spirits that kept a link between the past and the present, as for most forest peoples the souls of ancestors were thought to reside in the tiger. The cult of the tiger linked beliefs throughout the land of the tiger, from the Manchurian taiga to the Indian forest and the Sumatran jungle.

More than one billion people live in twenty-first-century India. It also boasts half the world's tiger population, half the world's Asiatic elephant population, and an array of other living creatures. One might argue that these animal populations might not have survived at all if these people had not maintained a core belief in nature's power. The Asiatic elephant invoked the specter of Ganesha, the elephant god; the tiger was the vehicle of Durga.

I firmly believe that true conservation values exist in a nation because of the religions, rituals, myths, and legends that abound in the traditions of the people. Enormous damage has been done to the tiger in the last fifty years as changes have affected the cultural fabric across Asia, and this process has accelerated rapidly in the last fifteen years as new economic models increasingly dot the landscape. One of the primary reasons that the future of the tiger is now in question has to do with our apparent inability to integrate the needs of business (and the human communities it serves) with preservation of our natural environment.

In Times Past

Romila Thapar

The goddess Durga sits astride a tiger in this eighteenth-century painting. Durga's alliance with the tiger suggests an association with a potent and positive energy.

AT THE START OF INDIAN CIVILIZATION, the tiger was revered and woven into mythology, yet a few thousand years later it was hunted almost to extinction. The tiger was not an alien or exotic animal; it had long been appropriated into the semantics of power and myth in Indian society. What was it, then, that was so mysterious about this animal? Was it its habitat, the deep tropical forest, which made it virtually invisible and allowed it to be a loner, as compared, for example, to India's lions, which were usually part of a pride? The tiger was initially associated with the power of

A rock painting of a tiger discovered by the author in a cave deep within the forests of Satpura National Park in the highlands of central India. It was probably painted between 4000 and 2000 B.C.E.

the shaman—the ritual specialist, the healer, the person who could communicate with deities and spirits. The shaman rode the tiger, and this linked him to powers beyond the normal. And through all the centuries when the tiger was being hunted, he remained the mount of the goddess Durga. The seeming contradiction of an animal that is worshipped and hunted, venerated and killed, might become more comprehensible if we trace its representation in early Indian history. It might also help us to clarify the relationship between people and the tiger.

The earliest representations of the tiger were in rock art all over the Indian subcontinent, although many of the highest concentrations are in hilly areas with many rock shelters and caves. These were the natural habitat of both the earliest human society and their predators. The dates of the rock paintings range over some ten thousand years, and paintings from prehistoric periods have been juxtaposed with or overlaid by more recent ones, making any chronology imprecise. Members of the *Panthera* family—particularly leopards—seem to be depicted at many sites, but the clearly recognizable tiger occurs more rarely.

Perhaps the best known of these sites is Bhimbetka, in Madhya Pradesh in central India. The hill here has an intricate network of caves and rock shelters, ideal for prehistoric settlements but also used as a temporary home by nomads and as a hideout in later times. The paintings, therefore, are from various periods, but very occasionally there are inscriptions in an early and widely used language, Prakrit, written in the earliest deciphered Indian script, *brahmi*. In one case, these suggest that the shelter may have been used by Buddhist monks, perhaps in the rainy season when they could not go out to collect alms.

In the nearby Mahadeo hills, there is a painting depicting a tiger-like animal just outside what appears to be a settlement with some cattle. If the predator was seen as a threat, it was attacked with swords and daggers. Elsewhere there are scenes of a tiger being hunted with bows and arrows. Compared with depictions of other animals, such as those of the deer and the boar families, which are drawn with considerable sophisticated detail, the tiger is shown in a less specific way, its identity merely suggested by its size and its stripes. It was obviously seen at close quarters less frequently than were herbivores. The presence of the tiger near such settlements is also indicated by a few remains of tiger bones found at archaeological sites in the northwest of the subcontinent, in Maharashtra and on the western Ganges plain.

Rock art in many parts of the world is linked to societies that depended on hunting and gathering or were moving toward the early stages of agro-pastoralism. This has led to the general assumption that one of the functions of these paintings and engravings was sympathetic magic. Frequently, the scenes are of humans hunting animals, generally those that are normally eaten, such as deer and boar. It is thought that these paintings were created in an effort to ensure the success of the hunt and that they became the objects of ritual attention prior to the hunt—and presumably after the hunt as well, should it have been successful. The hunted animals are painted with a remarkable degree of precision and stylistic verve, whereas the humans are matchstick men, more figurative than realistic. The focus was clearly on the animals, not the hunters nor the forest itself, which is not depicted directly. Sympathetic magic can be associated with shamanism, where the representation acts as a communication with the supernatural world and imbues both painters and hunters with special powers.

The paintings of the tiger hunt, although infrequent, are therefore curious, as the tiger was not eaten regularly. They suggest perhaps an early use of the tiger's body parts for magical and medicinal purposes. Possibly the claws and the skin had already acquired magical properties, and the meat may have been eaten as a special treat. It is well known that pastoralists, for example, do not indiscriminately eat the flesh of even their domesticated animals. They do so only to mark special rites and occasions, as is attested for the eating of cattle flesh among the Nuer in East Africa and in the earliest textual source in India. Eating the flesh of a valued animal was possible only to those of special status. Among some Naga clans of northeastern India, tigers were invoked by the shamans but were killed only on ceremonial occasions.

The shift to agriculture is indicated by a few designs common to rock paintings and the pottery associated with farming societies. There is also the occasional painting of yoked cattle and of chariots—rather reminiscent of the Daimabad bronzes from Maharashtra, supposedly from the later period of the Indus civilization, about three and a half thousand years ago. But perhaps a more obvious signal of change is the depiction of a tiger-like face on a form seated like a human. The overlapping of tiger and human had begun—the tiger was entering human mythology. Terracotta masks suggesting the face of a tiger have been found in some of the cities of the Indus valley.

The Indus Civilization, circa 3000 to 1700 B.C.E.

The tiger comes into its own during the period of the Indus civilization, as part of what seems to have been the mythology of the cultures of Mohenjo Daro, Harappa, and other cities. Together with the elephant, rhinoceros, and water buffalo, the tiger became a familiar animal. At this time, the plains of the Indus and Gujarat, where the urban centers were located, were covered with tropical forest, the natural habitat for these animals. Despite the deforestation of the last few centuries, tigers were seen in the gallery forests of the Indus as late as the nineteenth century. There is, however, little evidence for the presence of the other great animal of the wild, the lion. A couple of terra-cottas, identified with some uncertainty as heads of lions, may have come from farther west, where the lion was well-known. Perhaps the ecology of the Indus as it was at that time, prior to heavy deforestation, was not a congenial habitat for lions. Seals from the time that depicted animals show in the main the elephant, rhinoceros, gharial or Indian crocodile, and bull; each of these appears about four times as often as the tiger. But if numbers indicate importance, then a presumably mythical single-horned unicorn-like animal was the most significant. However, the tiger does not occur only as a standing figure, and often there is a scene suggestive of a story.

The tiger's most frequent occurrence is on seals made largely from steatite or soapstone. These are usually flat, two to six centimeters (roughly one to 2.5 inches) across, square or rectangular in shape—very occasionally cylindrical—with a boss on the back. It is known that these were used for sealing packages, but they may have had other uses, too. Clay tablets of approximately the same size and copper amulets also have depictions of the tiger, with similar themes.

In contrast to its depictions in rock art, the tiger here is clearly recognizable, often highly stylized and in one case in a strikingly elegant stance. Among the many forms in which it is represented is one where it is standing open-mouthed but not looking particularly fierce. That there were mythologies associated with the tiger is evident from the forms in which it occurs. Thus, three tiger heads are joined to a single body, forming a decorative motif, a kind of imagery that occurs with other animals in other cultures. A standing human figure has the rear half of a tiger attached to it, forming a tiger-man or tiger-woman. On one such figure there seems to be a branch either sprouting out of the head or placed behind it. Would a tree be a symbol of the forest? Ritual associations are suggested on other seals where the tiger is shown with the horns of the zebu (the humped bull), standing before an object that has been interpreted as a kind of altar and that often occurs with the unicorn-type animal. A variation on this theme is a tiger without horns standing in front of what looks like a feeding trough. Could this represent a domesticated tiger? A seal portraying a tiger and cub might suggest the same. On another seal, a horned tiger is shown being attacked near a tree by a bovine-human.

Other scenes suggest more complicated symbolism. There is the much-cited seal, sometimes known as the Pashupati Shiva seal, after the manifestation of Shiva in which he is viewed as the lord of the animals of the forest, and variations of it—such as one of a person seated on a stool with his legs in a yogic position, wearing a horned headdress and surrounded by four animals: rhinoceros, elephant, water buffalo, and tiger. The tiger is in profile and seems to be leaping toward the center. On the base of the stool are deer, making the scene reminiscent of the depiction of the Buddha preaching his first sermon in the deer park at Sarnath.

Another scene, found on more than one seal and on clay tablets from Harappa, shows a female figure—though on some seals it is a male—holding apart two tigers, one on each side. The animals are standing up on their hind legs and are in profile. The tablet additionally has an elephant below the main scene and a wheel above it, which could be a pictogram. It is unclear what this scene represents, but there is an interesting parallel seal from Mesopotamia that shows a man grappling with two lions. It is significant that the lions and tigers were interchanged in the two civilizations, probably depending on which animal was more familiar to the local people. The tiger is not generally associated with western Asia, where the lion was the animal linked with power and majesty. The story

With his arms outstretched, a warrior fends off a pair of tigers on this Mohenjo Daro seal of the Indus civilizations, 3000 to 1700 B.C.E.

depicted here seems to have had a widespread meaning, as it occurs not only in Mesopotamia, where in one case the hero plunges a dagger into the lion, but also in central Asia, where a winged deity is depicted between two lions. It is noticeable that the images of the tiger are not crafted as aesthetically as those of the lion in western Asia nor those of the zebu or the one-horned animal on other Indus seals.

Another repetition of similar scenes on seals and tablets shows a man sitting on a branch of a tree with a tiger standing on the ground beneath, looking up at him. What is the link between the two? There is sometimes a gharial in the upper register, which must be connected with the story. Recent interpretations of the scenes on the tablets suggest that there was probably a continuous depiction, with the man in the tree above the tiger followed by a man spearing a water buffalo below the gharial and then by the man in a yogic position. But even if so, what would have been the story behind this, since none of the features is repeated?

The pictograms on the many seals depicting this scene are not identical and therefore cannot have been captions. One could argue that the depiction indicated a fear of meeting the tiger in the jungle and therefore drew a demarcation between man and tiger, but this is contradicted by the tiger-man/woman image, endorsing the unity of human and tiger. That the hero combats felines is obviously a way to underline his power. The woman combating tigers seems to signify other aspects of power and allies fertility with divinity. Was she a priestess, or did she encapsulate the kind of power associated with goddesses, which has been an underlying feature of Indian civilization throughout the centuries? Was this a thread of belief that continued from earlier times when the shaman claimed that he rode the tiger?

Mythologies draw on multiple sources and contribute to others, particularly when there is much coming and going of people, goods, and ideas. City dwellers such as the Harappans tend to romanticize animals with which they have little to do, and their narratives and depictions have to be read at many levels. Further, commerce encourages meeting people in distant places, and it is known that the Harappans had contact with people living in Mesopotamia and in northeastern Iran. Doubtless some of their myths were parallel while some grew out of cultural interactions. But the next phase of the presence of the tiger in Indian history was rather different.

The Tiger in the *Vedas*, circa 1500 to 500 B.C.E.

The Vedic corpus consists primarily of the four *Vedas*— *Rigveda*, *Yajurveda*, *Samaveda*, and *Atharvaveda*—and a few additional texts of the mid-first millennium B.C.E. They reflect cultures with diverse concerns that are not identical with those of the earlier Harappans, although some myths and rituals may have been handed down. The earliest is the *Rigveda*, the authors of which write about and were familiar with an area that extended from the Indo-Iranian borderlands to the edge of the Indo-Gangetic watershed— what was called the *sapta-sindhu*, the seven rivers of the Indus system. The geographical horizon of the *Rigveda* was distinct from that of the more easterly later Vedas, which included the Ganges plain.

The societies mentioned in the Vedic corpus were agro-pastoral, primarily herding cattle and sheep in their settlements but practicing agriculture as well, with groups gradually migrating from the northwest to the middle Ganges valley. The settlements were small and used horses for herding and transportation. Their language, Vedic Sanskrit or Indo-Aryan, points to the incorporation of forms and words from Munda and Dravidian languages, resulting from interaction between migrants and the earlier local settlements. The people were generally organized in a system of clans, with the clan chief position slowly evolving into a local king. It is possible to trace the evolution of states as the clans gradually became more complex, culminating in the Mauryan empire in the fourth century B.C.E. Changes in the attitude to the tiger reflect some of these broader changes.

The *Rigveda* does not mention the tiger—the word for tiger, *vyaghra*, does not appear until the later Vedas. This word derives from a root that means "to scent out," and thus it seems to have arisen from careful observation of tiger behavior. However, the lion does feature in the *Rigveda*, leading to the suggestion that the original authors lived in the Indo-Iranian borderlands or other areas where lions were common. Sharduli, the mythical mother of the cat family and later linked to tigers, is mentioned, but at this stage *shardula* could have indicated a lion, panther, or leopard. Not only is the lion referred to earlier on, but it is respected and treated with awe.

Although the tiger, too, is respected, it is also feared as a predator of cattle, sheep, and people. In one hymn that lists categories of hostile pairs, the tiger's hostility is said to be directed toward cattle. The lion is also a predator but is not mentioned as such as often as the tiger is. Safety is sought from tigers, other wild beasts, and thieves. Large herds of cattle, even in stockades, would be prey to tigers. Though it is hard to believe when one sees the denuded northern Indian plain of the present day, the area was at this time densely covered with monsoon forests. Establishing a settlement involved cutting down forest and inevitably coming face-to-face with the tiger population.

The Vedic corpus contains the first references to a dichotomy between the two contrasting categories of what have been called the settlement and the forest. This dichotomy was described initially as being between the *grama* (village) and *aranya* (wilderness) and in later times as being between the *kshetra* (field) and *vana* (forest). At a literal level, the contrast is between the ordered, organized human settlement and the unknown, disorderly existence of the forest, which has its own laws and patterns of behavior. But at a more metaphorical level, it has been argued that these are not merely spatial differences. Stability in the settlement grows out of the cohesion of the human group encapsulated in the practice of ritual and the observance of social norms within the concept of an ordered world. The forest lacks this cohesion, being less definite in space; it is the habitat of those who do not live by social norms, such as thieves and brigands seeking refuge there, as well as the forest people, whose norms are different. The forest therefore is remote and wild.

One can argue that this was a way of establishing metaphorical boundaries. The tiger within the forest observed the rules of natural order among animals, and from the perspective of human society it was admired and could be an object of worship. But when it strayed into the settlement it was a threat, since the rules of the settlement were different and the tiger's transgression of these rules made it an object of hostility. One may not agree with the starkness of the dichotomy, for in a sense the forest, too, has its rules, but these are not always accessible to human understanding. Nevertheless, the metaphor occurs repeatedly in Indian civilization and it was central to legitimizing the gradual spread, over many centuries, of ordered civilization into areas that were forested and unknown.

In its association with the unknown, the tiger comes to be linked with sorcery and power. The *Atharvaveda* mentions the grinding up of the teeth, eyes, mouth, and claws of the tiger, the snake, the wolf, and the sorcerer. This action presumably has something to do with protection through sorcery, and the *yatudhanas* (sorcerers) were much feared. The *Atharvaveda* contains many references to such activities. The force of an amulet is attested to by saying that with it a person can attack a tiger. The household fire is described as a tiger that guards the house.

But the power of the tiger now also begins to be eulogized. When the god Indra drank the hallucinogenic ritual drink *soma*, parts of his body were converted into wild beasts; the contents of his innards became the tiger and his blood became the lion. The tiger is said to be the *kshatra*, the epitome of power, among animals of the forest. Gradually, the chief of the clan, the *raja*, aspired to the power of the tiger. At the royal consecration, his seat was covered with a tiger skin. Since the tiger was said to be born through the deities Soma and Indra, he is formidable, and his strength and power are internalized by the *raja* at his consecration.

The *Mahabharata* and the *Ramayana*, circa 400 B.C.E. to C.E. 400

Some of the attitudes initially expressed in the Vedic corpus become crystallized in the immense oral tradition of the two great Indian epics, the *Mahabharata* and the *Ramayana*. The dichotomy of settlement and forest is brought out strikingly, with the settlement being the location for the capitals of kingdoms, while the forest is the place of exile, where life is lived without the facilities or laws of the settlement. It is far removed from the complexities of civilization but nevertheless has complexities of its own. In the epics, the forest is a central space crucial to the imagery of the poet, the place where fantasies can reign.

In both epics, the perception of the tiger is expressed through a series of similes. Dasharatha, before becoming the father of the hero Rama, performs a special sacrifice in

This eighteenth-century painting reflects the deep spirituality of the natural world. Surrounded by elephants, a tiger, a leopard, a peacock, and a variety of other animals, a group of ascetics meditate in the hermitage, or nature's sacred grove.

order to obtain sons. Out of the fire emerges a great being sent by the god Prajapati, who is described as stepping out in the fashion of the tiger. The *rishi* (sage) Vishvamitra takes Rama to the forest inhabited by *rakshasas* (demons); the forest is described as deep and dreadful, filled with the screaming and the roar of ferocious animals, including tigers, lions, elephants, and boars. The forest is again unknown and lawless, but it is also the required background to the royal hunt, and in the culture of the royal hunt the naturally hostile pair is not the tiger and a domesticated animal like a cow, but the tiger and the deer. This is a frequent source for comparison in the epics.

When Rama's stepmother, Kaikeyi, demands that Rama be exiled, Dasharatha is stunned, and his condition is compared to that of a deer at the sight of a tiger. Rama's

mother, Kaushalya, bidding him farewell, prays that the lions should protect him and the tigers not harm him in any way. The *rakshasas* of the forest take a terrible toll on the animals on whom they feed. In one case, the demon has speared three lions, two panthers, four tigers, ten deer, and a huge elephant. Rama's wife, Sita, kidnapped by a *rakshasa*, is kept in captivity in Lanka, where she is surrounded by women guards and described as being like a doe surrounded by tigresses. When Rama's ally Sugriva sends out search parties for Sita, he tells one of them to look among those who have the form of a half-man half-tiger. This is reminiscent of similar forms depicted on the Harappan seals. But there is also a gentler image of the tiger. A touching description of the sage Nishakara has him seated in his hermitage with lions, tigers, bears, reptiles,

The presence of a tiger represented an affiliation with the most powerful and positive force for good in the natural world. Local people believed the tiger was the intermediary between heaven and earth.

and the like surrounding him like supplicants around a patron. Among the objects required for the coronation ceremony of Rama, specific mention is made of an entire tiger skin. (In later centuries, too, the tiger skin and that of the lion covered the king's seat at a royal consecration.)

The highest compliment to the prowess of the hero is the simile commonly used in the *Mahabharata* of *purushavyaghra*, which translates as "tiger among men" but has variants such as "tiger among kings" and "tiger among sages." Comparisons are made between heroes rushing at each other and tigers rushing at elephants and buffalo. Lesser warriors flee from the heroes like small animals fleeing from tigers. Tigers are known to fight one another, but tigers and lions in combat with one another are not mentioned.

The gentleness and absence of violence from the *rishis*' hermitages was conveyed by the image of deer grazing safely in the presence of tigers. This may also have had to do with the origins of the hermitages, which may have grown out of the earlier idea of sacred groves, with trees dedicated to a particular deity, whose presence was said to ensure the meekness of predators.

The peace and calm of the hermitage, although in the heart of the forest, contrasted with the turmoil created by the *raja* and his entourage out on a hunt. The famous narrative of the young woman of the hermitage Shakuntala being wooed by the *raja* Dushyanta opens with him hunting in the neighboring forest, accompanied by heavily armed soldiers and hundreds of horses and elephants, almost as if going into battle. Whole families of tigers and deer are killed, and wounded elephants trample on the forest in their pain. So fierce is the slaughter that animals that are normally the prey take refuge with the predators. This is reminiscent of another vivid description in the *Mahabharata* of the destruction of the Khandava forest to clear land to build the capital of the Pandavas at Indraprastha. The five Pandava brothers claim their inheritance of part of the kingdom from their cousins, the Kauravas, and the Khandava forest is part of the territory ceded to them. One of the brothers, Arjuna, and his mentor, Krishna, invoke the help of the fire-god, Agni, in order to burn and thereby clear the forest. Fire rages for days and eats everything that comes in its way, from birds to *rakshasas*. So great is the carnage that even the gods ask whether the day of the ultimate destruction of the universe—the *mahapralaya*—has arrived. Again and again, hunts are described as wars against nature, with trees being uprooted and many lions, tigers, elephants, bears, boars, and lesser animals being killed.

The forest was unknown and therefore dangerous, but it had also to be cleared to establish a settlement and to obtain its resources: timber, elephants for the army, semi-precious stones, ores from the mines, and other produce. Both the ferocity of the hunt and the burning of the forest are preconditions to resources and power and as such are not merely symbolic. Deforestation is a crisis that goes back many centuries.

The people of the forest are frequently described as strange and even animal-like, and there is often a demonizing of those who look different and live in ways that seem alien to people from settlements. Hermitages were the vanguards of settlements, seen as encroachments by the people of the forest and therefore attacked. This may explain the threats to the *rishis* by the *rakshasas* in the early part of the *Ramayana*, when Vishvamitra calls upon Rama and his brother Lakshmana to ward off these attacks.

These were societies mutating from small, locally organized clans to the more extensive and distanced systems of kingdoms. New territories were settled, with agriculturists and artisans contributing to the revenue of the state. The cutting down of forests was the first step. Hunts were surrogate raids and also provided training for small-scale campaigns and particularly target practice. The hunter par excellence was a heroic ideal, and in the forest the tiger was seen as the match for such a hunter.

On other occasions when a tiger threatened a settlement, the man who warded off the predator and was killed in the combat was memorialized on a stone slab, which was ritually installed and worshiped. These "hero-stones," as they have come to be called, were originally memorials to those who had died in battle. But the defense of the settlement was equally important, and the local hero who protected the village became a legendary figure, the subject of epic poems, immortalized by a sculpted representation of his heroic act.

Yet despite the tiger being a predator, there was also a remarkable awareness of the symbiotic relationship between it and the forest. They are seen as inherently bonded—it is significant that the tiger is chosen as the animal that protects the forest from desecration. Although the two sets of cousins in the *Mahabharata* are enemies, the Kauravas are said to be like the forest and the Pandavas like the tigers—the bonding of kinship is implicit. In its natural habitat, the tiger was respected and worshipped as a powerful spirit. The hostility was only to it crossing the boundary of its own habitat and threatening the settlement.

Uneasiness with the alienness of the forest does not preclude some poetic descriptions of life there as idyllic, with the most beguiling reconstructions of trees, plants, and flowers. In such descriptions, the forest is a haven of quietude and beauty, often rendered all the more exalted by the evocative language and imagination of court poets. The forest lent itself to a remarkable mythology of imagined creatures, some fierce and fantastic and some gentle and fulfilling of every wish.

The Mauryan Period, circa Fourth to Second Century B.C.E.

In the Mauryan period, the state adopted a policy toward forest and wildlife, attempting for the first time to exert control over both. The great work of statecraft from this time, the *Arthashastra*, was written by Kautilya, minister to the first Mauryan king, Chandragupta, but was edited in the subsequent centuries and is therefore relevant to later periods as well. It prohibits the cutting of forests without permission from the state. More than likely, this was not because of enlightened conservation policy but rather to ensure that all land newly brought under cultivation was registered for the purposes of taxation. It was also a method of keeping peasants tied to the land they cultivated and preventing them from migrating to new settlements. And it might have been an attempt to curb shifting cultivation among communities that were not peasant cultivators. Kautilya also advocates the settling of *shudra* (low caste) peasants on wasteland, thereby extending agriculture and increasing revenue. All cultivated land had therefore to be registered.

According to the *Arthashastra*, the director of forest produce is required to collect produce in the form of plants, poisons, and animal parts and set up places where items made from these products can be manufactured. Skin, bones, eyes, teeth, horns, and hooves of various wild animals are mentioned, and their uses are varied. Would the suggestion that animal skins were to be collected by the director indicate that they were the object of poaching, as

tiger skins were? That there was a demand for skins is evident from the way the elite draped themselves in them and lined their chariots with them. Various poisons and traps were recommended for killing tigers once they became a threat. Medical treatises from around this time prescribe the meat of tigers for calming the mind and giving energy.

During this period, there was considerable interest in the tiger in the writing of the Hellenistic world of the eastern Mediterranean and western Asia, largely in Greek and recording comments of visitors to India. These writers were more familiar with the lion—tigers became better known in the early Christian era, when they were brought to Rome as exotic animals for entertainment. But prior to this, strange stories circulated about weird animals from the east. A Greek physician at the court of the Persian Achaemenid king, writing in the sixth century B.C.E, describes an amazing animal that some have thought was actually a tiger. He calls it the *matrikhora*, a predatory animal with three rows of teeth and a sting in its tail. Gradually, as familiarity with Indian fauna increased, descriptions of the tiger became more realistic. The largest, said to be found in the east, were twice the size of lions and so powerful that even a tame one had to be led by four men. Another text states that leopards, tigers, and elephants were common to the peninsula, but no mention is made of the lion.

In the Mauryan period, the tiger is still associated with heroism and prowess, but royal majesty is linked to the lion. The reasons for this have not been fully explained, but some of the capitals of pillars set up by the Mauryan emperor Ashoka, on which he inscribed his later edicts, have lions sculpted on them. A famous example from Sarnath, in whose deer park the Buddha preached his first sermon, shows four seated lions facing the cardinal directions and supporting the *dharmachakra*, the wheel of law. In later Buddhist teachings, this came to be associated with the symbolism of the Buddha as the universal ruler, his teaching as the roar of the lion, and the turning of the wheel of law as the central focus of what he taught.

The lion as the symbol of majesty and royalty may have resulted from Mauryan closeness to the Achaemenid and Hellenistic worlds through exchanges of envoys, through trade, and through the extension of the Mauryan empire as far as Afghanistan. In western Asia in the first millennium B.C.E., from Assyrian to Achaemenid times, the lion was the royal animal par excellence. Whatever the reason for its preeminence, it now also attained this status in India.

In recent writing, Ashoka has sometimes been put forward as the first conservationist in India. This is perhaps misleading, though he was averse to hunting, and he planted many shade-giving trees along the royal highways. His Fifth Pillar Edict, which lists the animals that are not to be killed, is frequently quoted. It is a curious list; the animals included are birds, waterfowl, bats, ants, tortoises, small animals of the field, deer, rhinoceroses, and those quadrupeds that have no utility or are not eaten. Goats, ewes, and sows that are with young or giving suck are not to be killed, and capons are not to be made. It is difficult to find an explanation for this list, since it does not conform to what conservation might have required; it may have had to do with medicinal or ritual connections. On specific days of the month, considered auspicious by certain sects, other animals, including fish, are inviolate by a decree that included a ban on castrating animals that were eaten and on branding horses and cattle on certain days. The emphasis is on the specific days as much as on the animals. Ashoka also states that forests must not be burned in order to kill living beings or without good reason—a rather different perspective from that behind the burning of the Khandava forest.

Outside the Mauryan domain and in the far south of the subcontinent, Ashoka mentions the chiefdoms of the Cheras, Cholas, and Pandyas clans flourishing until the beginning of the Christian era. Their earliest literature in Tamil—the *Shangam* poems—has been described as heroic poetry. The clan systems evolved into kingdoms, but these and other names persisted. In references to the animals of the forest, the tiger consistently remained preeminent. The lion is mentioned but not as frequently, and this may well be because the ecology of this region was more conducive to the presence of the tiger. The tiger preys on deer, but there is also some hostility between the tiger and the elephant, which may have had to do with the usual competition for territory and water.

Tigers are associated with the mountains, and their lairs are in caves, but they stalk the jungle. Here, the tiger is again the counterpart of the hero, and the herd of deer that is hunted is compared to people. A mother who is asked where her son has gone replies that although her womb was once his lair he is now seen only on the battlefield. The simile emphasizes the superiority of the chief among the clansmen, but implicit in it is also some animosity between the two. There is, however, another reference to a tigress giving her teat to a baby antelope. A certain empathy with the tiger comes through in an occasional remark, such as that a particular amber liquor is the color of a tiger's eyes. In the later literature, there are many references to kings and deities wearing tiger skins as marks of status. The son of the chief or king is compared to the tiger's cub. The children of hunters wear necklaces of tiger teeth. The curving stripes of the tiger are often mentioned in the poems.

Buddhist Texts, circa 300 B.C.E. to C.E. 500

The link between people and tigers changes in some of the Buddhist teachings of this period. The associations of prowess and status continue—as, for instance, in the prohibition on monks sleeping with coverlets embroidered with figures of the tiger or made of tiger skins and on riding in chariots lined with tiger skins. The monk was not to aspire to worldly symbols of luxury and status.

Since the Buddhist monks traveled through forests and initially lived in remote areas, the tiger was always near at hand. Monks were cautioned about the animal's ferocity and tended to avoid wandering alone in jungles. Consequently, in many stories the tiger comes to symbolize the threat or obstruction to the attainment of nirvana or supreme knowledge. The ploughman keeps working the field of knowledge even though the tiger advances toward him. But the tiger, too, has his moments of being unaware, and it is said that a person who is gathering flowers is carried away by death just as a sleeping tiger is carried away by a stream.

The threat of the tiger is also a test of the monk's commitment to Buddhism. In the time before monasteries were built, monks often lived in forests. In one case, thirty monks were dwelling in a forest but kept a vow of silence. Early one morning, three of them dozed off, and even though they were carried away by a tiger they kept silent. It was then decided that if a tiger came, the monk should be allowed to call out. Later, a young monk was caught by a tiger; he called out to the others, but the tiger sped with him up to a precipice that the monks could not reach. Before dying, the young monk called out that he had kept his vows and therefore was not afraid to die. The message is presumably that one should not fear death but should stand fast by one's vows and the Buddha's teaching. Here, the tiger is the challenge to both.

Among the more famous stories, repeated not only in the Buddhist texts but also in the accounts of Buddhist travelers to India, are those of the *bodhisattvas*—the Buddhas to be—sacrificing themselves in acts of piety. A *bodhisattva* is generally born into a family of status, is learned in the texts of religion and philosophy, and is highly respected. But he finds all this purposeless and gives up home, wife, and son to become a monk and follow the teachings of the Buddha. The test comes when he feels that he has to help another human being by sacrificing a part of his body, such as giving his eyes for a blind person or parts of his flesh for a dove, which in this context represents the natural world; ultimately, he may sacrifice his entire body. The classic story tells of a *bodhisattva* who sees a starving tigress. She is so hungry that she is about to eat her cubs. Sending his disciple away on an errand, the *bodhisattva* offers himself to the tigress and her cubs, who feed on him and save themselves. Such stories encapsulated Buddhist ethics; in addition to being frequently told, they were

included in the narrative art that adorned such monuments as the Nana-Buddha shrine in Nepal. Compassion toward all living beings was a central component of these ethical values and extended even to those who were normally regarded as hostile predators.

The Period of the Guptas and Later, circa C.E. 400 to 1000

The Buddhist ethic was not universally adopted, and soon the symbolic power of the tiger was seen as competing with the prowess of the hero and the king. Violence became essential to claims of kingship, and one expression of this was the depiction of the king subduing the lion and the tiger. The Gupta rulers of the fourth and fifth centuries C.E. issued a superb series of beautifully crafted gold coins depicting some of their activities. Among these are coins showing an early king of the dynasty, Chandragupta, slaying a lion; those issued later show the kings Samudragupta and Kumaragupta killing a tiger. The legend *vyaghra-parakramah*—"overpowering the tiger"—is inscribed on some coins that show Samudragupta shooting an arrow at a tiger at close range. The reverse of the coins often depict a goddess standing on a crocodile—the vehicle of the river goddess Ganga—or on a lotus.

The coins from the period when the Chola dynasty ruled in southern India, at the end of the first millennium, frequently carry three symbols: the fish, the bow, and the tiger. These have been explained as emblems of the Pandyas, Cheras, and Cholas, and presumably when all three occur on Chola coins with a prominent tiger the Cholas claim overlordship of the other two. This is underlined on one coin on which the tiger is depicted sitting under a canopy with a bow on the left and a pair of fish on the right. The tiger remained the emblem of the Cholas throughout their reign, a persistent symbol of power. It appears on coins and on some seals, the latter holding together inscribed plates of copper that were the legal documents recording grants of land made by royalty to the owners of the plates.

An eighteenth-century painting of a tiger hunt. The bow and arrow gradually gave way to the gun.

Changes in the Political Economy from the Late First Millennium C.E.

After about the eighth and ninth centuries, substantial changes occurred in the societies and economies of many parts of the subcontinent. The system of opening up new areas to settlement gradually became more widespread and intensified. Land was granted on a large scale, generally as gifts to brahmans and sometimes in lieu of salaries to officers of the administration. Originally, the grant was largely of the revenue from the land and did not confer ownership rights, but in the course of time ownership came to be assumed. There were many categories of land grants: some consisted of land already under cultivation or even villages, where the revenue and dues to the grantee were

readily forthcoming; but grants in more remote areas required clearing the land before it could be settled and brought under cultivation. The second category covered either wasteland or, perhaps more often, forest areas. Such grants became the base for the acquisition of more territory and rights by the grantees, who after a few generations set themselves up as rulers. Dynasties claiming brahman origins and associated with forest kingdoms were not unheard-of in these times. New lands were cleared and brought under cultivation; settlements were established, and some grew to be towns; exchange introduced commerce, which meant more routes cutting through forests—all of which contributed to the taming of the forest. Such settlements are sometimes described, as for instance the Shabara village is in Banabhatta's *Harshacharita*, the biography of the king Harshavardhana, written in the seventh century, which provides insight into the gradual assimilation of "tribal societies" into the caste system and peasant economies.

Deforestation meant confrontations with the tiger and the lion. *Simha* as a title or part of a name came into use, especially among the *kshatriyas*—those claiming royal or aristocratic status—and has persisted to modern times. Its use may not have so much to do with confronting lions as with claims to power, sometimes presumed. *Vyaghra* as a personal name and a title emerged in inscriptions at this period but was popular for a shorter time. Mention is made of rulers named Maharajah Vyaghra, Vyaghraketu, and Vyaghradeva, among others. Place-names such as Vyaghra-tati-mandala, Vyaghraviraka, Vyaghracoraka, Vyaghra-agrahara, and Vyaghrapallika also occur.

Mythologies of the First Millennium

The interplay of human and tiger, with each taking on the presumed characteristics of the other, surfaces in a myth from the *Vishnu Purana*, one of a number of *Puranas* composed at this time that were repositories of myths, presumed histories, and sectarian religious observances. It concerns the *raja* Saudasa, who goes hunting in the forest and sees two tigers mating. He kills one, who on dying turns into a ferocious *rakshasa* and swears revenge. When the king is performing a major sacrificial ritual, the *rakshasa* magically assumes the form of the priest Vasishtha and demands human flesh for food. The king is puzzled but has to meet the demands of the priest; otherwise, the ritual will be nullified. When human flesh is provided, the real Vasishtha arrives; horrified, he curses the king to become a *rakshasa* himself and live on human flesh. But when he realizes who the other Vasishtha is, he modifies the curse so that it lasts only twelve years. The king-turned-*rakshasa* moves to the forest. One day, he sees a brahman and his wife making love and catches the man. The wife pleads with him when she recognizes that he is a

king, but he eats the brahman in the manner in which a tiger would eat a man. The woman curses him and says that he, too, will die when making love. The king therefore, even when he has returned to a human form, cannot procreate and has to appeal to Vasishtha, who grants his wife a son.

The story echoes many themes from the narratives of the *Mahabharata* and the Puranas: the killing of one of a mating couple, thus preventing procreation; the curse converting human to demon; the serving of human flesh; and the period of twelve years. But the interchangeability of human and tiger and their behavior is striking. The tiger becoming a *rakshasa* and eating human flesh could be seen as natural behavior; the man being demonized and eating human flesh is a reversal of it. Yet in a sense, the ultimate triumph lies with the tiger who initiated the events, since the king can no longer procreate, which is a disaster for any king. Such myths allude to how people appropriate what they believe to be the characteristics of the tiger.

The Tiger in Other Manifestations

Establishing settlements in the forest meant having to accommodate existing forest-dwelling societies, which were incorporated into caste society and allotted statuses. The hunters among the forest dwellers who stalked and killed animals for food were often recruited for royal hunts. But their caste status was kept low, the explanation often being that they were killers of animals. However, the same activity carried out by kings was much applauded, treated as heroic, and made not the slightest dent on their caste status.

The people of the forest imprinted their culture on caste society in the assimilation of their religious cults; these were either incorporated into the many cults and sects that constituted Hinduism or used to create new ones. This brought about an abundance of deities, beliefs, and practices and also led to a reinforcement, or on occasion even a reformulation, of the powers of the existing major deities. Among these was the great goddess in her manifold forms, one of which was Durga, who is often shown riding a lion or a tiger. Durga's association with the lion has been traced back to the goddesses of ancient western Asia, who may have been popularized in northern India from Kushana times (first century B.C.E. to third century C.E.) into the early Christian era. But her association with the tiger may go back to Harappan times, when a similar figure is shown grappling with tigers. This is not to suggest that the Harappan representation be read as Durga but that a thread of mythology may have wound its way through the centuries, embedded in the substratum religion of the unorthodox, and found expression in a manifestation of Durga at this time. Durga in her manifestation as *maheshasuramardini*—"slaying the buffalo demon"—was doubtless both popular and credible, and the buffalo is the natural prey of both lion and tiger.

Durga is often shown riding a tiger amid other animals of the forest, and there seems to be a nexus between her, the tiger, and the forest that could draw on earlier times. It could be argued that this was a subterranean religion of Indian society, widely accepted but with fewer spectacular representations than the worship of Vishnu and Shiva. This might explain why a deity riding a tiger is an image not exclusive to Durga and Hinduism. In Islam, some Sufi mystics are said to ride a tiger, which is believed to encapsulate proximity to the experience of the divine and to the defeat of evil.

Above all, the largest number of people involved in this worship are those who observe no formal religious boundaries but revere pious men, often associated with the tiger and the forest. One example out of many is Ghazi Sahib, who in the forests of the Sundarbans is linked with the worship of the tiger-god, Dakhin Rai, and the goddess of the forest, Bonobibi. Figures such as these are worshipped by Hindus, Muslims, and others alike, and the mythology derives from a multiplicity of religious sources.

The hunting of the tiger is mentioned more frequently in later times. The royalty that evolved with the Mughals, whether Mongol, Rajput, Turk, or Afghan, was portrayed in paintings as actively hunting tigers. It has been said that this was linked to the exoticism of the animal, but more likely it was in the tradition of the hero overcoming the tiger—*vyaghraparakramah*. Gradually, the bow and arrow and spear gave way to guns as weapons of the hunt. In the last couple of centuries, the tiger has been viewed either as a predator to be exterminated or as a spectacular trophy of big-game hunting. But the coming of the gun led to the near extinction of the tiger. Those who hunted animals with guns were not heroes but exterminators.

A longer-range view points to a relationship that once existed between the forest, people, and the tiger, one that could also be extended to many denizens of the forest. Over the centuries, human activities have changed this relationship, sometimes legitimately but not invariably so. Perhaps we need to reflect on the nature and reasons for the changes. Should we continue relentlessly to exterminate the forest and those who live in it, or should we recognize that the relationship remains viable and should be sustained, perhaps to enhance the creativity of human society, as it once did? This possibility becomes all the more poignant when one realizes that hovering in the background of many Indian traditions was an extraordinary sensitivity toward the tiger and the forest, as expressed in the *Mahabharata*: "The forest which has tigers should never be cut, nor should the tigers be chased away from the forest. Not living in the forest is death to the tiger, and in the absence of the tiger the forest is annihilated. The tiger protects the forest and the forest nurtures the tiger."

ROMILA THAPAR is Emeritus Professor of History at the Jawaharlal Nehru University in New Delhi. She has worked on early Indian history and has published a number of monographs. Among these is the Penguin history entitled *Early India* and a collection of essays on early India, *Cultural Pasts*.

La Rentrée des Felins dans le Cirque
by Jean-Léon Gérôme

CHAPTER 5

Tiger and Man

Throughout the ages, the tiger has commanded people's wonder and respect. Our fascination with this and other powerful, elusive animals has inspired an insatiable inquisitiveness. As a result, hundreds of thousands of exotic animals from every corner of the globe have been collected as specimens and tribute for powerful families. Our earliest records indicate that magnificent animals have long been given by rulers as gifts to other rulers, to cement political alliances, or to mark special occasions. These gifts often formed the basis of royal menageries—the forerunners of our modern zoos. Historically, tigers' fearsome strength and unusual appearance—more than three meters (ten feet) long from nose to tail, paws like dinner plates, canines the size of a middle finger, and intensely probing eyes—have made them popular additions to captive collections and much coveted status symbols.

For more than six thousand years, people have collected and enjoyed animals for their entertainment. Records of aviaries date back to 4500 B.C.E. in what is now Iraq; by 2500 B.C.E., elephants were held in captivity in India; and one of the earliest recorded wild-animal collections dates from about 2000 B.C.E. in Mesopotamia. The ancient Egyptians trained cheetahs to help them in their hunting expeditions. Around 1000 B.C.E., the emperors of China were collecting and displaying animals in their palaces, and Emperor Wen Wang established a zoo of 1,500 acres (about six hundred hectares), which he named the Ling-Yu or Garden of Intelligence. It was considered a peaceful and sacred place.

Around 300 B.C.E., King Seleucus of Syria, a former general under Alexander the Great, presented the people of Athens with the first captive tiger ever seen in Europe. No other tigers appear to have reached the lands of classical civilization until 19 B.C.E., when the Roman emperor Augustus received some from an Indian entourage visiting him on the island of Samos. Some years after that, the tiger began to appear in the amphitheaters of Rome. Paola Manfredi, an Italian anthropologist, explores the tiger's introduction to the West.

The Tiger in the Ancient World

Paola Manfredi

The peacock came from India to Greece, where it appeared for the first time in 450 B.C.E. So stunning was this bird with its golden-shaded plumage that it became the sacred bird of the goddess Hera and was kept at her temple on the island of Samos. But it was not until Alexander the Great's conquests in Asia in the fourth century B.C.E. opened up intensive interchanges between the western and eastern worlds, with great economic and cultural impact on both sides, that other Indian animals and birds became known in Europe. Alexander's expeditions and his own great curiosity fostered the advances in geography and natural history that became the root elements in those fields of knowledge for centuries to come.

Nearcos, one of Alexander's generals, wrote about India, its people, its social institutions, and its extraordinary fauna, among which elephants and tigers figured prominently. His description of the capture of wild elephants in India is a remarkable document. He did not see a live tiger, but he saw a tiger's skin, and Indians told him that the tiger was an animal much stronger than the elephant, bigger than the biggest of horses, and that no other creature could match it in speed and strength, not even the elephant. In the event of an encounter between a tiger and an elephant, he was told, the tiger could jump on the elephant's head and easily strangle it.

It was believed by some at the time that the phoenix, an animal often depicted with the body of a tiger and the head and feet of a bird of prey, was to be found in India. One legend has it that Alexander did not actually die but was taken to heaven by one of these mythical beasts.

The founding of Greek cities in Asia and the opening up of trade routes facilitated the flow of people, ideas, artifacts—and animals. From the earliest records, India's fauna was a favorite subject for the Greeks, and the Indians' ability to capture and tame elephants was acknowledged and admired, as was their skill in training other wild animals. In the centuries following the death of Alexander, elephants, tigers and an array of other exotic creatures such as rhinoceroses, apes, and even parakeets reached the western world, thus corroborating India's reputation as a land of marvelous creatures.

In Greece, on the occasion of religious festivals, it was customary to organize processions in honor of the gods—though in fact these events were little more than spectacles of public entertainment. When the gods being honored were connected with nature or fertility, as were Dionysus and Artemis, all kinds of animals, tame and wild, native and foreign, were paraded free or in cages. In Egypt, a similar tradition developed during the reign of the Ptolemies, a dynasty of Greek origin and vast wealth. Indian and native Egyptian pageantry probably combined to add further magnificence to the traditional processions, like one held at Alexandria under Ptolemy II that displayed a fantastic variety of fauna, part of the royal collection of wild animals, which were mainly from North Africa, Syria, and North Arabia.

The parading of exotic wild animals on religious occasions was a tradition that originated in an ancient and deep reverence for nature, but under the influence of first the Egyptian kings and later the Roman emperors it evolved into a display and celebration of power over faraway lands and populations. This was best represented by the diversity and strangeness of the creatures displayed. The collections of exotic beasts and birds in Roman Italy on one level reflected the history of Greek and Roman expansion and the policies of the imperial power. On another level, they threw light on existing knowledge concerning wild animals, such as the methods of capture and transport and the skills required to keep, breed, and train them, to mention only a few. Furthermore, they reveal approaches to nature and to wild animals in the Hellenistic culture that range from the religious, inquisitive, utilitarian, or affectionate to the cruel, savage, and bloody, manifested in the hunts and fights staged in imperial Rome's amphitheaters for the delight of frenzied and bloodthirsty crowds.

The continual hunting of wild animals, such as leopards or lions, for use in the amphitheater was responsible for these species becoming extinct in parts of North Africa, though this, far from being perceived as a problem, was seen as a positive development, as it made more land safe for agriculture and facilitated the settling down of nomadic populations such as the Numidians.

The Tiger in Some Classical Texts

According to literary sources, the tiger became known in the western world quite late. It is not mentioned in the Bible, and the ancient Greeks do not seem to have had much contact with it. The only mention of the tiger in Greek mythology is in connection with the name of the river Tigris. According to the story as retold by Plutarch, Dionysus fell in love with the nymph Alphesibe and tried to seduce her by changing himself into a tiger in order to help her cross the river, which has ever since been called the Tigris.

Alexander the Great entrusted to his tutor Aristotle the task of studying and writing on the nature of animals. Aristotle picked up information from thousands of people from all over Alexander's vast realm, people who lived from hunting, birding, and fishing, or whose profession involved animals in various capacities, so that the information would be accurate and comprehensive.

According to some sources, Aristotle compiled seventy volumes, according to others only fifty, on the history of animals and related zoological topics. Most of his writings would have been lost if it had not been for the Roman writer Pliny the Elder, who in the first century C.E. summarized most of Aristotle's knowledge about zoology in his own encyclopedic *Historia naturalis*, adding to it previously unrecorded information. These writings reveal an accurate knowledge of the animal kingdom and natural history along with imaginative descriptions of real animals from distant

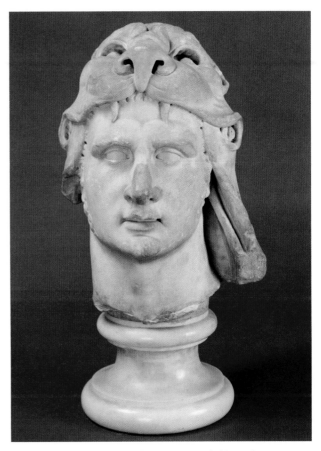

A bust of Mithradates VI (132–63 B.C.E.), king of Pontus.

lands and of mythical creatures then perceived — and therefore treated — as real ones. Pliny's work remained the authority on such matters up to the Middle Ages.

Pliny maintains that tigers come either from Hyrcania, a wild region south of the Caspian Sea, or from India. The poet Virgil, however, talked of tigers from Armenia. Pliny summarized knowledge of the tiger from the oldest written records of his time, and it is clear that the information available was very scanty, compared, for example, with the lengthy description of the Indian elephant, both in the wild and in captivity. The tiger must have been relatively rare, especially if compared with the thousands of recorded lions and leopards in the Roman world, and therefore remained to a large extent mysterious throughout the centuries that followed.

Capturing tigers for the Roman arena by enticing a tigress to pursue her stolen cub, a detail from the "Worcester Hunt."

Pliny's description of the tiger is mainly concerned with capturing cubs; in the process, some information about the animal itself does creep in—ancient knowledge maintained, for example, that the male tiger was not concerned about the young cubs, which were always born in large litters. According to Pliny, cubs were to be stolen by a hunter riding a horse. The horse had to be a very fast one, and a few more fresh and fast ones had to be kept ready for the hunter to switch to, while running from the fury of the tigress when she realized that her den had been raided. The tigress would immediately throw herself in pursuit of the thief, following his scent. When he heard her furious roars, the hunter had to let down one of the stolen cubs, as the tigress would stop to collect it in her mouth and "as if the weight of the cub would add to her energy and speed" take it back to the den. Once it was safely deposited, she would turn around and run again after the hunter and the other cubs. This continued till the hunter reached the shores of the sea where a ship was waiting for him. Finally, the tigress would be left behind on the shoreline, furious and now powerless to catch him or rescue her cubs. This story, which might have been anecdotal, became the accredited version of how to procure tiger cubs and escape the tigress's wrath.

In a few variations on Pliny's story by other classical authors, the structural elements of the narrative remain unchanged, but other anecdotes are added. Not only does this story epitomize the knowledge and perception of the tiger in the ancient world, it also codified distinctive features of the tigress's temperament that have survived even into some contemporary expressions. The devotion of the tigress to her cubs has become legendary, as have her terrifying rages when her cubs are lost. In Roman literature and art, the tiger is generally a female, and the Latin word for "tiger" is of the feminine gender, although the masculine is also occasionally used. Juvenal compares a cantankerous woman to a tigress whose cubs have been stolen. In a tragedy by Seneca the Younger, Dejamire, mad with jealousy, rises up "furious and vicious as an Armenian tigress" who, seeing her enemies, springs up on the rocks where she has just delivered her cubs. In another text, the desperation of a mother who has lost her son is compared to a grief-stricken tigress who cannot stop licking the place inside the den where the cubs used to be. Medea's passion and rage make her pace aimlessly like "a tigress whose cubs have been stolen, and she would then roam furiously in the jungles of the Ganges." Silius Italicus described the Carthaginian general Hannibal as being furious like a tigress who in only few hours crosses Caucasia, then takes a giant leap across the Ganges, racing as quick as lightning, till she picks up the scent of her stolen cubs and dashes down on the enemy. Valerius Flaccus, a Latin writer, in a brief description of the tiger hunt among the Sarmatians, explains that when the hunters with their loot are able to take refuge on the waters, they are safe, as the tigress will not follow them there.

Although the following text from Aelian's *On the Characteristics of Animals* is only indirectly connected with the tiger, it still is a fascinating part of the knowledge about the tiger in the ancient world. In it, the Indian hound is said to be bred from tigers:

Huntsmen take thoroughbred bitches which are good at tracking wild animals and are very swift of foot to places infested by these animals; they tie them to trees and then go away, simply, as the saying is, "trying a throw of the dice." And if the tigers find them when they have caught nothing and they are famished, they tear them to pieces. If however they arrive on heat and full-fed they couple with the bitches, for tigers too when gorged turn their thoughts to sexual intercourse. From this union, so it is said, a tiger is born, not a hound. And from this tiger and a bitch again a tiger would be born, although the offspring of this last and of a bitch takes after its dam, and the seed degenerates and a hound is born. Nor will Aristotle contradict this. These hounds which can boast a tiger for a sire scorn to pursue a stag or to face a boar, but are glad to rush at lions and therefore to give proof of their pedigree.

It is said that the Indians gave Alexander a test of the strength and power of endurance of one these hounds, and in the text there is a gory description of a hound that, despite being progressively cut to pieces, would not release his grip on his prey: "Alexander was deeply amazed and grieved that the hound in proving its mettle had perished and that contrary to the nature of things had met his death because of its courage. The Indians, touched by Alexander's grief, presented him with four hounds of the same breed. He was delighted to receive them and gave the Indians a suitable gift in return."

Aelian also mentions that the people of India offer to their king tigers that have been trained.

The Tiger and the Emperor

Roman menageries and zoological parks developed under Greek and Egyptian influences, but, once tigers reached Rome, their principal role became to take part in practices such as the *venatio*, the staged hunt in the amphitheater; the *ludi* (games), in which animals were forced to fight against one another or against *bestiarii* (beast hunters) or *venatores* (hunters); and the *damnatio ad bestias*, which was the public execution by wild animals of a person convicted of a capital crime. Gladiators did not fight animals, only other gladiators. Conversely, the *bestiarii* and *venatores* were specially trained to fight animals and never fought gladiators. To make sure the animals gave a good show and were suitably aggressive toward their victims, tigers and lions were starved for three days before entering the arena. If a beast was lucky enough to kill its prey and survive, it would usually have to go to a second round with an armed *bestiarius*. However, some of the more exotic and difficult-to-collect animals, such as tigers, were kept for another day of fighting and entertainment. In among all this extravagance, someone still had an eye on the purse strings.

The *venationes* and the *ludi* used elements of various origins—Greek animal processions and bullfighting, gladi-

A Roman hunt, probably in Roman North Africa. Plate 10 from Venationes Ferarum, Avium, Piscium

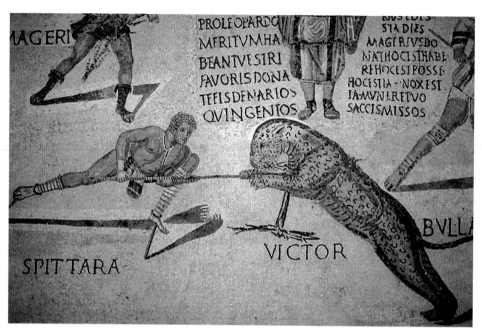

Detail from a third century C.E. mosaic from Smirat, Tunisia.

atorial combats from Etruria, which became very popular in Rome, and also elements of ritual hunts that were traditionally held in Rome at the time of religious festivals. These entertainments were either private or state sponsored and could be held to celebrate festivities and important events, such as victories in war or the triumphs of a general or emperor; they might also serve as memorials to distinguished persons who had died, or they might be intended to win the favor of the masses before or after elections. Not only were they very expensive affairs; they also required such elaborate organization that only people who enjoyed or commanded a vast network of connections could afford to present them.

The mightiness of the sponsor was emphasized by the number of animals presented, or alternatively by their rarity and the elaborate arrangements of the performances. In the *venationes* the amphitheater was dressed so as to give the illusion of natural surroundings that matched the homelands of the animals or sometimes re-created some extravagant or mythical environment. Archaeological findings have revealed complex systems under the

amphitheater in Rome that would have allowed for spectacular scenic tricks. The Roman public was a demanding one, not easy to impress and quick to voice its disappointment if an act was not up to standard. In a crescendo of competition, each sponsor had to outdo the previous one, and the games in the arena became more and more extravagant, spectacular, and, of course, bloody. As far as the audiences were concerned, the more blood spilled the better the entertainment, and as the centuries rolled on the number of deaths in the ring had to increase to keep the audience from rioting.

Hundreds of animals could be slaughtered in a single day, although on one occasion it was recorded that the public took pity on a group of elephants. Having put up stiff resistance and apparently understanding that they were doomed, the animals clustered together to support one another and started trumpeting in such a heartbreaking way that the public, far from finding this exciting, was for once revolted by its own cruelty.

According to Pliny, the first tiger ever seen in Rome was a tamed tigress kept in a cage and exhibited by Augustus in

The Christians Thrown to the Beasts by the Romans
by Louis Felix Leullier

First century C.E. mosaic from Castro Pretoria, Italy, depicting a tiger and two trainers.

11 B.C.E. during the festivities for the dedication of the Theater of Marcellus. When Egypt formally became a Roman province in 30 B.C.E., it became one of the chief sources of Indian animals for the arenas, since it had already established trading relations with India. Tigers soon became a more frequent sight in Rome, though they were always something of a rarity. The emperor Claudius (C.E. 41–54) presented four tigers in one of his shows, an event that Pliny described as unprecedented. Although we cannot be sure what happened to these tigers, the animals that appeared in the arena or in the triumphal procession were not always killed. Many undoubtedly were, but others were far too precious to be disposed of, and they were kept in menageries or trained to perform repeatedly in the amphitheater. It is about at this time also that we find mention of the tiger being used for capital punishment. This passage refers not to a specific execution, but to the general practice: "strange ravening creatures freight the fleets and the padding tiger is carried in a gilded palace, to drink human blood while the crowd applauds."

There are reports that Indian trainers worked with the tigers there. Many of the wild animals made to perform in the arena—whether for hunts, animal fights, or the killing of convicts—in front of thousands of excited and howling spectators were trained, since the most likely reaction of an animal not used to such a commotion would have been total fear, and that could have compromised the show.

In C.E. 80, the great amphitheater of Rome, the Colosseum, was inaugurated and dedicated with unforgettable shows and spectacular ceremonies, during which the most marvelous and exotic creatures were presented to match the splendor and the glory of the Roman empire. Thousands of animals were shown, five thousand in a single day, and nine thousand were killed in the hundred-day-long celebration.

An unexpected happening caught the attention of the first-century satirist Martial, and thus we know of a fight between a lion and a tame tiger, during which, unexpectedly, the lion was killed. In an interesting footnote to the episode, Martial remarked that the tiger's ferocity was probably due to its "familiarization" with human beings! In C.E. 93, at the celebrations for the return of Emperor Domitianus from war on the Danube, a number of tigers were again exhibited in Rome. How many is not clear, as Martial says only that there were more than two, for more than two tigers were attached to chariot of Bacchus/ Dionysus when he celebrated his triumph over the Indians. The number must have been rather more than two, though, as Martial, in his usual witty style, says that now Rome has seen more tigers than any tiger hunter by the Ganges had to fear and that the city could not even count her treasures. In his writing, Martial also refers to tigers on leashes.

There is no more mention of tigers in surviving writings until the reign of Antoninus Pius (C.E. 138–161), a quiet and respectable emperor, unlike so many of the others. In one show of this period, it seems that a remarkable collection of wild and exotic animals, such as elephants, hyenas, lions, tigers, rhinoceroses, crocodiles, and hippopotamuses, were exhibited. While Antoninus's successor, Marcus Aurelius (C.E. 161–180), was horrified by the cruelty of the bloodthirsty Romans, his own son and successor, Commodus (C.E. 180–192), was so passionate about sports in the amphitheater that he took the title the Roman Hercules:

He collected rare animals for slaughter at Rome and the historian Dio, who witnessed his performances, describes him killing elephants (three are mentioned altogether), six hippopotami, rhinoceroses, a giraffe, a tiger and, in one day only, one hundred bears! He killed also one hundred lions and ostriches; these were with a special crescent-shaped arrow, which would cut off the head, while the decapitated body of the animal would keep on running throughout the amphitheatre, to the delight of the spectators!

At the funeral games to honor Quintillus Plautianus, during the reign of Septimius Severus (C.E. 193–211), ten tigers were killed during fights in the arena.

Caracalla (C.E. 211–217), who had a great admiration for Alexander the Great, loved to parade around surrounded by symbols of his power:

He was accompanied on journeys by an escort of elephants, and owned many lion[s], some of which he had always with him, particularly a tame lion named Acinaces (Scimitar) which was his table companion and slept in his room. The greater part of his reign was spent away from Italy: he made senators pay for *venationes* and chariot-races in the cities where he stayed, and was himself a keen *venator*. [The historian] Dio mentions a zebra among the animals killed in the amphitheatre early in Caracalla's time and the others recorded are an elephant, a rhinoceros and a tiger.

Heliogabalus (C.E. 218–222), who was, to put it mildly, another extravagant Roman emperor, is represented in the *Historia Augusta* as "having a taste for keeping animals and employing them in childish amusements and very disagreeable practical jokes. He is said to have driven in harness lions, tigers and even stags." Breaking stags to harness is particularly difficult, and great credit must be given to the animal trainers of those times.

During the games held to celebrate the emperor's marriage, the many beasts killed included an elephant and fifty-one tigers; it is suggested that the elephant was killed in a fight with three or four tigers. This is by far the largest number of tigers ever mentioned in any of the ancient records, and Dio believed it to be unprecedented.

Heliogabalus is also said to have harnessed tigers to a chariot on which he himself posed in the guise of Bacchus, the Roman god of wine. For fun, he would put lions and tigers whose teeth and claws had been extracted into the bedrooms of his drunken guests—several of whom, on awakening, not surprisingly died of fright. Possibly the eastern campaigns of Septimius Severus, who himself exhibited ten tigers on one occasion, had somehow made it easier for the Romans to obtain this animal from the Persian plateau, Hyrcania.

At the secular games held by Philip the Arabian in C.E. 248, the list of animals shown in the amphitheater mentions thirty-two elephants (probably from Persia as the spoils of war), ten elk, ten tigers, sixty tame lions, thirty tame *leopardi* (maneless lions), ten hyenas, six hippopotamuses, one rhinoceros, and ten *argoleontes* (wild lions). At the triumphal procession of Aurelian, the conqueror of Zenobia of Palmyra, in C.E. 274, the list includes twenty elephants, two hundred tamed animals of different sorts from Africa and Palestine (distributed after the show to private citizens in order to save the treasury the cost of their keep), four tigers, one giraffe, one elk, and "other such animals."

This is the last record of tigers exhibited in imperial Rome. On the whole, the tiger, which had to be sought beyond the boundaries of the empire and at such a great distance from Italy, continued to be a rarity. From the time of Diocletian (C.E. 284–305), with the exception of the reign of Maxentius (C.E. 306–312), Rome ceased to be the regular residence of the Roman emperor, and although animal shows and *ludi* in the amphitheater continued, the magnificence of the *venationes* offered by the emperors could be matched only rarely.

In the fourth and fifth centuries, the cruelest side of the animal shows gradually disappeared, giving way to performances in which animals would entertain spectators with tricks and skills — although there is mention of *venationes* being given in the Colosseum in the later years of the reign of Theodoric (C.E. 493–526). But these shows had very little in common with the spectacular public slaughters of the earlier times; instead, they were the forerunners of our circuses.

When the Colosseum was excavated in the middle of the nineteenth century, large quantities of animal bones were found in the ancient drains. They were analyzed and identified as belonging to ostriches, horses, asses, goats, bulls, camels, stags, deer, bears, dogs, wolves, hyenas, lions, and tigers. In total, there were the bones of twelve lions and three tigers — gruesome reminders of what must have taken place two thousand years ago.

PAOLA MANFREDI has a background in anthropology, and she has been working in India for over twenty years on textiles, history, and cross-cultural influences on textiles. She also designs and produces handmade white-on-white embroidery. She has been associated for several years with the Ranthambhore Foundation, and she is active in the conservation of endangered environments and species, particularly the tiger. She is the author of various articles on textiles and embroidery and she edited the book *In Danger: Habitats, Species and People*, published by the Ranthambhore Foundation in New Delhi in 1997.

Kublai Khan's Tigers

After three hundred years of watching slaughter, the crowds became harder to impress. As the emperors changed, so did some of the animal acts. Elephants were trained to bow before the royal box and draw pictures in the sand with their trunks, while tigers licked the hands of their keepers and pulled chariots. But the majority of creatures that entered the arenas were expected to kill or be killed. The more noble beasts, like tigers, lions, and elephants, were used only in the amphitheaters of Rome. Provincial circuses had to make do with wild dogs, bears, and wolves.

It was neither moral enlightenment nor the impact of Christianity that finally put a stop to the massacres in the circus amphitheater, but rather a chronic shortage of victims. And with the fall of the Roman Empire, the event disappeared, though some of its terminology and legacy survived in more recent blood sports such as bullfighting and cockfighting, the origins of which are in the Roman arena.

After the fall of Rome, tigers disappeared from western literature for nearly one thousand years, reappearing when Marco Polo, perhaps the most famous of all medieval travelers, ventured into China and entered the service of the Mongol emperor. Kublai Khan, who reigned from 1260 to 1294, had a huge collection of wild animals in his palace, including elephants, hippos, tigers, camels, and birds. Most were kept simply to be admired, but he trained some, such as the big cats, to go hunting with him. The young Marco Polo described how Kublai Khan's men trapped tigers (which he thought were striped lions, reinforcing the idea that Europeans had forgotten about the existence of tigers over the previous centuries) either by digging ditches into which the cats were lured by the bait of a white dog or by using dogs to hunt them down:

> There are so many lions, that no one may sleep out of doors at night, for the lions would instantly devour him. And I will also add that when people travel on this river and stop somewhere for the night, if they do not keep at a good distance from the banks, the lions will spring on to the boat, and snatch a man, and go away and devour him. But . . . there are dogs in that country that have the pluck to attack them. There must, however, be two of them. . . . One attacks him from behind, and the other barks in front of him. The lion turns now towards the one, and now towards the other, but the two dogs do not let themselves be caught. And so the lion, seeing that he cannot catch them, ends by going away. But as soon as the dogs see that the lion is going away, they run after him, and bite him in the thighs or the tail. The lion turns fiercely, but cannot catch hold of them, for the dogs know well how to defend themselves. . . . Meanwhile the man takes his bow, and shoots one, two, or more arrows, as many as are necessary to kill the lion. In this way they kill many of them. For a lion can put up no defense against a man on horseback with two good dogs.

He also describes a scene with these hunting tigers: "You must know that the Great

Khan . . . has many very big lions . . . much bigger than those of Babylon; they have very fine coats, and are of a beautiful color, being striped lengthways in black, red, and white. They are trained to take wild boars, wild oxen, bears, wild asses, stags, fallow-deer, and other beasts. And I assure you it is a splendid sight to see those lions catch their quarries."

It is clear from Marco Polo's accounts that Kublai Khan loved his tigers and that "tigers bowed to the great Khan." On special occasions, unchained tigers were led into the emperor's presence, and at the sight of him they lay down—a sign of great veneration.

MENAGERIES

Although a few European powers kept small collections of wild beasts during the Middle Ages, the period was generally a barren one for exotic animals in the West. The first recorded tiger kept in captivity in England belonged to King Henry I (1100–1135), who established a menagerie at Woodstock, near Oxford, in 1120. The collection was enhanced a century later, in the reign of King Henry III (1216–1272), with gifts from foreign parts—including, in 1250, a tiger presented by Frederick II of Germany, who was himself a great collector. Two years later, Henry III had the zoo transferred to the Tower of London, where it remained until 1834 and where he sponsored fights between lions and tigers, billed as contests for the title "King of the Beasts."

The royal menagerie at the Tower waxed and waned according to each succeeding monarch's whim. In the sixteenth and seventeenth centuries, Elizabeth I and James I ordered animal fights at Windsor Castle, where they pitted wild beasts such as lions, tigers, bears, and elephants against domestic animals—bulls, mastiffs, horses, cows, and donkeys—as a way of measuring whether wild beasts were stronger than domesticated animals. Recent excavations at Paris Gardens, a public arena on the South Bank of the Thames, have also shown that tiger baiting went on during James I's rule.

It was not until the eighteenth century that visitors were allowed in to see the animals in the Tower, offering their pet cats and dogs to the inmates as payment. It was also at this time that the hymn-writing Methodist preacher John Wesley (1703–1791) performed a crude experiment on the big cats to discover whether they had souls. He had a flute played to them, and the result was interesting, though inconclusive: a tiger leaped over a lion, returned under its stomach, then leaped back over it, repeating the cycle again and again.

In 1830, a lion and two Bengal tigers were accidentally allowed into the same enclosure, where they fought viciously. The frantic keepers tried to stop them by jabbing heated irons into their nostrils and mouths. Eventually, they were separated, but the lion died from its injuries a few days later. The public, as well as the keepers,

The ferocity of the fight between the lion and two tigers at the Tower of London is captured in the lithograph Extraordinary and Fatal Combat.

decried this unfortunate event. Four years later, the royal menagerie was closed down, and its 150 animals found a new home at the newly opened Regent's Park Zoo.

The Duke of Cumberland (1721–1765), third son of King George II, was an infamous general and also a keen animal collector, though for no other reason than to pit them against one another in battle. He created a menagerie at Windsor Great Park, where the zebra and tigers famously painted by George Stubbs (1724–1806) were housed alongside other exotic gifts the duke received from his military contacts around the world.

Another English royal to come under the spell of tigers was the young Queen Victoria, who in 1839 visited the Theatre Royal in Drury Lane five times to watch a show by Isaac Van Amburgh. Van Amburgh was one of the original animal tamers, whose method was to thrash his beasts mercilessly with an iron bar until they cowed to his wishes. Born in Kentucky, he dressed like a Roman gladiator in toga and sandals and emphasized his domination over the animals by thrusting his arm into their mouths, daring them to bite. When he came under attack for spreading cruelty and moral ruin, he quoted the Bible: "Didn't God say in Genesis 1:26 that men should have dominion over every animal on the earth?" To enhance his case, he acted out scenes from the Bible, forcing a lion to lie down with a lamb and even bringing a child from the audience to join them in the ring. He enjoyed worldwide notoriety and brought his performance to England's noblest spectators. The queen was so impressed that she asked the artist Sir Edwin Landseer (1802–1873) to paint Van Amburgh and his cats.

RIGHT: *A tiger housed in the royal menagerie at the Tower of London is depicted in* Fanny Howe, Whelp'd in the Tower *(1794).*

BELOW: Portrait of Mr. Van Amburgh as He Appeared with His Animals at the London Theatre *(1847), by Sir Edwin Landseer.*

Ritual Entertainment in European Colonies

Even in now-colonized lands where the tiger had been held sacred, the rulers—both local and European—were also catching tigers for entertainment. In seventeenth-century Java, the Dutch decided to rid their colony of these large and troublesome carnivores. Since they did not hunt tigers (probably because they did not have trained and domesticated elephants to take them through the thick tropical jungle), they created huge pits in the jungle that tigers would either fall or be baited into. Two rituals were enacted to exterminate the tiger. The first involved fights between tigers and buffalo: the animals were led into a ring and forced to fight to the death—the buffalo usually winning, goring, and trampling the tiger. In the second ritual, called tiger sticking, several ranks of men with spears formed a large square. A tiger was then released into the square, and as it tried to escape it was repeatedly speared; these tigers often died slow and painful deaths. Several tigers would undergo the same ordeal, released into the square one after another, until they were all dead. The success of these rituals contributed to making Javan tigers rarer and harder to find in the twentieth century, thus ending these brutal practices.

In India, too, tigers were made to fight other animals to entertain nobility. Rang-ghar was the first amphitheater in Asia, built in Upper Assam in 1746 by King Pramatta

In this late-eighteenth-century painting from India, a nawab seated in a riverside pavilion watches the fight between two tigers and several water buffalo.

The brutal ritual of tiger sticking involved releasing a tiger into an open square surrounded by men with spears. The tiger eventually succumbed to the repeated spearings.

combat.

D'un tigre auec des elephants quelque fois l'on voit L'éléphant prendre auec sa trompe
Le tigre par le milieu du corps et le jetter en l'air, quand Son cornac ou l'homme
qui est dessus lui ordonne il le foule auec les pieds ou le reçoit sur ses dents. Le
tigre tâche principalement de prendre la trompe auec ses griffes et l'éléphant

This eighteenth-century watercolor belonged to the king of Siam (modern Thailand), and the caption reads: "The elephant sometimes wraps its trunk around the middle of the tiger's body and flings it into the air when its handler or rider orders it to do so. It tramples the tiger with its feet or gores it with its tusks. The tiger endeavors to sink its claws into the elephant's trunk."

Singha. It was a two-story, oval-shaped pavilion in which members of the royal family watched fights between elephants and tigers and between elephants and elephants, as well as buffalo fights and wrestling matches in the field below.

EARLY HUNTING

Of course, the form of entertainment that slaughtered most tigers over hundreds of years was hunting—a sport that goes back as far as 3000–4000 B.C.E.; the Bhimbetka cave paintings reveal a tiger surrounded by hunters in the wild forests of India. In Egypt, Pharaoh Amenhotep III hunted big cats more than three thousand years ago. So did the ancient Assyrians, using dogs so large, powerful, and catlike in their movements that some believed they were the offspring of a bitch who had mated with a tiger. In 800 B.C.E., the queen of Assyria brought back eight thousand tiger skins from her campaign in India to grace the floors of the hanging gardens in Babylon. In India during the reign of Samudra Gupta (C.E. 335–380), a series of gold coins shows the king hunting the tiger with bow and arrow. On the obverse is the inscription *Vyagra-Parakrama*, "slayer of tigers." Thus we understand that tigers have been trapped or poisoned for thousands of years.

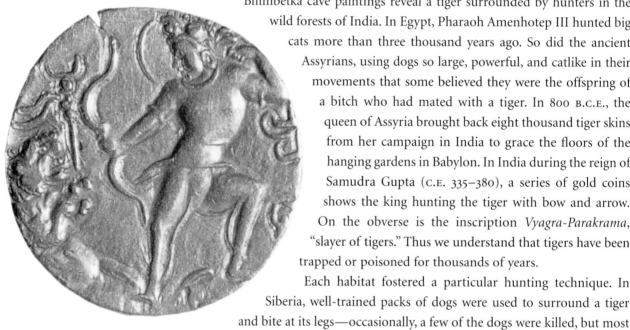

This two-thousand-year-old coin shows Samudra Gupta hunting a tiger.

Each habitat fostered a particular hunting technique. In Siberia, well-trained packs of dogs were used to surround a tiger and bite at its legs—occasionally, a few of the dogs were killed, but most of the time the tiger concentrated on trying to escape. Sometimes, a pack of dogs could tree a tiger and keep it there until the hunter arrived to dispatch it. In that freezing climate, another approach was to exhaust the tigers by tracking them through the snow in shifts, two trackers at a time. The trackers followed each other's tracks. When the first pair tired out, the next pair took over a few hours later. Such hunting required untiring efforts and a detailed knowledge of tiger behavior. The pursuit of a single tiger could take weeks.

In India, killing a tiger had been a sign of a warrior's ability for hundreds of years. But by the time the Mughals came to power in the sixteenth century, hunting tigers for sport with spears and horses was fully developed. A painting from the *Akbarnama* shows Emperor Akbar (1556–1605) on horseback, slaying a tigress with his sword. The painting recalls the first time that Akbar killed a tiger (and all five of her subadult cubs), when returning to Agra from Malwa in 1561. One of the cubs depicted is of lighter tone, and some observers have said it is a white tiger. I disagree. Many tigers of

A late-sixteenth-century painting from the Akbarnama *of Akbar hunting a tiger near Gwalior, India. The light-colored tiger has been mistaken for a white tiger by various specialists.*

lighter tone are found in the wild, and these are natural variations. Eleven years later, Akbar killed a tiger while on a pilgrimage to the shrine of Chisti in Ajmer. On another occasion, his divine look at a tiger is said to have made the animal cower and tremble, his stare alone melting the beasts of the jungle into submission.

Hunting graduated from swords, lances, and bows and arrows to the gun. Akbar's successor, Emperor Jahangir (reigned 1605–1627), regularly used muskets to hunt lions and tigers. However enthusiastic the Mughal hunters were, however, they were retiring compared to the colonial rulers who followed. By 1757, the British in Bengal had started giving special rewards—known as bounties—for each tiger killed. The modern ecological historian Mahesh Rangarajan, looking at the way the tiger has declined over the last century, wrote in *India's Wildlife History* (2001):

Nawab Muhammad Abdul Ramman Khan, on horseback in the center of the painting, spears a tiger. In the background, elephants carry dead tigers and a deer.

Bounty-hunting aided the decline of species but its impact was uneven depending on the region and the animal. Its impact on the tiger cannot be seen in isolation from hunting for sport. Sportsmen often saw elimination as their great "achievement." Far from simply being an adjunct to expanding cultivation, vermin-killing carried the battle well beyond the borders of the cultivated arable land. Any tiger anywhere was better dead than alive. For a time, no place in British India was sanctuary for such vermin. Preliminary figures do not minimize the latter as the two were inseparable for a long time. But the extension of agriculture (as in the Indus basin) also exerted a powerful influence on the fortune of the species. Given its large body size and its need for forest cover, even an animal as resilient as the tiger found it difficult to survive. The decline of prey species in forest areas may have been a powerful contributory factor.

THE EIGHTEENTH CENTURY

One of the earliest accounts of a grand tiger hunt with elephants was written by Sir John Day in a letter dated April 1784 and published in *Oriental Memoirs* by James Forbes:

> Matters had been thus judiciously arranged: tents were sent off yesterday, and an encampment formed within a mile and a half of the jungle which was to be the scene of our operations. . . .

An eighteenth-century Rajasthani painting of a maharajah hunting. The tigress has just left her den and her cub is visible on the right.

We had not proceeded five hundred yards beyond the jungle, when we heard a general cry on our left of "Baug, baug, baug!" On hearing this exclamation of "tiger!" we wheeled; and forming a line anew, entered the great jungle, when . . . a scene presented itself confessed by all the experienced tiger hunters present to be the finest they had ever seen. Five full grown royal tigers sprung together from the same spot, where they had sat in bloody congress. They ran diversely; but running heavily they all crouched again within new covers within the same jungle, and all were marked. We followed, having formed a line into a crescent, so as to embrace either extremity of the jungle: in the centre was the houdar (or state) elephants, with the marksmen, and the ladies, to comfort and encourage them.

When we had slowly and warily approached the spot where the first tiger lay, he moved not until we were just upon him; when with a roar that resembled thunder, he rushed upon us. The elephants wheeled off at once and shuffled off. They returned, however, after a flight of about fifty yards, and again approaching the spot where the tiger had lodged himself, towards the skirts of the jungle, he once more rushed forth, and springing at the side of an elephant upon which three natives were mounted, at one stroke tore a portion of the pad from under them; and one of the riders, panic struck, fell off. The tiger, however, seeing his enemies in force, returned, slow and indignant, into his shelter; where, the place he lay in being marked, a heavy and well-directed fire was poured in by the principal marksman; when, pushing in, we saw him in the struggle of death, and growling and foaming he expired.

We then proceeded to seek the others . . . and with a little variation of circumstances, killed them all; the oldest and most ferocious of the family had, however, early in the conflict, very sensibly quitted the scene of action, and escaped to another part of the country.

The chase being over, we returned in triumph to our encampment.

THE NINETEENTH CENTURY

In the early part of the nineteenth century, tiger-hunting parties were out all over India. One of the first books on hunting, Captain Thomas Williamson's *Oriental Field Sports*, appeared in 1807. It contains this description of how local people hunted and killed tigers:

> Such is the velocity of the arrow, and so quick does this simple contrivance act, that tigers are, for the most part, shot near the shoulder. Generally, tigers fall within two hundred yards of the fatal spot, they being most frequently struck

through the lungs and sometimes straight through the heart. If the arrow be poisoned, as is most frequently the case, locality is no particular object; though without doubt, such wounds as would of themselves prove effectual, unaided by the venom, give the shecarrie least trouble. The poison never fails to kill within an hour.

As soon as the tiger is dead, no time is lost in stripping off the skin; for, were it suffered to remain until the heat might taint it, nothing could effect its preservation; it would rot a certainty; and, even were it not to do so, rapidly the hair would loosen and fall off.

The Tiger at Bay *(1807) by Samuel Howitt. Elephants were trained to surround tigers in order to give the hunters a shot.*

It must have been a strange time for the local people who had feared and revered the tiger for so long; now its slaughter was beginning to shake the very root of their beliefs. The Gond people, hired to be part of a hunt, would spend a large portion of their wages to make sacrifices for the animal they were helping to kill.

In *Pen and Pencil Sketches, Being the Journal of a Tour of India,* Captain A. Mundy

Tiger Hunt, *1892. A cornered tiger attacks the elephant and*
gets shot at close range.

had this to say about a tiger shoot in 1827: "Thus in the space of about two hours, and within sight of the camp, we found and slew three tigers, a piece of good fortune rarely to be met with in these modern times when the spread of cultivation and the zeal of the English sportsmen have almost exterminated the breed of these animals."

In the 1860 publication *Wild Sports of India* by Major H. Shakespear, an English lady described a shooting expedition in 1837 into the Rajmahal Hills of Bengal with 260 attendants and twenty elephants. Writing to a friend, she said:

> They do say that there are hills in Bengal, not more than a hundred and forty miles from here; and the unsophisticated population of these hills is entirely composed of tigers, rhinoceros, wild buffaloes and, now and then, a herd of wild dogs. There, I'm going to live for three weeks in a tent. I shall travel the first fifty miles in a palanquin and then I shall march; it takes a full week to travel a hundred miles in that manner. . . .
>
> We had thirty-two elephants out this morning to beat the jungles and to be sure, they were jungles that required beating. What is called high grass jungles, the grass being the consistency of timber; it seems to me, so very much higher than elephant, howdah, and human creature, nothing to be seen of them at five yards distance, nothing heard but the crunching of reeds by the elephants as they break their way through.

The richness of the habitat had to be astounding, as rhinos and tigers were constantly flushed out by these expeditions. *Wild Sports of India* records another diary entry of 1839 that offers the following detail: "William arrived yesterday; he looks uncommonly well. . . . He and Mr. A have killed 36 tigers, the largest number ever killed in this part of the country by two guns, and his expedition seems to have answered very well."

THE SLAUGHTER REACHES ITS PEAK

New records continually replaced old ones. A Colonel Rice killed and wounded ninety-three tigers between 1850 and 1859. Lieutenant Colonel Gordon Cummings killed 173 tigers in 1863 alone. Mahesh Rangarajan estimates the figures of animals killed between 1875 and 1925 as "80,000 tigers, more than 150,000 leopards and 200,000 wolves. . . . It is possible this was only a fraction of the numbers actually slain."

This carnage soon brought about local extinctions. By 1913, there were no tigers left in the Punjab, for example. Some rulers seemed to be willing to wipe out their entire tiger population in their hunger for trophies. Many places in Rajasthan were giving bounties for shooting big cats—ten rupees for tigers and twenty-five for lions; the latter were also disappearing fast. Nor was this attitude confined to India: in Burma, now Myanmar, in 1923 there were reports of tigers being killed in the capital city of Rangoon. (In India, too, tigers were hunted in the outskirts of Delhi.) By 1929, the bounty on a tiger's head in Burma had resulted in the killing of 1,100 tigers in three years.

A notable description of hunting tigers during an earthquake that must have occurred in the Punjab in about 1916 appears in George Hogan Knowles's book *In the Grip of the Jungles* (1932). The writer is positioned up a tree on his machan, with an elephant and mahout nearby:

> Suddenly, a swift clammy gust of wind rustles by and whirls over the high rocks over my head, leaving in its wake an upheaval of fine gritty dust, like the warm whirlwind of an express train dashing by at full speed. Hardly has this gust passed, when breaking through the jungle at headlong speed, the frightened sambhur [sambar] dash away in terror, bellowing as they go. I can hear the crashing through the undergrowth a long distance till it dies away. Terrible silence then follows—not a sound—everything as still as death, and then—what is it? I look round. A low murmuring sound like deep guttural thunder seems to be traveling under the hills from the west; and then again, a few seconds of awful depressing silence. Suddenly, the grass in front of me heaves up . . . and, at that very instant my tree—too—shakes violently, a rush and a deafening roar nearly paralyze me. To my breathless astonishment, while I am clinging to the tree with my "machan" at all angles, I see a lame tiger in furious rage out before me from somewhere, to protect his kill. His hair stands, bristling up on his arched back. . . . Being heaved about on top of the tree, to get in a shot is out of the question; and, to my terrible disappointment, I see the monster with his ears savagely back, standing over the carcass broadside on, trying to balance himself: he suddenly falls; and then, with a terrific roar, he lurches up, and gallops back into the cover again, just next to me, but out of sight the very moment that the shaking stops. . . .
>
> Just as the cause of the last shaking dawns on me, I see the dark mountains in front of me, breathing like great upheaving breasts, and then comes a shaking that throws me into a panic! . . . My "machan" is giving way! I am clutching the tree and my rifle in grim desperation when, suddenly, the ropes burst, and the string-laced bed hangs and swings in the air. Down falls the balance of my things, carrying my heavy ulster with them, sprawling on the ground. The great lame tiger lifts his head at the noise, sees the falling things, and then on to my ulster and quilt he comes in a terrible rage, spitting and giving tongue in short gasps, and stumbling over the shaking ground. And now, with thundering roars, he is tearing my things to shreds. At this terrible moment I hear big stones rattling down the hill-side behind me, and I look up. There to my unspeakable

The Prince of Wales, later King Edward VII (1901–1910), shooting a tiger during a hunting expedition in India. From the Illustrated London News, *March 1876.*

Dead tigers were commonly transported on top of elephants, as shown in this photograph from the 1920s.

*The Prince of Wales, later
King Edward VIII, poses
with his first tiger, Nepal,
December 1921.*

horror, I see the bare hill brows almost knocking against each other—swaying like the heads of drunken men! . . .

I notice, for the first time, that my tree is bent slightly forward, and realize that it is the result of the earthquake shocks. I have thought of slipping down to look for some open flat ground for safety, but the presence of the ferocious lame tiger makes the attempt far too risky, and I decide to cling to the tree whatever happens.

Suddenly, within fifteen paces to my left, without the stir of a blade of grass or the crackle of a dry leaf being heard, the huge monster appears—as if by magic—and stalks out to his kill. My rifle is already loaded, and I rise from my clinging position across a thick branch and shuffle round slowly inch by inch. How my heart leaps with excitement! The tiger is taking his time to stalk, so slow and gradual that the movement is barely perceptible. He is giving me an exhibition of that wonderful soft tread, the power of which is possessed only by his species. In trembling anxiety I am waiting for the beautiful striped brute to take but a few more paces forward to give me a clear, unhampered shot, when, suddenly, that ghastly rumbling, intensified in volume and duration, sends a terrorizing warning through the jungles for the third time. The tiger halts to listen. With his ears cocked forward, and fierce whiskers streaming away on either side of his wide panting nostrils, his great handsome head lifts in noble defiance, and turns slowly to the right and then to the left; and now he is gazing steadily in front of him far over his kill as if in lofty meditation! The picture is magnificent! . . .

The spot where I am is like an island between mighty rivers of rolling shale—the hill has given way! I have fixed my rifle round the bole of the tree, which gives me the only support possible, and I cling for dear life with my legs wrapped round a branch lower down. In between the terrible din of falling earth and crashing boulders, the furious roars of the tiger can be heard in the cleft below. . . . I am now lost in a dense fog of fearful dust, and feel my tree going slowly. I do not know where, and do not know whether it is the tree or I that am falling until suddenly I hear the top branches above me gently bumping the ground. I can hardly credit my good fortune, though the vibration of the timber sends a nerve-racking jar through me. But next moment the dust rising below me—as if it came from just under my body, stretched out on the top of the tree trunk—makes me realize my awful situation! My tree is lying across the crevice like a bridge, and I am stretched on the top of that uncanny intermedium, looking down into the dark cavernous space close below me, where the savage lame tiger lies wounded.

Perhaps the most extravagant record of a hunting expedition describes a December 1921 shoot held for the Prince of Wales (later King Edward VIII and subsequently Duke of Windsor). *Menu and Food at the Hunt of Prince of Wales—H.R.H. The Prince of Wales's Sport in India* (1925) notes the arrangements and food for that event:

The greatest attention to detail was displayed in the lay-out of the camp, and every provision was made for the comfort and convenience of the guests. The roomy tents, which were beautifully furnished and fronted by garden terraces, flanked an open lawn scattered with chairs and tables where people might sit in the evenings. Here also a huge bonfire flared all night, and the giant log blazed—quite the biggest I have ever seen. The whole camp, both inside and outside, was lit with electricity, from the great arc lamps, which hung picturesquely from the trees (under which all the trophies shot during the day's sport used to be shown before being handed over to the ministrations of the skinning camp), down to the little reading lamp by one's bedside, which one could switch off before turning in.

The Royal suite of apartments was simple, yet all that could be desired, and ornamented, as befitted the occasion, with emblems and trophies of the chase. The floor of the mess tent was carpeted with leopard skins, pieced together as a great mat; the effect, as can be gathered, was extremely rich and striking. The very appointments of H.R.H.'s [the prince's] writing table were all mementoes of sport in Nepal, being made up from rhino hoofs, horns and hide, and even the waste-paper basket was made from the lower joint of a rhino's leg. The albums on the tables of the mess tent held the photographic record of many a famous shoot in the Nepal Terai.

This dinner menu was served to the prince in the impenetrable jungle of Nepal, miles from civilization: Consomme printanière, Saumon à la grand duc, Suprême de poulet mascotte, Selle d'agneau, Perdreaux sur canapés, Haricots verts à l'Anglaise, Crème Viennoise, Petites rissoles Nantua, Dessert, Café.

And the total "bags" of the prince and his staff on their Indian shoots of 1921 and 1922 included thirty tigers, six leopards, three bears, three elephants, ten rhinoceroses, twelve sambar, and seven wild boars. Of the above the Prince of Wales himself shot five tigers, two rhinoceroses, and one sambar.

Wherever you looked across the land of the tiger, hunting was reaching its peak. In 1929, a tiger that had swum in from the Thane Creek just outside Bombay was shot dead. It was the last recorded wild tiger in Bombay. European hunters had taken their toll on the Bali tiger to the extent that it was nearly extinct—the first subspecies to fall to the hunters' gun. Others would follow. Even hunters who could appreciate the beauty of the creature could not resist the temptation to add it to their trophies. Mary Hastings Bradley shot and killed her first tiger in Vietnam in 1929, and recorded her experiences in a book called *Trailing the Tiger*.

> There was a feeling in the air that the day was done. And then, as I looked out, realizing every moment slipping by as something palpable, bearing forever away the chances it might have held—I saw something.
>
> Out of the wall of distant shadows came a gleam of gold and black—vivid as lightning against the green—and the tiger walked out of the jungle.
>
> Never in my life had I seen such a picture. Elephants by moonlight, lions at dawn, gorillas at blazing noon I had seen, but nothing was ever so beautiful and so glorious to me as that tiger walking out of his jungle. He was everything that was wild and savage, lordly and sinister.
>
> He seemed to materialize like something in a dream and for a moment I could imagine I was dreaming. He stood, projected vividly against the forest, and he looked enormous. The great striped roundness of him was like a barrel. Then he moved, and seemed to flow along the ground, nearer and nearer.

Her account is not unique. Other hunters shot hundreds of tigers in Indochina, Indonesia, Malaysia, and all across Asia.

The rajah of Mandas (inset) and the pelts of the more than twenty tigers he killed.

NEAR EXTINCTION

And yet in India, one of the most destructive times in the history of the tiger only began in the mid-1930s. Every dignitary visiting India insisted on a tiger shoot. English royals joined their Indian counterparts in seeking tiger trophies. In 1935, Prince Azam Bahadur shot thirty-five tigers in thirty-three days in the forests of Adilabad in southern India. The prime minister and maharajah of Nepal shot 295 tigers between 1933 and 1939. One of the most appalling records comes from a shoot in Chitwan, just four months after he took office. He recorded that in just two days—January 12 and 13, 1933—"five tigers, all shootable (i.e., over seven feet) were shot on the first of these days, but this number was actually exceeded on the second day when no less than six tigers were killed. This made the phenomenal bag of nineteen tigers in four consecutive days. . . . Nowhere else in India or Nepal would it be possible to shoot nineteen tigers in four days over such a comparatively limited range." On this shoot, forty-one tigers and fourteen rhinos were shot in twenty-one days. In 1938–1939, in company with Lord Linlithgow, the British viceroy of India, the maharajah killed 120 tigers in the space of ten weeks.

In 1935, the first conference on protecting the tiger and Indian wildlife took place. Jim Corbett, the famous killer of man-eating tigers, and F. W. Champion, a forest officer, actively campaigned to protect both the tigers and their forests. But at the end

RIGHT: *A Nepalese maharajah with his day's bag of three tigers.*

BELOW: *A maharajah from central India poses atop a tiger with his two sons.*

Queen Elizabeth II and Prince Philip pose with the maharajah and the maharani of Jaipur, probably in Ranthambhore, the private hunting preserve of the erstwhile rajahs of Jaipur.

of the 1930s, the journal Corbett edited folded after only three issues due to the lack of support for tiger preservation.

There was no sign that, despite the efforts of men such as Corbett and Champion, this barbaric form of "entertainment" was ever going to end. In 1938 alone, 891 tigers were killed in India. The maharaja of Gwalior killed seven hundred in the course of his career.

India was fighting for independence while the Second World War was being fought in Europe. The war effort entailed cutting of vast amounts of timber, making the 1940s one of the worst periods for India's forests and wildlife. Conservation measures continued to suffer when India gained independence in 1947. Subsequent rapid development and huge river valley projects fueled the further decline of India's rich forests. By the 1950s thousands of travel agencies mushroomed across India, inviting hunters around the world to shoot tigers and other exotic beasts that lived in India's forests. In the 1960s, conservationists were convinced that India's wildlife had little chance of survival. Fortunately, when Indira Gandhi became prime minister in 1966 she brought to her position a great love for both the forest and all its inhabitants. By the end of the 1960s the first signs of positive change started to emerge.

THE MODERN CIRCUS

The word "circus" in Latin means "circle" or "oval," and it was the Romans who first entertained themselves with animals in a circus arena. The Roman circus was, of course, unlike our modern version with its tent, clowns, acrobats, and performing animals.

Clowns, acrobats, and animal shows had existed for centuries but were not put together into the formulaic show we know as the circus until 1768, when an English ex-military officer named Philip Astley put his horse-riding skills into action, alongside those of other performers. His performance skills notwithstanding, creating the circus ring itself was his greatest contribution to the modern circus. When he decided to use a covered arena for his shows, Astley realized that centrifugal force would make it much easier for the performers to balance on top of a horse galloping in a circle. It also provided the entire audience a clear view.

When Astley's circus grew in popularity, he was invited to France to perform before the court and so delighted Marie Antoinette that she invited him to return. Soon, imitators were producing rival shows and touring the world with them. Many military-trained riders, theater producers, or former students of Astley's Riding School became circus entrepreneurs. The circus spread around the world, becoming popular in the Russia of Catherine the Great in 1793. In that year, the circus also reached the infant United States and shortly thereafter spread to Canada, Mexico, and the rest of the world.

Although Astley is regarded as the father of the modern circus, exotic and wild animals, which we now consider essential to a circus performance, were not used in the shows until after his death in 1814. The introduction of these "jungle acts" created the circus we know today.

As popular as circuses were in Europe, it was in America that circuses really took off. One of the greatest is Ringling Bros. and Barnum & Bailey, which has been going strong since the 1870s. (The two operations merged in 1919.) At its peak, it had one of the largest shows on Earth, with more than one thousand performers and dancers in three-ring tents, which could hold as many as fifty elephants at a time, along with the usual dancing horses, trapeze artists, clowns, and all the rest.

HERCULES P. COUTALIANOS
IN MONTEVEDEO, LOUROUYIE
IN THE YEAR OF 1873 SOUTH AMERICA

Ringling Bros. and Barnum & Bailey also produced some of the most famous tiger trainers the world has known. One of the first was, unusually, a woman named Mabel Stark. A petite woman in a white leather suit and long black boots controlling her tigers in the old-fashioned manly way, with whips, guns, and fear, she attracted large crowds. She enjoyed a long career, went through five marriages, and survived dozens of maulings by tigers.

The next Ringling hero was the notorious Clyde Beatty, the big star of the 1930s, 1940s, and 1950s. He worked on the knife-edge of safety, in a big cage often surrounded by large numbers of dangerous animals such as tigers, lions, leopards, pumas, hyenas, and bears. He, too, was of the old school of "training," using the whip, gun, and chair to goad his cats into snarling and lashing out at him, demonstrating to his audience how fierce they were and how brave he was. He had a "fighting act" in which he controlled forty lions and tigers at once, which must have been an awesome sight. So famous was he in his day that he starred in a 1933 Hollywood film, *The Big Cage*, based largely on his exploits.

After the civil rights movement, political turmoil, and social upheaval of the 1960s, attitudes toward animals changed once again, and Gunther Gebel-Williams, yet another Ringling star, revolutionized animal training, making it more like what it is today. He rejected the old "fighting style" of training animals with pain and violence and instead adopted a gentler and friendlier approach. Although still a typical "dominant male" in the center ring, with big animals performing breathtaking stunts, he used more encouragement than fear to get his tigers to ride elephants, jump through hoops, and climb pedestals. You were less likely to see his animals cowering from him as he entered the ring.

Tiger trainer Sara Houcke, the "Tiger Whisperer."

A current tiger trainer, Sara Houcke, is known to her admirers as "the Tiger Whisperer." With the public more concerned about animal welfare than they have ever been, the circus has had to adapt its acts in order to stay afloat. To achieve the kind of relationship she has with her tigers, Houcke spends hours each day in clothes that have the tigers' scent on them, hugging and petting her tigers, feeding them by hand, and generally befriending them. When she performs, she does not enter the stage with a whip or chair, shouting and encouraging her beasts to show off their ferocity. Instead, she literally whispers, enticing her seven tigers to do her bidding. There are no pedestals or flaming hoops. Houcke relies simply on the natural fascination that tigers hold.

Today, the circus can be found in every corner of the globe, but there has been a worldwide decline in animal acts. Non-animal circuses appear to be on the increase. With animal-rights groups lobbying governments, the public knowing how animals should look in their natural surroundings, and people generally having a more compassionate attitude toward animals, this trend is understandable. The use of animals in entertainment has already been restricted or banned in several European countries, including Sweden, Finland, Switzerland, and Denmark; Austria is following suit. In the last couple of years, first India and then Singapore have also banned tigers and other exotic animals in traveling circuses. New Zealand has no circus tigers even though it has not yet banned their use, nor does Australia. Where animal acts still exist, laws on animal welfare are instituting more restrictions, and some individual cities are banning circuses. In the United Kingdom, there are now just twelve animal circuses, of which only one has some young Amur tigers.

Siegfried and Roy with three white tiger cubs born at the Mirage in Las Vegas, October 2002.

Of course, not every country has the same ideals and views, and in North America there are still an estimated two hundred tigers being used in circuses. It is impossible to know for sure, since no regulatory agency keeps records of the trading of animals (which is widespread) nor of their births and deaths.

One of the most exotic animal shows of all time, Siegfried and Roy, was cancelled indefinitely after a seven-year-old white tiger named Montecore attacked Roy Horn during a performance at the Mirage in Las Vegas on October 3, 2003. The tiger had performed in the show for years, and Horn himself, a trainer and magician, had performed with tigers in more than 30,000 live shows by the time of the incident. For reasons that are not known, the tiger refused a command to lie down and then clamped its jaws on Horn's right arm. The magician struck the head of the tiger with his microphone repeatedly. The tiger then lunged at Horn's neck and dragged him offstage. Crew members backstage sprayed the animal with a fire extinguisher to force the cat to release its grip.

The frightening incident prompted both sympathy for Roy and criticism of the show. Dan Mathews, vice president of People for the Ethical Treatment of Animals, wrote in a letter that "a brightly lit stage with pounding music and a screaming audience is not the natural habitat for tigers, lions, or any other exotic animals."

Notwithstanding (and perhaps because of) the risks involved for both trainer and animal, many people in North America and several European countries, including Spain, Portugal, France, and Germany, continue to enjoy exotic animal performances. Little is known of tiger welfare in Russia and China. On the whole, while there seems to be a general decline in animal acts worldwide, there are still many exceptions.

TRAINING TIGERS FOR FILM ROLES

Thierry Le Portier and one of his charges.

The techniques of animal trainers from around the world explain something about how a mere person can control the king of beasts. One of the premier trainers, Thierry Le Portier, who grew up in Paris and Toulouse, has been infatuated with animals, and with big cats in particular, all his life.

"When I was eleven, I thought I would buy a baby lion, a baby tiger, a baby puma, a baby leopard, everything when I grew up—because with me it's all or nothing. And I'd train them and they'd be like my dogs." His first break came at the age of sixteen, when he got a poorly paid job with a seventy-three-year-old big-cat tamer. Le Portier explains: "I did all the hard, dirty work. After six months, he pushed me into the cage with the lions, in front of the public, and said, 'Okay, off you go'—and I did the whole act, without any help from him. I'd observed closely everything he did."

Le Portier spent time refining his dangerous craft in circuses all over Europe and even performed with his big cats at the casino in Monte Carlo and the Folies Bergères in Paris. His first brush with the cinema came with the renowned director Pier Paolo Pasolini on the film *Flower of the Arabian Nights*. His abiding memory of that experience

was being treated to lunch by the director—a man famous for never buying so much as a cup of coffee for anyone on his crew.

Ten years later, he worked on a television miniseries with James Mason and Ava Gardner called *Anno Domini*. This was memorable for a three-day drive across France during the 1984 truck drivers' strike. There were blockades everywhere. They swiftly parted to let Thierry through when he threatened to open his truck and release his tigers and leopards, saying they had not eaten for three days.

Le Portier began to collect some impressive credits: television commercials with French director Jean-Jacques Beineix, using a black panther, which people still remember today; France's version of the famous Esso tiger ads; the film *The Bear*, directed by Jean-Jacques Annaud; *The Ghost and the Darkness* with Michael Douglas. By this time Thierry's personal collection of working big cats had reached thirty.

Then came *Gladiator* and arguably cinema's most famous big cats, the tigers that fought Russell Crowe on the sands of Rome's Colosseum, reconstructed in Malta. "I was busy watching the World Cup," Le Portier recalls. "The phone rang, and it was the producer, who said, 'We're doing a Roman film, called *Gladiator*, with Ridley Scott directing, and we need some tigers—can you do it?' Naturally I said yes."

Le Portier trained his tigers for those gladiatorial scenes using a different technique from the usual one of offering meat rewards for doing the right thing. He exerts total control—even over a 225-kilogram (495-pound), potentially lethal cat—through his uncanny ability to "read" it and know what it's thinking: "If you can do that, you always know just a little bit in advance of him what he's going to do." Le Portier does not believe that this is something you can be taught. "It's impossible. It's only you who can learn it." How many animal behaviorists have that skill?

Thierry Le Portier directs one of his tigers on the set of Two Brothers.

"Not even an animal behaviorist can really read an animal. They know certain signs mean certain things—the tiger looks like it's going to charge—yes, but when? Now? In ten minutes? And is it going to be a mock charge to intimidate you, or does he want to kill you? Is he going to head off in another direction and attack you from behind? You can't read that from the flicking ears or the twitching tail. Me, I know when he's going to charge—and the tiger can even charge without any warning sign."

The secret of his method—and that of all successful trainers—is dominating the animal. While modern trainers usually use a whip, they do so not to thrash the animal but to direct or discourage it. Le Portier explains his approach as follows: "I never hurt or maltreat my animals. It's about control. I have to give off aggression—and that means I can give them a little tap with the whip—because it's my aggression that becomes a punishment for the animal. That's how it behaves with others. I can't bite it—I must make it afraid of me. But three minutes later, it's all forgotten. It's only a transitory fear of me that the animal has. Even after a violent scene between us for the cameras, ten minutes later the animal comes over to be caressed."

After *Gladiator*, Le Portier began work on another movie, *Two Brothers*, a shoot that reunited him with director Jean-Jacques Annaud. Le Portier's skill with tigers, lions, and the other glamorous big cats has them doing their scenes over and over, in exactly the correct position for the cameras, until everything is right. And Le Portier says that, like good actors, they just get better all the time.

Filming Tigers

Mike Birkhead

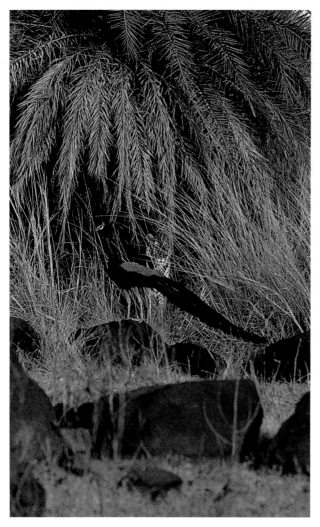

The peacock is unaware of the tiger watching in the background.

It ALL BEGAN IN THE EARLY 1990S, when I wanted to make a film on peacocks.

I had been a research scientist for a few years and had specialized in animal behavior, in particular bird behavior, so any excuse to make a film on birds suited me. Peacocks are about as good as they get—big, colorful, and sexy. I thought that would be good enough.

The British Broadcasting Corporation had said they liked the idea of a peacock film, but as peacocks somehow were not big enough or sexy enough for them, they said they would take the film if I included tigers in it! So instead of a film called *The Tale of the Peacock*, I found myself at work on *The Tale of the Peacock and the Tiger*. I set off to India for the first time, armed with lots of indigestion tablets and a great deal of trepidation. India had been a no-go area for filmmakers for a while after a disagreement with BBC led to a ban on filming for several years. I knew where to go to find peacocks there, but where to go for tigers— that was the question. A little bit of research led me to Valmik Thapar's books on tigers, so Ranthambhore National Park, the locale of many of his books, was to be one of my first stops. Now I was excited—maybe peacocks could be bettered.

Well, a few weeks on and there I was in Ranthambhore—the best place in the world to watch tigers, or so all the guidebooks said. Five days later, no tigers. In fact, all the talk was of something strange going on—but what was it? All the wonderful tigers of the 1980s seemed to have disappeared, but no one was sure why. There were rumors and counter-rumors, politics, and more. This turned out to be a good introduction to India and Ranthambhore, in fact. No one seemed to accept that the tigers were gone— I couldn't quite understand it, and neither could the other visitors. All the officials were quite sure the tigers were just hiding, or at least that is what they were telling everybody.

That seemed reasonable to me—after all, they were wild animals. Then, one evening I was having a drink at Fateh Singh Rathore's house—he is Valmik's tiger guru and was at the time the man in charge of the park—when he got a message on his radio. At least one man, one of his forest guards, had been shot dead while trying to recover a tiger skin from a poacher's house. It soon became clear this was the start of the "tiger crisis."

Just a few days later some more forest guards were killed in tiger-poaching-related incidents in Corbett National Park. Evidently, tigers were being killed in great numbers, not for their skins but for their bones, which were needed in the Chinese medicine trade. The peacock film was put on the back burner, and so started ten years of making films in India, many of which have been on the tiger. These include *Tiger Crisis*, *Land of the Tiger*, *Tiger's Fortress*, *Danger in Tiger Paradise*, and, of course, *The Tale of the Peacock and the Tiger*, which had started it all off.

One place we originally avoided due to politics and the "tiger crisis" was Ranthambhore itself, but eventually we did decide to film there, and over the course of five or six years we accumulated some very interesting information on the special tigers of that region.

In Ranthambhore tigers could be watched during daylight hours—an important factor to consider in filming. Ranthambhore was particularly known for its tigers of the 1980s, but some of its most impressive tigers—Genghis, Nikki, and Noon—had all disappeared, and when we started filming there in the mid-1990s, the newer tigers were not as well known, and it was like starting all over again. At its peak, Ranthambhore had nearly fifty tigers and at it worst probably ten—maybe more, maybe less.

Our tiger films tend to be specific stories about individual tigers, and for that of course you need to be able to recognize them as individuals. That is not easy, but we manage to do it by using our film and photographs to help us pick out recognizable features. The females are reasonably straightforward, as they tend to stick to fairly small territories, so if you find a female tiger in a certain area it is likely to be the same one you saw there earlier. But you also soon identify certain characteristics: a nick in the ear, a broken tail—we have even had a tiger whose stripes above the eyes formed a "52": a clear 5 over one eye and a 2 over the other. Of course, you always have to be careful to check that other tigers don't have similar markings. In Ranthambhore from 1997 to 2003, we recognized a number of individuals and from that learned a lot. We are not pretending this is science, but it is worth recording, and then it is up to scientists to see if they can make use of it.

I remember arriving on day one for *Tiger's Fortress* and meeting Colin, Valmik, and Fateh. It was such a thrill: at last, here we were, trying to film tigers. You never know what it is going to be like. We had taken a gamble—Ranthambhore was meant to have tigers again, not unlike the mid-1980s. There was even talk of tigers hunting in the lakes as they had done in their heyday. This was what I was really hoping for.

When we first arrived at Ranthambhore, there was a female who occupied the territories around the lakes. We called her the Lady of the Lakes. She was known to be the mother of three cubs of around twenty to twenty-four months old, two of whom had already left their mother's territory. The third cub was a female, and we called her Machli. We could recognize her due to the idiosyncratic stripe patterns on her face. She was to be the star of the films *Tiger's Fortress* and *Danger in Tiger Paradise*.

In the first film, *Tiger's Fortress*, we followed Machli as she fought with her mother, the Lady of the Lakes, for a slice of her territory. This is what tigers do. The female offspring tend to live in parts of their mother's territory in what is described by scientists as an extended pride—it is rather like a lion's social system but on a larger, more diluted scale. Tigers are less social than lions, and the females seem to prefer space to themselves, though they need to fight for this space from their mothers—or so it seems from our experiences in Ranthambhore. On at least two occasions, we filmed serious conflicts between Machli and the Lady of the Lakes. Eventually, the two tigresses came to an "agreement": Machli inherited part of her mother's territory around the lakes, and her mother moved to an adjacent area away from the lakes. Valmik and Fateh had witnessed similar behavior in the 1980s when Noon had given up part of her territory to her daughter. We do not know, of course, if the mothers are happy with these arrangements. But we did not witness further aggression once separate territories had been adopted. At some point, it seems mothers and daughters manage to live peacefully in neighboring territories.

Over the next few months, we watched Machli grow up in her own territory, with which she was already familiar, for her mother had taught her the best places to hunt, rest, hide, or whatever. She also knew the local territorial males. Of course, there would be a chance that one of them was her father, if he was still around, but we are fairly sure the first male Machli mated with was Boombooram—not her father—a tiger of some reknown in Ranthambhore, as he is said to be the one President Clinton saw when he visited the region in 2000.

Machli eventually had two cubs, the appearance of which tied in with her mating (given the three-month gestation period) with Boombooram, so we assumed he was the father. This is not proof, of course, but it is the best you can do sometimes. Boombooram died or disappeared soon afterward, so we were left with a very interesting situation of a novice mother alone with her cubs. In tiger terms, this is not good. The loss of the territorial male means new males will try to move into the vacant territory. They don't do this because they like the view or the lakes to dip their toes in; they do it to acquire the two, three, or four females they will get to mate with if they succeed in taking over the territory. They may have fought and killed the last ruling male—this is not uncommon. Indeed, in Khana we filmed a huge dead male that we suspected had been killed by rivals.

Once a new male moves in, every tigress, especially the ones with small cubs sired by the last male, needs to be

Boombooram *by Rose Corcoran.*

careful. An experienced female may stand a better chance of dealing with this, but we were not sure about a first-time mother like Machli.

Machli was vulnerable, and so were her two three-month-old male cubs. We followed them over a period of about eighteen months to see what was going to happen. We also wondered if male cubs were more in danger than females would have been—after all, one day they may be competitors to the new male. All in all, Machli was in just about the worst position a young tigress could be in. In fact, there seemed to be two mature males moving in on her territory: one called Nick, a young male we had known since he was born, and an older, bigger guy we called the Chiroli male. Nick eventually seemed to get the territory, and Colin filmed some remarkable interactions between him and Machli. We put forward the idea that Machli used a combination of seduction and aggression to keep her small cubs safe from the new males. We saw her mating with Nick when it was unlikely she was in estrus, and we know she didn't have any cubs as a result of the liaison. Also, Colin filmed her in a terrific fight with Nick when he was getting too amorous. We called it, tongue in cheek, a game of cat and mouse, Machli trading off sex and/or fighting the big male to keep her cubs safe long enough for them to mature, leave her, and fend for themselves. Of course, we know we over-anthropomorphize—that is what we do when making films so that they are appealing to the viewing public. We do not want to present dry science, but we do want to keep to the facts as we see them.

Machli's two cubs survived until they were at least twenty months old; remarkably, one of the last things we filmed was these huge cubs suckling or at least trying to suckle from their mother—a most unusual sight. Then they disappeared, and we did not see them again for five or six months. Nick did successfully mate with Machli, and presumably he managed to frighten off these two males. Eventually, we did find one of the cubs, now a pretty big male whom we could easily identify, Broken Tail.

I am always aware that we need to tell new stories through our films, and I think they work best when we team up with people such as Valmik, Ullas Karanth, or Fateh Singh Rathore, who have spent a great deal of time studying tigers. Raghu Chundawat was a particular help on the series *Land of the Tiger*. He is an extraordinary field biologist who had studied snow leopards in the Himalayas and then decided in the mid-1990s to switch his attentions to the tiger full-time. We filmed his team collaring a tiger in 1996, right at the beginning of his studies. Chip Houseman was the cameraman. We had dedicated eleven days to getting the sequence, but by the eleventh morning we still hadn't gotten it. Chip called to say he might miss the plane, as he wanted to give it one last try that morning. It was a good decision, and the team caught its tiger. It proved to be good for our films, too, as we returned there seven years

later to make a film on Raghu's research; the tigress they caught that day—the female with the distinctive eyebrows, 52—had provided Raghu with his most important subject. She is still alive today, and we caught one of her daughters just last year. But I wanted to make a film with Raghu that would help tell us more about male behavior, so I asked if we could catch a male. Raghu and his trusted colleague, veterinarian Pradeep Malik, agreed to try.

Since the time that Raghu had started his study, there had been one big male that ruled the park. But it was clear that he was coming to the end of his reign. At least one big new male was now known to be around, and he was the one we were going to try to catch. I was excited to be part of the operation. I decided to allow fourteen days for filming the event, knowing how close we had come to failing the last time. Just how do you catch a tiger? Well, you need a huge Indian elephant, a mahout (an elephant handler), someone to fire a tranquilizer dart into the tiger, and someone brave enough to be first off the elephant to check that the tiger is asleep—that would be neither Valmik nor I, that would be Raghu. You find the tiger on a kill and then fire the dart into it from about twenty paces away from the safety of the back of the elephant.

I wanted to film Raghu and Valmik together witnessing the whole thing, which promised to make it even more difficult. Filming tigers, elephants, wolves, or whatever species is challenging enough, but trying to include a person in the same shot as the animal makes it so much more difficult. Over the years, the films I had done with Valmik relied more and more on such shots, however. In Ranthambhore, we had had a great deal of success and managed to get Valmik juxtaposed, as we say in the business, with a number of nice tigers. My favorite is definitely the one we shot on the day we found a tigress with four tiny cubs. Just to film this tigress and her family would have been a big success, but to get Valmik in the same shot talking about them was what I really wanted. It was a fairly typical quiet morning in Ranthambhore—once you are away from the popular lakes you do not see many people. We got a report from Colin and

Salim that they had found the tigress and her cubs on a fresh kill just up ahead! Fantastic—it sounded perfect, as it so often does until you get there. We entered a small, tight valley the sides of which rose about eighteen to twenty meters (sixty to sixty-five feet) on either side. Down the middle was a narrow track surrounded by trees and bushes.

Well, around the last bend we drove, straight into a tourist traffic jam more like something you encounter in a city than in the Indian jungle: twenty, thirty, forty jeeps and lots of excited chatter. My heart sank—I didn't think there would be any chance of getting any useful shots with all these tourists as keen to see the tiger as we were. We could not move, which was a limiting factor. The only good thing was that we were at the end of the line of traffic, just about the last people to arrive there. We could see the tigress and hear the cubs, but the undergrowth was quite thick, and all I could see us getting was a few nice shots. It was nevertheless exciting—we counted the cubs slowly as they appeared from amid the vegetation. The tigress was carrying the remains of a freshly killed chital stag, with two cubs following her. Then she left the kill and moved down the slope closer to us. Two more cubs appeared, and they, too, moved toward their mother and closer to us. This was starting to get really exciting. Colin and Salim were just ahead of us, but there were a couple of jeeps in between.

If we were to film Valmik and the tigers together, Salim had to get his jeep next to ours. The tourists and drivers in Ranthambhore are so helpful—it always amazes me—in part because they now recognize Valmik from the films he has been in. So a few maneuvers later, Colin and Salim were right behind us. And after we sent up a few prayers, the whole family—one lovely tigress and four little cubs—toddled out onto the road in front of us, Colin filming, Salim recording sound (and driving), Valmik speaking to the camera, and me lying on the floor trying to keep out of the shot! All our Christmases had come at once—we got two or three pieces with Valmik and that extraordinary family. It is undoubtedly one of my luckiest tiger encounters

and probably the best we have ever filmed with Valmik and tigers. But would we have the same luck trying to catch the big male with Raghu?

Each day, we set off and searched for the big male and also the famous 52, whom Raghu wanted to catch, as she had recently lost her collar. After eight or nine days, we had not caught a single tiger. I was beginning to get worried. But Raghu was as patient as ever, as was Pradeep Malik. We knew the tigers we wanted to catch were around. We had been following their pugmarks, or tracks, and found their kills, so I knew that it was only a matter of time. Eventually, we did catch 52. Raghu knew her to be quite fierce, and she charged us and our elephant a few times. It was fantastic to see the tigress up close once we had caught her. She was huge, but Raghu said she was small compared with the male we wanted to catch. But before I knew it Pradeep said, "Antidote in—get back on the elephant and leave." That meant the tranquilizer was being counteracted, and we had less than eight minutes left on the ground; that was not enough time to film a good sequence with Valmik explaining what was going on. But we had the key shot at least—Valmik stroking a big tiger that had just been caught and collared. We even got a nice shot of her getting up and leaving after the antidote took effect.

A day or so later, we caught up with the big male feeding on a kill. He was so big he looked like a different species than the female. Raghu and Pradeep estimated he weighed 250 kilograms (550 pounds), and his head was enormous. He was so confident that he did not run away from us or our elephants, though he did hide in the bushes. And this, so it proved, created a bit of a problem. A blade of grass or a leaf can easily deflect the delicate tranquilizer dart. You cannot afford to miss the tiger—even though it is a big animal, the vet is trying to hit a specific spot about the size of a tennis ball on the tiger's torso. You also have to have enough time to "process" the tiger and release it afterward in the daylight. At three o'clock, Raghu was about to call the hunt off and declare that it was too late, even though we were just twenty paces away from the tiger. There were a few big branches in the way, making the shot a bit too risky.

Elephant mahout to the rescue. He instructed his four-ton charge to delicately remove a few branches from an intervening tree, and at last Pradeep had a clear shot. He wasted no time and shot the tiger. The big male was off. He didn't like the surprise. For me, at least, this was the worst time. The elephant we were on was instructed to follow the tiger wherever it went at all costs, but no one had told us that. So as soon as we had filmed the dart being fired, the tiger took off, and so did we. We seemed to demolish everything around us, small and large trees alike. But the big tiger didn't get far—in fact, only about one hundred paces. Pradeep's tranquilizer worked like a dream. We had twenty minutes to film the sequence we were after while Pradeep and Raghu put a radio collar on the tiger and took a few measurements. I think the tiger was an extra-large. His neck was more than ninety centimeters (thirty-six inches) around, his canines were about 7.5 centimeters (three inches) long, and he had feet literally the size of dinner plates.

Once again, we managed to capture an exciting sequence, this time with Valmik, Raghu, and Pradeep in the shot. This was not easy at all—all the plans you make before the event usually go out of the window, because the scientists have to consider their own agendas as well as our needs, and they cannot afford for things to go wrong. But this time it was about as good as it can get: we got our sequence, and Pradeep and Raghu seemed happy, too.

Over the past ten years or so we have captured some amazing tiger moments on film; we have also learned a lot about tiger behavior. I feel it is important to document these special moments. The cameramen I work with spend an inordinate amount of time watching, following, and getting to know the animals—up to and sometimes more than two years for each film. Normally, only scientists spend as much time as that—and very often they are not under the same pressure we are to find the animals. I hope that some of the films have had positive effects and helped preserve the tiger's existence in some parts of India—as I think *Tiger Crisis* did. I also hope that films like the series *Land of the Tiger* inspired people to visit India and see the magnificent wildlife that incredible country still has despite its huge population—now more than one billion people.

MIKE BIRKHEAD earned a doctorate at the University of Oxford and spent two years there doing postdoctoral work in the Department of Zoology. He subsequently joined London Weekend Television in 1984. Since 1988 he has worked as an independent producer/director, producing more than twenty-five wildlife films for BBC, PBS, HTV/Partridge Films, National Geographic, WNET, Discovery, and Animal Planet. His award-winning productions include: *Danger in Tiger Paradise* (2002), The *Tigers' Fortress* (2000-01), *Tiger* (1998), *Land of the Tiger* (1997), *Grand Canyon—From Dinosaurs to Dams* (1995), *Tiger Crisis* (1994), and *Land of Giants* (1992). His most recent documentary film is *The Ultimate Guide to Tigers*.

TIGERS AS PETS

From the earliest records of the capture and slaughter of tigers to their use in theatrical acts, humans have long tried to domesticate tigers. A new trend is the keeping of tigers as pets. Motivations for doing so are varied. Some private owners simply like being different, while others find the sleek feline almost erotically intoxicating. There are even stories of tigers being used as "guard cats" by drug dealers.

The startling fact is that in the United States alone there are reckoned to be more tigers in captivity than survive in the wild in the rest of the world. More than ten thousand big cats live as pets in the United States, of which half are tigers. Not only is it legal to keep a pet tiger in most states, but, as with the animals performing in circuses, it is also largely unregulated. In most jurisdictions, only local municipal or county bylaws similar to those prohibiting people from keeping roosters or other farm animals as pets restrict the keeping of tigers.

This lackadaisical attitude has led to disastrous results, because most people do not comprehend the commitment required to truly tame a tiger. Owners should expect to be with the tiger constantly, even when it is asleep. The tiger must be bottle-fed as many as five times per day for six months, by which time it will weigh about one hundred pounds. By six to seven months, the tiger will weigh approximately two hundred pounds. By the time a tiger is three years old, depending on its gender, it will weigh between four hundred and eight hundred pounds. Monthly costs run over $2,000 for food, veterinary care, horsetails, and other toys to chew on. Almost invariably, people who adopt tiger cubs as pets end up changing their minds after the acquisition, and at best the animal lives out its life caged, in varying conditions, until it dies or, more often, is put down. At worst, they are let loose.

From 2000 to 2004, at least seven people were killed by tigers in the United States, and reports of children being bitten and maimed are not uncommon. A blaze of publicity surrounded the case of a fully grown tiger that was living in an apartment in New York City in 2003. The "pet" was discovered because its owner sought medical treatment for the injuries it had inflicted on him.

In a chilling incident that was reported in November 2003, former circus trapeze artist Joan Byron-Marasek, known as the "Tiger Lady," was arrested near Trenton, New Jersey, after a four-year court battle waged by the state Fish and Wildlife Division authorities. The owner of twenty-four Bengal tigers, she was charged with running a substandard and unhealthy facility. The tigers were eventually moved to the Wild Animal Orphanage near San Antonio, Texas.

There are instances of cruelty, as well. Some big cats end up in the "canned hunt" ranches, where for two to twenty thousand dollars "big-game hunters" can bag their trophy of choice. Success is all but guaranteed, as the tiger is hunted at close range, sometimes even in a cage. There are more than one thousand such ranches in the

United States. But perhaps the grimmest story, which hit the headlines in 2003, was the discovery at the home of a Californian who ran a so-called tiger rescue center for thirty-five years. When police invaded his premises, they found ninety dead tigers either rotting on the grounds or stuffed in freezers. Others, including tiny cubs, were tied up and emaciated.

Excluding these kinds of isolated horrors, recent changes in the treatment of tigers demonstrate the power of public opinion. Mistreated for centuries, hunted ruthlessly, its habitant diminished, and decimated to the brink of extinction, the tiger's plight has begun to galvanize a number of concerned people around the world to preserve the tiger's habitat and ensure its survival. This growing interest, along with progress in tiger research, increasingly provides us with the motivation and knowledge to act responsibly toward this enigmatic and fascinating animal.

The power and intense sanctity of the tiger is reflected in this nineteenth-century painting of the Deva with Siva and Bhairava.

CHAPTER 6

The Tiger in Art

Ever since man first set eyes on the tiger, this magnificent striped cat has mesmerized people around the world and inspired their artistic creations. The first representation of tigers in western art coincided with the appearance of live tigers in Greek or Roman processions and in the amphitheaters of the Roman world. As anthropologist Paola Manfredi describes below, the tiger seems to have been featured in only one ancient art form—the mosaic.

From the seventeenth century onward, Mughal artists in India produced some intriguing composite paintings, some of the most famous of which are the intricate miniatures described in this chapter by Archana Verma, a research scholar working on Indian art history.

Although this tiger imagery appeared across South Asia, it percolated only slowly through to the western world. As late as the seventeenth century, Europeans were unfamiliar with the tiger, and most artists were drawing from descriptions brought back by adventurers. However, by the late 1700s, more tigers were being kept and displayed in the capitals of Europe, and artists were able to witness these beautiful and exotic animals firsthand. Rose Corcoran, a painter who specializes in big cats but focuses particularly on tigers, describes the western artists and tiger paintings that have been an inspiration to her.

Scenting *by Rose Corcoran*

ABOVE: *A centaur fights wild animals in this Roman mosaic from the Emperor Adrian's villa at Tivoli, 118–128 C.E.*

OPPOSITE: *A Roman mosaic from the Villa Hermes, Aquincum (Budapest), Hungary, fourth century C.E.*

218

The Tiger in Ancient Mosaics

Paola Manfredi

From early Hellenistic times to the late Roman empire period, very few tigers appear on artifacts such as statuettes, vases, plates, sarcophagi, and paintings. What representations we have are found mostly in a number of beautiful mosaics discovered throughout the Roman empire but particularly in the North African provinces, Sicily, and Byzantium, where some of the most striking images survive. The art of mosaic developed enormously, both stylistically and technically, in the Hellenistic world and during the Roman empire and the Byzantine period; though a very exclusive and luxurious product in the earlier centuries, it became a more affordable commodity from the beginning of the Roman empire—virtually every house of a certain standard was decorated with mosaics. With different styles and schools, different techniques, and with themes derived from mythology, religion, or everyday life—whether in urban or rural surroundings and whether depicting celebrations of special events, heroes of the amphitheaters, landscapes, hunting scenes, or naturalistic or geometric decorations—the repertoire of ancient mosaics is amazingly wide. Although the mosaic craftsmanship came mainly from North Africa, the shows in the Roman amphitheaters had a huge impact throughout the empire, bringing life and vibrancy to the image of the tiger.

Studies have revealed that books of sample drawings, showing many variations of the most popular subjects, circulated among painters and mosaicists. It is for this reason that multiple versions of the same image can be found in parts of the empire distant from each other, such as two replicas of centaurs killing wild animals, in which a tiger occupies the center of the scene. One of these was found in an African province, while the other was in the villa of the Emperor Adrian at Tivoli, near Rome, and is now housed in the Staatliche Museum in Berlin.

Dionysus and the Tiger

The mosaics depicting tigers can be grouped into those featuring the tiger in association with Dionysus or with other mythical figure and events, and those with a more naturalistic flavor, such as portraits or scenes of tigers being hunted, being captured, or fighting with other animals. Over two thousand years on, it would be impossible to find a surviving example of every kind of image of the tiger. It is particularly difficult to find clear

"tiger images" in the *emblemata*—small, self-contained scenes, arranged as individual medallions, framed by borders, and en masse forming a much wider mosaic floor. But after searching through hundreds of photographs, many of them old and foggy and faded from the years, I was amply rewarded, as images of tigers started to pop up from almost every corner of the Roman empire.

The ancient Greeks believed that the Indians had been blessed, in some mythical time, by the "civilizing" deeds of the god Dionysus. According to legend, Dionysus had gone to India, which was then inhabited by a nomadic people whose life was very primitive. He succeeded in subduing them, founded cities and laid down laws, and granted them the greatest present of all: wine. He donated seeds to cultivate the land. Then he taught the people to attach bullocks to the plough and to sow and grow plants; he gave them weapons and taught them to honor the gods, particularly himself, by playing cymbals and drums and by dancing. Having organized all this and chosen a good king for the Indians, Dionysus went back to the West. In Mediterranean countries, from Tunisia to Spain, this story is represented in beautiful mosaics showing Dionysus coming back from India triumphant in a chariot pulled by tigers, amid a very colorful cortege.

According to the scholar Luis Foucher, "It is certainly in Ptolemaic Egypt that the representation of Dionysus' chariot drawn by tigers started, as it evoked both the triumph of Dionysus over the Indians as well as Alexander's victories in the Indus valley." The Ptolemaic dynasty (from 322 B.C.E. to the Roman conquest in 30 B.C.E.) arose in the wake of Alexander's conquest of Egypt and promoted the identification of Alexander with Dionysus in order to benefit from such divine association. Ptolemy IV even took the additional name "Neos Dionysus."

Dionysus was worshipped as Cosmocrator, a manifestation of the god taming the wild beasts. The Latin author Statius, in his *Thebaid*, written in the first century C.E., described Dionysus as pushing a chariot drawn by tigresses that "lick" their reins wet with "must." The first and second centuries C.E. Roman emperors Trajan, Hadrian, and Antoninus Pius strongly supported the cult of Dionysus, and their patronage certainly contributed to its popularity. Later, Heliogabalus, in an attempt to be identified with Dionysus/Alexander, even drove lions and tigers around in harness, escorted by elephants bearing the symbols of the "divine" emperor.

A mosaic found on the island of Delos and dated to the second century B.C.E. is among the oldest images in the western world that features the tiger. It depicts a young Dionysus, who, "ivy crowned, winged, and brandishing a thyrsus, rides on a magnificent tiger, whose neck is wreathed with wine-leaves and grapes." Actually, the head of this animal looks more like that of a leopard, but the body is unmistakably striped. The image of the god ivy-crowned and riding the tiger is found in Spain, France, England, Germany, Italy, and the Balkans, as well as, of course, the North African provinces. In Tunisia, in particular, there are many beautiful mosaics depicting Dionysus as a child riding a tigress. The child on the tiger's back looks like a baby held on by a nurse or like a young boy who is part of a Dionysian procession.

ABOVE: *Triumph of Dionysus, a Roman mosaic from the House of Virgil, early third century* C.E.

OPPOSITE: *The child Dionysus riding a tigress, from the central section of a Roman mosaic in the peristyle of the House of the Dionysian Procession, mid-second century* C.E.

221

A second century B.C.E. mosaic from Delos, one of the oldest representations of the tiger in western art.

Other mosaics narrating the triumph of Dionysus feature the god, surrounded by satyrs and maenads and tame and wild animals, standing on a chariot that is usually drawn by two tigresses, although the sex of the tigers is not always clear. The magnificent panel in the Sousse Museum in Tunisia, dated third century C.E., is unique, with its four mighty tigresses. These images represent the golden age of Dionysus, during which peace prevails everywhere, even among the wild animals. As Luis Foucher puts it:

From his travels in India, Dionysus had brought back the tiger, which therefore is often associated to his cortege, and it must have tempted the artists for the exotic note that introduced in the composition. However, it seems that the artists were not very confident in replicating an animal which almost certainly they had never seen and which they drew copying from sketches more or less accurately.

The most lively of the series, unfortunately damaged, is the one from the House of Dionysus at Delos, which dates from the second century B.C.E. . . . Generally speaking, the African mosaics tend in their reproduction of the tiger to exaggerate the size of the hump on the back of the neck. . . . On the mosaic of Dionysus Pais riding a tigress, the boy's left leg hides this detail. The stripes on the neck and on the legs, in this mosaic, are drawn quite artificially, and the hind portion of the animal is rather heavy; in this respect the tigresses of the triumph of Dionysus from Sousse, which, like this one, seem to be tamed, come from a better reference.

Another favorite mythological theme is that of Orpheus playing such divine music on his lyre that all the animals, including the tiger, gather around him, mesmerized by the heavenly melodies.

Catching and Hunting Tigers

A mosaic of a "tiger walking in front of an olive tree," dated third century C.E., also from Sousse, shows a tiger with a large hump on its back. An even larger one appears in a mosaic featuring the "tiger attacking wild ass," from El Djem; it is as if the image of a walking tiger, with the typical protuberance on its back, had been copied onto the otherwise stretched body attacking the ass.

A beautiful and well-known panel from Ostia, near Rome, now housed in the Musei Capitolini, uses the *opus sectile*—a sort of inlay technique—and shows a "tigress savaging a calf." This panel was actually part of a pair, the second showing a "tigress savaging an antelope," though this second panel is partially damaged and of much inferior pictorial quality.

Mosaic floors featuring hunting themes became very popular in North Africa between the third and sixth centuries C.E. It has been suggested that the widespread preference for hunt mosaics can be ascribed to the allegoric significance of hunting as an image of the fight against evil and an emperor's triumphs over it. In Roman militaristic society, hunting was considered "an effective teacher of war," and hunters were "blessed and worthy of admiration." As one scholar put it, "Hunt mosaics are vivid testimony to the passion with which the ancient world pursued hunting as entertainment, leisure activity and virtue."

The tiger in hunting mosaics is generally portrayed as in the episode of the capture of the cubs, mentioned in chapter 5. This episode, with variations, remained a favorite for more than three centuries. The "Dermech Hunt," from Carthage, dated third or early fourth century C.E., shows a horseman with a cub in his hands, escaping from the enraged mother up the gangplank of a ship. From Antiochia and Apamea in Syria come some very interesting floor mosaics dated circa 450–520 C.E.: the "Worcester Hunt" mosaic decorated a large reception hall and also features the capture of a tiger cub. In this case, two small cubs accompany the tigress as she chases the huntsman, who is holding out the stolen cub as if to provoke the mother to follow him. The "Honolulu Hunt" was originally in a smaller room adjacent to the Worcester one—here the tigress has one cub and is also seen chasing a stag and doe. Classical scholar Christine Kondoleon explains, "Both floor mosaics are executed in what is known as the carpet style, an innovative phase in the development of late Roman mosaics in which figures and landscape elements are spread across a neutral background." In the "Megalopsychia Hunt" mosaic, a dramatic and pathetic note is introduced into the narrative: a huntsman armed with a spear is about to strike a tigress with two small cubs running next to her; one of the youngsters looks up to his mother as if searching for directions as to what to do.

Another very interesting and unusual mosaic, dated from the late fourth to early fifth century C.E. and found in the Carthaginian suburb of Khereddine, "The Offering of the Crane," represents a sacrifice to Apollo and Diana. In

TOP: *A tiger attacking two wild asses. A Roman mosaic from the triclinium of the House of Dionysian Procession, mid-second century* C.E.

BOTTOM: *A fourth century* C.E. *mosaic from Ostia, near Rome, depicts a tiger attacking a calf.*

ABOVE: *The "Worcester Hunt."*

OPPOSITE: *A detail of the "Great Hunt," an immense mosaic in the ambulatory of the Villa del Casale, Piazza Armerina, Sicily, 310–315 C.E.*

the register immediately above the gods is a pictorial description of a tiger hunt. In a naturalistic setting, one rider is about to spear a tiger that is holding onto its prey, while on the other side another rider is aiming his bow at a crouching tiger. This mosaic is remarkable for its overtly pagan content at a time when Christianity had already triumphed.

The most spectacular mosaic concerning the tiger is undoubtedly the "Great Hunt," from the Villa del Casale in Piazza Armerina, Sicily, which has been dated to circa 310–315 C.E. The Villa del Casale is a very large complex with a repertoire of floor mosaics of such impressive quality that many scholars have suggested that it could have been the residence of a Roman emperor.

The "Great Hunt" has many similarities to the "Dermech Hunt," and it seems probable that the same line of Carthaginian mosaicists worked on both. It occupies a corridor more than sixty meters (about two hundred feet) long, with an exedra (a recess in the wall) at either side.

Each mosaic presents a central feminine figure surrounded by animals. One, extremely damaged, has been identified as Mauritania, the other as India. India is surrounded by the animals best representing her—the elephant, the tiger, and the phoenix—and she holds an elephant tusk in her hand.

The narrative develops from the exedrae and converges towards the center, depicting hunting episodes positioned as if on different levels—some in the foreground, and others in the background.

Although it is called the "Great Hunt," in this long and complex narrative all sorts of exotic animals, such as leopards and lions, ostriches and an antelope, an elephant, a rhinoceros, a huge bull, a tiger, and a phoenix, are depicted as captured alive and carried within boxes or driven aboard ships, probably to be taken to Rome, where all these species would be shown in the amphitheater. A man, elegantly dressed and with assistants on either side, supervises the operations.

Here also we see the favorite subject of the huntsman

One of the exedrae, representing India, of the "Great Hunt,"
at the Villa del Casale, Piazza Armerina, Sicily.

holding a tiger cub while escaping from a tigress and riding up the gangplank of a ship, but in this variation the tigress is looking into a round object, inside of which is depicted a small tiger. There have been various interpretations of this image. The round object has been seen as a mirror, a shield, or a glass sphere in which the tigress could see her own reduced reflection, mistaking it for the stolen cub. A text of the fourth century C.E. by Saint Ambrose narrates the story as told by Pliny, with the variation of a glass sphere instead of the cub being thrown at the tigress. This trick would allow the huntsman to ride away to safety, taking the cubs with him.

One interesting interpretation of the "Great Hunt" sees it as a huge geographical map in which each animal is representative of the place it comes from. As C. Settis-Frugoni puts it, "Because all the places are so distant from each other, the result is an indirect glorification of the august buyer who can command such a costly operation."

The Great Palace of the Byzantine emperors in Istanbul has spectacular mosaics, which, according to some, are even more outstanding than those in the Piazza Armerina. They have been dated to the fifth century C.E. The tiger appears in three episodes: on one occasion, it attempts to devour a man; on another, a warrior attacks a tiger with his sword; and on third, a large and very fine tiger is being attacked by two men with spears. There is also a remarkable image of a phoenix with a tiger-like body devouring a lizard. All the animals in this mosaic are "conceived with a feeling for naturalism which is seldom equaled elsewhere."

This is only a brief overview of the surviving images of the tiger in ancient Roman mosaics. I believe it is the first time such a compilation has been done, and there is a tremendous scope in the future to develop this research and go into further detail about the amazing impact of the tiger in ancient times.

A detail from the "Great Hunt."

PAOLA MANFREDI has a background in anthropology and has been working in India for over twenty years on textiles, history, and cross-cultural influences on textiles. She also designs and produces handmade white-on-white embroidery. She has been associated for several years with the Ranthambhore Foundation, and she is active in conservation of endangered environments and species, particularly the tiger. She is the author of various articles on textiles and embroidery and she edited the book *In Danger: Habitats, Species and People*, published by the Ranthambhore Foundation in New Delhi in 1997.

A ragini (part of a musical score) in human form touches a pair of tigers. Indian musical traditions often assimilated the sounds of nature. The meter called "Sardula Vikridita" is based on the idea of tigers playing together. This eighteenth-century painting reflects the harmony that music can create between man and his environment.

The Tiger in Miniature Painting

Archana Verma

MUGHAL MINIATURES IN INDIA, typically ranging from four to ten inches in width and six to twelve inches in height, derived from the rulers' Persian predecessors. Babur (reigned 1526–1530), the founder of the Mughal empire, was a great connoisseur of art and carried with him to India as many paintings as he could from the library of his ancestors, the Timurs. Although many of these returned to Persia after Nadir Shah, the last of the great Central Asian conquerors, captured Delhi in 1739, Persian influence remained, most significantly that of Bihzad (born circa 1460) and his pupil Sultan Muhammad. Indian miniatures dating from before the time of the third Mughal emperor, Akbar (1556–1605), are very rare and are all versions of a Persian original. During Akbar's reign, few portraits were made—most of the portraits of Babur, Humayun (1530–1556), and Akbar that we have today are later copies of originals that are either no longer extant or themselves imaginative and stylized depictions.

Here we will look at the extraordinary richness of medieval Indian miniature art and show the various ways in which the tiger was perceived and depicted in these paintings.

Court Art as a Narrative of Imperial Grandeur

It was during Emperor Humayun's reign that two painters from the Persian or Safavid (as the ruling dynasty was known) palace, Abd-as-Samad and Mir Sayyid Ali, joined the Mughal court, first in Kabul (in modern Afghanistan) and later in India. But it was Humayun's son Akbar who really diversified the art of Mughal painting by asking these two artists to head a workshop and train court painters,

Tigers were often captured and brought alive to the royal court to symbolize the power of the ruler, as is depicted in this eighteenth-century painting.

known as Kitab Khana, in the Safavid tradition. Gradually, the Indian Mughal style became distinct from the previous traditions that had originated in Turkey and Iran.

Akbar loved this art and personally supervised the work of his painters, looking at the material every week and conferring rewards for excellence. He also identified particularly talented individuals, such as the Hindu painter Daswanth. The workshops functioned as a collective, with up to three artists executing a single work—one handling the coloring, another working on the composition, and the third the actual painting. Painters began to specialize, with some focusing on court scenes, others on battle scenes, and some on flora and fauna. Miskin was one prominent painter of birds and animals.

The life of those times emanated from the artist's

Akbar on a tiger hunt, from the Akbarnama.

brush. As miniature painting grew in popularity, hundreds of local artists were recruited from across Gujarat and Rajasthan. Local painting schools began to flourish—color mixing improved, and finishing touches became ever more exquisite. Akbar ensured that the artists got the best paper, brushes, and pigments. Names like Basawan, Kesu, Sanwala, and Mansur became famous ones. The most accomplished painters held privileged positions in the imperial court. Over the centuries, thousands upon thousands of miniature paintings were produced, and the survivors now live in hundreds of museums around the world.

In the early part of his reign, Akbar favored the illustration of literary and poetic works. His painters decorated manuscripts such as the *Hamzanama* (the story of Hamza, which relates the semimythical adventures of an uncle of the Prophet Muhammad). Executed between about 1562 and 1577, this work originally took 1,400 paintings, divided into fourteen volumes. In the 1580s, Akbar became interested in history, and alongside the literary works he had a series of historical texts written and illustrated, notably the *Tarikh-I-Khandan-Timuriyya* or *Timurnama*, the history of the Timur family, begun in 1584. The Mughal emperors claimed descent from Timur (or Tamerlane, the great Mongol conqueror), and this text narrates the story of the family up to the time of Babur, Humayun, and Akbar himself. A close study of the 137 illustrations shows that the artists were attempting to establish the Timur–Mughal connection, depicting the Mughals as the legitimate heirs to Timur's vast and glamorous empire and as the just and rightful rulers of India. Thus, art was placing itself at the service of Mughal ideology, with the painters becoming active promoters of their emperor patrons.

Around the same time, the *Baburnama*, the life of Akbar's grandfather, was translated from Turkish to Persian and presented to Akbar by Abdul Rahim Khan-I-Khanan, commander in chief of the Mughal army and an accomplished poet. At least four copies of this text survive, all richly illustrated with Mughal miniatures. Some time around 1590, Akbar's artists began work on the *Akbarnama*, the official version of his own reign. This work presents an unquestioning glorification of Akbar's political ideals. A second copy was made in 1604.

Portraying the Emperor

Akbar also started the genre of portrait painting. He sat for his own portrait and ordered portraits to be made of all his courtiers. Encouraged by this, the Kitab Khana gradually adopted an increasing realistic approach to portraiture.

Portrait painting became really popular during the reigns of Emperor Jahangir (1605–1627) and Shah Jahan (1628–1658). The figure is usually standing, with the face in profile. One of the most significant aspects of Jahangir's patronage was his patent determination to exorcise past

The tiger skin was thought to keep away evil and those who sat on it gained the power of the tiger, as this seventeenth-century painting of Hamza depicts.

An eighteenth-century painting of a tiger in its natural habitat in the dry deciduous forests of the Kota region of Rajasthan.

mistakes—such as his rebellion against his aging father, Akbar—through elaborate pictorial representations. Not only were artists expected to extol his grandeur, they were also required to give a glorified interpretation of historical events that often diverged from reality. Akbar is often painted in the form of a soul or in some mythical association with Jahangir, offering him the globe, a crown, or a royal insignia and thus symbolically legitimating his son's rule.

Another image that became popular during Jahangir's reign was one indicating the emperor's deep reverence for the holy men of India, both Hindu and Muslim. Paintings often depict him visiting and consulting sages, again symbolizing the rightfulness of his reign and also the supremacy of the spiritual realm over the temporal one. They were conscious attempts to obliterate the memory of

his rebellion and the murder of Akbar's venerable minister and chronicler, Abul Fazal.

Jahangir's son, Shah Jahan, continued the family tradition of commissioning paintings that extolled the legitimacy of the Mughals and documented the symbolic transmission of power from one monarch to his heir. But toward the end of his reign, it became fashionable to imitate all things European. The emperor obtained European paintings and had them copied by his court artists, and a European style began to pervade the Mughal miniatures. Halos appeared around the heads of the emperor and prominent sages, and European styles of depicting landscapes, perspective, and decorative elements were adopted. Great attention was also paid to minute and intricate details.

An eighteenth-century Kangra painting in which the tiger is an essential component of the progression of a narrative in the wilderness. The princess asleep in the forest and her waking when the prince leaves are part of a story that tells of complex exploits in the company of the tiger.

A twentieth-century painting of a hunting party
shooting at tigers both on land and from a boat.

Rani Budhawati hunts tigers in this eighteenth-century painting.

Hunting the Tiger—Image of a Powerful Royalty

Another way in which the Mughals' power was depicted was through hunting scenes in which the emperor or prince was shown fighting or killing a wild animal—often a tiger. The tiger in India has been symbolic of royalty and strength since very early times, and scenes depicting a royal Mughal overpowering or killing a tiger underlined both his sovereignty and his military prowess.

The hunting scenes were set either in a forest environment or in the dueling arena of the fort. Thus we find paintings depicting men on buffalo fighting tigers for the entertainment of the royal family. Although Mughal princesses were often given martial training, including training in hunting skills—Nur Jahan, the wife of Jahangir, was known to be a skilled huntress—Mughal paintings

of royal women rarely exhibited this aspect, since the portrayal of a princess often idealized her "womanly" qualities, which meant suppressing any sign of martial skills. However, we do have some paintings showing a woman shooting tigers or lions from the palace, suggesting that this was regarded as a suitable form of entertainment.

Miniatures from this period were varied in nature and showed the many ways in which a tiger could be hunted. Spears, swords, and guns were used. Swordsmen did the fighting, while gunmen stood by ready to shoot the tiger from behind. A hunter on horseback or elephantback might also pierce the tiger with a spear. The emperor is also shown hunting the tiger from the back of an elephant or a horse.

Some works do show sensitivity toward the tiger. There is an interesting painting of a deer being hunted by archers

An eighteenth-century painting of the story of the hunt for a tigress. The two cubs are unaware of their mother's predicament.

An eighteenth-century depiction of a maharajah hunting a pair of tigers from a tree as one tiger is in the process of killing its prey.

while a tiger hides in the grass, escaping their notice. In another painting, a feeding tiger is being shot at, and in another of the same group the artist has provided a ladder for the tiger to climb up a tree while a gunman shoots at him. These images underline the martial prowess and valor of the hunter and at the same time depict the tiger both as a symbol of strength and ferocity and as an animal used for sport and as a living creature in danger of being killed.

Diversification—the Rajput Genre

What is known as the Rajput miniature genre is an offshoot of the Mughal miniature school that developed in the early nineteenth century, when artists migrated in their thousands from the Mughal courts to various Indian principalities and received patronage there. The Mughals and the Rajput rulers had close alliances, encouraging a synthesis of their various art forms.

The Rajput school falls into two broad categories: the Pahari school, which came from the hills, and the Rajasthani school, from the plains. Within each category, a large number of local centers produced many variations. The Rajput school subject matter is taken largely from the repertory of the mythological and musical traditions of India. Some of the sources for the mythological themes were the great epics the *Ramayana*, the *Mahabharata*, the *Bhagavata Purana*, the *Gita Govinda*, and the *Pancatantra*. Poetic translations of ragas produced the *Ragamala*, an essentially Indian form of the "painting of music."

Depictions of the tiger in Rajput miniatures take different forms—the traditional symbolism of royalty and power; cultic and mythological images; and more realistic depictions of the tiger as a wild animal and in composite forms with other animals.

A painting of the school of Rajput miniatures of the eighteenth-century in which the goddess and the tiger defeat the buffalo, which represents evil.

An eighteenth-century painting of the goddess Durga on her mount. The tiger was believed to be the most powerful animal, and harnessing its power facilitated the defeat of any evil or dark force.

The Deity as Controller of the Tiger—an Image of Divine Power

In the paintings based on Hindu mythology, the tiger is depicted in association with the three major manifestations of the goddess: Parvati, Durga, and Kali. Some interesting paintings show Kali with a tiger or astride a tiger as Mahisasuramardini ("image of the goddess killing the buffalo demon"), while the traditional theme of Kali astride Siva (one of the Hindu trinity, depicted as an ascetic and often associated with the cremation ground) also appears. This shows Siva lying on a tiger skin, his usual garment in Hindu mythology. In early Hindu tradition, the lion was more often associated with Durga and Parvati, while Siva in the form of a corpse was linked with Kali. However, in the course of the medieval period, first Durga and then other manifestations of the goddess came gradually to be shown with the tiger as their vehicle. In the miniature paintings, it is almost always the tiger that is associated with the goddess.

One painting depicting Siva's household uses the tiger as a predominant motif. One section of it shows Siva and Parvati lying on a tiger skin, while another has Siva wearing a tiger skin. Their children, Ganesa and Karttikeya, are playing with Siva's vehicle, the bull-god Nandi, while Parvati's vehicle, in this case a tiger, sits nearby. Paintings of this type accentuate the image of Siva as an ascetic who associates with the animals of the forest and has their skin for his personal use. The presence of the tiger—the king of all land animals—underlines Siva's power.

ABOVE: *This painting lauds the power of the god Siva through both the skin of the tiger and its living presence.*

OPPOSITE: *An eighteenth-century Kangra painting of the god Siva's forest household.*

241

The Esoteric Image of the Tiger—Cult and Occult

Siva as a god associated with the forest creatures is an even more important concept in the Tantric cult (a cult that uses magical rites and rejects ordered social space, often following Kali as its patron deity with an aspect of Siva as her consort) and its art. It was easy for people to relate to this identity of Siva as an ascetic who stays in the cremation ground, smears himself with ash, drinks wine, and has spirits (*Ganas*) of various shapes and sizes as his attendants. The association of the animals of the forest with the spirits of the cremation ground was possible because of the fear and mystery inspired by both places. Often, the spirits were depicted along with animals such as the tiger and the snake, to make explicit their dangerous powers, which the Tantric practitioner aimed to control. One painting shows a *Gana*-like figure leading a group of elephant and tigers, demonstrating his power over these animals. Another shows a man with the face of an elephant holding the hair of a man who is thrusting his arm inside a

tiger. Yet another has two tigers being stabbed by a horned creature riding a horse. There is also a depiction of a tiger chariot, meant for the rider who can successfully harness the strength of the tiger. Paintings of this type reflect the conflict between the practitioner and the powers that he is attempting to master. It is a Tantric belief that before being subjugated, these creatures afflict the practitioner in many ways; he has to overcome their assaults before they accept his authority.

Because of the magical and mysterious qualities associated with the tiger, its image imparted an aura of a force that could destroy as well as empower the follower. Several miniatures highlight this aspect. One striking painting shows a tiger with a woman's face. Throughout history, woman has been perceived as a procreative and nurturing figure but also as a disruptive force in society if she is not controlled. Depicting a tiger with a woman's face highlights both its destructive and its protective qualities.

The Tiger in Legend and as a Symbol of Power

Miniature paintings also depicted various legends associated with the tiger. A very fine example of this is the Jodhpur palace collection, painted in the early decades of the nineteenth century with stories from the *Pancatantra* (an ancient text written by Visnusarma, which collated folktales with the intention of imparting to the sons of noble families both worldly wisdom and an understanding of government). These legends clearly depict the tiger as the king of the forest, showing him in a dominant position in relation to other animals, preaching to a group of jackals and leading them to a river. His prowess is also shown in his contest with a boar and in a painting of two tigers facing each other. In another painting, an owl that has been accepted as the king of birds is shown addressing an assembly of birds while standing on a tiger skin. This is a continuing motif from very ancient times, since in early historical texts the king was supposed to step onto a tiger skin at the time of his coronation. The Jodhpur palace collection also contains the famous painting of a donkey whose owner covered him in a

ABOVE: *A depiction of a ritual enactment of a folk story about good and evil in which tiger-striped animals are central to the fray.*

LEFT: *In this nineteenth-century work, the halo surrounding the head of a royal figure in a chariot signifies the special status that the tiger imparts.*

OPPOSITE: *An eighteenth-century representation of the feminine force of the tiger, showing the head of the tiger replaced by a woman's head.*

243

244

ABOVE: *An eighteenth-century painting of demons and a composite elephant from the Murshidabad district of West Bengal. The tiger's body and its tail merge perfectly with those of the elephant, thus lending power to the elephant.*

OPPOSITE: *An eighteenth-century composite painting from Murshidabad in which the camel has been stuffed with tigers to empower it to protect the princess on its back from evil.*

Three nineteenth-century
paintings from Jodhpur
illustrating the folk tales of
the Pancatantra.
RIGHT: *A donkey is dressed
like a tiger to give it power
and ferocity.*
BELOW: *An owl gives a
discourse to a flock of birds
while sitting on a tiger skin,
which provides it the
necessary power and status
to dominate.*
OPPOSITE: *A tiger bestows
his blessing on a cow by
tapping it gently on its head.*

smallest. The tiger is the most important element of this equation, for, as the *Mahabharata* says, "Without the tiger there is no forest, without the forest there is no tiger." When a princely figure is depicted riding such a camel, he is seen to embody the strength of the mightiest creature in his realm and also to sustain the ecological balance of the environment. The king is thus portrayed not only as a powerful controller of his territory but also as a channel for sustaining the life cycle of his kingdom.

Tiger: A Metaphor of Human and Natural Forces

The forms of depiction of the tiger in the miniature paintings in the medieval period of Indian history show that tiger was perceived not only as a powerful animal but that likenesses of it could be used to define the image of the ruler which underlined his martial qualities, his regal and often divine status, and his potential to control and sustain the territory he ruled. Often these images used violent metaphors to transmit this definition through the visual language. Notions of nature as omnipotent and mysterious, which the tiger represented, were also often intertwined with these images of power, especially in the cultic paintings. Scenes depicting human attempts to control and to hunt this animal, then, also communicate the human desire to control nature.

tiger's skin and turned him out to graze in the fields, where the people mistook him for a tiger and were afraid to drive him out. The *Pancatantra* paintings thus utilize the image of a tiger as a powerful creature whom the other animals recognize as their superior.

The miniature paintings also use the concept of a tiger's strength to show the prowess of a Rajput ruler. Thus, we have a painting of a king harnessing a tiger along with many other animals—an obvious indication of the monarch's power and strength.

There is also an interesting depiction of a camel carrying riders. The body of the camel is composed of several tiger figures, who are shown devouring smaller animals, linked to one another in a kind of food chain that forms the leg of the camel. At the end of the chain, the smallest animals, such as the hare, form the feet. This imagery symbolizes the "tiger-like" strength of the camel, which is capable of traversing the difficult desert terrain of Rajasthan. It also highlights the ecological equation represented by the "food chain," which begins with the tiger, the most powerful animal of the forest, and ends with the

ARCHANA VERMA completed her Ph.D. from the Centre for Historical Studies, Jawaharlal Nehru University, New Delhi, and is currently a visiting assistant professor in the School of Arts and Aesthetics there, teaching history of art. She has published a research article on the Bagh Caves in Madhya Pradesh and has presented a paper on the interface between the folk and colonial knowledge systems at the Indian Institute of Technology, Kanpur, in a seminar. She will present her work on the imaging of the goddess in Madhubani paintings at an International Conference on South Asia in Sweden in July 2004.

The Tiger As Inspriration

A View of the Tiger in Western Art

Rose Corcoran

Ranthambhore *by Rose Corcoran*

THE TIGER IS A FIERCE YET BEAUTIFUL ANIMAL, a creature that embodies all that is wild, an animal that fills our imagination. It has inspired artists throughout the centuries. But what exactly are the qualities that have provided this inspiration and how has the artist responded? To answer this question, I will examine some of the images that have inspired my own journey as an artist of the big cats. From the eighteenth century to the present day, science, history, drama, imagination, the artist's own psyche, and the partic-ular concerns of each era are reflected in the depictions of this fascinating animal.

To begin the journey, we literally go beneath the skin of the tiger and take a look at the extraordinary anatomical drawings of George Stubbs (1724–1806). Throughout his career, Stubbs was fascinated by anatomy, and though associated primarily with horses, he was also drawn to investigate more exotic species. As a result, his 1763 painting of the tiger kept in the menagerie at Blenheim Palace looked a lot more realistic than anything that had been offered up a century before. At the end of his life, he embarked on the immense task of comparing the structure of a human body with those of a tiger and a common chicken. This scientific approach reflected the growing curiosity of his contemporaries concerning the natural sciences and the desire to investigate and classify the vast array of species in the natural world. Stubbs's anatomical drawings of tigers are exceptionally beautiful. He strips the body down layer by layer and draws what he sees until he reaches the animal's bare bones. He records the workings of the tiger's vascular system, its musculature, its tendons, and finally its skeleton, and thus he begins to understand the functioning of this exotic creature and goes beyond mere observation to a more complete knowledge. His drawings are detached and painstakingly observed; they must have involved considerable physical effort for a man in his seventies. However, his anatomical studies should not be seen only as aids to his painting. Throughout his life, Stubbs felt that nature itself was the truest source of inspiration, and it was this that compelled him to investigate the fundamentals. Stubbs's approach and these informative yet beautiful drawings have been essential inspirations in my own quest to understand the workings of a tiger's body.

Portrait of the Royal Tiger *by George Stubbs*

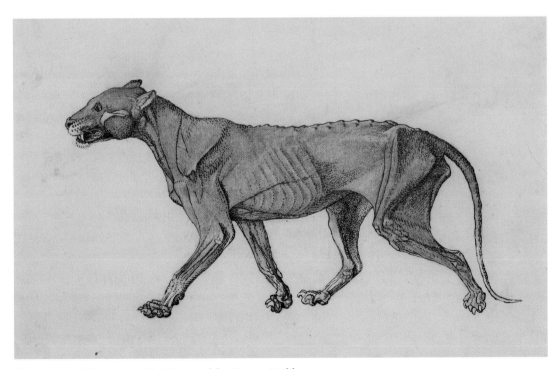

Tiger, Lateral View, Partially Dissected *by George Stubbs*

Isaac Van Amburgh and His Animals *by Sir Edwin Landseer*

Study of a Tiger *by Sir Edwin Landseer*

Though perhaps best known for his lion sculptures in Trafalgar Square, the Victorian painter Sir Edwin Landseer (1802–1873) was another brilliant observer of animals. He often gave his subjects human attributes and had a tendency to sentimentalize or romanticize what he saw. He prided himself, however, on his practical knowledge of both domestic and wild animals, and like Stubbs, he dissected them. (He once had a dead lion delivered to his house, where it was studied, then subsequently stuffed and the skeleton articulated and set up for future study.) In 1839, he painted *Isaac Van Amburgh and His Animals*, which I first discovered as an image on a postcard in the Victoria and Albert Museum. Struck by its beauty and the fact that it portrays not only tigers but leopards and lions as well, I have had it stuck to the wall of my studio ever since. Isaac Van Amburgh was an extraordinarily talented animal trainer of Dutch/American descent who took London by storm in 1838. It was said that he could lie down in a cage with all his big cats, whom he was said to rule with love, though Queen Victoria, who was much taken with him, remarked that the animals "seem to love him, though I think they are in great fear of him." In the painting, the relationship between Van Amburgh and the tiger is particularly interesting. The snarling beast with its ferocious teeth and claws has been placed in the center of the picture, and it draws us into the scene, but Van Amburgh's hand is firmly clasping the skin on the tiger's head, and he is clearly the dominant force. Gone is the objective observation of Stubbs's approach; although Landseer had an exceptional gift for the depiction of animals, he was also a man of his times, and this painting seems to reflect the Victorian urge to dominate and subdue the wilder and more exotic forces of nature.

In contrast, a French contemporary of Landseer, Jean-Léon Gérôme (1824–1904), painted nature in a realistic but more detached manner, concerned with "what" he saw rather than "how" he saw it. He traveled widely in Turkey, Egypt, North Africa, and Spain, painting the exotic scenes that he encountered, including many wonderful paintings of big cats. There are two in particular that I find both fascinating and moving. The first, *The Grief of the Pasha* (1882), is an illustration of a poem, "La Douleur du pacha," from *Les Orientales* by Victor Hugo. In it, the poet repeatedly asks why the pasha is so sad, only to be answered by the recurring line, "Son tigre de Nubia est mort." The painting shows a dead tiger laid out surrounded by roses on an oriental carpet in a Moorish courtyard. By his side sits the mourning pasha with his head in his hands. The heaviness of the beautiful dead animal reflects the weight of the pasha's grief—the loss of this great and noble creature has touched his soul. Gérôme has realized an image of overwhelming sadness with such sensitivity that it has acquired the magical quality of a scene from the *Arabian Nights*.

The Grief of the Pasha *(top) and* Whoever You Are, Here Is Your Master *by Jean-Léon Gérôme*

251

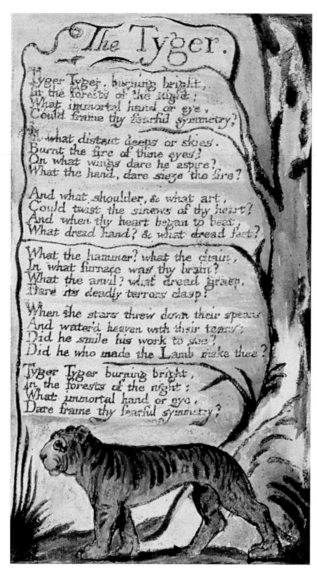

"The Tyger," plate 43 from Songs of Innocence and Experience *by William Blake*

The second work—*Whoever You Are, Here Is Your Master* (1889)—depicts an angel standing amid a group of big cats. The cats are all looking at the angel except the lion, who is looking at a tiger rolling around in the foreground and who himself is looking at the viewer. The tiger is clearly a compositional tool to bring the viewer into the painting, but it seems significant that it is only the tiger who seems unruffled, and perhaps even a little mischievous, in the presence of the angel; the other cats are curious but made slightly nervous at the strange apparition. In the time leading up to this work, Gérôme had lost several members of his family and close friends in a flu epidemic, and it is possible that the painting contains a spiritual element, showing his awareness of the power of God and of death. Unlike Landseer, who emphasizes man's will to dominate the wilder forces of nature, Gérôme here seems to reflect on a higher level on the inherently spiritual power of nature.

Thinking of my own sources of inspiration, I have been unable to ignore the poem "The Tyger" by William Blake (1757–1827). Blake as both an artist and a poet was able to express his imagery with equal power in either words or pictures, and he dressed his poems in color and design to make an artistic whole. "The Tyger" is a wonderfully evocative poem that I have known for as long as I can remember, and it is always there in the back of my mind when I am drawing. Blake is concerned with so much more than mere wonder at the tiger's existence. He presents a universe in which great cataclysmic contradictions exist side by side—dark and light, creation and destruction, rage and celebration. He imbues the tiger with all of these qualities, so that it not only becomes a creature of dark primeval energy but also reaches to the stars and the sublime and so symbolizes the most extreme forces in human nature and the world. At the time Blake wrote the poem, reports of the French Revolution were horrifying people in Britain; the revolutionaries were often described as ravening beasts and even specifically referred to as tigers. However, I feel that in this case the image does not match up to the strength of the words of the poem.

A Young Tiger Playing with Its Mother *by Eugène Delacroix*

Later, Blake foreshadowed a new direction in the arts that was to result in Romanticism when he wrote "the tigers of wrath are wiser than the horses of instruction." Eugène Delacroix (1798–1863) was the greatest French painter of the Romantic movement and reacted against the formality and rigidity of the neoclassical painting of his time. He believed in expressing his imagination, thoughts, and feelings in his work. It is not therefore surprising that throughout his life lions and tigers fascinated him, because they seemed to personify his philosophy that art should be wild, free, and untrammeled by constraints such as those of the neoclassicists. He was even described as looking like a tiger by Théophile Gautier, a leading critic, who said Delacroix "had tawny, feline eyes, with thick arched brows and a face of wild and disconcerting beauty; yet he could be as soft as velvet and could be stroked and caressed like one of those tigers whose lithe and awesome grace he excelled in portraying."

Early in his career, Delacroix produced a beautiful painting, A *Young Tiger Playing with Its Mother*, which was unusual in that later he preferred to emphasize the power and ferocity of the animals and avoid literal truth to nature, as in *Two Studies of a Struggle Between a Lion and a Tiger*. This early work is life-size and shows how Delacroix was training himself to observe animals accurately and to gain a deeper understanding of them. He drew constantly from life, working in the Jardin des Plantes in Paris and with the animals owned by the trainer Henri Martin. The mother tiger in this painting was drawn from one of Martin's, named Atir, of whom it was said that, "though large and powerful, it was neither ferocious nor cruel, as its reputation would suggest, but affectionate and playful." In 1829, Delacroix made an exquisite study of a resting tiger and another of one alert and seeming to look straight out of the picture. In just a few strokes, Delacroix captured the gentleness and beauty of the resting tiger and the arrogance, dignity, and sheer presence of the alert one, who stares out with a boldly uncompromising gaze.

(Detail) Two Studies of a Struggle Between a Lion and a Tiger *by Eugène Delacroix*

Tiger *by Eugène Delacroix*

However, most of his work on lions and tigers appeared after 1840, by which time he was giving a lot of thought to humanity's relationship with nature. Unlike in Landseer's conception of humanity's place in the scheme of things, in Delacroix's scenes of lion hunts and Arabs being attacked by lions, people do not dominate. Instead, they reflect what Delacroix saw as the eternal battle between humanity and animals, civilization and nature, reason and passion—in other words, between the ideals embodied in neo-classicism and those of Romanticism. There is no doubt that Delacroix was truly inspired by felines when he wrote, "Tigers, panthers, jaguars, lions . . . whence comes the movement caused in me by the sight of them?"

Delacroix often drew in the Jardin des Plantes with the sculptor Antoine Louis Barye (1796–1875). Like Delacroix, Barye was drawn to the feline form, and he sculpted representations of the big cats throughout his life. He drew constantly from nature and studied anatomy, gaining an encyclopedic knowledge of the structure of animals. "Observe nature," he said. "What other professor do you need?" Delacroix greatly admired him and said, "I shall never be able to give the curl to a tiger's tail as that fellow can." Barye, too, was a Romantic, and for him the animal was not purely a subject but a means of conveying his ideals. In 1831, he produced *Tiger Devouring a Gavial*, about which Théophile Gautier was inspired to exclaim, "What energy, what ferocity, what a thrill of satisfied lust for killing shows in the flattened ears, the savage gleaming eyes, the curved nervous back, the clutching paws, the rocking haunches and the writhing tail of the tiger, and how the poor scaly monster doubles in agony under those cutting teeth and jaws." Here Barye embraced the image; this is a tiger in all its predatory ferocity, its faculties alert and channeled, strong, muscular, and true to its nature. In startling anatomical detail he portrays the victor and the vanquished not only as parts of an allegory of life

Tiger Devouring a Gavial *by Antoine Louis Barye*

Great Royal Tiger *by Rembrandt Bugatti*

Siberian Tiger *by Rembrandt Bugatti*

and death but as accurate renditions of exotic animals and their behavior.

Thirty years after Barye's death, Rembrandt Bugatti (1884–1916) emerged to take on his mantle as a passionate sculptor of the feline form. Like Barye, Bugatti was an avid student of zoology and drew and sculpted directly from the animals in the Jardin des Plantes and in the Copenhagen Zoo. The Copenhagen Zoo was quite literally his studio. He became friendly with the keepers and was allowed into the zoo when it was closed to the public, and he spent hours feeding and talking to the animals. From my own experience, I cannot emphasize enough the importance of studying animals from life, for without intimate knowledge of their energy and agility and their individual characteristics, one cannot successfully portray them. Bugatti's sculptures have a quality that I constantly strive for in my own work. His *Siberian Tiger* vividly captures the strength

of this great cat, so that one can almost see it pacing around its cage. Similarly, his *Great Royal Tiger* seems to hold in its lithe, strong body and powerful shoulders all that the sculptor had observed in his years of study. It is infused with a feeling of pent-up frustration, vividly evoking the image of a great cat in the confines of captivity. Bugatti had not failed to notice that tigers would not settle into new surroundings in quite the same way as other cats. For me, his simple impressionistic sculptures convey the very essence of the soul of the feline; he is one of the most inspirational and gifted animal artists of the twentieth century.

I cannot write about tigers in art without mentioning Henri Rousseau (1844–1910). Rousseau seems to have been an enchantingly naïve and gentle soul who lived mostly in his imagination and only partly in the real world. Philippe Soupault said of Rousseau that he was "a Painter in every sense of the word ... not anxious to paint for the

Tiger in a Tropical Storm *by Henri Rousseau*

sake of painting. . . . For him there was no question of technique or influence—he had only to dip his brush in his heart." Rousseau and other French artists of the eighteenth and nineteenth centuries had great enthusiasm for exotic animals, which they painted realistically and in naturalistic landscapes. Like other artists, such as Delacroix, Barye, and Bugatti, Rousseau spent hours in the Jardin des Plantes in Paris, which housed a zoo as well as the botanical gardens that gave the park its name. There, they were able to study big cats at close quarters. Rousseau added the luxurious greenery that he found in the hothouses of the gardens, even though these did not represent the type of vegetation in which a big cat would really be found. Though Rousseau never ventured outside France he was a great reader of travel books. His study trips to the Jardin des Plantes sent his imagination spinning off into another world, out of which came paintings such as *Tiger in a Tropical Storm*. It was the ferocious nature of the tiger that inspired him—in this picture the tiger is a wild, frightening beast with large white teeth, blood-red gums, and staring eyes. According to Guillaume Apollinaire, "[Rousseau] sometimes frightened himself so much when he was painting his wild animals that he had to rush to the window for fresh air." This tiger is savage and only partly real, living in a strange jungle, and its nature seems to be reflected in the raging tropical storm. The whole scene is like a child's fantasy, permeated with a poetic magic, as if the viewer were looking through a window into a wonderland. As Grey Roch said, "His pictures are his dreams as the character of his brain ordained he should reveal them."

While Rousseau appeared to live in his imagination freely and unselfconsciously, Salvador Dali (1904–1989), a generation later, made a wholly intellectual decision to attempt to transcribe onto canvas the images thrown up from his unconscious. As a contributor to the Surrealist movement, he aimed to present irrational, dreamlike, or nightmarish images from his psyche in a hyperrealistic manner. His painting *Dream Caused by the Flight of a Bee Around a Pomegranate, One Second Before Awakening* (1944) is a typical example of his work. Here, two splendid tigers burst forth from the mouth of a fish, which in turn is emerging from a pomegranate. The tigers are violently aggressive, seeming to leap out of the canvas roaring, their teeth bared and their claws unsheathed. In a way similar to Blake's, Dali uses the tigers to represent a thought or feeling, but for him they are not grand universal concepts but personal projections of his unconscious mind; for ourselves, we can make of them what we will. Collectively, we will unquestionably understand that Dali's fearsome image represents a powerful, ferocious, and dynamic urge.

William Blake said, "Inspiration and vision was then and now is and I hope will always remain my element and my eternal dwelling place." For the artist, inspiration is what animates the work; without it, true creativity is impossible. Here, I have looked at a handful of artists inspired by the tiger who have been influences on me. Through their responses to this magnificent animal, it has been possible to see something of themselves, their imaginations, and their attitudes to nature, as well as of the times in which they lived. As an artist of the twenty-first century, I am confronted primarily with the potential tragedy that the tiger, this great source of magic and inspiration to so many millions of people the world over, faces the real possibility of extinction. I am only too aware that, in the words of William Beebe, "The beauty and genius of a work of art may be reconceived, though its first material expression be destroyed; a vanished harmony may yet again inspire the composer; but when the last individual of a race of living things breathes no more, another heaven and another earth must pass before such a one can be again."

ROSE CORCORAN graduated from London's Royal College of Art in 2000 and has had exhibitions in Paris and London. Working predominantly in charcoal and pastels on a large and at times monumental scale, she seeks to evoke the essence and vitality of the big cats. Her work takes her to India on a regular basis.

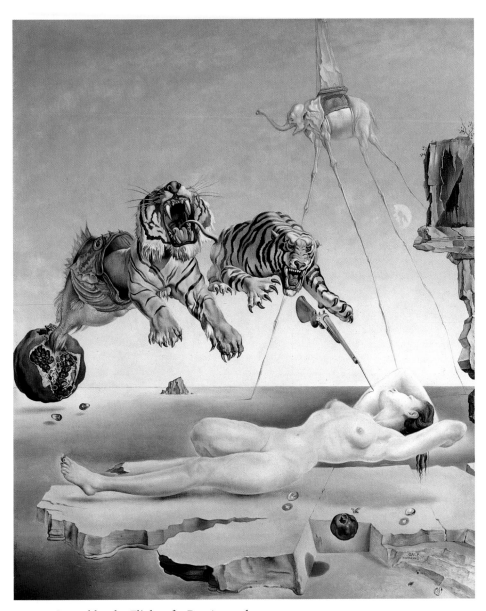

Dream Caused by the Flight of a Bee Around
a Pomegranate, One Second Before Awakening
  by Salvador Dali

CHAPTER 7

The Tiger in Western Literature

EMBLEM, PRISONER, FICTION

Ruth Padel

THE TIGER FIRST ENTERED WESTERN LITERATURE as a fanciful, third-hand, distant image based on travelers' tales: a creature of imagination, like a dragon. What changed over time was how people saw this image: how it mutated and grew when they actually saw tigers; what they brought to their idea of it; and how they used the image then.

The energy of western writing often depends upon its imagery. At least, Aristotle thought so, back in the fourth century B.C.E. Sanskrit, however, which is so rich (I am told) in the vocabulary of art, has many words for imagination (such as *kalpana*, meaning "fancy"), which have rather more varied verbal roots. In the *Balaramabharatam*, a text on dramaturgy dating from the eighteenth century, the art of the actor or creative artist consists in *Bhavananubhava*: imaginative experience. *Bhavana*, "the power of imagining," has an important connection to *bhava*, "feeling." There may be enormous and fascinating gulfs here between cultures and languages in the ways they perceive imaginative understanding and relate imagination to other areas of experience. But among the western heirs of practical-minded ancient Rome and of Greece, whose word *phantasia* is related to *phainomai*, "I appear," the visual image is the prime basis of that perception. For better or worse, English is the language-home of the empirical tradition. Its concept of "imagination" is related to Latin *imago*, "appearance": meaning "what is seen," either with the physical eye or with the inner one. The real tiger was unavailable, so the image, at first, was everything. The changing ways in which European writers saw and imagined tigers is deeply intertwined with the ways painters represented them.

So how did painters represent tigers? In the Middle Ages, most Europeans who saw a picture (or received a physical description) of a tiger got it from a bestiary, a didactic book based on the classical Physiologus (produced by Aristotle, among others) of animals both real and (as we now know) imagined. Bestiaries were illustrated by people who had little to go on and drew griffins, basilisks, and snakes with legs, as well as animals we now agree are real. Their point was allegorical and symbolic. Their beasts were emblems for moral or spiritual truths about human beings.

In the bestiary as in heraldry, where an animal's supposed shape and nature symbolized human traits, biological errors abounded. Lion cubs were supposedly born dead; their parents breathed life into them. But every bestiarist enjoyed refuting his predecessor. "It hath been falsely supposed," said Edward Topsell combatively in his early-seventeenth-century *Historie of Foure-footed Beastes*, "that all Tigers be female and engender by copulation with the wind."

Even early on, in Anglo-Saxon texts, "tiger" is a byword

for cruel ferocity. A tiger is bloodthirsty, savage as a force of nature. The distant unknowable places inhabited by tigers added to the power of their image. "Egre as is a tygre yond in Ynde," wrote Chaucer in the fourteenth century. Shakespeare's Romeo, in the sixteenth, breaks into Juliet's tomb to kill himself. His "fierce intents" are "savage-wild," he says; fiercer "than empty tigers or the roaring sea." Macbeth wants the ghost to take any terrifying shape but that of murdered Banquo. He would not tremble, he boasts, at "the rugged Russian bear, / The armed rhinoceros or the Hyrcan tiger." But tigers are also occasionally said to be brave in their raging. "Imitate the action of the tiger," Henry V tells his troops before battle.

The bloodthirsty-ferocity cliché persisted for centuries. In Bach's *St. Matthew Passion* (1727), Jesus in the dock is "a lamb in the tiger's claws." An eighteenth-century encyclopedist who never saw a tiger explained that it was "more ferocious, cruel and savage than the lion": "Though gorged with carnage, his thirst for blood is not appeased. He seizes and tears in pieces a new prey with equal fury and rapacity, the very moment after devouring a former one; he lays waste the country he inhabits."

Behind this rhetoric, mixed in with mistakes, are traces of travelers' tales that included real observation: "When he kills a large animal, as a horse or a buffalo, he sometimes does not tear out the entrails on the spot; but to prevent any interruption, he drags them off to the wood, which he executes with incredible swiftness. This is a sufficient specimen of the strength of this rapacious animal." But the author corrupts this nugget of observation with ignorant moral judgment: "Neither force, restraint or violence can tame the tiger. He is equally irritated with good as with bad treatment: he tears the hand which nourishes him with equal fury as that which administers blows: he roars, and is enraged at the sight of every living creature. Almost every natural historian agrees in this horrible character."

As tigers came into European menageries, the bestiary tradition was supplemented by observation. Menageries became an exciting resource for visual artists—for Albrecht Dürer, for instance, and for Leonardo in Milan. This had a knock-on effect on writers, too.

By the beginning of the seventeenth century, there were zoos all over Europe. James I's favorite item in the Tower menagerie was a tiger presented to him in 1613 by the ambassador of Savoy. It arrived on July 1 with a lioness and the remains of a lynx "that died upon the road." Other royal tigers in London were housed at Bankside at the Paris Gardens.

In the eighteenth century, the tiger's literary profile in the West, and people's feelings about tigers, began to expand. One of the "leopards, or tygers" in the Tower menagerie (as in many languages and cultures, spots and stripes are often confused) had been there "ever since Charles Second's time but is now in decay," said John Strype, writing the entry in a new edition of John Stow's *Survey of London* on this (no doubt horrible) royal zoo: "The other very beautiful and lovely to look upon, lying and playing, and turning upon her back wantonly when I saw her." By 1741, two tigers named Will and Phillis were kept there. So was their son, a lone cub named Dick. The playwright Oliver Goldsmith (1728–1774) described the Tower's tigers as "fierce and savage beyond measure," but he, clearly, was seeing what he expected to see.

William Blake (1757–1827) was a very different story. He added many things to the ferocity cliché, and among them, at last, beauty. For centuries, beginning with the Greeks, the West had endowed the tiger only with the thin, crass image of cruelty. Now, in the masterpiece of a genius, it got a whole glittering tapestry of emotional and religious symbolism all at once.

Blake may have made the effort to see the Tower tigers. He could also have seen the tiger exhibited in Leicester House during his early years as a child; his parents lived around the corner in Green Street. His tiger painting in *Songs of Experience* (which were published in 1794) is a more accurate shape than many seen at the time. But he may simply have known George Stubbs's painting of a tiger in a menagerie. It hung in Pars' Drawing School in

London's royal menagerie, 1816.

London, which stood at 101 the Strand, and acted as the preparatory school for the Academy of Painting and Sculpture in St. Martin's Lane; and this was where his parents sent him when he was ten.

Whether he saw this painting or real tigers in a cage, Blake was a true Enlightenment artist. To understand his tiger, we need the full layout of his imagination. Born the son of a hosier in a Dissenting and nonconformist household—that is, one holding strong Protestant views, but reacting against Church of England coziness and gilded ceremony—he was later caught up in the anti-Catholic Gordon riots. He was passionately excited by the French Revolution and spiritual radicalism, but also fascinated, technically and emotionally, by all aspects of physical creation. He illustrated the *Botanic Garden* of Erasmus Darwin; he took a keen interest in contemporary scientific ideas and new technologies, like geology, the production

of iron, the power of magnetism, volcanoes, electricity, and the stars.

But though he explored profoundly the scientific rationalism of the day, Blake cared most about the spirit. He was deeply conscious of the parallel between human art and divine creation, and identified God's creative process with that of the human artist. Plato had imagined the world created by a demiurge; Blake saw the Creator in similar terms, as a divine blacksmith, rather like the Greek god Hephaestus, the gods' furniture-and-statue maker. Blake's God is the connection between the technological, or the making of the world, and the moral: a connection that bears crucially upon the problematic nature of human beings.

Blake also thought deeply about physical making. That was his job. He was a printer, working with metal, fire, and words. But as the son of a nonconformist urban artisan, he also thought passionately about the social and industrial misery he saw around him. He felt its causes were demonic. Satan, he said, was "prince of the starry mills." Factories in his poem "Jerusalem" were "dark Satanic Mills." His images of beautiful creation had to address the origins of destruction, pain, evil, and savagery, in man and in the world.

This is where the tiger comes in. Blake imagined the *Songs of Experience* as a satire on his *Songs of Innocence*, published five years earlier. Formally, ostensibly, they were (or were like) children's poems. He etched some of them on the back of the copper plates on which he engraved the *Innocence* poems, writing backwards.

He had to write backwards, as part of the printing process. But "backwards" is also a metaphor for the way *Experience* resees the material of *Innocence*. Together, said his title, the two sets of poems showed "The Two Contrary States of the Human Soul," the coexistence of good and evil, in ourselves.

For Blake, too, was going to use the tiger emblematically, as an image of nonanimal qualities. It is very hard not to, when an animal has come from an unknown, mainly unimaginable other world. In his *Proverbs of Hell*, Blake says, "The tigers of wrath are wiser than the horses of instruction." Unless you see the real tiger in its own wild context, the animal's potential as a symbol for ideas about human things will outweigh what you learn about its reality.

Of all the relations between the poems that speak to one another across these two sequences, *Innocence* and *Experience*, that of "The Tyger" to "The Lamb" best encapsulates Blake's whole point: the relationship of knowledge (including knowledge of evil) to lamblike innocence.

Within that relationship, Blake's tiger took up an intricately ambiguous position, becoming capable of representing many different, maybe incompatible, things at once. Having stood simply and crudely for ferocity, the tiger now blossomed as a symbol into many open-ended and uncertain possibilities of meaning. Critics have interpreted

"the tyger" as industrialization; as the French Revolution, the violence of which was intended to redeem an oppressed society; as nuclear power and the splitting of atoms (Blake is credited with clairvoyance here); as technology; as the narcissistic self-admiration of our own human savagery. This is one of the most argued-over poems in the English language, and there is no right answer to its questions nor to understanding the ways in which it may mean them. Yet whatever else it is "about," "The Tyger" is concerned with creativity and with its use of the supreme creative and destructive world force, fire. It suggests that wherever there is a making, there is also pain and the potential for violent destroying. Ferocity and vulnerability, risk and beauty, creation and destruction, all come into the "tiger" package.

One question the poem is certainly asking is, Where does creating come from? ("What the hand, dare seize the fire?") If God is the benign Creator and His world is good, why bloodshed, violence, burning? Why war imagery and the need for pity? Why *did* stars throw down spears and water heaven with tears?

Blake's tiger fire also seems to be imagination: maybe human, maybe divine. The tiger is becoming an image for imaging itself. Imagination, too, has to be approached cautiously: what you make with it, whether a poem or a revolution, can turn and rend you. The created tiger, "burning bright," is kin to the violence that made it. Whoever created it had to "seize" something both beautiful and lethal:

> *What the hammer? what the chain?*
> *In what furnace was thy brain?*
> *What the anvil? what dread grasp*
> *Dare its deadly terrors clasp?*

This ambiguous poem could not have been made without the poet's sense of the animal's overwhelming beauty, yet its explicit awe is for the physicality behind it and a divine physique that made the tiger:

And what shoulder, & what art,
Could twist the sinews of thy heart?
And when thy heart began to beat,
What dread hand? & what dread feet?

Despite its beauty, the animal stands also for destructive violence. The combination of its qualities, as Blake imagined them, sum up the created coexistence of good *and* evil, beauty *and* savagery, both in ourselves and in the world God made.

Emblem of Energy, Sexuality, Imagination

By the nineteenth century, the British presence in India meant new physical consciousness in Britain of tigers, if only as animals to be shot. Tiger skins flooded into cities. The tiger's beauty was appreciated, but as a trophy or drawing-room ornament. To the hunters, the tiger was the highest animal adversary, so the military values of the day meant it became an image of courage as well as of savagery, something to be admired as you destroyed it.

Yet the tales of shooting did include some naturalist's observation, some understanding of the tiger's own motivation. It was not simply all the time a cruel, bloodthirsty monster. This dynamic was embodied by Jim Corbett, whose natural gifts as a writer made *Man-Eaters of Kumaon* (1944) a literary classic that also offered insights into what made tigers man-eaters, the pressures on them, their real lives, and their sufferings.

This came after a century in which Europe developed a slow-growing compassion for, and the beginnings of understanding of, all animals. At the same time, there were social reforms about how to treat animals, a move expressed in literature by seeing things from the animal's side, giving animals voices. These works can come across as sentimental now. Anna Sewell's *Black Beauty* was written in 1877, Felix Salten's *Bambi* in 1926. But as writing they were innovative, imaginative, and influential. *Black Beauty* had enormous impact on horse management in England.

And this writing often appeared in the newly dynamic genre of children's literature. It may not be an accident that both "The Tyger" and Rudyard Kipling's *Jungle Books* (1894–1895) were ostensibly aimed at another unfranchised class that was slowly being given a voice: children.

Shere Khan the tiger is, of course, a villain in *The Jungle Book*. But he is also the vehicle by which Mowgli comes to the jungle, as if the tiger's jaws were a necessary part of arriving where you belonged. In *Winnie-the-Pooh* (1926), A. A. Milne translates tiger ferocity into the undirected excess energy of Tigger; he is well meaning but bouncy: ferocity turned funny and cuddly. The early twentieth century is aware, of course, of the irony. In Evelyn Waugh's *Brideshead Revisited* (1945, but set in part in 1920s Oxford), the cynical Anthony Blanche sees through the hero's jungle paintings. They are, he says, simply "creamy English charm, playing tigers." And so are the endless soft toy tigers today.

In popular western imagination, and therefore in its literary imagination, too, the clichéd tiger ferocity gradually mutated into admirable wild energy. This could be associated with out-of-control drunken dreams—in the nineteenth century, a dive that sold illegal alcohol was called a "blind tiger." But it was also a sacred, yearned-for energy. "God invented the cat," said Victor Hugo, "so man could touch the tiger."

Why should we want to touch the tiger? Because the tiger was becoming the West's extreme image of physical, exquisite, savage energy, at a moment when the western world was beginning to worship the jungle (or, rather, how it perceived the jungle.) The century's music was ignited by "African" jazz rhythms in Stravinsky's *Rite of Spring* (1913). Harlem clubs in the 1920s were advertised as re-creations of jungles.

The tiger is still not itself in all this; it is an emblem for a human quality, but its perceived qualities are newly valued; in, for example, the 1967 film *Le Samouraï*. "Only the tiger in the jungle," says Alain Delon, "is as lonely as the samurai." Esso and Exxon still tell us to "Put a tiger in your tank." Gird yourself in tiger energy, pour it into your

BULDEO LAY STILL, EXPECTING EVERY MINUTE TO SEE MOWGLI TURN INTO A TIGER, TOO.

Illustration from a 1901 edition of Rudyard Kipling's The Jungle Book.

car. Or into yourself: Kellogg's tiger on the cereal box zooms in over amber wheat flakes in the bowl, to show what energy you will have when you eat them. The upper notes in a recent orchestral piece by the British composer Judith Weir titled "Tiger Under the Table" (2002) are underpinned by what she describes as a "furious bassoon," which refers, she explains, to the "exceptional energy in the bass register." "Tiger economies" are all-conqueringly energetic. The phrases "paper tiger" and "shabby tiger" suggest ferocious energy faked or betrayed.

But the twentieth century evolved another aspect to this energy, a quality that the West, increasingly explicitly, admired. The essayist and novelist G. K. Chesterton (1874–1936) called the tiger a symbol of "terrible elegance," but it was not only beauty that made tiger skins

popular in Britain before the Second World War. The mix of tiger beauty with tiger energy led to a third quality, which still hangs around the tiger's image in the West today. We do not say, "He's a lion in bed." He is a tiger. In the early twentieth century, the tiger became a symbol of rampant sexuality.

In 1907, the romantic novelist and Brighton beauty Elinor Glyn published a novel called *Three Weeks*. It was not a brilliant bit of writing, but it shocked everyone and enjoyed rocketing sales, mainly because it described a love affair consummated on a tiger skin. It inspired the anonymous lines, "Would you like to sin / On a tiger skin / With Elinor Glyn?" Glyn later wrote *It*, which became a silent movie about sex appeal that made Clara Bow famous, and three other novels with racy female protagonists. But despite her fame (and the sales of *Three Weeks*), Glyn was annoyed by the reception of her tiger-skin effusions. "The minds of some human beings are as moles," she wrote crossly, "grubbing in the earth for worms. Those who look beyond will understand the deep pure love and Soul in *Three Weeks*."

Deep pure love, however, was up against the zeitgeist, and its appetite for tiger eroticism. In prewar bohemian London, a model called Betty May made her career out of playing tigers. Her party trick was lapping a saucer of brandy on all fours, and she was known as Tiger Woman. "I am sure I am born for adventure," she says in her 1929 autobiography of that title, which carries a photo of her, black hair over her face like an unbrushed Mowgli about to bite. Born in the East End, May caught the eye of the sculptor Joseph Epstein, modeled for him, joined the Parisian underworld, tangled with cocaine, and landed up in Aleister Crowley's Satanist cult in Sicily. She did have competition: a blond dancer called Jessica Valda nicknamed herself Puma. But a puma cannot compete with a tiger, and Betty May remained the most famous of the many bohemian beauties courting a precarious living in the prewar Café Royal.

Imagination and the Cage

George Stubbs may have unwittingly painted the cage bars he saw into his tiger's stripes; Eugène Delacroix and Henri Rousseau gave their zoo tigers a wilderness or jungle background; twentieth-century poets, however, focused on what they saw standing between them and the wild animal: the cage itself. They identified with the animal's imagined fury at it. Reared on the taking-the-animal's-side pulse in children's literature, they brought to the big-cat image all sorts of other associations, including anger and frustration at being enclosed, as Bagheera the black panther was held in a king's cage at Oodeypur in *The Jungle Book*. He had a bare place on his throat where the jeweled collar had rubbed; eventually, he set himself free: "I broke the silly lock with one blow of my paw."

In September 1905 a young German poet became secretary to the sculptor Auguste Rodin. One day, he confessed to his master that he had a block; he had not written a poem for a long time. Go to the zoo, said Rodin, following the tradition of the visual artist inspired by the menagerie. Go and look at an animal "until you really see it."

The result was one of the twentieth century's most famous poems, "The Panther," in which Rainier Maria Rilke (1875–1926) marvels at a leopard's power and beauty:

> *the movement of his powerful soft strides*
> *is like a ritual dance around a center.*

He sees the leopard's jungle vision dimmed by the bars. "There are a thousand bars, and behind the bars, no world."

Half a century later, Ted Hughes responded to Rilke in his poem "Jaguar":

> *His stride is wildernesses of freedom:*
> *The world rolls under the long thrust of his heel.*

Hughes picks up Rilke's image of a beauty and power that belong in the wild but stresses the rage as well as cage.

In a sense, these poems are on a continuum with Blake's "The Tyger." They look intensely at the wild cat; they "really see," in Rodin's words, its living beauty. They also see how misplaced it is in a cage. But they, too, implicitly use the animal as an image for something in the human spirit: not destructive (the twentieth century knew more about human potential for destructiveness even than Blake) but imprisoned, unfulfilled.

And yet, ever since Blake, there had been another aspect of the tiger image running through western imagination, though not one that was obvious to British subalterns, trooping out with guns to shoot a tiger. In the West, a tiger was the most glamorous representative of the nonindigenous wild. And so tigers became a conscious image for the exotic, the elsewhere; or for imagination creating the elsewhere in oneself.

To the American Imagist poet Wallace Stevens (1879–1955), imagination was "the power that enables us to perceive the normal in the abnormal, the opposite of chaos in chaos." His poem "Disillusionment of Ten O'Clock" (1923) pictures conventional people at home at the end of their day, pressured to be like everyone else. Even in dreams they are caged, not free. They do not "dream of baboons and periwinkles." Out on the street, however, an old sailor, "Drunk and asleep in his boots," conjures up in his stupor the exotic dreams he once had in far-off places. In his alcoholic haze, he "Catches tigers / In red weather."

That "red" could mean many things, but it certainly suggests the power of imagination. Unlike the people caged in their houses, and in boring "white night-gowns," the tramp-like sailor is colored and enriched; saved, by dreaming of tigers, from the caging "disillusionment" of modern living. Catching tigers in red weather is an image for imagination and dream.

And with dream, we move on to the tiger's greatest western fabulist.

"There Are No Words That Can Rune the Tiger"

Jorge Luis Borges (1899–1986) sums up western experience of tigers. Meeting them in images, words, and zoos, he thrilled to them in imagination, investing them with the motifs of his extraordinary internal universe.

Borges was born in Buenos Aires but learned English before Spanish; his imagination was European and he was profoundly influenced by English and American literature. His mother was a translator, his father a lawyer and psychology teacher of Italian, Jewish, and English heritage. He grew up in a house with a library and garden, which laid down important external features of his imaginative landscape. In 1914, the family moved to Geneva, where Borges learned French and German and received his degree. After World War I, the family lived in Spain, where he published his first poem, in the style of Walt Whitman.

In 1921, he settled back in Buenos Aires and began his career as a writer. From the late 1930s to 1946 he worked at the Buenos Aires Municipal Library. Sacked by the Perón regime, he was appointed poultry inspector for the municipal market but from 1955 to 1970 taught literature at Buenos Aires University.

Borges was entranced by the idea of the philosopher George Berkeley that the sensible world consists only of ideas that exist as long as they are perceived; that the "real world" may be only one in an infinite series of realities. These ideas inform his fictions. So, side by side with them, do tigers. He was obsessed with tigers in childhood, and they often appear in his work.

As a child, Borges drew tigers incessantly. He adored going to the Buenos Aires Zoo. It always smelled, he wrote, "of candy and tigers," and he had to be dragged away from the tiger cage. In Borges's work, the tiger often symbolizes unattainably absolute physicality: pure sensuality, which lives in a world without language. He was not afraid of tigers, but he was afraid of mirrors. There were three large ones in his bedroom as a child. "I saw myself in the dim light thrice over," he once wrote, "afraid the three shapes would begin moving by themselves." He was scared, apparently, of being repeated or replicated. Mirrors became his emblems of the other, the double: what might happen on the other side of reality and the possibility of different identities.

In the short story "The Writing of the God" (1949), the markings on a "tiger" contain a secret divine message. The story is told by an Aztec priest imprisoned by the Spanish. In the next cell, there is a jaguar (*tigre* in Spanish), "which with secret, unvarying paces measures the time and space of its captivity." The prisoner remembers that on the first day of creation his god wrote a magic phrase somewhere, and one of the names of his god was *tigre*: "I imagined my god entrusting the message to the living flesh of the jaguars, that web of tigers, that hot labyrinth of tigers, bringing terror to the lanes and pastures in order to preserve the design."

Over the years, he learns the spots on the "tiger's" skin

by heart: "Black shapes mottled the yellow skin. Some made circles; others formed transverse stripes on the inside of its legs; others, ringlike, occurred over and over again—perhaps they were the same sound, or the same word." Gradually deciphering the sacred text, he reads the secret of the universe hidden in the markings on the "tiger." But he no longer remembers who he was, because now that he has seen "the burning designs of the universe," he has a different identity. So, he says, "Let the mystery writ upon the jaguars die with me."

"Blue Tigers" (in *Shakespeare's Memory*, 1983) is set in India in 1904 and told by a Scottish professor of eastern and western logic at the Lahore University, whose love of tigers brought him from Scotland to India. It opens with the idea that "there are no words that can rune the tiger," and draws on Borges's childhood obsession with tigers to sketch the speaker's character:

I have always been drawn to the tiger. As a boy I would linger before one particular cage in the zoo; the others held no interest for me. I would judge encyclopedias and natural histories by their engravings of the tiger. When the *Jungle Books* were revealed to me I was upset that the tiger, Shere Khan, was the hero's enemy . . . In my dreams I always saw tigers.

He reads that a blue tiger has been discovered in the Ganges delta and starts to obsess about tigers again, though has apparently done nothing about this love that drew him to India since he came to Lahore. He wonders what "blue" means. Could the animal be a black panther? The London press published a fantasy, a blue tiger with silver stripes, which was obviously rubbish. He starts to dream blue tigers, whose color, like the tiger itself, could not be described in words. "I saw tigers of a blue I had never seen before, and for which I could find no word."

Then a colleague says he has heard there were blue tigers in a village some way away from the Ganges. He decides to go see and arrives at a village below a flat hill. Praising the locality emptily, by saying that its fame has reached Lahore, he sees the villagers' faces change. He

feels they possess some secret. Maybe, he thinks, they worship the blue tiger and he is not supposed to know. He says he wants to see it. They look at him strangely, stupidly; they seem frightened. Then he says he wants to capture it, and they seem relieved. They start waking him at night, saying it has been seen. But he always turns up just as the tiger has gone. They show him a track, a pugmark, broken twigs; he begins to suspect these signs are faked.

These traces remind Borges's reader of that first idea, that no words can "rune" the tiger: that it is impossible for marks made by human writing (as opposed to the divine writing on the tiger's skin in the earlier story) to represent the reality of the world, or of the tiger.

He is told the hill cannot be climbed. There are magical obstacles blocking the path. He would be in danger; he might see some divinity he should not see, or go blind, or mad. So he climbs it alone at night and finds a crevice filled with little stones, which are exactly the same indescribable blue as the blue tiger of which he originally dreamed. He pockets a handful of them and returns to his hut.

The stones begin to send him mad, for they are obsessively impossible to count. They keep multiplying: they are another Borges image of sinister, ungraspable replication. The villagers say they are "the stones that spawn," whose color they are forbidden to see except in dreams. He leaves the village and keeps trying in vain to count the stones, but they "destroy the science of mathematics," and he, of course, is a logician. He prays in a mosque to be free of them and off-loads them on a blind beggar, who assures him he may now "keep wisdom, habits, the world"—everything he felt the blue stones taking from him.

The blue tigers of this fable are an open image. Like all symbols in Borges's mysterious fictions, they could stand for many things. But one thing they certainly stand for is the beautiful danger—which Borges associated with tigers—of an obsessive dream. It can deprive you of your "habits," your sense of order and logic, of "the world."

The voice of Borges's more apparently autobiographical

piece "Dreamtigers" (*The Maker*, 1960) says that when young, the writer was "a fervent worshipper of tigers." Like the speaker in "Blue Tigers," he lingered for hours in front of their cage at the zoo and judged encyclopedias "by the splendor of their tigers." "The tigers and my passion for them faded" after childhood, "but they are still in my dreams." When he realizes he is dreaming he says to himself, "I am going to bring forth a tiger." But it never works. "Oh incompetence. My dreams never seem to engender the creature I so hunger for. The tigers that appear are all wrong. Too small, wrong shape, or flimsy." Again, the Borges tiger is connected with the limit and failure of dreams, with how impossible it is truly to visualize or write the real.

Borges's poem "The Other Tiger" also argues that human imagination cannot make the tiger real. The poet imagines a tiger and longs to touch the physical, language-less animal itself; but he cannot. He is not in a jungle. He is in that archetypal Borges space, a library. Writing a poem about a tiger, this poem discovers, means failing to write the real tiger, its power, innocence, and footprints in the mud. Thinking of the tiger puts the library's books at a distance for the poet, between the poet sitting in a library in South America and a real tiger in India beside the Ganges. All he can do, he tells the tiger, "is dream you." But the tiger he dreams is "made of symbols and of shadows." It is "a set of literary images, / scraps remembered from encyclopedias." The poem tries to conjure the real thing, the tiger living its tiger life, but only succeeds in making what human beings do make, a fiction. The real tiger is "out of reach of all mythologies."

This poem is about reaching for the reality behind the symbol and never being able to get there, not even with all the resources imagination can draw on: tradition, language, a library, encyclopedias (that great Borges image of the ordered but bafflingly endless repository of knowledge), or poetry and myth.

There is a cage here, but it is not the physical bars that Rilke and Hughes saw around the animal. The animal is fine, and free. It is human imagination that is caged, doomed to the "ancient, perverse adventure" of struggling to touch reality in language, bridging the gap between the image and the real.

The poet rejects the image tiger, created out of fragments floating from the leaves of encyclopedias. He yearns to see the tiger as, in Rodin's words to Rilke, "it really is."

But he never can. Borges's tiger is the image of all images that most brings human imagination, and human words, up against their own limit, reminding us that we cannot reach the real.

As It Really Is?

So where does this leave the tiger in western literary imagination? Throughout, it has been an image for things other than itself, in which developing western literary consciousness saw reflections of human nature through the centuries. Once the animal's living beauty made an impact, there was a shift from symbol of simple ferocity to other symbolizing: it could stand for creativity, imagination, or the reality that imagination cannot reach. It came to symbolize more human qualities as more accurate information about tigers, and personal zoo observation, trickled into the tradition, and especially as the culture changed—as savagery, associated with energy and sexuality, was increasingly admired. But as Borges's poem points out, human self-images and verbal secondhand ideas do not really come up to the tiger itself.

I suspect that Blake did see tigers in the Tower menagerie. His poem, more than any other, is full of awe at the tiger's presence. But his main purpose, like everyone else's, is symbolic. Apart from "The Tyger," no western writing breathes the sense of the tiger *as itself* that you get, for example, from the passage below from Jim Corbett.

Corbett is engaged not in allegory but in compassionate observation, writing not about himself or human nature but about a tiger. It is not great literature. But it does have writerly power, which comes from the fact that in his often rather stiff, conventional language, Corbett implies but never foregrounds his own (clearly very strong) feelings about what he sees. Above all, he is writing, as none of the others did, about what he knew.

In the following passage from *The Temple Tiger* (1954), Corbett is tracking the Chuka Man-Eater, who killed a lot of people in the Ladhya valley in 1936. He is up a tree watching a kill. But the tiger that arrives is not the one he expects.

A tigress came into view, followed by two small cubs. This was quite evidently the first occasion on which the cubs had ever been taken to a kill, and it was very interesting to see the pains the mother took to impress on them the danger of the proceeding and the great caution it was necessary to exercise. Step by step they followed in her tracks; never trying to pass each other, or her; avoiding every obstruction that she avoided no matter how small it was, and remaining perfectly rigid when she stopped to listen, which she did every few yards....

Passing by my tree she lay down on a flat piece of ground overlooking the kill and about thirty yards from it. Her lying down was apparently intended as a signal to the cubs to go forward in the direction in which her nose was pointing, and this they proceeded to do. By what means she conveyed to them the information that there was food for them at this spot I do not know, but that she had conveyed this information there was no question. Passing their mother—after she had lain down—and exercising the same caution they had been made to exercise when following her, they set out with every appearance of being on a very definite quest....

The blowflies disclosed its position and at length enabled them to find it. Dragging it out from under the leaves the cubs sat down together to have their meal. The tigress had watched her cubs as intently as I had and only once, when they were questing too far afield, had she spoken to them. As soon as the kill had been found, the mother turned on her back with her legs in the air and went to sleep....

When the cubs finished their meal they returned to their mother and she proceeded to clean them, rolling them over and licking off the blood they had acquired. When this job was finished she set off ... for there was no suitable cover for the cubs on this side of the river.

I did not know, and it would have made no difference if I had, that the tigress I watched with such interest that day would later, owing to gunshot wounds, become a man-eater and a terror to all who lived or worked in the Ladhya valley and the surrounding villages.

How Borges would have loved to be up that tree with Corbett. Blake, too. We can only wonder what, had they been, they might have written.

RUTH PADEL is a British poet and a Fellow of the Royal Society of Literature. She has won the U.K. National Poetry Competition and published six poetry collections. A classical scholar, she taught Greek at Oxford, Cambridge, London, and Princeton universities.

The author is grateful to Ayappa Paniker for his observations on the conceptual relationship between Bhava *and* Bhavana.

CHAPTER 8

The Future of the Tiger

In the twenty-first century, saving wild tigers poses an enormous challenge. As human populations encroach more and more on traditional tiger ranges, economic, political, and conservation issues intensify, escalating the need for strategies for preserving the delicate balance between human and wildlife communities. This chapter outlines the historical conflicts between man and tiger that nearly wiped out the tiger in the last few centuries—especially the hunting of tigers that not only killed untold numbers but injured and disabled thousands more, resulting in sharp increases in man-eating. In examining the encounters that gave rise to the wholesale decimation of some tiger species and the serious depletion of others, we will better understand how to protect this majestic animal, and what is at stake for human beings should we fail to do so.

THE MAN-EATER

People came into conflict with the tiger as many as two hundred years ago, when human populations began to grow at an exponential rate, thus encroaching on the tiger's territory and consuming the prey that tigers depended upon. Perhaps the most dramatic result of this shift was the sharp increase in the incidence of tiger attacks on and consumption of people. One of the earliest records is that of Sir Hector Munro's son in the Sundarbans. This extract appeared in *The Gentleman's Magazine* in 1793.

OPPOSITE: *A tiger bounds through a grassy meadow in central India.*

> I heard a roar, like thunder, and saw an immense tiger spring on Munro who was sitting down. In a moment the head was in the beast's mouth and he rushed into the jungle with him. . . . Mr. Munro came up to us, all over blood and fell. We took him on our backs to the boat. . . . He lived twenty-four hours in the extreme torture; his head and skull were torn and broken to pieces and he was wounded by the claws all over the neck and shoulders.

In the nineteenth century, the conflict between tigers and people reached its peak, as thousands of tigers who were wounded but not killed by hunters' bullets became unable to kill their usual fleet-footed prey.

ABOVE: *An early-nineteenth-century hand-colored engraving of a tiger attacking people on boats in the Sundarbans of eastern India.*

Singapore and the surrounding area was a network of swamps and jungles. Tigers had crossed the straits from the Malay mainland and established themselves there. As more people arrived, conflicts with tigers started as lands were claimed for human use, much as had happened in the Sundarbans in India. By the 1840s, two hundred to three hundred Chinese laborers were killed each year, and on some of the small islands between Singapore and the mainland the figure was said to be six hundred to eight hundred. These numbers naturally dropped off over the course of the next century as humans exterminated tigers from the islands.

Korea reported some man eating as well. In 1891 eighteen people were killed in one village alone. As forests were cleared and railroads created, many of the first settlers on the borders of Russia and China lost their lives to tigers, though there was little evidence of man-eating tigers in the regions themselves.

While this problem cropped up across the tiger's range, India, which had a high density of both tigers and humans, was the site of the most intensive tiger hunting, reporting vastly more incidents of accident and death due to tiger-human conflict. In 1822, in the Khandesh district of Bombay Province, five hundred people and twenty

N° 633   Dimanche 17 Janvier 1909   Prix : 15ᶜ

Journal des Voyages

JOURNAL HEBDOMADAIRE
146, Rue Montmartre, PARIS (2ᵉ)

et des Aventures de Terre et de Mer

LA MORT DE SAÔ
PAR MARCEL PIONNIER.

Derrière cette jungle impénétrable, « Ong-Kop », monseigneur le tigre ! achève l'horrible drame en dévorant sa proie ..

N° 633. (Deuxième série.)   N° 1645 de la collection.

thousand head of livestock were killed, chiefly by tigers. In 1877, when tigers killed 798 people in India, only sixteen were killed in Burma. Few such incidents occurred in Thailand and Sumatra. There were some tiger-related deaths in Vietnam, but nothing compared to the frequency of man eating in India.

In the early part of the twentieth century, Jim Corbett pursued some of the most notorious man-eaters in India. He describes the fear people felt of such tigers: "Every one of the hundred or more inhabitants of Thak had fled, taking their livestock with them. So hurried had been their evacuation that many of the doors of the houses had been left open. On every path in the village, in the courtyards of the houses, and in the dust before all the doors were the tigress's pugmarks."

In 1908, human fatalities totaled 909. A single tigress held the record of killing seven hundred people; she was herself killed in 1915. The United Provinces were home to the Champawat tigress, who killed 436 people, and several other tigers who accounted for more than 150 human deaths each. At this time man eating accounted for an average of eight hundred to one thousand human deaths per year. And the figure crept up: in 1922, it was 1,603, though in 1927 it came back down to 1,033.

An 1807 engraving of a tiger entering a village in India in search of vulnerable prey, human or animal—an increasingly common phenomenon as humans encroached on the tiger's traditional hunting grounds.

In Malaysia in 1930, fifteen people were killed by tigers, compared to more than one thousand in India in the same year. South China was a problem area—in 1922, sixty people were killed in the space of a few weeks in Fukien Province, where there was little prey left, the tiger's forests were being pulled down, and tigers stalked the villages. According to the missionary H. R. Caldwell, the man-eater on this occasion was "blue" in color. Local people called man-eaters "black devils," so they could have been black tigers, which are rare but still found today. According to one source, nearly seven thousand deaths caused by tigers were reported in a five-year period in the 1930s.

In all, between 1800 and 1950 across the tiger's range, more than 130,000 people died from tiger attacks. In the same period, at least 160,000 tigers were killed. The numbers increased with the arrival of the automobile, which made the forests more and more accessible. In aggravating the situation by cutting farther and farther into the tiger's territory, man was creating man eaters. By the mid-1940s, however, tiger attacks had become exceedingly rare, though in February 1943 a tigress in the Nowgong district of Assam in India attacked eighteen people within thirty-six hours, killing eleven of them.

The invention of the motor vehicle made more forest areas accessible to the hunter and led to a sharp decline in tiger populations across their range. They were killed by the thousands and strapped to bonnets of cars in what was thought to be "royal style."

In another case in Assam in 1950, a tiger attacked fourteen people in a single night, killing three of them. But both of these tigers are thought to have been rabid.

When tiger shooting was banned in India in 1970, the incidence of aggression toward humans and man eating had decreased drastically, except for ten to twenty fatalities in the Sundarbans each year. The infrequent incident of a tiger stalking and killing a human does still occur: in the late 1970s, for example, a tiger in Dudhwa National Park plucked a motorcycle rider from his vehicle and killed him. But ever since the ban, there have been fewer bullet-injured animals roaming around, desperate for food and unreliable in temperament because of the pain they are suffering. When human disturbance is minimal, tigers are much less likely to be aggressive. When humans are no longer in the role of tiger killer, the tiger no longer plays the role of human killer.

THE FIRST LEGISLATION

The earliest laws concerning forests and game were the Elephant Preservation Act of 1873 and the Wild Birds and Game Protection Act of 1878, which was revised in 1912. For the first time in India, hunting quotas and closed seasons were introduced; there were times of year when it was permitted to shoot a male deer, for example, but not a female, who was likely to be breeding. These laws were initiated by, and passed largely for the benefit of, the hunting lobby, which had begun to realize that its quarry was in danger of being wiped out.

By the 1920s, demands for the creation of "protected areas" were growing, spurred by an act of carnage even more devastating than the massacre of the tigers. World War I had rocked the world and wiped out a generation of young men. It had also taken a toll on India's forests. A vast amount of timber had been cut down to built ships and railroads, destroying huge tracts of wildlife habitat. The automobile was now making its entry on the tiger-hunting scene, causing ever more disturbance. In the 1920s, human populations rose sharply, with birth rates soaring and mortality levels coming down. Pressure on the forest increased, and those who sought to protect India's wildlife embarked on an enormous struggle.

For the first time game preservation became an issue in India. The Bombay Historical Society, founded in 1883 and today the largest nongovernmental organization (NGO) on the Indian subcontinent engaged in nature-conservation research, played a vital role in triggering the debate—its leaders wrote to forest officers and sportsmen for their opinions, and a series of editorials in the society's journal created an awareness of the need for conservation. People had finally begun to notice that wildlife numbers were decreasing. (Remember that by this time uncontrolled hunting had exterminated tigers from the Punjab, for example.) There was much discussion about the concept and feasibility of game sanctuaries. But those who cared remained in the minority—few people yet believed that there was any need for protected areas.

However, the years between 1927 and 1937 saw a sudden spurt in writing about what some considered a rapidly developing wildlife crisis. The Indian Forest Act of 1927 contained new rules and guidelines. Discussions about shooting rules, closed and open seasons, the creation of game-preservation societies, the protection of monitor lizards, and how different regions should create new laws to protect species became frequent—all largely due to the development of the Indian infrastructure. As the railway network expanded rapidly, its demand for wooden sleepers kept up the pressure on the forests. At the same time, a major program of road building caused havoc to wildlife as hunting cars specially designed for the maharajahs entered the forests.

By 1939, Great Britain, which still ruled India, was engaged in World War II, which brought with it another period of seemingly endless timber cutting; the contractors involved eliminated wildlife with a vengeance, ignoring the regulations that governed any given area. The war overrode all other concerns, and what attention the British could spare from it was occupied by the indigenous struggle for independence. It is estimated that more than three hundred thousand cubic meters (10.6 million cubic feet) of sal wood alone was cut in the war years. India gained its independence in 1947, shortly following the end of World War II. As the British prepared to leave, the priorities of the moment relegated concern for the forests to oblivion.

POSTINDEPENDENCE INDIA

The years following independence brought devastation to Indian wildlife. Travel agencies, mushrooming across the world, lured hunters from far and wide. Forests were rapidly cleared in the name of the magic word "development." The maharajahs sought to fulfill their dreams of hunting tigers and creating records. It was a free-for-all in which few laws were followed or enforced. Even worse, every forest officer's training commenced by shooting a tiger. One such officer was Kailash Sankhala, who later became India's first director of Project Tiger. When the head of India's forest service ordered, "Shoot your first tiger in your first year," Sankhala went out to do so. He describes the event:

> I levelled the "cannon" and as he switched on his torch I fired. With a deep-throated "Oonooh" the animal jumped into the bush. Peacocks called and langurs whooped, then after a time there was silence. The smoke of the black powder persisted over the machan as I flashed my torch over the buffalo carcass. It was not there. A moan came from the bushes; evidently the tiger had been hit. A thousand thoughts flashed through my mind: the tiger cubs which used to come to our house, the mock beat of forest trainees as they tried to flush animals from the forests adjacent to Forest College. Was it courage, or cold-blooded murder in the dark? The picture of the tigress's beauty haunted me, and with every groan from the bushes my feelings of guilt increased. Not surprisingly I did not sleep, and when the crows called and sunlight lit the valley once more I found it difficult to wear a brave smile when I saw the tiger dead, his legs up and his eyes open. He seemed to look in my eyes and ask the reason for his death. "Is this sport, when all the rules are in your favour?" I could not even bluff myself that he was a man-eater or even a cattle-lifter. Humbled in guilt I touched his body to beg his pardon. Even today the scene is as fresh as it was that morning, and the open eyes of that tiger have haunted me all my life.
>
> I never repeated that murder, and to overcome my guilt I have dedicated my life to the cause of tiger preservation.

Sadly, few people felt as Sankhala did, and many tigers met their deaths at the hands of forest officers.

One of the biggest battles fought in post-independence India was to initiate the creation of a department of wildlife. R. W. Burton, an Englishman who stayed on after independence, spearheaded this battle, sending two long notes along the corridors of power in New Delhi. Burton saw the solution to India's wildlife problems very clearly. He wrote, "Without a wildlife department as suggested herein the survival of much of the wonderful wildlife of India is inconceivable and a great national asset will disappear never to be regained, as the majority of the unique species will become extinct."

By this time it was clear to many conservationists that saving wild tigers meant creating the right laws and enforcing them, as the only deterrent to the future depletion of wildlife. The Bombay Historical Society and an early Indian conservationist named Humayun Abdullali played an important role in drafting and steering through the groundbreaking legislation that became the Wild Animals and Wild Birds Protection Act of 1951. This in due course formed the basis of the Wildlife Protection Act of 1972. Indeed, most of the spadework for current Indian wildlife legislation was done in the early 1950s.

The years 1953 to 1955 were critical for India's wildlife. Big dams and hydroelectric projects were undertaken, which Prime Minister Jawaharlal Nehru believed were the temples of modern India and would lead to rapid development. These ripped apart large tracts of irreplaceable forest; Nehru was not aware of the vital importance of wildlife and the forest. India had to wait another decade for a politician who cared about the tiger—ironically, it was Nehru's daughter.

In the meantime, it was the beginning of the end for the tiger in China. Where its population was around four thousand in 1950, it fell to hundreds by the late 1960s. Over the decades, the tiger had been treated as a pest to be exterminated. It never recovered. And although India remained the most popular destination for tiger-shooting safaris, hunters also went into the forests of Southeast Asia. By the 1960s, the tigers of Bali were extinct, shot out by hunters. The tiger in Java soon followed. All that was left of one subspecies were the tigers of Sumatra.

IN THE NICK OF TIME

In India, however, things were about to change. George Schaller had just finished the first scientific study of the tiger, which was completed in 1965, and some of his findings were startling enough to have an impact on conservation. The era of the hunter was about to end.

In 1966, Indira Gandhi became prime minister, and by 1968 she had taken quick action to save tigers and the wilderness. The export of tiger skins was banned in 1968, and a ban on tiger shooting followed in 1970. The 1972 Wildlife Protection Act precipitated a tiger census, and most tiger watchers were shocked to find that only 1,800 remained in the wild in India. A special project to save the tiger, born out of a 1969 International Union for the Conservation of Nature and Natural Resources (IUCN) conference in New Delhi, was launched in September 1972 by Prince Bernhard of the Netherlands. It was known through most of the world as Operation Tiger, and in India as Project Tiger. The campaign traveled across the world, and it soon became socially unacceptable in many countries to use or wear tiger skins. Ceremonial drummers of the armed services in Britain replaced their tiger-skin aprons with artificial ones. Also at this time, the IUCN created CITES—the Convention on International Trade in Endangered Species of Flora and Fauna—which, among other things, compiled lists of endangered species. The CITES agreement, which outlines a complete ban on the trade of some animals and regulates the terms of trade of plant and select animal species, was quickly adopted by several countries and has since been ratified by more than 150 more.

In eighteen months, Operation Tiger raised $1.8 million, out of which a substantial donation was made to India's Project Tiger. By 1973, India had nine tiger reserves. Malaysia, Thailand, and Indonesia all expressed their desire to create more tiger reserves. Bhutan created the Manas Tiger Reserve in Assam. Nepal also banned tiger shooting and created its first protected areas. Radio telemetry had just been invented, and from 1973 tigers were tracked using radio collars in Chitwan National Park in Nepal. Thirty tigers were radio-collared over the next decade. Scientific studies began to pick up across the continent. India followed in the steps of this research, but not until much later. It was also in 1972 that Indonesia protected its vulnerable population of Sumatran tigers, and by 1976 peninsular Malaysia had done the same. Sadly, it was too late to save the Javan tiger.

In 1979, even China decided to join IUCN and became a member of CITES. Bangladesh, Nepal, and the USSR started special tiger-protection schemes, enlarging some of their forest tracts into reserves. Guy Mountfort spearheaded Operation Tiger and oversaw the first years of its success. Looking back, he wrote in his book *Saving the Tiger* (1981):

> It was a remarkable demonstration, by a large number of relatively poor Third World countries, of their awareness of the importance of protecting their natural heritage. Can we in the affluent West question their decision to spend money and effort on such a cause? Was it wrong to hasten to help them achieve such a goal? I think we had a duty to do so, because, as the Prime Minister of India said at the 1979 Symposium, the tiger campaign "was not just for the survival of our heritage of wildlife, but also for the survival of man." And this, I believe, is the real answer to the question.
>
> As for the cost involved, one has only to compare it with what the nations of the world are willingly spending on new weapons of destruction. In 1978 military expenditure amounted to £212,000 million ($530,000 million). Saving the tiger and its habitat will have cost, taking everything into account, less than the price of a single short-lived modern bomber aircraft. Or to put it another way, the equivalent of about the cost of seven miles of a six-lane highway. One may ask which of these represents the best long-term investment for humanity. The tiger is part of everyone's heritage and I, for one, am proud to have played a part in the crusade to save it.

INDIRA GANDHI AND THE IMPACT OF HER POLICIES

The 1980s were perhaps the best decade of modern times in India for the tiger. Indira Gandhi's policies were beginning to have an impact, and the tigers were flourishing. The 1980 Forest Conservation Act played a crucial role in preserving habitat. By 1984, it was believed that there were four thousand tigers in India, compared with 1,800 in 1972. But when Indira Gandhi was assassinated in 1984, India's forests, tigers, and wildlife lost their greatest supporter and spokesperson.

Without Indira Gandhi there surely would have been no ban on the export of furs in 1968 or on hunting in 1970. There would have been no Wildlife Protection Act of 1972 and no Project Tiger in 1973. The hunters would have continued to enjoy a free-for-all, and by 1975 they would have taken a toll from which the tiger might never have recovered. Without the Forest Conservation Act of 1980 I doubt if any of India's primary forest would have survived another five years. India would have been a desertified and barren landmass with no wildlife. Critical water problems would have been magnified and river systems severely depleted. Rampant diseases, infection, flood, and drought would have followed. India would probably have ended up with ten or twelve national parks and twenty sanctuaries instead of the seventy-five parks and 475 sanctuaries in existence today. A natural treasury would have been plundered unmercifully, and extinctions would have been frequent.

The laws and amendments that were made in Indira Gandhi's era were checks and balances to the total anarchy that followed. Many politicians have subsequently tried to weaken them, but fortunately, in the absence of political will, judicial will came to the fore to interpret the existing laws correctly and keep the forests of India protected. Of all the politicians who followed Indira Gandhi, only her son Rajiv Gandhi tried to strengthen the environmental laws and amended the Forest Conservation Act in 1988. Since his party lost the election of 1989, little has happened except for some controversial amendments that dilute the processes for the final legal declaration of National Parks and Sanctuaries to the Wildlife Protection Act in 1991. In fact, much of the impact of conservation legislation has been diluted administratively and through government orders.

If India has any ecological security left, it is because of Indira Gandhi. Her vision surpassed that of all the conservationists around her, and because of this vision we have something left to fight for. No people's movement could have achieved the same. In the 1960s, Indira Gandhi steered India on a course that saved the forests and wildlife of the country for at least another fifty years. At the time of her death, she left many things in the pipeline, probably the most important of which was the creation of a new Ministry of Environment and Forests out of the existing Department of Environment. There was also discussion of the possibility of an environment-protection act to control industrial pollution and minimize the negative impact of haphazard development.

Indira Gandhi and her son Rajiv Gandhi. Both were prime ministers of India between 1966 and 1989, and in their tenure India created all the laws that govern forests, wildlife, and the environment.

After the defeat of Rajiv Gandhi at the polls in 1989, India rushed into the 1990s without any political leadership to defend the tiger or its forests. The goals of the decade were all economic. By 1992, another tiger crisis was raging across India, and its tentacles were spreading across the globe. This period was traumatic and torturous and is described here by acclaimed natural history writer Geoffrey Ward. Ward was writing about India, but his words also reflect the world of the tiger in the 1990s.

Massacre

Geoffrey C. Ward

IN LATE JUNE 1992, I received a letter and a set of newspaper clippings from Fateh Singh Rathore. Several poachers had been arrested at Ranthambhore; they had confessed to the police that they had shot more than fifteen tigers there over the past two years. And they were not alone. Several other poaching gangs, they said, were at work in and around the park.

Rumors of tiger poaching had swirled around Ranthambhore since 1990, but the chief wildlife warden of the state had dismissed them all as "baseless," the products of "vested interests" (by which he seems mostly to have meant Fateh, the former field director whose stubborn ingenuity had cost him his job, and who was noisily unhappy at what was happening to the sanctuary he still considered his). Some thirty-one thousand tourists, more than half of them foreigners, visited the park during the winter of 1990–1991, an all-time record, and a good many complained that they had seen no signs of tigers, let alone the tigers themselves. Noon—the tigress who had mastered the technique of killing in the lakes, the animal I had watched feeding with her cubs in the grass two years earlier—seemed suddenly to be missing. So was the magnificent Bakaula male. So were other individual animals well known to Fateh and Valmik [Thapar] and to the guides and jeep drivers who made locating tigers their business.

The Trade in Skin and Bone

A story about the mysterious dearth of tiger sightings at Ranthambhore appeared in the *Indian Express* in February 1992. The field director claimed there was nothing to worry about: because of an unusually heavy monsoon the previous summer, the tigers were simply keeping to the hills. In March, the erstwhile maharani of Jaipur, whose hunting reserve Ranthambhore once had been, also expressed her concern. She, too, was told nothing was

Noon and one of her subadult cubs in the tall grasses of Ranthambhore National Park.

wrong, and when the census was taken that summer, sure enough, the official total was forty-five tigers, one more than had been claimed the year before.

Fateh made more trouble for himself by publicly denouncing the count's accuracy: if there were that many tigers, why weren't they being seen? He was sure there weren't more than twenty tigers left in the park.

The rumors persisted. During our visit to Ranthambhore that winter, the corpse of Badhiya, a forest guard who had been one of the most knowledgeable and dedicated members of the forest staff, was found sprawled along the railroad tracks outside the park. There were whispers he'd been murdered because he knew too much about poaching.

Something was very wrong. Even the forest department began to worry; when the census was undertaken the following May, Valmik Thapar was asked to help conduct it. The results were devastating: he could find concrete evidence of only seventeen tigers in the park, and tentative evidence suggesting there might be three more. Again, the chief wildlife warden denied everything. The census was faulty, he insisted, botched by the same amateurs he himself had asked for help.

But then came the arrests. Gopal Moghiya, a member of a traditional hunting tribe who ordinarily worked as watchmen for local herdsmen, was seized by the Sawai Madhopur police, along with the skin and bones of a freshly killed tiger he had shot.

Fateh was devastated. He wrote me:

Geoff, it is a massacre. When the police chief showed me the skin, I could not control myself. Tears were rolling down my cheeks. He had to take me away. It's heartbreaking and sometimes I feel guilty that I taught them to have faith in human beings. . . . All the tigers were shot at point-blank range, just innocently looking at the man with the gun. . . . Every day some bad news is coming. . . . Somebody shot a tiger two years ago and somebody else shot one three months before that. It shows that nobody bothered about these animals.

I called Fateh. He was again in tears. "I sometimes think it was my fault," he shouted over the long-distance line. "I taught my tigers not to fear people and see how they have been repaid."

Gopal Moghiya's confession led to the arrests of several others, including his own brother, a Muslim butcher, and four Meena herdsmen, who admitted killing four tigers to protect their livestock.

The forest department's initial instinct, as always, was to cover things up. One or two animals might have been killed, it said, but poaching on such a large scale was impossible. Gopal Moghiya did eventually recant his con-fession, yet he had airily bragged of his poaching skills to several disinterested journalists before doing so.

But the facts could not be denied: eighteen tigers and leopards were already gone from Sariska, perhaps twenty tigers missing at Ranthambhore, and reports of more poaching were filtering in from everywhere. In Uttar Pradesh, for example, where the forest department stubbornly insisted that Dudhwa and its adjacent forest still held 104 tigers, Billy Arjan Singh estimated there were now no more than twenty.

Valmik did a hasty calculation of the total number of tigers thought to have been poached, based on just five years' worth of official seizures of skins and skeletons. It came to 120 animals. And it seems reasonable to assume that several times as many more went unreported.

At that rate, the Indian tiger is surely on its way out. Tigers have always been poached. Villagers poison them to protect themselves or their livestock, and some skin smuggling has continued despite an international ban on the trade. But compared to the twin menaces of expanding population and dwindling habitat, poaching has been a relatively minor threat to the tiger's survival. Now that has changed. If allowed to continue at its current pace, poaching will swiftly undo whatever good Project Tiger has managed to do over the past few decades.

The immediate crisis was caused by the peculiar demands of Chinese medicine. For hundreds, perhaps thousands of years, tiger bones and other tiger by-products have played an important part in Chinese healing. The catalog of physical ills that tiger bones and the elixirs brewed from them are supposed to cure includes rheumatism, convulsions, scabies, boils, dysentery, ulcers, typhoid, malaria, and even prolapse of the anus. Tiger remedies are also said to alleviate fright, nervousness, and possession by devils. Ground tiger bone scattered on the roof is believed to bar demons and end nightmares for those who sleep beneath it. A miraculous "medicine" made from tiger bone and sold in Vietnam and elsewhere promises "six love makings a night to give birth to four sons."

*A poisoned tiger is brought ashore in Ranthambhore
National Park. Many tigers were poisoned in the 1990s
because they had killed domestic livestock.*

The demand for these products is enormous, not only in China and Taiwan but in South Korea and in Chinese communities throughout Southeast Asia and some western communities as well. A single brewery in Taiwan imports two thousand kilograms (4,400 pounds) of tiger bones a year—perhaps 150 tigers' worth—from which it brews one hundred thousand bottles of tiger-bone wine.

The Chinese themselves have finally run out of tigers: wild populations that once ran into the thousands have been reduced to fewer than one hundred animals, and so they have begun importing tiger bones on a massive scale, ignoring the complaints of conservationists, and are willing to pay prices smugglers find irresistible. From the Indian reserves, where tribal hunters are paid a pittance to take the risks and do the actual killing, shadowy middlemen, perhaps with the connivance of some forest department and police officials, spirit the bones of poached tigers northward across the Nepal border, then on into Tibet and China.

More because of the inefficiency of this process, evidently, than out of concern for the wildlife of other countries, the Chinese have set up a tiger-breeding farm near Beijing. There, using Siberian tigers obtained from North American zoos, they are now raising carnivores whose only raison d'être is to be disassembled, ground up, and sold to clients at home and abroad. Its managers predict they will have bred some two thousand tigers in the next seven years, and they have recently asked the Convention on International Trade in Endangered Species (CITES) for a permit to peddle their tiger products overseas. "If we don't get the permit," one official told a visitor to the breeding farm, "we'll just kill all the tigers."

Sentiment aside, some urge that the Chinese breeding program should be encouraged, since its success might relieve the pressure on dwindling wild populations. Opponents argue that farms will never be able to provide enough tigers to satisfy Chinese demands, while legitimizing trade in tiger products would only make it easier for poachers and smugglers to continue their deadly work.

The Ranthambhore scandal could not have come at a worse time for Project Tiger. Nineteen ninety-three was to be its twentieth anniversary, and a celebration was already planned at which a brand-new national census figure was to be announced: 4,300 animals, almost two and a half times the number there had been when the project began.

Debate and Discussion

All the old problems still persisted. The hostility of local people had intensified: arsonists had recently set fires raging through the hearts of Kanha and Nagarahole, where K. M. Chinnappa, the ranger responsible for defending it for so long, had been forced to flee for his life. And there was already one disturbing new problem, a sad side effect of the national struggle with sectional and ethnic separatists that threatens to tear apart the Indian union. Armed militants of one kind or another had taken shelter in seven of the nineteen reserves, intimidating forest staff, slaughtering animals for fun or food or profit, making a mockery of the parks' supposed inviolability.

Now massive poaching has been added to that already bleak mix. A three-day international symposium on the tiger was to be held in New Delhi in February 1993. Nearly 250 delegates were coming from every region of India and many parts of the world, and the government's more strident critics predicted little more than a desperate exercise in defensiveness. They were wrong. The new all-India census figure of 4,300 was bravely announced, though almost no one believed it; three thousand tigers seemed a far more realistic figure, according to most of those with whom I spoke, and even that may now be far too high. The delegates were also made to sit through an appallingly self-congratulatory film: "Forest cover is increasing," the narrator intoned. "The tiger reigns supreme," and in the reserves "all is well."

Everyone in the hall already knew that all was anything but well, and for the first time in my experience Indian government officials were willing to say so in front of one another and in public. The forest secretary, R. Rajamani, set the tone of candor: the anniversary conference, he said, "should be an occasion for introspection, not celebration."

For three full days, the tiger's champions talked and argued and agreed to disagree. Billy had come all the way from Dudhwa, looking out of place as he always does once he leaves his jungle. "I don't know which will outlast the other, the tiger or me," he said with a grin. I told him my money was on him.

Fateh was there, too, newly reinstated in the forest department by the courts. "I have my dignity back," he said, though he was relegated for the moment to a desk job. He kept his trademark Stetson on inside the assembly hall and, while delivering a paper on the problems of censusing tigers, mimicked in cunning pantomime a forest guard trying to trace a pugmark when he had never before held a pencil. Ullas Karanth, the researcher from Nagarahole, eagerly shook the hands of Billy and Fateh and other tiger wallahs he had only read about, and he lobbied hard for a more scientific approach to tiger management. Research should be free and unfettered, he said; India needed objective facts upon which to make its hard decisions.

Valmik Thapar seemed to be everywhere, delivering a battery of papers, demanding complete honesty about poaching and other potential embarrassments, and vowing to defend those forest officials willing to bring them to the public's attention.

Everyone seemed to agree that a much greater effort had to be made to involve local people in the creation and management of parks. The poaching crisis would never have occurred had local people felt they had any stake in the tiger's survival. And both central and state governments seemed serious about undertaking ambitious eco-development projects — electricity, water power, alternative forms of fuel — to provide benefits at last to the people who live in and around the parks. Some plans seemed so ambitious, in fact, that Ullas Karanth gently pointed out that the government already had access to 96 percent of the country on which to experiment with economic uplift and might do better to leave alone the mere 4 percent left

over for wildlife. Similarly, one field director suggested that before the government came to the aid of the herdsmen he'd been trying to keep out of his park, he hoped it would at least provide trousers for his forest guards.

There was also a good deal of what seemed to me to be very romantic talk about the importance of maintaining intact the ancient "sustainable lifestyles" of the tribal peoples who live in and around the besieged reserves. I couldn't help but remember the Gujjars whose herds I'd seen avidly eating up what was left of Rajaji National Park, in the foothills of the Himalayas. Their lifestyle was ancient all right, but it was no longer remotely sustainable; if Rajaji is to survive, some creative alternative will have to be found for them. If it is not found, the forest will vanish, and so will they. And though every park is unique, it is hard for me to see how the same won't ultimately be true for most if not all of the people now living within India's reserves.

In any case, I left the Delhi conference in better spirits than I had expected. The poaching crisis had brought together the tiger's most eloquent advocates. They were talking to one another now, working together instead of on their own, for the first time more united than divided. Before flying home to the States, we wanted to revisit Ranthambhore and Dudhwa once again. It had been five years since I had sat on the roof of Valmik's farmhouse watching the village women heading home while he tentatively outlined his plans for the Ranthambhore Foundation. I had been sympathetic then but privately unconvinced that the hardscrabble landscape around his home could ever be coaxed back to life, let alone that the gulf between wildlife enthusiasts and villagers might one day be bridged.

A New Beginning

I could not have been more wrong. Valmik's house is now the heart of a green oasis, alive with birds and small animals, shaded by some fifty species of trees, many of them native varieties grown from seeds gathered in the forest. A lush nursery grows half a million seedlings for villagers to plant during the monsoon. And a cluster of outbuildings behind the house constitutes a full-scale demonstration farm, with a sleek, stall-fed murrah buffalo, already the father of hundreds of handsome progeny scattered through nearby villages; a herd of cross-bred cattle whose milk yield is ten times that of the ordinary Indian cow; and heat for cooking provided by a bio-gas plant powered by the animals' dung. Just down the road, village women of all castes and faiths meet in their own handsome, mud-walled building, producing handicrafts that provide needed extra income to some sixty households.

Villagers from as far as fifteen miles away are asking for seeds with which to reforest their land. In at least two villages, the people themselves have formed forest-protection societies with nurseries of their own. The people of Sherpur, Valmik's nearest neighbors, asked for and then helped dig a cattle ditch two kilometers long so that their approach to Ranthambhore at least can be made as green again as it was in the time of their ancestors.

Valmik is the executive director of the Ranthambhore Foundation and divides his time between his farm and his home in New Delhi, from which he does almost ceaseless lobbying on behalf of wildlife in general and Ranthambhore in particular.

The man in charge of day-to-day activities around Ranthambhore is Goverdhan Singh Rathore. He is Fateh's son and has his father's chesty swagger and Rajput mustache, but he is a tiger wallah of a different kind: he seeks to serve the tiger by ministering to the needs of those whom he hopes will one day be its protectors. Five mornings a week, he climbs aboard a medical van and sets out for one of fifteen villages. He and his medical team have now offered immunizations and basic health care—heavily dosed with messages about family planning and the importance of preserving the forest—to more than twenty-five thousand people, and more villages have expressed their interest in participating in the program.

The Ranthambhore Foundation is just one of many nongovernmental agencies now at work around India's parks, but partly because of the park's fame at home and abroad the foundation has become a symbol for a new kind of Indian conservation effort. The Indian branch of the World Wildlife Fund has launched a similar project of its own just down the road, and as part of a large-scale eco-development plan intended to serve as a model for other parks, the Rajasthan forest department has begun planting fodder to be given away to grazers so that they needn't take their animals into the park.

It is the foundation's work with children that seemed to me to hold the brightest promise. When foundation workers began taking jeeploads of them into the park, the children liked the birds and animals well enough, but what first struck most of them was the novel sight of seeing so many intact trees in one place. Born and raised within a kilometer or two of Ranthambhore, in the heart of what had once been a thick forest, many had never seen more than two or three lopped trees at a time and had never realized before just what had been lost to cattle and goats and the woodcutter's ax.

On our last evening of Ranthambhore, Goverdhan took us to the mud-walled children's educational center that the foundation constructed beneath a huge tree on the outskirts of a nearby village. Lit by the white glare of a hissing kerosene lamp, fifteen boys sat in a circle while one of them rattled out a steady rhythm on the bottom of an upturned kettle. They all sang a specially written song about the wonder of trees and the importance of caring for the wild animals that lived beneath them. These boys had come from miles away to spend the weekend, and some had ridden two different buses to get there. Represented among them were several of the communities that live around the park—Meenas, Gujjars, Malis, Muslims—all eating from the same pot, singing about the same forest.

As we watched and listened from just beyond the circle of light, other voices could suddenly be heard moving along the dark road behind us. Several more boys, hurrying home to their village, had been moved to join in praise of the forest, which ultimately only they can save.

With Billy Arjan Singh

From Ranthambhore, we returned to Delhi, then made the long drive to Dudhwa to visit Billy. The court cases against him seemed at least momentarily forgotten, and late one afternoon he did something he does only rarely these days: he accompanied us into the park.

Dudhwa seemed especially handsome as dusk approached. As we drove through the red-brown grass—tiger-striped by the smoke from fires deliberately set to char the undergrowth and allow fresh green shoots to spread for the deer to eat—thousands of swallows and bee-eaters tumbled through the air in pursuit of their evening meals.

But the few animals we saw—chital, a herd of thirty swamp deer, a lone sambar calf somehow separated from its mother—seemed frantic with fear, plunging deeper into the forest as soon as they spotted us, evidence perhaps that they had recently been shot at from vehicles that resembled ours. And only once, along all the miles of dusty road we traveled, did we see a set of tiger pugmarks.

Gloom seemed to settle almost palpably around Billy's shoulders as we turned off the metaled road that leads out of the park and onto the rutted track to Tiger Haven that runs for two kilometers along the Neora. The sun was hanging very low in the sky now, and as we came around a bend in the river, wisps of mist rose from the elephant grass, and its damp sweet smell filled our nostrils.

A big male tiger lay motionless atop the riverbank, fifty feet across the river, his brassy coat burnished by the dying sun, his opaque eye fixed upon us.

I stole a look at Billy as he watched the tiger. It seemed almost an invasion of his privacy: head cocked to one side, smiling, he was rapt, adoring, his face lit up as if he had unexpectedly come upon a lover.

The tiger gazed back at him for a time, then rose slowly to his feet and—stretched out to an almost unbelievable length, belly nearly touching the ground—slipped into the underbrush and disappeared. Under Billy's vigilant eye, this tiger, at least, still occupies his range and still reminds us of what will be lost if the new hopes stirred at the Delhi conference are allowed to die away.

As the Land Rover started up again, Billy beamed at me and raised one thick thumb in silent delight.

GEOFFREY C. WARD is an American historian, biographer, and screenwriter who spent several boyhood years in India and has written about its wildlife for *Audubon*, *Smithsonian* and *National Geographic* magazines. He is also the author of *The Year of the Tiger* (with Michael Nichols) and *Tiger Wallahs* (with his wife, the writer Diane Raines Ward) and serves on the board of the Save the Tiger Fund.

People and Tigers

Just as Geoffrey Ward found the beginnings of conservation work with local communities and the tiger, some three thousand miles away Dale Miquelle was seeing some amazing connections between people and tigers. Everyone knew that the future of the tiger would depend on its relationship with humanity. It is clear that, whether in India or Siberia, traditional links with the tiger were still the basis of a bond between the human being and the tiger. A remarkable relationship of trust between man and tiger has developed across the tiger's range. Most local communities view the tiger as the guardian and protector of the wilderness.

VLADIMIR

Dale Miquelle

"THERE'S A REPORT OF TWO CUBS down on a farm at Zolotaya Polyana." Nine times out of ten you arrive at such a site to find out that, well, yes, there have been tigers here, and they are sure to come back, but the last sighting was, well, last week, but gosh, you've got to do something. Nonetheless, we have to check such reports out. A Canadian film crew, with us for this week in February 2001, is, of course, game. We send Sasha Reebin, a member of our staff, back for the capture equipment, just in case, and ask him to find Boris Litvinov or a member of his Tiger Response Team of Primorski Krai, the state entity that has legal responsibility for such situations and with which we work closely in all such encounters.

It takes nearly an hour to get to Zolotaya Polyana, where there are a number of "cottages" and agricultural fields for people from Plastun village. We managed to find the decrepit-looking building that might be described as a farmhouse, and there were people outside, apparently waiting for us. I got out and approached them.

"We heard a report of some tigers around here?" I asked. This is normally when they tell you how you just missed them, they're sure to come back, and it was only a few days ago that they were terrorizing them. Instead I got: "Yes, you want to see him?"

A woman came forward hurriedly and said, "He came here asking for help. You have to give him some medicine," and then the whole family (or, I should say, the whole group of people, because it was hard to figure out who was related to whom and how—an older man, looking like he was getting towards his seventies, a not-unattractive woman in her forties, and three kids, ages sixteen to twenty, perhaps) proceeded around the back of the house, with our entourage in tow. The house sat on the embankment of the Sheptoon River, and the foundation was exposed on the back side, with an opening in it for a door into the cellar. In place of a door, however, was a set of bedsprings laid on end to cover the doorway, with a metal pipe leaning against them, apparently to hold in the cub.

John Goodrich and I peered through the bedsprings. In one corner was a pile of pinecones (a good nut crop this year). A tarp hung from a post, hiding much of the corner but visible to the side of the tarp was the huge head of a tiger. "Oh my God" was all I could say. I stood there, almost frozen and speechless, waiting for the tiger to charge at us, obliterating the flimsy excuse for a cage door. The family was standing around, perfectly at ease in the presence of this tiger, excitedly telling us the story of how they had seen a tiger walking at the edge of their yard last night. Later, the old man had heard some noise down in the cellar and had gone down there with a flashlight, fumbling around, only to hear the growl of a tiger. He, of course, left quickly, with no bad consequences, and this morning put the bedsprings up. But there was another tiger, too, they said, that they also saw this morning, not thirty yards from the house. I'm looking at the tiger the whole time—its eyes are blinking, but it is showing no reaction to the nine people standing just outside this entryway—and I'm thinking that we don't have any idea what his status is and that if he walked in here last night, he certainly has the strength in him for one last rush, one angry attack. And I am dumbfounded by the attitude of this entire family. They are not in the least bit frightened that a tiger is in their cellar—on the contrary, they are talking about it as if it is one of their dearest pets that fell ill and needs veterinary attention. I think they're all nuts.

I ask everyone to back off and return to the front of the house. This is a potentially explosive situation. The old man takes John and me out to the edge of their yard and shows us tracks of where the tiger was seen last night. John notes that in a couple of places there are tracks suggesting that

another tiger walked nearby but then slunk back into the low oak-shrub fields surrounding the area. And they show us tracks where, this morning, the other tiger was just twenty or thirty yards from his or her son/brother/buddy in the cellar, seemingly waiting for him to get up and move on out of here. So not only do we have a tiger of unknown status in the cellar, but there is another one lurking somewhere nearby—potentially a defensive mother.

Sasha shows up with the immobilization equipment, but without Litvinov (in Vladivostok) or Anatoly Khubotnov (not home), so we send him off immediately to find Zheny Tsarapin (the other member of the response team) in Plastun. Meanwhile, we try to keep people from walking out back ("There's no danger from him," insist the family) or away from the farmhouse, where another tiger may be waiting.

Today is the first break in the miserably cold weather of this winter, and we can't do anything on our own, so we lounge in the sun waiting, still stunned that there is a full-grown tiger lying in the cellar of the house in front of us.

It's after 1:00 p.m. when Sasha returns with Zheny Tsarapin. John and Sasha prepare darts while I take Zheny out back and try to explain what is going on. I find myself having a hard time making sense of the situation to him—it's just too surreal.

Sasha recommends that we drive my car around to the downstairs entry and back up to the door so that he can fire the dart gun out of the rear window. This sounds like a safe plan. Of course, the film crew wants to be down there, so we get them set up as far away as we can, and they do a good job of staying out of the way. When I've got Sasha backed right up to the door, he starts scanning the cellar room, saying he cannot find the tiger. I can't see back there from the driver's seat, but I say, "What do you mean you can't see him, he's right there on the pinecones." No, he isn't, says Sasha. The tiger has moved, and now we know he is still mobile and expect him to come lunging out from one of the corners that we cannot peer into. Sasha leans out the rear door to get a better view—I am waiting for that explosive roar and powerful rush of an enraged and frightened predator. John and Zheny walk up on each side of the car and are peering through the bedsprings screen, flares and rifle ready. It is only now that they realize there is a second room built into the foundation. The tiger must be behind that wall.

Now what? We all agree you can't walk in there, in the dark—it would just be too risky. We discuss options but can't come up with a reasonable way to deal with this situation. Finally, we ask the family, "You don't, by any chance, have a trapdoor to the cellar?" Most root cellars in Russian homes are accessed through such a trapdoor, but this is not really a root cellar.

"No, but we can make one!" comes the almost gleeful reply, and within minutes they are ripping out their flooring and have the chainsaw revved up to cut through the main floorboards. As the saw roars upstairs, I am again stunned by the lengths to which this family is going for this tiger.

Sasha and I stand below, expecting to see a tiger come roaring out of that black back room, hell-bent on escape from the screaming chainsaw overhead. Our task, should that happen, is to keep him contained—how we would do that is not quite clear. But we see no tiger, and no sign of movement by him, despite the raucous din just above him.

They finally get the hole cut, and John can see the tiger now. He is not responding to the light or people above him, so Sasha goes upstairs to try to get a dart in him. The hole is small, and of course not in the right place—Sasha has to wedge himself into the hole up to his waist, hang upside down, and shoot the dart gun with one hand. He is expecting the tiger to leap at him in response to the ketamine dart, and now, with Zheny down at the doorway with me, we are again expecting the tiger to come charging out. But, Sasha later says, except for a slight flinch there was no response.

In just a few minutes, we walk in, still cautious, with rifle cocked and ready, but the tiger is immobilized, both with drugs and sickness. We carry him out into the light. He is a young male but fully grown, with the huge head that I first saw lying on the pinecones. However, he is the most emaciated animal I have ever seen—a real bag of bones, every rib and every limb bone traceable through the skin and coat; his pelvis sticks so far beyond his emaciated muscles in the hindquarters it is almost grotesque. On all his legs the hair has been lost, probably due to mange.

We collect blood, take body measurements, and weigh him in at 186 pounds—a healthy animal of this size would weight at least 250, maybe 300. I have the blood tubes in my hand and need to label them. I ask the old farmer, "What's your name?" and he tells me, "Vladimir." I write this name for this tiger on the tubes. One of the boys explains to his elder that the tiger has been named after him, and the old man seems pleased.

Now, what do we do? Our initial plan was to bring the tiger in the back of the pickup to Plastun, where Zheny has a cage that is nearly ready. We could bring him directly to Litvinov's, in the village of Terney, not much farther away, where they have constructed a cage especially for problem tigers. The warm midday sun is gone, and we're afraid our patient won't hold up well in the freezing wind in the back of a pickup, so we fold down the backseats and slide him into my jeep. We will have our hands full if he decides to get up in the next hour.

We get out of there as fast as we can and negotiate the icy roads quickly. Sasha is in back with the tiger, constantly testing it—ear twitches, jaw resistance, breath rate—for any sign of recovery from the drugs. When we are only five kilometers from Terney, Sasha thinks we need to provide a supplemental dose of ketamine. In town, we quickly add the final touches to the cage, fill it with hay, get a dish wired into the corner, and transfer the tiger into it. Meanwhile, John and Sasha pump a few liters of saline solution into the tiger subcutaneously. Ideally, we would have this patient hooked up to an IV and be feeding him glucose and a saline solution, but that is simply impossible given a wild tiger and existing supplies. Even before we can cover up the cage, people start arriving: "I've never seen a tiger in my life. Can I have a look?" Terney is a small village, and word does indeed travel fast.

John and I return home and eat our first meal of the day, then return for a final inspection just before dark. Vladimir is lying in the same position, his breathing labored. It is hard to tell where the effect of the drugs leaves off and the sickness takes over. Prospects look bleak.

In the morning, we see he has changed positions, but there is no indication that he has drunk any of the chicken broth that was provided last night. A couple of pieces of boiled chicken were thrown in, but it is impossible to tell if he ate them (later, we learn, surprisingly, that he did). Neither John nor I think this animal is simply starving to death, and we are both thinking of canine distemper, which is killing half the dogs in Terney. (One of the dogs at the farm was dragging both hind legs, and we later learned that he died the next day.) Canine distemper had wiped out half of the Serengeti lion population, and we are concerned about a potential outbreak of the disease in the wild tiger population, since there are reports of distemper in zoo tigers. John suggests that the greatest value of this animal may be in its ability to provide information about the illness afflicting it. In any case, we realize that it will require heroic efforts to attempt to save this life, and we are not equipped for it.

In the afternoon, preparations are made to send Vladimir to Ussurisk, where the Krai veterinarian clinic is situated and which is also, coincidentally, the home of the person who does necropsies of tigers for the Committee for Environmental Protection. With the crew driving there we send a set of specific questions to be addressed, including a request that they do a virus culture to look for distemper.

We load a small wooden crate into the back of the Ural truck. Just a month ago, this same crate had carried two tiger cubs to Vladivostok for transfer to Moscow Zoo. (Abandoned by their mother and captured by our team, they were also victims of this tough winter.) The cage is not strong enough to hold a healthy adult tiger, but it should do for this one. The main advantage of this cage is its smaller size, which allows the tiger to ride in the warmth of the back cabin of the truck.

At this point, just before the truck leaves, we search for remains of the boiled chicken in the cage and find that Vladimir not only ate but readily chewed up the bones. Just before they leave, I warn Kolya Reebin, Sasha's brother, who will be traveling down, to be careful opening up the back cabin—the tiger found the strength to walk to the rear room of the cellar yesterday and eat chicken last night, but the rest of the time he is in an almost comatose state. Perhaps sometimes he comes out of it, in which case he could be capable, and therefore dangerous, for short periods of time.

Such optimism and concern prove unnecessary. Just outside Dalnegorsk, one third of the way to Ussurisk, they stop to check on the tiger: no movement and no breathing.

The pathologist receives a fresh corpse to examine, and we are hopeful that, in time, we will learn more explicitly what happened to Vladimir. But I can't stop thinking about that woman back on the farm who kept saying, "He came to us humans asking for help. We've got to do something for him." It is reassuring to know that such people are still out there, living with the tiger, in an accepting, almost loving way. It was those people who had the right attitude toward this tiger, and it was I who had it all wrong, in spite of my good intentions. I feel as if we let her, and of course him, down. This time, it seems, there was nothing we could do, and I apologize to both of them.

DALE MIQUELLE was born and raised in New England, and received a B.S. at Yale University, an M.S. from University of Minnesota, and a Ph.D. from University of Idaho. He spent a year working on the Smithsonian Tiger Ecology Project in Chitwan National Park, Nepal, before joining the Hornocker Wildlife Institute's Siberian Tiger Project. Now country coordinator for the Wildlife Conservation Society's Russia Program, Miquelle coordinates Siberian tiger research and conservation in both the Russian Far East and nearby northeast China.

THE CRISIS DEEPENS

Siberia in 1992–1993 was in a period of transition, postperestroika; rising crime, anarchy, and drugs enveloped the former Soviet Union. Little attention was paid to tiger conservation, even though the first scientific studies on the Amur tiger started with the radio-collaring of a tigress in 1992. Since then, radio-collared tigers have revealed important information about their needs, which was necessary since the

Well-developed protection strategies and excellent patrolling have led to successful seizures of tiger skins in the Siberian wilderness.

Amur tiger was effectively invisible to researchers—even camera traps rarely succeeded in taking pictures because of the low population density. According to E. N. Smirnov and Dale Miquelle, who have followed the tiger in Siberia for many years, "The key to ensuring survival of the Amur tiger will be the development of a connected network of protected and managed lands that will provide for a minimum population and management of additional lands through a zoning process that will allow human uses of the landscape that are compatible with tiger conservation." They both believe that the future of the tiger depends on how much of the habitat is effectively protected and how poaching can be discouraged.

In 1993, the Chinese government finally banned trade in tiger bone and rhino horn. Throughout the world, in countries that were part of the tiger's ranges and countries that were not, nongovernmental organizations flourished. Companies such as Exxon, which had used the tiger as a symbol for decades, started "Save the Tiger" funds. Governments allocated more money to protecting wild tigers, and the media covered the crisis as never before. However, as wildlife biologist Alan Rabinowitz, described in *Riding the Tiger* (Seidensticker, Christie, and Jackson, eds.), "the idea that tigers are protected simply by establishing protected areas is no longer a valid concept, if it ever was. Even in the largest remaining forest area, poaching and the wildlife trade continue to be the most insidious threats to the remaining tiger population."

At the end of 1993, a time when huge hauls of tiger bones and skins were being recovered from illegal traders, Mike Birkhead and I met to discuss producing a film on the crisis. The following year, *Tiger Crisis* was shown all over the world. For tiger conservationists, the years that followed were some of the busiest. Every effort was made, every initiative tried.

New Initiatives

In August 1995, the Russian prime minister passed a national decree to save the Amur tiger. At roughly the same time, India, in partnership with the Global Environment Facility and the World Bank, initiated a seventy-million-dollar eco-development project aimed at involving local communities in conservation. (Sadly, the program proved to be an expensive failure.)

Excellent scientific research was under way throughout the land of the tiger. Ullas Karanth, India's most senior wildlife biologist, had begun a survey across the country to estimate tiger population densities. In 1996, Raghu S. Chundawat started the second major research project in central India using radio telemetry. The government was persuaded to create a Tiger Crisis Cell, a group of experts organized to monitor the crisis and provide practical solutions to the tigers' problems. India initiated the Global Tiger Forum, an association of all tiger-range states. In 1997, more than 320 members of the Indian Parliament across party lines signed a petition to save the tiger, and this was handed to the prime minister. The chief election commissioner of India banned the use of forest jeeps or personnel during local or federal elections in order to limit the mobility of poachers. There were endless crisis meetings in and outside of government.

There was much camaraderie in the conservation community, because all across the tiger's range we were facing similar problems. India was losing a tiger per day to poachers and timber mafias. Siberia was losing precious forests, and tiger poaching had reached a peak. The rest of Asia was no different. Nearly every wildlife organization on the planet was doing its best to save tigers. There must have been glimmers of hope in the late 1990s, but as the century ended I realized that many of us were living in some kind of illusion—little had really changed, even though tens of millions of dollars had been thrown at the issue. In most countries, the root of the problem was bad governance, and this was an area too complex for NGOs to enter.

Probably the most positive aspect of the mid-to-late 1990s was the tremendous spurt in research across the land of the tiger and the fascinating information that it produced. Ullas Karanth and Raghu S. Chundawat in India, Dave Smith and Charles McDougal in Nepal, Dale Miquelle, John Goodrich, and Howard Quyley in the Siberian snows, Tim O'Brien in Sumatra—the list of dedicated scientists in the field goes on. If anything good can be said to have come out of the tiger crisis, it is that it triggered some of the finest scientific research ever on wild tigers.

The End of a Century

Many of the studies produced recommendations, but governments seldom took much notice. Few in power wanted to reform or restructure the existing system, and there was more rhetoric than action. In India, it took months for funds to be disbursed into the field, where they could be put to practical use—and in other tiger-range countries it was much worse. What saved India's tigers and forests from total disaster were orders that regularly emanated from the supreme court, protecting large chunks of Indian forest from the axes of timber merchants. Between 1995 and 2000, there were nearly two hundred such orders. At this pivotal moment, the court had taken over the role of people like Indira Gandhi.

But generally the mood was of one of exploitation. As the twentieth century drew to a close, as a tiger conservationist I felt a sense of despair such as I had never felt before. I thought this century would close with a celebration of the extraordinary recovery of the wild tigers of Ranthambhore.

Instead, on December 19, 2000, I woke up to news that, purely by accident, the sales-tax inspectors in Ghaziabad, a small town in northern India, had intercepted a truck and found, instead of illegal garments, fifty leopard skins, three tiger skins, and a handful of other skins. Although the news came and went, many of us in and out of government remained in shock for several days. It was probably the second-largest seizure of big-cat skins since Indian independence, and it brought home the fact that our precious wilderness was vanishing.

I went to Ghaziabad with some of the most senior officers of the Ministry of Environment and Forests. At 7:00 A.M., the smog and mist of the filth of Delhi and all its satellite towns were only just lifting. We drove for more than an hour and then into the sprawling mess of Ghaziabad's lanes until we arrived at the district forest officer's residence. I was with the inspector general of forests, and after we stepped out of the car and walked a few yards around a corner, there in front of us were laid out and hanging the skins of so many dead leopards that the first sight of it took the breath away and stunned all of us into silence. In a numb state, we looked at what must be only the tip of an iceberg in the ongoing massacre of India's wildlife. (How many thousands of mornings I have waited even for the faintest sign of a leopard in India's forest. I have craved to see even a glimpse of them.) In twenty-five years I have probably seen twenty-eight leopards, yet I found myself surrounded by fifty dead ones. Some were enormous, the skins shining in the early morning sun. There were hardly any marks in them; they had probably been poisoned or electrocuted, and a couple appeared to have been caught in foot traps and then smashed on the head, as the congealed blood suggested. They all looked freshly killed—probably within the last six months. They had been cured somewhere and waxed and even had the signature of the artist on the back. They were folded perfectly, like tablecloths. It was a bloodcurdling sight. Standing silently in the midst of the skins, my head, my heart, my every pore seemed to collapse. I realized that the recovery of Ranthambhore was probably only an illusion.

Fifty leopard skins and three tiger skins were recovered from a poacher in Ghaziabad, northern India. Unfortunately, such seizures continue to this day.

I touched, looked at, and turned over some of the skins. My colleagues from the ministry were shocked, too. We were close to tears. I moved to an enormous tiger skin—its foot looked as if it had been punctured in a foot trap, and its flank had spear or knife marks, suggesting that the tiger had roared in fury and pain from the trap, and the poaching gang had come by and speared it down. My vision of the end of the century had been ripped apart, torn in pieces; it was covered in blood. There was no doubt that hundreds of leopards and tigers were being decimated by the coordinated working of poaching gangs all across India. Were skins being ordered like garments? Why were exactly fifty leopard skins booked from Delhi to Siliguri, a small town close to the border of Nepal? Are there other such consignments? How many gangs are out there engaged in this horrific slaughter?

THE TWENTY-FIRST CENTURY

One century ended, another has begun; we as a conservation community have failed. The federal government, the ministry, the states, the NGOs, and people like myself have entered the twenty-first century without information; we are impotent because there is no effective mechanism of wildlife governance and enforcement. Our laws are violated with impunity. We are mute spectators to a massive slaughter in every forest of India. Big business has ripped apart India's wilderness for mining, illegal traders have picked out our precious wildlife for commerce, and none of us has worked out a way to counter either. Our natural treasury is being devastated. There is no room for lip service any more, no room for complacency. There is only one goal ahead: those who care must engage in the battle to save some of India's natural treasures and secure their future.

THE CARNAGE CONTINUES

There was more to come. On January 12, 2000, a day I will never forget, a police party with wildlife inspectors, acting on a tip that must have resulted from the December 19 seizure, raided three premises in Khaga, Fatehpur, in Uttar Pradesh, and seized seventy leopard skins, four tiger skins, 221 blackbuck skins, 18,000 leopard claws, and 132 tiger claws. The two seizures appeared to be linked. The three premises were illegal factories involved in the tanning and curing of skins. By January 15, more than 185 kilograms (407 pounds) of tiger and leopard bones had been recovered from around these premises, revealing the horrifying state of affairs. Wildlife governance was in a complete state of collapse. As if what had been found so far was not enough, by May two more seizures in Haldwani resulted in the recovery of the skins of eighty more leopards and innumerable other animals. Never before in the history of India had there been a haul of this magnitude. I cannot bear to imagine what had been processed in these factories over the last decade.

We are already losing at least ten thousand square kilometers (nearly four thousand square miles) of dense forest each year to timber mafias and developers. I believe that at least $12 billion in resources—not only wood, but mineral wealth, fodder, and other commodities—are taken, legally and illegally, from India's forests each year, and I am convinced that hundreds of tigers and leopards are trapped, poisoned, and poached so that their skin, claws, and other derivatives can feed the insatiable international market. This abuse is not India's failure alone. We have failed globally. Much of the responsibility must fall on our international organizations, both intergovernmental and nongovernmental. India's wilderness heads for disaster. To avoid total annihilation requires global will and urgent reform in the enforcement mechanisms that prevent illegal trade across the world.

The following two essays provide testimony from people currently working to protect the tiger from poaching and illegal trade. Belinda Wright is the executive director of the Wildlife Protection Society of India and is actively involved in the prevention of poaching; John Sellar is the senior enforcement officer of CITES.

Poaching and the Illegal Trade in Tiger Parts

Belinda Wright

The ingenuity of tiger poachers knows no bounds. For years, tigers have been poisoned, shot, and trapped. Now they are also victims of the widespread theft of electricity in India, as is shown by one of the most tragic incidents of recent times. Villagers in Melghat Tiger Reserve in central India laid wires attached to an overhead electrical line across an animal track. Their intention was to kill deer. Instead, they electrocuted a heavily pregnant tigress. When her body was found on February 3, 2003, four aborted cubs lay dead beside her.

As the demands on tiger habitat increase, so do such "accidental" killings. But far more alarming is today's network of highly organized wildlife criminals who send their agents out to the remotest corners of India in search of tiger parts. Over the past three years, field investigators working for the Wildlife Protection Society of India (WPSI) have uncovered an incredible degree of sophistication among hard-core wildlife criminals. Large sums of money (in one case a half million rupees, about $10,800) have been found on arrested criminals, along with cell phones and modern small firearms.

India's tiger parts are destined entirely for foreign countries—most often China, where they are processed and then smuggled to other countries. The demand has led Indian traders to collaborate closely with their counterparts in neighboring countries, in particular with citizens of Nepal and the Tibet Autonomous Region of China, a number of whom have been arrested in tiger-related wildlife cases in India over the past three years. Myanmar is also an important trade route. In November 2001, police in China stopped a truck near the Myanmar border that was said to contain jellyfish. Instead, they found a huge haul of skins—23 tigers, 33 leopards, and 134 otters. Although reports initially said that the skins had come from Bangladesh, WPSI later learned that this was a translation

error and that the skins were in fact those of "Bengal tigers," most likely having originated in India.

Another huge seizure of skins took place in China in October 2003—31 tiger skins, 581 leopard skins and 778 otter skins were found in a truck in Angren County. Most of the skins were wrapped in Indian newspapers, and the three people who were arrested told the Chinese authorities that they had collected the skins at the Indian border. These two seizures alone represent perhaps 2 percent of India's entire population of wild tigers.

The trade in tiger parts is in the hands of a few well-connected individuals, the dons of this aspect of organized crime, about whom a fair amount is now known. In fact, the tragedy is that there is probably now enough information available for these individuals to be apprehended, which would largely put an end to this illegal trade. But sadly, there is little determination by the authorities to do this, so the trade continues. The dons' links crop up in all the big seizures. These include their legal representation. The dons clearly look after their underlings—as soon as a big seizure takes place, an aggressive and experienced lawyer is dispatched to represent the accused and seek bail. This has happened with alarming swiftness in a number of cases, including the huge seizure in January 2000 in Khaga, Uttar Pradesh. With good legal representation, such a case can drag on for up to fifteen years, which makes a conviction extremely unlikely, as the case is weakened by time: judicial changes confuse the flow and documentation of the case, files are lost, witnesses and the accused die or disappear, and the seized items deteriorate.

One man in this system stands out. He is Sansar Chand, born in 1958 and a resident of Delhi. He has been convicted once, in April 1982, when he was sentenced to one and a half years' imprisonment for a 1974 seizure that included tiger and leopard skins. After losing his appeal, Chand was

A huge recovery of tiger and leopard bones in the town of Khaga in northern India in the year 2000.

finally sent to jail in Delhi in 1994, but he was released after six months when he appealed his Delhi High Court conviction in the Supreme Court. They allowed his release, pending payment of a fine, on the grounds that he was only sixteen years old in 1974. His father, mother, brother, uncle, cousins, and brother-in-law, along with various other close associates and employees, have all been accused in a number of wildlife cases throughout India. His and his wife's phone numbers appear time and again in diaries

recovered from wildlife criminals. Chand has about fourteen cases pending against him in the states of Delhi, Rajasthan, Uttaranchal, Uttar Pradesh, and Andhra Pradesh.

Perhaps the largest concentration of professional tiger poachers and carriers occurs near the city of Katni in the central Indian state of Madhya Pradesh. WPSI has amassed a dossier on 262 known and suspected poachers who are mostly based in just thirteen villages in the Katni district. As many as 142 of these individuals have been arrested in states as far afield as Karnataka, Andhra Pradesh, Maharashtra, Gujarat, Uttaranchal, and Haryana, as well as in Madhya Pradesh. They usually hire or purchase a small bus to travel long distances, with their families, to tiger and leopard habitats. Traveling cash is hidden in children's clothing (and in one case in a plaster cast). The families put up simple camps near the jungle, frequently selling cheap toys and plastic flowers as a cover. Working with local villagers, they lay steel-spring traps along animal paths to catch their prey. Tiger and leopard skins are then carried back by the women to Katni, either by train or bus. From there, they are taken by trusted couriers (also usually women) to the dons in Delhi.

WPSI makes every effort to investigate all known tiger deaths in India. In 2001, we recorded details of seventy-two illegally killed tigers. The following year, we recorded forty-three tigers killed, and up to mid-July 2003 there were twenty-six. It is difficult to gauge the real magnitude of tiger poaching—but, for the record, the Indian customs authorities' method is to multiply known offenses by ten.

Effective measures have not been—and perhaps cannot be under the present system—put into action to stem this slaughter. The forest department is neither trained nor equipped to handle hard-core wildlife crime, and wildlife court cases (and tiger-related cases in particular) have an appallingly low conviction rate. In the state of Maharashtra, for instance, it is a meager 1.8 percent. Wildlife cases are badly prepared and not vigorously pursued by the authorities. The cases are further weakened by the sheer time they take to conclude. In addition, political interference on all sides—at the central and state government level, ministers or senior bureaucrats may act in the interests of the corporate sector, while at a local level a politician or bureaucrat may be doing a friend a favor—prevents us from protecting our natural resources.

Failing to apprehending city-based wildlife criminals—the masterminds and benefactors of the tiger trade—is still India's biggest shortcoming. One positive step would be to set up a well-funded and -equipped central wildlife-crime unit to investigate and act on information received anywhere in India. The conservation community has lobbied vigorously for this since WPSI first proposed the idea in July 1995. Eight years later, a unit has indeed been set up by the Ministry of Environment and Forests—but it consists of a single forest officer based in Delhi without any facilities or backup.

The late prime minister Indira Gandhi once said, "For countless centuries our country has been the home of a magnificent array of wild creatures. Our ancestors had learned to live with them in mutual respect. We hold this great heritage in trust for future generations. Let us prove worthy of it." But as the years go by, I wonder if we—or the world—really deserve to be the custodians of such a splendid animal as the tiger. Despite all the fanfare, the problems of protecting the tiger have increased. Our success is that we now know a lot. Our failure is that no one is acting on that knowledge. India's Band-Aid efforts may have kept the situation from deteriorating further than it would have otherwise—but that is thanks not to us but to the resilience of the tiger.

BELINDA WRIGHT, renowned tiger conservationist and wildlife campaigner, is the Founder and Executive Director of the Wildlife Protection Society of India. She has pioneered investigations into the illegal wildlife trade in India and helped expose the trade in tiger parts. The work of Belinda and her colleagues has been instrumental in the arrest of hundreds of wildlife criminals and plays a critical role in the development of new conservation strategies. Born in Calcutta, Belinda has spent her entire life working with wildlife in India. Before turning to full-time conservation work in 1994, she was a wildlife photographer and an Emmy Award–winning documentary filmmaker who worked for many years for *National Geographic*.

Tackling the Tiger Takers and Traders

John M. Sellar

TIGERS HAVE ALWAYS BEEN PERSECUTED. That persecution is, to an extent, understandable. The tiger is a dangerous creature that can pose considerable hazard to humans and to their livestock. Consequently, substantial numbers of animals have been killed, legally and illegally, through what is often described as "problem animal control." They have been shot, snared, speared, trapped, and poisoned. It is not uncommon for "problem" tigers to be found where they were killed illegally, with no effort made by the killers to use the carcass in any criminal fashion. Adequate response by government agencies (including compensation schemes) should be able to eliminate much of this persecution.

For decades, the tiger was also a prized target for big-game hunters, and many thousands ended up as trophies. The hunting of tigers is now illegal in all tiger-range states. Live tigers, particularly cubs, are sometimes found in the illegal exotic-pet trade.

Almost every part of the tiger can be used in traditional medicine, from the bones to the whiskers to the penis. The preparation of such medicines, which involves dissolving the bones or other body parts in alcohol or boiling the bones in water or oil until a gluey consistency is achieved, leaves few traces for forensic scientists.

The skins (whole and in part), claws, and teeth are used as talismans and for decorative purposes. It is rumored that some Chinese gamblers believe that possessing the collarbone of a tiger brings success. It is said that members of the Russian mafia love to adorn their Moscow apartments with tiger skins. The demand for such items is so strong that some persons engage in making and selling fake skins and fake teeth. Additionally, the teeth and claws of other cat species are often falsely sold as those of tigers.

It took a long time for conservationists, and subsequently governments, to wake up to how badly tigers were being affected by trade in their skins and other body parts.

Fortunately, trade in tigers, in general terms, is now banned throughout the world. Yet illegal trade continues.

Who Are the Consumers?

Wherever there are users of traditional medicine, one will find products claiming to contain tiger parts, whether that is in Asia or among the Asian ethnic communities elsewhere in the world (never forgetting that alternative medicines are increasingly popular among non-Asians). However, the apparent ready availability of these products, in such numbers and so relatively inexpensively, brings into question how many of them truly contain tiger parts. It seems more likely that the "genuine article" is being secretly traded to specialist suppliers who are delivering to customers willing to pay high prices to ensure they get "the real thing." A black-market trade is also likely to exist where consumers in countries such as Japan still want to obtain penises that they can dissolve in alcohol, believing that this liquor provides strength and acts as an aphrodisiac.

Seizures demonstrate that there are trade routes for skins and bones from the tiger's remaining stronghold in India to China through Nepal, Myanmar, Cambodia, and Vietnam. This is despite the fact that China banned domestic trade in tiger products in 1993. It is also known that tigers are being kept in captivity illegally in several countries in Southeast Asia. It is rumored that a demand exists for skins and live animals in the Middle East. Unfortunately, it also seems that there is a "black hole" into which live tigers, skins, and bones disappear, since surprisingly few seizures are made of products that genuinely contain tiger or of processed and tanned tiger skins, except for those made in countries where tigers are still found in the wild. Once the tiger (live or dead, whole or in parts) is smuggled from its native home it seems to be gone forever.

These facts, combined with other evidence and intelligence, indicate that there are highly organized criminal groups engaged in the poaching, processing, smuggling, and trading of tigers and tiger parts. There can be little doubt that some government officials in conservation and enforcement positions are colluding with such criminals and acting corruptly. This is all the more despicable when one considers the considerable courage and commitment displayed by the majority of such officials, who are dedicated to tackling the takers and traders. Of course, not every tiger that is killed illegally enters the sophisticated supply chains run by criminal networks, but sufficient numbers do to justify much greater attention being given to these criminals than has been the case in the past. That such organized groups seem to trade in other endangered species and engage in a range of criminal activities also makes them worthy targets for police, customs, and wildlife law-enforcement officers.

What Have We Done About It?

Common to many tiger-range states is a situation that does not lend itself to an efficient response to wildlife crime. Historically, especially in those countries that were previously colonies of western nations, wildlife was seen as the property of the rulers, the aristocracy, the military and forestry-officer cadres, and the political elite. Wildlife, or the wildlife that could be "bagged" in sport hunting, was reserved for them. There was no overt racism in this; the very same situation existed in the West. A working-class man in England knew very well that it was not his place in life to take up a shotgun and kill a brace of pheasants for supper, just as a clerk in an office in Calcutta knew that tiger hunting would never be for him.

With such a clear division in society, where everyone "knew their place," there was little need to deploy well-equipped or intensively trained enforcement staff. Field staff in the forests of Asia carried sticks (almost as much a symbol of office as a weapon) and patrolled "beats," just as police constables and gamekeepers in Yorkshire did. These officials were there to deter and detect those people who

A street vendor tries to sell tiger claws to a prospective buyer in the Himalayan region of India. Robust illegal trade in tiger parts remains an ongoing challenge.

would, from time to time, forget their stations in life and seek to take their share of nature's bounty, be that an animal or wood for their fire. They were there to deal with the nuisance element that might spoil a day's hunting or reduce the chances of a really good total for the day. Alongside their enforcement duties, these officers were heavily engaged in recording population numbers, maintaining roads, helping control timber harvesting and planting, and watching for fires and fighting them when they occurred.

This was, and still is, an inhospitable environment in

which to work: often baking hot, sometimes disease-ridden, full of difficult terrain, and populated by creatures that did not appreciate that they were being protected and were just as dangerous to official personnel as they could be to poachers, who for their part could also be dangerous and could both threaten and deliver violence to a forest guard and his family. Plus, whenever there were administrative cash-flow problems, it was the forest guard's wages that failed to arrive, not those of the white-collar workers in the state and federal capitals.

Modern changes in society, whether brought about by national independence or by other factors, brought with them alterations in the attitudes toward wildlife. They also brought the realization that, in some places, there wasn't a lot of wildlife left. The reduction in big-game hunting also, at least for a period, led to a reduction in the monitoring of species' populations and even in interest in the species themselves. It was during such times that the poachers and the unscrupulous dealers moved in. By the time governments realized the seriousness of the scale of illegal activities, the situation was almost out of control in some places and, very importantly, wildlife crime was increasingly organized and of a nature that traditionally deployed enforcement personnel were not intended to combat.

What Are We Doing About It Now?

It is all too easy, yet also true, to reply, "Not enough." However, a great deal has been achieved, and significant sums of money have been spent by governments and by NGOs. Regrettably, some of the money has not always been used wisely, and some has not reached the personnel in the projects it was designed to aid; because of a variety of factors ranging from poor management to corruption. Some governments also have reason to be embarrassed by the fact that NGOs in their countries (often consisting of very few people) have achieved considerably more than the hundreds, if not thousands, of government officials whose jobs encompass tiger conservation. NGOs have played, and continue to play, a vital role in assisting enforcement

personnel and alerting governments to problems at every level: international, regional, subregional, national, state, and district. It is equally vital, though, that governments do not leave it all to NGOs or abdicate their responsibilities to such groups.

More and more governments are taking those responsibilities seriously; have instigated legislative changes; have engaged in public-awareness campaigns; and have promoted the use of alternative ingredients in traditional medicines. The more technologically advanced nations have assisted not only with funds but also through in-kind assistance, such as forensic science research and support. The U.S. Fish and Wildlife Service's forensic laboratory has established an international repository for ballistic evidence, which can be used by tiger range states to identify repeat offenders, provide evidence of cross-border poaching, and assist prosecutions.

The Convention on International Trade in Endangered Species (CITES) has helped focus the world's attention on the illegal killing and trade in tigers and has undertaken a number of initiatives related to this species. The CITES secretariat has coordinated technical missions to twelve of the fourteen tiger-range states. This helped outlaw the sale of tiger products in Japan, where domestic sales had remained legal until the late 1990s. The CITES Tiger Enforcement Task Force has provided guidance on the gathering and reporting of wildlife crime at the field level, as well as on the collation, analysis, and dissemination of intelligence; it has also designed a training program for enforcement staff.

Wildlife crime and the illegal killing of and trade in tigers still remain a low priority for the primary enforcement agencies, police and customs, in most countries. All too often, combating these crimes remains the work of wildlife and forestry departments that are not adequately trained or equipped to deal with it. They do not have the infrastructures or policies in place that facilitate cooperation with other enforcement agencies, even at national levels, let alone internationally. Very often, they do not have sufficient numbers of staff in the towns and cities where the illegal trade takes place. Risk assessment, profiling, targeting, and intelligence-led operations are terms and procedures unknown to too many senior managers and field staff. Until these tools become better known and understood, organized crime and criminal networks will continue to find wildlife crime all too easy, because it will remain all too free from the risk of detection. In many countries, the judiciary needs to be sensitized to the seriousness of poaching and illicit trade, and thus alerted to the need for penalties that will reflect the threat to species such as the tiger and act as an effective deterrent. Judges and prosecutors should also learn that enforcement staff are fed up with arresting the same offenders time after time, only to see them released on bail and then waiting months or years for cases to come to conclusions in court.

In May 2002, CITES organized a two-week training course for twenty-eight operational staff, many with supervisory responsibilities, from twelve tiger-range states. Very appropriately, it was held at the National Police Academy of India, and its faculty, staff, and lecturers from around the world sought to provide the policing skills that are not taught in the wildlife, forestry, and conservation departments of the participants' home countries. It is too early to measure the results of the initiative, but if nothing else the event provided for the establishment of an important informal network that students might use in their future work.

More and more use is being made across the globe of specialized units and multiagency approaches to combating the threats to tigers and other endangered species. The Inspection Tiger Brigades of the Russian Far East have shown themselves to be highly successful. Properly trained, adequately equipped and funded, and with the absolutely essential ingredient of political support, a few good men and women can achieve a lot.

While it may be true that the world has not done enough to eliminate threats to tigers, there is reason to be satisfied with some significant progress in what, after all, has been a relatively short time since the seriousness of the situation became widely apparent. This is especially true when compared to action against other organized criminal activities. There is, however, no room whatsoever for complacency.

It is understandable that policymakers might concentrate on those other criminal activities, such as the cultivation, manufacture, smuggling, and sale of narcotics. However, the war against drugs will inevitably be a series of long-term battles. Many endangered species cannot wait for enforcement agencies to win long-term battles, and the war against wildlife crime will be lost for species such as the tiger if urgent action is not taken in the immediate future.

JOHN SELLAR served for twenty-three years in the Scottish Police Service before joining the Convention on International Trade in Endangered Species (CITES) as secretariat in 1997. As secretariat he assists signatory parties to the convention in enforcement matters, including providing technical advice and assistance, training, and conducting assessment and verification missions to parties. He also serves as the contact at CITES for Interpol and the World Customs Organization. Since joining CITES he has made over one hundred missions to forty-eight different countries (including missions to twelve tiger-range states as the leader of the CITES Tiger Missions Technical Team). He also serves as the coordinator of the CITES Tiger Enforcement Task Force.

*The decimation of the tiger's natural habitat is perhaps
the greatest threat to its survival.*

Solutions for India?

I have followed the trail of the tiger for twenty-seven years, and it has led me over the richest part of India, the forests. This forest land contains a vast amount of timber, marble, gems, manganese, iron ore, bauxite, and many other minerals. Everyone wants a bit of the land. Builders of big dams, organizers of infrastructural projects, and land developers want their pieces, too. The forest covers 20 percent of India—the most neglected sector of the country. But although we seem not to be able to create effective mechanisms for protection, we excel at mechanisms for exploitation. We must work out ways to change this, putting public pressure on our political leadership to focus on real issues. For instance, take the federal arm involved with saving tigers in the Ministry of Environment and Forests: 95 percent of its time, effort, and money is spent on clearing public- and private-sector projects and dealing with city pollution. Forested India has been allocated a tiny, insignificant wing to deal with its issues. The richest part of India never has a decent allocation of money from the Planning Commission, which creates five-year plans for the utilization of the country's finances. The richest part of India has no ministry to protect it.

We must start from scratch and restructure all our mechanisms for wildlife and forest administration. To start, we need:

- a new federal ministry for the protection of forests and wildlife.
- a refocusing of the Indian Forest Service on the protection of biological resources, perhaps with the establishment of an independent subcadre for wildlife.
- a national armed force of forest officers, on call like any other police force, to minimize the enormous damage to our natural treasury.
- financial mechanisms that will disburse money rapidly from the federal structure to the field for better management.
- to declare this sector essential so that the huge vacancies that plague forest staff are filled and the gates to looting are closed.
- to disband Project Tiger, which over the decades has become only a disburser of money and has no power to govern. Instead, under this new ministry, a Tiger Protection Authority of India must be created, one that is empowered under the law to appoint, recruit, transfer, and assess all officers in tiger reserves from the rank of ranger upward. This authority must also be able to disburse money directly to the field and have the final say in the management of all twenty-seven reserves.

Only when these mechanisms are actually and effectively put in place can we even begin to start tackling the details of the most vital and most seriously neglected area of our planet: the forests. Land-use policy, community conservation schemes, joint forest management, and so much more require innovative brainstorming. The first priority is to set into motion the six measures outlined above. The rest will follow. Only then will we be on the path of saving wild tigers.

The Present—and the Future

As of the end of 2003, the South China tiger is probably extinct. The tiger crisis continues across the world. The tiger's future is directly dependent on how much land is protected and kept inviolate: unless human disturbance is kept minimal in the forests of the tiger, the tiger will not survive. This is exceedingly difficult for countries like India and China, with their combined human population of 2.5 billion. The needs of these people have completely overwhelmed the natural world. In other countries, the surviving fragments of forests are under pressure from timber merchants, miners, or poachers. To keep tigers alive anywhere requires the political will to protect their homes fully—when this is done, there is immediate success. Large tracts of forest in Siberia are protected by Operation Amba, a semiofficial antipoaching force begun in 1994, and frequent scientific study and monitoring in these forests resulted in small increases in the tiger population. In India, the last decade has been riddled with political problems, and the protection of forests has been abysmal. The system of governance is defective—it requires urgent correction. The same is true in other tiger-range countries.

After at least six meetings and expenditure of more than one million dollars, the strategy of the Global Tiger Forum is still fast asleep. There are other well-meaning but misguided projects, too—in 2003, two captive-born South China tiger cubs (from a pool of about sixty that survive in Chinese zoos) were flown to South Africa so that a team of conservationists could teach them to hunt and survive in the wild, before returning them to their native habitat in China. Although there may be a few South China tigers left in the wild, the population is far too small and fragmented to be viable, and most experts believe that these conservation efforts should be concentrated on strengthening the tigers' gene pool by improving breeding facilities in Chinese zoos.

The root of the problem is that too few countries want to work together in the tiger's interest. Success has come only to microcosms because of individual efforts, whether in scientific research or in management. But this process has been ad hoc. The institutions that govern wildlife are weak. Laws are seldom enforced, and violators seldom convicted. Proper punishment for abuse of the tiger's world does not exist— so there is more exploitation and slaughter than ever before. Just the problem of livestock grazing in India's tiger forests has been a nightmare. I believe that between 1900 and 2000, nearly one thousand tigers were poisoned in revenge for their killing of cows and buffalo. There are multiple layers of problems to tackle.

How do we stop the crisis? How do we save tigers? I believe the answer lies in doing small and practical things: not by focusing on the larger idealistic picture but by supporting the right individual strategically. It could be an individual who manages a forest or a wildlife biologist who works for an NGO. Let's consider a plan for a tract of forest with a moderate density of tigers. First, we should make sure the area is fully protected by law. Then, using all the available goodwill, we must ensure that the right person is posted to manage the area, and that he or she has a good team. Then we would have to see if an NGO could deliver any required infrastructure, such as vehicles for protection or antipoaching patrols. At this point, it would be really useful to have a scientific team undertake some innovative research in the area and to establish a small training school to conduct six-to-nine-month courses for local people in forest-related activities that preserve rather than destroy. Even if only ten members of a local community are trained like this each year, it will have a positive impact on the habitat.

People-centered ideas for conservation typically end up as rural-development strategies and are therefore in the long run counterproductive to conservation. The Global Environment Facility spent nearly seventy million dollars in six prestigious wilderness areas of India, and the result came to nothing. Much of the money was wasted and pilfered, and staff members who should have been protecting the forest were used for village work. All the selected sites have suffered tremendously in the last six years. Rest houses and bathrooms were tiled, air-conditioned vehicles were purchased for park staff, but no one created a true menu for tiger protection.

Above, I have suggested six points as simple initiatives that could make a real difference to the future of the tiger. They are universal, common-sense approaches that will work in Sumatra or Siberia or India. Each country must fine-tune its mechanisms of governance to deal with changing and local problems, but the basics are there, and they should be implemented without delay. The first priority is not money. It is finding a team—be it government or nongovernment—that is committed to saving tigers, and then this team needs to work for five to seven years without transfers or changes. There has to be enough political goodwill to ensure this, and when there isn't we have to hope that the judiciary will fight for the interests of the tiger, as the Supreme Court of India has done. Saving the tiger is all about the right person in the right job. It is all about minimizing human disturbance. It is all about protection and training local people to protect. If most of this happens, tigers will continue to survive in protected areas across Asia. If not, the tiger will vanish.

One of the world's most eminent conservationists, George Schaller, conducted the first serious research into wild tigers forty years ago and continues to inspire all those who fight to save this most magnificent of creatures.

The Future of the Tiger

George B. Schaller
Wildlife Conservation Society

I HAVE WATCHED TIGERS feeding on a buffalo kill during a moonlit night in India and tracked them through snowbound forests in the Russian Far East. Each time I encounter a tiger, even if just a glimpse of one, the fire in its eyes, its massive power, its dignity, and its beauty inspire respect, awe, and admiration for its sheer magnificence. I can well understand how local people once worshipped and feared tigers, how the animal entered dreams and visions, legends, and myths. The soul of the tiger in life and spirit permeated Asian culture and wilderness. Today as over the centuries, the Hindu goddess Durga rides a tiger to defeat the evil that plagues the world.

During the past century or two, the traditional lives of people have changed. Tigers had survived in part because of beliefs in their magical powers. With fading traditions and changes in attitudes, the tiger in much of its range was doomed. Instead of being revered it was considered a pest, one that occasionally killed livestock and people. Where once the species roamed unhampered from Turkey eastward through India and China to Russia, its range contracted and its forests became degraded, fragmented, and invaded by settlers and livestock. Tigers were relentlessly hunted, and their natural prey, such as deer and wild pigs, were also decimated. Tiger numbers plummeted. Today the tiger is endangered, with perhaps 5,000 to 7,500 remaining in the wild, more than half of them in India. When I meet a tiger, I not only marvel that it has survived but also feel anxiety for its future and sadness as well as guilt that humankind has so persecuted this icon of our natural world.

The tiger's situation is grave, but the future of the species is not all bleak. Large forest tracts remain in which tigers could recover their numbers. The cats are resilient and adaptable; populations can recover rapidly. All they need for security is space with shade and water, an ample supply of wild prey, and safety. Surely we can offer them that. Unfortunately, the tiger is gone or almost so even from various large forests. This I noted during weeks of trekking in eastern India, Laos, Vietnam, Myanmar, and China during the past two decades. Tigers had simply been exterminated along with their prey. Sometimes the cats are killed because they pursue livestock, but in recent years the demand for hides and for bones has made them the focus of commercial poachers.

In spite of numerous conferences that set goals for tiger conservation, the efforts to map priority areas for protection, the dedication with which the illicit trade in tiger parts is being monitored, and the many organizations that promote awareness of the cat's plight, the fact remains that we still have little hard information on the species. Status reports for a number of countries are based on little more than intuition. Numbers and distribution—or even just information on presence or absence—are unknown for a considerable part of the animal's range. In India and Nepal—countries that have done the most for tiger conservation—the cat and its prey have been studied and monitored in only a few reserves. Laos and Vietnam have done little for the species; China dithered for a quarter century, watching the tiger almost vanish before showing concern; Myanmar, with perhaps only one viable site left, is now taking action. However, tigers in the boreal forests of Russia are on the increase, as shown by a decade of study, because of vigorous protection; it is the only country that can legitimately make such a claim.

Overall, habitats and tiger numbers continue to dwindle. There are far too few skilled persons active in the field as guardians of tiger forests. Such persons are needed to census and monitor tigers, train local staff, resolve conflicts and promote coexistence between tigers and local people,

and collaborate with officials. The tiger will not be saved by deskbound conservationists, no matter how dedicated they are. India has twenty-seven Project Tiger reserves. How many of these are wholly secure: fully protected, safe from intrusive development, with humans and livestock strictly regulated and wildlife accurately monitored? Tiger reserves in other countries sometimes do not have any staff.

It has become axiomatic that to save tigers we must manage their living space. This implies that there is a need to devise tactics that uniquely suit the management of an area, including involvement with the problems and aspirations of the local people. So far we know only how to protect tigers, not how to manage them. What does one do when tigers in a small forest area become inbred or wander into villages to prey on livestock or fill their habitat beyond capacity?

Conservation is politics. The tiger needs more than legal protection. We need the willpower and long-term commitment of governments in the form of effective protection of both the species and its habitat. Key areas in every country must be managed and treasured by society as a whole in partnership with governments, scientific institutions, and local people. Every nation has ample funds: it merely depends on having the moral vision to give priority to its natural heritage. Religion must also become associated with conservation again to help recapture the spiritual and cultural values and feeling of responsibility that once bound people to nature and the tiger. Our goals are clear. Now there must be action. If we carelessly permit the tiger to descend into the dark abyss of extinction, future generations will revile us for the lack of compassion toward the species and lack of foresight that deprived them of one of the most dramatic and beautiful creatures this world has seen. Our options remain open, and because of this hope still burns bright for the tiger.

GEORGE SCHALLER is a field biologist with and vice president of the Wildlife Conservation Society in New York. He spends most of his time in the field in Asia, Africa, and South America. He is the author of fifteen books, among them *The Year of the Gorilla*, *The Serengeti Lion*, *The Last Panda*, and *Tibet's Hidden Wilderness*. Schaller has collaborated for nearly two decades on the Tibetan Plateau with Chinese and Tibetan scientists working on behalf of the survival of the Tibetan antelope, wild yak, and snow leopard. In addition, he has conducted conservation projects in Laos, Myanmar, Mongolia, Iran, Tajikistan and other countries. His awards include the International Cosmos Prize (Japan) and the Tyler Prize for Environmental Achievement (USA).

Acknowledgments

I would like to thank several people who had a hand in bringing this book to fruition: Bobbie Fletcher researched many different aspects of the world of the tiger; Caroline Taggart put her pen to the first draft of the text; Mary Bahr edited and shaped the final draft. I must also thank Jeremy Eberts, the designer of the book, who put his heart and soul into this enormous venture.

This book has allowed us to present the work of some of the finest wildlife photographers in India. I would especially like to thank Kakubhai, whose photographs open a window into the secret world of the tiger. Special thanks also to Anish Andheria of *Sanctuary Asia* in Mumbai, who kindly allowed us to reproduce some photographs that have appeared in that magazine. Many thanks also to H. V. Praveen Kumar, M. D. Parashar, Fateh Singh Rathore, Toby Sinclair, R. G. Soni, Judith Wakelam, and Lu Zhi.

Museums and libraries around the world have been extraordinarily generous in permitting us to reproduce images from their collections. Special thanks to the National Museum of India in New Delhi, the Archaeological Survey of India, the Mehrangarh Museum Trust in Jodhpur, and Karan Singh. Thanks also to the Austrian Museum of Applied Arts/Contemporary Art (MAK), Vienna; the Bibliothèque nationale de France, Paris; the Koninklijk Instituut voor Tall-, Land- en Volkenkunde (KITLV), the Netherlands; the Royal Collection; the Trustees of the Chester Beatty Library, Dublin; the Worcester Art Museum, Worcester, Massachusetts; the Joslyn Art Museum, Omaha, Nebraska; the University of California, Berkeley Art Museum; the Asian Art Museum of California; the San Diego Museum of Art; the San Diego Natural History Museum; the McCord Museum of Canadian History, Montreal; and McGill University Libraries, Rare Books and Special Collections Division, Montreal. The tiger skull is courtesy of the Redpath Museum of McGill University, Montreal.

Thanks also to the School of Oriental and African Studies, where I spent much time absorbed in research in the early 1990s, and the Victoria and Albert Museum in London.

Thanks to Michael Slade at Art Resource, David Savage at Bridgeman Art, and Marie-Josée Samson at Magma for providing images from their collections. Thanks also to Ardea, London; Peter Arnold Inc., New York; Getty Images; *The China Pictorial*; Ringling Bros. and Barnum & Bailey Combined Shows, Inc.; and Erwin Neumayer.

Special thanks also to Rose Corcoran and the Sladmore Gallery, London, for permission to reproduce her exquisite tiger drawings.

I am indebted to the experts whose contributions have added a special dimension to the book. Whatever their field—natural history, anthropology, art, or history—their insights have made the tiger leap from the page. I thank you all profusely.

I also thank Paola Manfredi for her ongoing pursuit of the imagery of the tiger and its cult.

There are many others that make such books possible, among them Madan Mahatta, Mahesh Rangarajan, Vivasvat Chauhan, and Sunny Philip. I also thank the forest officers in the field for their commitment to the tiger. They are an inspiration.

Last but not least, I would like to express my thanks to Mike Birkhead for his special efforts with this book.

Notes

CHAPTER 4

157 "The Vedic corpus consists primarily of the four *Vedas*": These compositions were ritual texts largely hymns and exegesis on them and rituals and were preserved orally for many centuries through a meticulous technique of memorization.

167 "The forest which has tigers should never be cut": *Mahabharata*, Udyogaparvan, 29, 47–48.

CHAPTER 5

173 "Silius Italicus described the Carthaginian general Hannibal": J. Aymard, *Essai sur les chasses romaines des felins a la fin des Antonins* (Cynegetica). Paris, 1951.

173 "Valerius Flaccus, a Latin writer": Ibid.

173 "Alexander was deeply amazed and grieved that hound": Aelian, *On the Characteristics of Animals*, Book 8, 1.

173 "Aelian also mentions that the people of India": Ibid., Book 15, 14.

176 "strange ravening creatures freight the fleets": Petronius, *Satiricon*, 119.14, in G. Jennison, *Animals for Show and Pleasure in Ancient Rome*. Manchester, 1937, p. 72.

176 "An unexpected happening caught the attention": Martial, *Epigrams*, Book 18.

177 "How many is not clear, as Martial says": Ibid., Book 8, 26.

177 "The number must have been rather more than two": Jennison, *Animals for Show and Pleasure in Ancient Rome*, p. 76.

177 "He collected rare animals for slaughter at Rome": Ibid., p. 87.

177 "He was accompanied on journeys by an escort of elephants": Ibid., p. 90.

177 "having a taste for keeping animals and employing them": Ibid.

177 "Possibly the eastern campaigns of Septimius Severus": Ibid., p. 91.

178 "They were analyzed and identified": R. Rea, "Il Colosseo, teatro per gli spettacoli di caccia. Le fonti e i reperti," in A. La Regina, ed., *Sangue e Arena*, 2001, pp. 223–43.

CHAPTER 6

219 "One of these was found in an African province": *Mosaico e Mosaicisti nell'antichita'*. Roma, 1967, p. 11.

220 "It is certainly in Ptolemic Egypt": Luis Foucher, *Hadrumetum*. Paris, 1964, p. 218.

220 "The Latin author Statius": Ibid., p. 219. "Must" is a word generally associated with male elephants, who, when seized by sexual urge, emit a liquid from near their eyes.

220 "thyrsus": Staff carried by Dionysus shown as a stalk of giant fennel (nartex) segmented like bamboo, sometimes with ivy leaves inserted in the hollow end; in *Encyclopaedia Britannica*.

220 "ivy crowned, winged, and brandishing": C. M. Havelock, *Hellenistic Art*, 1971, pl. 8, in J. M. C. Toynbee, *Animals in Roman Life and Art*. London, 1971, p. 358, n. 68.

220 "The child on the tiger's back looks like a baby": K. M. D. Dunbabin, *The Mosaics of Roman North Africa*. Oxford, 1978, pp. 1775–81.

222 "associated to his cortege": Sometimes the chariot is drawn by leopards or lions.

222 "From his travels in India Dionysus had brought": Luis Foucher, *La Maison de la procession dionysiaque à El Jem*. Paris, 1963, p. 94.

222 "It has been suggested that widespread preference": *Mosaico e Mosaicisti nell'antichita'*. Roma, 1967, p. 21.

222 "In Roman militaristic society": Libanios, *Oratio*, Book 5, 20–21.

223 "Hunt mosaics are vivid testimony": Christine Kondoleon, *Antioch: The Lost City*. Princeton University Press and Worcester Art Museum, 2000, p. 160.

223 "smaller room": Nine feet six inches by nine feet three inches.

223 "Both floor mosaics are executed": Kondoleon, *Antioch*, p. 158.

225 "One, extremely damaged": A. Carandini, A. Ricci, M. Devos, *Filosofiana, la Villa di Piazza Armerina*. Palermo, 1982.

227 "A text of the fourth century c.e. by Saint Ambrose": C. Settis-Frugoni, *Il Grifone e la Tigre nella "Grande Caccia" di Piazza Armerina*, in *Cahiers Archeologiques*, 1975, p. 23.

227 "Because all the places are so distant": Ibid.

227 "The tiger appears in three episodes": D. T. Rice, ed., *The Great Palace of the Byzantine Emperors*, second report. Edinburgh, 1958, p. 139.

227 "conceived with a feeling": Ibid., pg. 136.

251 "It was said he could lie down in a cage": Lennie, Campbell. *Landseer: The Victorian Paragon*. London, 1976, p. 104.

253 "the tigers of wrath": Kenneth Clark, *Animals and Men: Their Relationship as Reflected in Western Art from Prehistory to the Present Day*. London, 1977, p. 41.

253 "had tawny, feline eyes": Ibid., p. 154.

253 "Though large and powerful": *Gazette des Beaux Arts*. France, September 1984, Vol. 104, Num. 1388, p. 70.

254 "Tigers, panthers, jaguars, lions": *Delacroix: The Late Work*, eds. A. Serullaz, D. Loit, E. Delacroix, J. J. Rishel, L. Prat, V. Pomarde. London, 1998, p. 450.

254 "Observe nature": Stuart Pivar, *The Barye Bronzes, A Catalogue Raisonne*. Woodbridge, 1974, p. 8.

254 "I shall never be able": James Mackay, *The Animaliers. A Collector's Guide to the Animal Sculptors of the 19th and 20th Centuries*. New York, 1973. p. 129.

254 "What energy, what ferocity": Pivar, *The Barye Bronzes*, p. 13.

256 "a Painter in every sense": Jean Bouret, *Henri Rousseau*. San Francisco, 1961, p. 168.

258 "[Rousseau] sometimes frightened": Ibid., p. 170.

258 "His pictures are his dreams": Grey Roch, Lefevre Gallery Catalogue. "Paintings by Henri Rousseau 'Le Douanier,'" October 1926.

258 "Inspiration and vision was then and now is": Hugh Honour, *Romanticism*. New York, 1979. p. 289.

258 "the beauty and genius of a work": William Beebe, *The Bird, Its Form and Function*. New York, 1906.

Bibliography

Books Published Between 1827 and 1965

Edward Hamilton Aitken. *A Naturalist on the Prowl*. Calcutta: Thacker, Spink, 1897.

Allen, Hugh. *The Lonely Tiger*. London: Faber and Faber, 1960.

Archer, Milfred. *Tippoo's Tiger*. London: Victoria and Albert Museum, 1959.

Baikov, N. A. *The Manchurian Tiger: Big Game Hunting in Manchuria*. London: Hutchinson, 1925/1936.

Baker, S. *Wild Beasts and Their Ways*. London: Macmillan, 1891.

Barras, J. *India and Tiger-hunting*. London: S. Sonnenschein, 1885.

Barras, J. *The New Shikari at Our Indian Stations*. London: Swan, Sonnenschein, 1885.

Bazé, William. *Tiger! Tiger!* London: Elek Books, 1957.

Bennet, E. T. *The Tower Menagerie*. London: Robert Jennings, 1829.

Berg, B. M. *Tiger and Mensch*. Berlin: Halltorp, 1934.

Best, J. W. *Forest Life in India*. London: John Murray, 1935.

Best, J. W. *Indian Shikar Notes*. 1922.*

Best, J. W. *Tiger Days*. London: John Murray, 1931.

Braddon, E. *Thirty Years of Shikar*. London: William Blackwood and Sons, 1895.

Bradley, M. H. *Trailing the Tiger*. New York: D. Appleton, 1929.

Brown, J. M. *Shikar Sketches: With Notes on Indian Field-Sports*. London: Hurst and Blackett, 1887.

Burke, W. S. *The Indian Field Shikar Book*. London: 1920.*

Burton, R. G. *The Book of the Tiger*. London: Hutchinson, 1933.

Burton, R. G. *Sport and Wild Life in the Deccan*. London: Seeley, Service, 1928.

Burton, R. G. *The Tiger Hunters*. London: Hutchinson, 1936.

Caldwell, H. R. *Blue Tiger*. London: Duckworth, 1925.

Campbell, W. *The Old Forest Ranger*. London: How and Parsons, 1842.

Champion, F. W. *The Jungle in Sunlight and Shadow*. London: Chatto and Windus, 1925.

Champion, F. W. *With a Camera in Tiger-land*. London: Chatto and Windus, 1927/1933.

Corbett, J. *Man-eaters of Kumaon*. Oxford: Oxford University Press, 1944.

Digby, G. B. *Tigers, Gold, and Witchdoctors*. New York: Harcourt Brace, 1928.

Eardley-Wilmot, S. *Forest Life and Sport in India*. London: Edward Arnold, 1910.

Eardley-Wilmot, S. *The Life of a Tiger*. London: Ames, 1911.

Ellison, Bernard. *The Prince of Wales in India*. London: Heinemann, 1925.

Evans, G. P. *Big-Game Shooting in Upper Burma*. London: Longmans, Green, 1912.

Fayrer, J. *The Royal Tiger of Bengal: His Life and Death*. London: J. and A. Churchill, 1875.

Felix. *Recollections of a Bison and Tiger Hunter*. London: J. M. Dent, 1906.

Fife-Cookson, Colonel J. C. *Tiger Shooting in the Doon and Ulwar*. London: Chapman and Hall, 1887.

Fletcher, F. W. F. *Sport on the Nilgiris and in Wynaad*. London: Macmillan, 1911.

*Full information is unavailable.

Forbes, James. *Oriental Memoirs*. 2 vols. London: R. Bentley, 1834–1835.

Forsyth, J. *The Highlands of Central India*. London: Chapman and Hall, 1889.

Gee, E. P. *The Wildlife of India*. London: Collins, 1964.

Glasfurd, A. I. R. *Musings of an Old Shikari*. London: John Lane and the Bodley Head, 1928.

Gouldsbury, C. E. *Tigerland*. London: Chapman and Hall, 1913.

Gouldsbury, C. E. *Tiger Slayer by Order*. New York: G. Bell and Sons, 1915.

Hamilton, D. *Records of Sport in Southern India*. London: R. H. Porter, 1892.*

Hanley, P. D. *Tiger Trails in Assam*. London: Robert Hale, 1960.

Hewett, J. P. *Jungle Trails in Northern India*. London: Methuen, 1938.

Hicks, F. C. *Forty Years among the Wild Animals of India, from Mysore to the Himalayas*. Allahabad: Pioneer Press, 1910.

Hingston, W. G., and G. R. Stevens. *The Tiger Kills*. London: Ames, 1944.*

Hornaday, W. T. *Two Years in the Jungle*. London: Kegan, Paul, Trench, 1885.

Jadho, K. R. B. S. *A Guide to Tiger Shooting*. London.*

Jepson, Stanley, ed. *Big Game Encounters*. London: Stanley Jepson, 1936.

Johnson, D. *Sketches of Indian Field Sports*. London: Robert Jennings, 1827.

Locke, A. *The Tigers of Trengganu*. London: Museum Press, 1954.

Maharajah of Cooch Behar. *Thirty-Seven Years of Big Game Shooting in Cooch Behar, the Duars, and Assam: A Rough Diary*. Prescott: Wolfe, 1993 (originally published in 1908).

Mockler-Ferryman, A. F. *The Life Story of a Tiger*. London: Adam and Charles Black, 1910.

Mundy, Captain G. C.. *Pen and Pencil Sketches, Being the Journal of a Tour of India*. London: John Murray, 1833.

Panwar, H. S. *Kanha National Park*. London: Cassell, 1964.

Perry, Richard. *The World of the Tiger*. London: Cassell, 1964.

Pocock R. I. *1929—February, a Lion Tiger Hybrid*. The Felid, 1929.*

Reid, M. *The Tiger-hunter*. New York: G. W. Dillingham, 1892.

Rice, W. *Indian Game (from Quail to Tiger)*. London: W. H. Allen, 1884.

Rice, W. *Tiger-shooting in India*. London: Smith, Elder, 1857.

Rousselet, L. *The King of the Tigers*. London: S. Low, Marston, Searle, and Rivington, 1888.

Sanderson, G. P. *Thirteen Years Among the Wild Beasts of India*. London: W. H. Allen, 1882.*

Singh, K. *One Man and a Thousand Tigers*. New York: Dodd, Mead: 1959.

Singh, K. *The Tiger of Rajasthan*. London: Robert Hale, 1959.

Smythies, E. A. *Big Game Shooting in Nepal*. Calcutta: Thacker, Spink, 1942.

Smythies, O. *Tiger Lady*. London: Heinemann, 1953.

Stacton, David. *A Ride on a Tiger*. London: Museum Press, 1954.

Stebbing, E. P. *The Diary of a Sportsman Naturalist in India*. London: John Lane, 1920.

Stebbing, E. P. *Jungle By-ways in India*. London: John Lane and Bodley Head, 1911.

Stewart, A. E. *Tiger and Other Game*. London: Longman's, Green, 1878.

Sutton, R. L. *Tiger Trails in Southern Asia*. St. Louis, C. V. Mosby, 1926.

Taylor, M. L. *The Tiger's Claw*. London: Burke, 1956.

Todd, W. H. *Tiger! Tiger!* London: Heath Cranton, 1927.

Trench, Philip. *Tiger Hunting: A Day's Sport in the East*. London: Hodgson and Graves, 1836.

Wardrop, Major A. E. *Days and Nights of Indian Big Game*. London: Macmillan, 1923.

BOOKS PUBLISHED AFTER 1965
(when conservation strategies for the tiger first began)

Alvi, M. A., and A. Rahman. *Jahangir: The Naturalist*. Delhi: Indian National Science Academy, 1968.

Amore, C. *20 Ways to Track a Tiger*. U.S.A.: Wildlife Worlds, 2003.

Barnes, Simon. *Tiger!* London: Boxtree, 1994.

Bedi, Rajesh, and Ramesh Bedi. *Indian Wildlife*. New Delhi: Brijbasi, 1984.

Bergmann Sucksdorff, A. *Tiger in Sight*. London: A. Deutsch, 1970.

Boomgaard, P. *Frontiers of Fear*. London: Yale University Press, 2001.

Booth, Martin. *Carpet Sahib: A Life of Jim Corbett*. London: Constable, 1986.

Boyes, Jonathan. *Tiger-men and Tofu Dolls: Tribal Spirits in Northern Thailand*. Chiang Mai, Thailand: Silkworm Books, 1997.

Breeden, Stanley, and Belinda Wright. *Through the Tiger's Eyes: A Chronicle of India's Wildlife*. Berkeley: Ten Speed Press, 1996.

Brunskill, C. *Tiger Forest: A Visual Study of Ranthambhore National Park*. London: Troubador, 2003.

Chakrabarti, Kalyan. *Man-eating Tigers*. Calcutta: Darbari Prokashan, 1992.

Choudhary, L. K., and S. A. Khan. *Bandhavgarh Fort of the Tiger*. Sandhya Prakash Bhavan, 2003.*

Choudhury, S. R. Khairi. *The Beloved Tigress*. Dehradun: Natraj, 1999.

Courtney, N. *The Tiger, Symbol of Freedom*. London: Quartet Books, 1980.

Cubitt, Gerald, and Guy Mountfort. *Wild India*. London: Collins, 1985.

Daniel, J. C. *The Tiger in India: A Natural History*. Dehradun: Natraj, 2003.

Denzau, Gertrude, and Helmut Denzau. *Königstiger*. Steinfurt, Teclenborg Verlag, 1996.

Elliott, J. G. *Field Sports in India, 1800–1947*. London: Gentry Books, 1973.

Fend, Werner. *Die Tiger von Abutschmar*. Vienna: Verlag Fritz Molden, 1972.

Forest, Denys. *The Tiger of Mysore: The Life and Death of Tipu Sultan*. London: Chatto and Windus, 1970.

Ghorpade, M. Y. *Sunlight and Shadows*. London: Gollancz, 1983.

Green, I. *Wild Tigers of Bandhavgarh—Encounters in a Fragile Forest*. Tiger Books, 2002.*

Gurang, K. K. *Heart of the Jungle: The Wildlife of Chitwan, Nepal*. London: Andre Deutsch, 1983.

Harris, H. A. *Sport in Greece and Rome*. London: Thames and Hudson, 1972.

Hodges-Hill, Edward. *Man Eater—Tales of Lion and Tiger Encounters*. London: Cockbird Press, 1992.

Hornocker, M., ed. *Track of the Tiger*. San Francisco: Sierra Club Books, 1997.

Israel, Samuel, and Toby Sinclair, eds. *Indian Wildlife*. Singapore: Apa Publications, 1987.

Ives, Richard. *Of Tigers and Men*. New York: Doubleday, 1996.

Jackson, Peter. *Endangered Species—Tiger*. London: Apple Press, 1990.

Jung, S. *Tryst with Tigers*. London: Robert Hale, 1967.

Lindblad, Jan. *Tigrata—Vart storsta aventyr*. Belgium: 1982.

Lipton, Mimi, ed. *The Tiger Rugs of Tibet*. London: Thames and Hudson, 1998.

Manfredi, Paola. *In Danger: Habitats, Species, and People*. New Delhi: Ranthambhore Foundation, 1997.

Matthiessen, Peter. *Tigers in the Snow*. London: Harvill, 2000.

McDougal, Charles. *The Face of the Tiger*. London: Rivington Books, 1977.

McNeely, Jeffrey A., and P. S. Wachtel. *The Soul of the Tiger*. New York: Doubleday, 1988.

Meacham, Cory. *How the Tiger Lost Its Stripes*. New York: Harcourt Brace, 1997.

Montgomery, Sy. *Spell of the Tiger*. Boston: Houghton Mifflin, 1995.

Mountfort, Guy. *Back from the Brink*. London: Hutchinson, 1978.

Mountfort, Guy. *Saving the Tiger*. London: Michael Joseph, 1981.

Mountfort, Guy. *Tigers*. London: Newton Abbot, 1973.

Naidu, M. Kamal. *Trail of the Tiger*. Dehradun: Natraj, 1998.

Niyogi, Tushar K. *Tiger Cult of the Sundarbans*. Calcutta: Anthropological Survey of India, 1996.

Peissel, Michel. *Tiger for Breakfast: The Story of Boris of Kathmandu*. New York: Dutton, 1966.

Perry, Richard. *The World of the Tiger*. London: Cassells, 1964.

Prater, S. H. *The Book of Indian Animals*. Bombay: BNHS, 1988.

Rabinowitz, Alan. *Wildlife Abuse: Chasing the Dragon's Tail*. 1991.*

Rangarajan, M. *India's Wildlife History*. New Delhi: Permanent Black, 2001.

Ranjitsinh, M. K. *Beyond the Tiger: Portraits of South-Asian Wildlife*. New Delhi: Brijbasi, 1997.

Sankhala, K. *Tiger!* London: Collins, 1978.

Sankhala, K. *Tiger Land*. New York: Bobbs-Merrill, 1975.

Schaller, G. B. *The Deer and the Tiger*. Chicago: University of Chicago Press, 1967.

Seidensticker, John, Sarah Christie, and Peter Jackson, eds. *Riding the Tiger*. Cambridge: Cambridge University Press, 1999.

Shah, Anup, and Manoj Shah. *A Tiger's Tale*. Kingston-upon-Thames: Fountain Press, 1996.

Singh, Bhagat. *Wild Encounters*. India: Pelican Creations International, 1999.

Singh, Billy Arjan. *The Legend of the Maneater*. New Delhi: Ravi Dayal, 1993.

Singh, Billy Arjan. *Tara, a Tigress*. London: Quartet Books, 1981.

Singh, Billy Arjan. *Tiger Book*. Delhi: Lotus Roli, 1997.

Singh, Billy Arjan. *Tiger Haven*. London: Macmillan, 1973.

Singh, Billy Arjan. *A Tiger's Story*. Delhi: HarperCollins, 1999.

Singh, Billy Arjan. *Tiger! Tiger!* London: Jonathan Cape, 1984.

Singh, Dr. L. S. *Tara, the Cocktail Tigress: The Story of Genetic Pollution of the Indian Tigers*. Allahbad: Print World, 2000.

Sinha, V. R. *The Tiger Is a Gentleman*. Bangalore: Wildlife, 1999.

Stracey, P. D. *Tigers*. London: Arthur Barker, 1968.

Sunquist, Fiona, and Mel Sunquist. *Tiger Moon*. Chicago: University of Chicago Press, 1988.

Sunquist, Mel, and Fiona Sunquist. *Wild Cats of the World*. Chicago: University of Chicago Press, 2002.

R. Thapar. *Early India, From the Origins to A.D. 1300*. Berkeley: University of California Press, 2003.

R. Thapar. *From Lineage to State*. New York: Oxford University Press, 1985.

Thapar, Valmik. *Battling for Survival*. New Delhi: Oxford University Press, 2003.

Thapar, Valmik. *The Cult of the Tiger*. New Delhi: Oxford University Press, 2002.

Thapar, Valmik. *The Land of the Tiger*. London: BBC Books, 1997.

Thapar, Valmik. *The Secret Life of Tigers*. New Delhi: Oxford University Press, 1998.

Thapar, Valmik. *Tiger: Habitats, Life Cycle, Food Chains, and Threats*. London: Wayland Publishers, 1999.

Thapar, Valmik. *Tiger: Portrait of a Predator*. London: Collins, 1986.

Thapar, Valmik. *The Tiger's Destiny*. London: Kyle Cathie, 1992.

Thapar, Valmik. *Tigers: The Secret Life*. London: Hamish Hamilton, 1989.

Thapar, Valmik. *Wild Tigers of Ranthambhore*. New Delhi: Vikas Publishing, 1983.

Thapar, Valmik. *With Tigers in the Wild*. New Delhi: Vikas Publishing, 1983.

Thapar, Valmik, ed. *Saving Wild Tigers*. New Delhi: Oxford University Press, 2001.

Tilson, R., and U. Seal, eds. *Tigers of the World—The Biology, Biopolitics, Management, and Conservation of an Endangered Species*. Park Ridge, N.J.: Noyes Publications, 1987.

Toovey, J., ed. *Tigers of the Raj*. Gloucester: Alan Sutton, 1987.

Turner, Alan. *The Big Cats and Their Fossil Relatives*. New York: Columbia University Press, 1997.

Tyabji, Hashim. *Bandhavgarh National Park*. New Delhi: 1994.*

Verma, Som Prakash. *Flora and Fauna of Mughal Art*. Mumbai: Marg Publications, 1999.

Ward, Geoffrey C., with Diane Raines Ward. *Tiger-wallahs*. New Delhi: Oxford University Press, 2002.

Ward, Geoffrey C. *Tiger Wallahs: Encounters with the Men Who Tried to Save the Greatest of the Great Cats*. New York: HarperCollins, 1993.

F. Zimmerman. *The Jungle and the Aroma of Meats*. Columbia: South Asia Books, 1999.

Zwaenepoel, Jean-Pierre. *Tigers*. San Francisco: Chronicle Books, 1992.

ARTICLES PUBLISHED BETWEEN 1892 AND 1965

Ali, Salim. "The Mohgul Emperors of India as Naturalists and Sportsmen." *Journal of the Bombay Natural History Society* 31(4) (1927): 833–61.

Bannerman, W. B. "Capturing Tiger with Birdlime." *Journal of the Bombay Natural History Society* 25 (1917): 753.

Biscoe, W. A. "Tiger Killing a Panther." *Journal of the Bombay Natural History Society* 9(4) (1895): 490.

Boswell, K. "Scent Trails and Pooking in Tigers." *Journal of the Bombay Natural History Society* 54(2) (1957): 454.

Boswell, K. "Following Up Wounded Tiger at Night." *Journal of the Bombay Natural History Society* 54(2) (1957): 454–45.

Burton, R. "Death Cry of a Tiger." *Journal of the Bombay Natural History Society* 48(1) (1948): 176–78.

Burton, R. "Rabies in Tiger—Two Proved Instances." *Journal of the Bombay Natural History Society* 49(3) (1950): 538–41.

Burton, R. "A History of Shikar in India." *Journal of the Bombay Natural History Society* 50(4) (1952): 845-69.

Burton, R. G. "The Tiger's Method of Making a Kill." *Journal of the Bombay Natural History Society* 49(3) (1934): 538–41.

Campbell, T. A. "Tiger Eating a Bear." *Journal of the Bombay Natural History Society* 9(1) (1894): 101.

Champion, F. "Tiger Tracks." *Journal of the Bombay Natural History Society* 33(2) (1884): 284–87.

Champion, F. W. "Preserving Wildlife in the United Provinces." In *The Preservation of Wildlife in India: A Compilation*. Edited by R. W. Burton. Bangalore, India, 1953.

Chaturvedi, M. D. "Future of the Tiger." *Indian Forester* 81(2) (1955): 7334.

Corbett, G. "A Tiger Attacking Elephants." *Journal of the Bombay Natural History Society* (7)1 (1892): 192.

Corbett, Jim. "Wildlife in the Village." *Review of the Week* (Nainital), 1932.

Fenton, L. "Tigers Hamstringing Their Prey Before Killing." *Journal of the Bombay Natural History Society* 16(4) (1905): 756.

Fraser, S. M. "Tiger Netting in Mysore." *Journal of the Bombay Natural History Society* 1902.*

Hearsey, L. "Tiger Killing Swamp Deer or Gond." *Journal of the Bombay Natural History Society* 35(4) (1932): 885–86.

Hubback, T. R. "Three Months after Big Game in Pahang." *Bombay Natural History Society.*

Littledale, H. "Bears Being Eaten by Tigers." *Journal of the Bombay Natural History Society* 4(4) (1889): 3416.

Morris, R. "A Tigress with Five Cubs." *Journal of the Bombay Natural History Society* 31(3) (1927): 810–11.

Pocock, R. I. "Tigers." *Journal of the Bombay Natural History Society* 33(3) (1929): 505–41.

Richardson, W. "Tiger Cubs." *Journal of the Bombay Natural History Society* 5(2) (1890): 191.

Toogood, C. "Number of Cubs in a Tigress Litter." *Journal of the Bombay Natural History Society* 39(1) (1936): 158.

ARTICLES PUBLISHED AFTER 1965

Choudhury, S.R. "Pragmatic Practice in a Tiger-tracer and Grass-tracer." In *International Symposium on Tiger*, pp. 358–65. New Delhi: Project Tiger, Department of Enviornment, Government of India, 1979.

Desai, J. H., and A. K. Malhotra. "The White Tiger." New Delhi: Publications Division, Ministry of Information and Broadcasting, 1992.

Dinerstein, E., E. Wikramanayake, J. Robinson, U. Karanth, A. Rabinowitz, D. Olson, T. Mathew, P. Hedao, M. Connor, G. Hemley, and D. Bolze. "A Framework for Identifying High Priority Areas and Actions for the Conservation of Tigers in the Wild." Washington, D.C.: World Wildlife Fund and the U.S. Wildlife Conservation Society, 1997.

Gilbert, R. "Notes on Maneating Tigers." *Journal of the Bombay Natural History Society* 4(3) (1989): 195–206.

Green, M. J. B. "IUCN Directory of South Asian Protected Areas." Cambridge, U.K.: IUCN, 1990.

Jackson, P. "The Bengal Tiger—Man-eater or Large-Hearted Gentlemen?" *TV Guide*, 1985.

Karanth, K. "Tigers in India: A Critical Review of Field Census." In *Tigers of the World—The Biology, Biopolitics, Management, and Conservation of an Endangered Species*, eds. R. Tilson and U. Seal, pp. 118–32. Park Ridge, N.J.: Noyes Publications, 1987.

Karanth, K. U. "Estimating Tiger: *Panthera Tigris* Populations from Camera-trap Data Using Capture-recapture Models." *Biological Conservation* 71 (1995): 333–38.

Karanth, K. U., and M. D. Madhusudan. "Avoiding Paper Tigers and Saving Real Tigers: Response to Saberwal." *Conservation Biology* 11 (3) (1997): 818–20.

Karanth, K. U., and J. D. Nicholas. "Estimation of Tiger Densities in India Using Photographic Captures and Recapture." *Ecology* 79(8) (1998): 2852–62.

Kronholz, J. "You Can Tell a Tiger by Its Face Stripes—but It Isn't Advised: Using Paw-print ID System, India Finds Its Bengals Are Burning Brighter Now." *The Wall Street Journal*, August 6, 1982.

Leyhausen, P. "What Is a Viable Tiger Population?" *Cat News* 4 (1986): 3–4.

Mills, S. "The Tiger, the Dragon, and a Plan for the Rescue." *BBC Wildlife* 12(1) (1994): 50.

Rabinowitz, A.. "The Current Status of Tiger Conservation—Where Are We Now?" Report on the Year of the Tiger Conference, Dallas, Texas, 1998.

Smith, J. L. D. "The Role of Dispersal in Structuring the Chitwan Tiger Population." *Behavior* 124 (1993): 165–95.

Sunquist, M. E. "Radio Tracking the Tiger" (originally titled "Radio Tracking and Its Applications to the Study and Conservation of Tigers"). Paper presented at the International Symposium on Tiger Conservation, India, 1979.

Sunquist, M. E. "The Social Organization of Tigers (Panthera tigris) in Royal Chitwan National Park, Nepal." *Smithsonian Contributions to Zoology* 336 (1981): 1-98.

FURTHER READING: TIGERS IN ART

Aelian. *Characteristics of Animals*. Boston: Harvard University Press, 1958.

Aymard J. *Essai sur les chasses romaines des felins a' la fin des Antonins (Cynegetica)*. Paris, 1951.

Benge, Glenn F. *Antoine-Louis Barye: Sculptor of Romanticism and Realism*. University Park: Pennsylvania State University Press, 1984.

Bindon, David. *The Complete Graphic Works of William Blake*. London: Thames and Hudson, 1978.

Bindon, David. *Songs of Innocence and Experience*. London: Tate Gallery Publication in association with the William Blake Trust, circa 1991.

Bouret, Jean. *Henri Rousseau*. London: Oldbourne Press, 1961.

Campbell, Lennie. *Landseer: The Victorian Paragon*. London: Hamish Hamilton, 1976.

Clark, Kenneth. *Animals and Men*. London: Thames and Hudson, 1977.

Doherty, Terence. *The Anatomical Works of George Stubbs*. London: Secker and Warburg, 1974.

Dunbabin, K.M.D. *The Mosaics of Roman North Africa*. New York: Oxford University Press, 1978.

Foucher, L. *Hadrumetum*. Paris, 1964.

Foucher, L. *La Maison de la procession dionysiaque a El Jem*. Paris, 1963.

Goudriaan, Teun. *Hindu Tantric and Sakta Literature*. Wiesbaden: Otto Harasowitz, 1981.

Havelock, C.M. *Hellenistic Art*. London: Phaedon, 1971.

Honour, Hugh. *Romanticism*. New York: Perseus, 1979.

Innes, Miller J. *The Spice Trade of the Roman Empire*. New York: Clarendon, 1969.

Jennison, G. *Animals for Show and Pleasure in Ancient Rome*. Manchester, 1937.

Kenoyer, M.J. "The Indus Civilization," in J. Aruz (ed.), *Art of the First Cities*. New Haven: Yale University Press, 2000.

Kondoleon, Christine. *Antioch: the Lost City*. Princeton: Princeton University Press and Worcester Art Museum, 2000.

Mackay, James. *A Collectors Guide to the Animal Sculptors of the 19th and 20th Centuries*. New York: E.P Dutton and Co. Inc., 1973.

Martin, F.R. *The Miniature Painting and Paintings of Persia, India and Turkey from the 8th to the 18th Century*. Vols. I and II. Delhi: Low Price Publications, 1993. (Reprint, first published 1912).

Mathpal, Yashodhar. *Prehistoric Rock Paintings of Bhimbetka, Central India*. New Delhi: Vedams, 1984.

Mosaico e Mosaicisti nell'antichita', Roma.

Neumayer, Erwin. *Prehistoric Indian Rock Paintings*. New York: Oxford University Press, 1984.

Ohri, Vishwa Chander. *On the Origins of Pahari Paintings—Some Notes and a Discussion*. Simla: Indian Institute of Advanced Studies, 1991.

Okada, Amina. *Imperial Mughal Painters*. Paris: Flammarion, 1992.

Ormonde, Richard. *Sir Edwin Landseer*. London: Thames and Hudson, 1981.

Pivar, Stuart. *The Barye Bronzes: A Catalogue Raisonne*. Woodbridge: Antique Collectors' Club, 1974.

Rea, R. "Il Colosseo, teatro per gli spettacoli di caccia. Le fonti e i reperti," in A. La Regina, ed., *Sangue e Arena*, 2001.

Ricci, A. and M. Devos. *Filosofiana, la Villa di Piazza Armerina*. Palermo, 1982.

Rice, D.T., ed. *The Great Palace of the Byzantine Emperors*. Edinburgh, 1958.

Serullaz, D. et al. *Delacroix: The Late Work*. London: Thames and Hudson, 1998.

Toynbee, J.M.C. *Animals in Roman Life and Art*. Ithaca: Cornell University Press, 1973.

Wilson, R.J.A. *Piazza Armerina*. Austin: University of Texas Press, 1983.

About the Author

Valmik Thapar, one of the world's leading tiger conservationists, earned a degree in social anthropology from Delhi University in 1972 and since then has dedicated his life to tiger research and preservation. Thapar has been associated with Ranthambhore National Park in Rajasthan, northern India, for nearly thirty years. He is the founder and director of the Ranthambhore Foundation, which he created in 1987, an organization devoted to maintaining the ecological balance necessary to protect the tiger and its habitats all over India.

Thapar is the author of ten books on tigers, most recently *Tiger: The Ultimate Guide* (2004), *The Cult of the Tiger* (2002), *Saving Wild Tigers* (2001), *Wild Tigers of Ranthambhore* (2000), and *The Land of the Tiger* (1997), which accompanied a major BBC-TV series of the same name. Thapar has also written *Bridge of God* (2001), about the Masai Mara National Park in Kenya, and *Battling for Survival* (2003), an ecological history of the forests of South Asia. Thapar has appeared in and contributed to a number of documentaries.

Since 1992 Thapar has been serving on several expert committees of the Indian government related to tigers and wildlife and is currently a member of the Central Empowered Committee, which was constituted by the Supreme Court of India to monitor forests and wildlife. He lives in New Delhi.

Contributors

Mike Birkhead earned a doctorate at Oxford University and spent two years there doing post-doctoral work in the Department of Zoology. Since 1988, he has independently produced and/or directed more than twenty-five wildlife films for BBC, PBS, National Geographic, WNET, Discovery, and Animal Planet. His most recent documentary film is *The Ultimate Guide to Tigers*.

Raghu S. Chundawat is one of India's leading wildlife biologists. He earned his doctorate in wildlife biology, focusing on the snow leopard. He now studies the behavior of wild tigers in Panna National Park in central India. His wife, **Joanna Van Gruisen**, is a wildlife photographer.

Rose Corcoran graduated from the Royal College of Art in 2000 and has had solo exhibitions in Paris and London. She works predominantly in charcoal and pastels on a large and at times monumental scale, dedicating her art to the conservation of animals and their natural habitats.

John Goodrich received a Ph.D. in zoology in 1994 from the University of Wyoming. In 1995, he began work for the Wildlife Conservation Society's Hornocker Wildlife Institute as field coordinator for the Siberian Tiger Project. He lives in Terney, in the Russian Far East, where he directs research and conservation projects on tigers, Asiatic black bears, brown bears, and the Eurasian lynx.

K. Ullas Karanth has studied tigers for nearly twenty years. He earned his doctorate in wildlife biology with a focus on predator-prey relationships in Nagarahole National Park in southern India. From his home in India he works with the Wildlife Conservation Society in New York.

M. Monirul H. Khan is a wildlife biologist studying the tiger and other wild animals of Bangladesh. He earned a Ph.D. from Cambridge University and conducted fieldwork on the ecology and conservation of the tiger in the Sundarbans of Bangladesh. He is the author of fifteen scientific articles and many popular articles.

Andrew Kitchener, curator of mammals and birds at the National Museums of Scotland, is conducting research that has led to the reclassification of tiger subspecies. He is a member of the Cat Specialist Group of IUCN, the World Conservation Union.

Paola Manfredi has been working in India for more than twenty years on textiles, history, and cross-cultural influences on textiles. Associated with the Ranthambhore Foundation, she actively supports the conservation of endangered environments and species. She edited *In Danger: Habitats, Species, and People*, published by the Ranthambhore Foundation in 1997.

Dale Miquelle received a B.S. at Yale University, an M.S. from University of Minnesota, and a Ph.D. from University of Idaho. He worked on the Smithsonian Tiger Ecology Project in Chitwan National Park before joining the Hornocker Wildlife Institute's Siberian Tiger Project. Miquelle is now country coordinator for the Wildlife Conservation Society's Russia Program.

Ruth Padel is a classical scholar and has taught Greek at Oxford, Cambridge, London, and Princeton universities. She is also a poet and Fellow of the Royal Society of Literature. She has won the United Kingdom National Poetry Competition and has published six poetry collections. The great-great-granddaughter of Charles Darwin, she is also a Fellow of the Royal Zoological Society of London. Her travel memoir about wild tigers will be published by Little, Brown in 2005.

Fateh Singh Rathore was the field director of Ranthambhore National Park from 1979 to 1987. He is largely credited for making the park the exceptional tiger reserve that it is. He has spent forty years working with wild tigers and continues to live near the park.

George Schaller is a field biologist and vice president of the Wildlife Conservation Society in New York. He is the author of fifteen books, among them *The Serengeti Lion* and *Tibet's Hidden Wilderness*. Schaller has conducted conservation projects in Laos, Myanmar, Mongolia, Iran, Tajikistan, and many other countries. His awards include the International Cosmos Prize (Japan) and the Tyler Prize for Environmental Achievement (U.S.A.).

John Sellar served for twenty-three years in the Scottish Police Service before joining the Convention on International Trade in Endangered Species (CITES) as secretariat in 1997. He has made more than one hundred missions to forty-eight different countries (including missions to twelve tiger-range states as the leader of the CITES Tiger Missions Technical Team). He also serves as the coordinator of the CITES Tiger Enforcement Task Force.

Billy Arjan Singh, who was born in 1917, is perhaps India's best-known tiger conservationist. He resides in Tiger Haven, his farm adjacent to the Dudhwa tiger reserve in Uttar Pradesh, India. He is the author of many books on tigers and continues to work on behalf of tiger habitat and species preservation.

Romila Thapar is Emeritus Professor of History at the Jawaharlal Nehru University in New Delhi. She has worked on early Indian history and has published a number of books, among them the Penguin history entitled *Early India* and a collection of essays on India, *Cultural Pasts*.

Archana Verma completed her Ph.D. from the Centre for Historical Studies, Jawaharlal Nehru University, New Delhi, where she is currently a visiting assistant professor in the School of Arts and Aesthetics. She has published a research article on the Bagh Caves in Madhya Pradesh and recently presented a paper on the imaging of the goddess in Madhubani paintings at an international conference on South Asia.

Edward J. Walsh is the Director of the Developmental Auditory Physiology Laboratory at the Boys Town National Research Hospital in Omaha, Nebraska. He also holds appointments in the School of Medicine and in the Department of Special Education and Communication Disorders at the University of Nebraska. In conjunction with colleagues at Omaha's Henry Doorly Zoo, he studies the utility of acoustic tools to reduce extinction pressures facing tigers in the wild.

Geoffrey C. Ward is an award-winning American historian, biographer, and screenwriter who spent several boyhood years in India and has written about its wildlife for *Audubon*, *Smithsonian*, and *National Geographic*. He is also the author of *The Year of the Tiger* (with Michael Nichols) and *Tiger Wallahs* (with his wife, the writer Diane Raines Ward), and he serves on the board of the Save the Tiger Fund.

Belinda Wright, a renowned tiger conservationist and wildlife campaigner, is the founder and executive director of the Wildlife Protection Society of India. She has pioneered investigations into the illegal wildlife trade in India and helped expose the trade in tiger parts. Before turning to full-time conservation work in 1994, she was a wildlife photographer and an Emmy Award–winning documentary filmmaker for *National Geographic*.

Conservation Organizations Focused on Protecting Wild Tigers

Bombay Natural History Society, Mumbai
www.bnhs.org

David Shepherd Wildlife Foundation, U.K.
www.davidshepherd.org

Environmental Investigation Agency, U.K.
www.eia-international.org

Global Tiger Patrol, U.K.
www.globaltigerpatrol.co.uk

Project Tiger (Government of India)
www.projecttiger.nic.in

The National Fish and Wildlife Foundation (Save the Tiger Fund), U.S.A.
www.NFWF.org

Sanctuary Asia Magazine, Mumbai
www.sanctuaryasia.com

U.S. Fish and Wildlife Service (Rhino & Tiger Conservation Fund), U.S.A.
www.fws.gov

The Wildlife Conservation Society, New York
www.wcs.org

Wildlife Institute of India
www.wii.gov.in

Wildlife Protection Society of India
www.wpsi-india.org

WWF India
www.wwfindia.org

WWF International, Switzerland
www.panda.org

Illustration Credits

ii   © Kakubhai

viii © H. V. Praveen Kumar

xii   Clockwise from top left: © Kakubhai; © Clem
      Haagner/ardea.com; © NHPA/Andy Rouse; © Joanna
      Van Gruisen/ardea.com

1   Tejbir Singh

2   Top: © John Daniels/ardea.com; Bottom: © San Diego
     Natural History Visual Reference Collection.
     Artist: Jim Melli

3   © Anup Shah/naturepl.com

5   © China Pictorial

6   © Erwin Neumayer

7   © Harappa Archaeological Research Project/Courtesy,
     Department of Archaeology and Museums,
     Government of Pakistan

8   Top: © Koninklijk Instituut voor Tall-, Land- en
     Volkenkunde (KITLV); Bottom: Private collection
     (Valmik Thapar)

9   © Roger Viollet/Getty Images

10   © Bettmann/CORBIS/MAGMA

16   © Fateh Singh Rathore

17   © Kakubhai

22   © Yale Center for British Art, Paul Mellon Collection,
     USA/Bridgeman Art Library

23   © N. C. Dhingra/Sanctuary Photolibrary

24   Top: Tiger skull courtesy of the Redpath Museum of
     McGill University, Montreal. Photo by Christine Guest;
     Bottom: © H. V. Praveen Kumar

25   © Lu Zhi

26   Top: © Daniel Cox/OSF; Bottom: © Chris
     Brunskill/ardea.com

27   © Valmik Thapar

28   © Kakubhai

29   © Gunter Ziesler/Peter Arnold Inc.

30   © Kakubhai

32   © Masahiro Lijima/ardea.com

33   © Kakubhai

34   © Rose Corcoran

35   © Valmik Thapar

36   © H. V. Praveen Kumar

37   Top: © Valmik Thapar; Bottom: © N. C. Dhingra/
     Sanctuary Photolibrary

38   © Dr. T. Shivanandappa/Sanctuary Photolibrary

40   © Kakubhai

41   Private collection (Valmik Thapar)

43   © Valmik Thapar

44   © K. M. Narayana Swamy/Sanctuary Photolibrary

46   © Joanna Van Gruisen

48   © Joanna Van Gruisen

50   © Judith Wakelam

51   © Valmik Thapar

52   © Valmik Thapar

53   © Fateh Singh Rathore

54   © Fateh Singh Rathore

55   © Fateh Singh Rathore

56   © Fateh Singh Rathore

57   © Kakubhai

58   © Kakubhai

60   © E. A. Kuttapan

61   © Valmik Thapar

62   © Toby Sinclair

65   © Valmik Thapar

66   © Sanat Shodhan/Sanctuary Photolibrary

67   © Kakubhai

70   © Kakubhai

71   © Kakubhai

72   © Kakubhai

75   © Kakubhai

77   © Valmik Thapar

78   © Lu Zhi

79   © Kakubhai

80   © Diane Raines Ward/Peter Arnold Inc.

81   © Valmik Thapar

82   © Fateh Singh Rathore

83   © Valmik Thapar

84   © Kakubhai

86   © Valmik Thapar

87   © Kakubhai

88   © Tom and Pat Leeson/ardea.com

91   © M. N. Jayakumar/Sanctuary Photolibrary

233 Courtesy National Museum, New Delhi
234 Private collection (Valmik Thapar)
235 Courtesy National Museum, New Delhi
236 Courtesy National Museum, New Delhi
237 © Victoria and Albert Museum, London/Art Resource, NY
238 Courtesy National Museum, New Delhi
239 Courtesy National Museum, New Delhi
240 Courtesy National Museum, New Delhi
241 Private collection (Dr. Karan Singh)
242 Private collection (Valmik Thapar)
243 Top and bottom: Private collection (Valmik Thapar)
244 © University of California, Berkeley Art Museum. Photograph by Ben Blackwell
245 © Asian Art Museum of California. Gift of George Hopper Fitch, 1991.9.a-.b. Used by permission.
246 Top and bottom: © The Mehrangarh Museum Trust, Jodhpur
247 © The Mehrangarh Museum Trust, Jodhpur
248 © Rose Corcoran
249 Top: © Christie's Images/CORBIS/MAGMA; Bottom: © Yale Center for British Art, Paul Mellon Collection, USA/Bridgeman Art Library
250 Top: The Royal Collection © 2004, Her Majesty Queen Elizabeth II; Bottom: © British Museum, London, UK/ Bridgeman Art Library
251 Top: © Joslyn Art Museum, Omaha, Nebraska. Gift of Francis T. B. Martin; Bottom: © Christie's Images/CORBIS/MAGMA
252 © Fitzwilliam Museum, University of Cambridge, UK/ Bridgeman Art Library
253 © Erich Lessing/Art Resource, NY
254 Top: © Réunion des Musées Nationaux/Art Resource, NY; Bottom: © The Burstein Collection/CORBIS/ MAGMA
255 Top: © Réunion des Musées Nationaux/Art Resource, NY; Bottom: Courtesy of the Sladmore Gallery, London, UK
256 Courtesy of the Sladmore Gallery, London, UK
257 © National Gallery Collection; by kind permission of the Trustees of the National Gallery, London/CORBIS/ MAGMA
259 © Nimatallah/Art Resource, NY. © 2004 Salvador Dali, Gala-Salvador Dali Foundation/Artists Rights Society (ARS), New York
260 © Kakubhai
263 © Historical Picture Archive/CORBIS/MAGMA
266 *The Jungle Book* by Rudyard Kipling. The Kipling Collection. Rare Books and Special Collections Division, McGill University Libraries, Montreal, Canada
272 © Vivek Sinha/Sanctuary Photolibrary
274 © McCord Museum of Canadian History, Montreal

275 Courtesy of Jean-Jacques Annaud
276 Private collection (Valmik Thapar)
277 Private collection (Richard Holkar)
283 © Bettmann/CORBIS/MAGMA
284 © Fateh Singh Rathore
286 © Fateh Singh Rathore
291 © Dr. Ajit Deshmukh/Sanctuary Photolibrary
292 © Kevin Schafer/Peter Arnold Inc.
296 © R.P.G./YEVGENY KONDAKOV/CORBIS SYGMA/ MAGMA
299 © BAGLA PALLAVA/CORBIS SYGMA/MAGMA
302 © S. C. Sharma
305 © Valmik Thapar
308 © A. Kothari
313 © H. V. Praveen Kumar
314 © Valmik Thapar
315 © Kakubhai

Index

adult skills, 69–73
advertising, 265–66, 296
Africa, 3, 6, 178, 219–20, 222
Akbar, Emperor, 186–87, 229–32
Akbarnama, 186–87, 230
Amur tigers (*Panthera tigris altaica*), 18, 20, 21, 88–89, 204, 296–97
ancient world, 170–78, 219–27
Anderson, Kenneth, 49, 136
art, 217, 248–58
    miniature paintings in, 229–47
    mosaics, 219–27
Asia, 5–8, 19–21, 114, 151–52, 156, 170, 287, 297, 304, 312
Asian tigers (*Panthera tigris tigris*), 18–19, 20, 21

Balinese tigers, 18, 21
Bandhavgarh National Park, 59, 141
Bangladesh, 94–97
Battye, R. K. M., 93
Bayre, Antoine Louis, 254–56
Bazé, William, 113
Bengal Civil Service, 134
Bengal Staff Corps, 99
Bengal tigers, 20, 29, 88–89, 180, 214, 301
Bergmann's rule, 19
Birkhead, Mike, 49, 135, 208–13, 296
birth, birth rate, 45, 89
Blake, William, 252–53, 258, 262–65, 267
blue or black tigers, 29, 269, 276
Borges, Jorge Luis, 268–70
Brander, A. A. Dunbar, 92, 126
Broken Tail, 76, 211
Buddhism, 163–64
Bugatti, Rembrandt, 256

Caldwell, H. R., 133
calls, *see* communication; sounds
canines, 25, 127, 144
captivity, *see* menageries and captivity
carnassials, 25, 122

carpal hairs, 31
Caspian tigers (*Panthera tigris vigata*), 7, 18–19, 21
cave, rock painting, 7, 154–55
Champion, Frederick W., 41, 99, 100, 126
Chesterton, G. K., 266
China, 3, 5, 18, 179–80, 281, 296, 301, 310, 312
Chinese medicine, 151–52, 209, 285–87
Chitwan National Park, 45, 82, 94, 140–41, 148, 281
chuffing, 35
Chundawat, Raghu S., 45, 46–47, 48, 83–86, 211, 297
circuses, 178–79, 202–6, 214
claws, 26, 122
cline, 18
clouded leopards (*Neofelis nebulosa*), 3
coat, *see* fur
communications, 32, 33, 80–81, 99–109
    sense of smell and, 36, 102–6
    social, 34–35, 72–73
    see also sounds
conservation and protection, 41–42, 96–97, 114, 149, 199–201, 204–5, 215, 287–89, 296–300, 310–14
    legislation on, 277–83
    see also specific parks
Convention on International Trade in Endangered Species (CITES), 280–81, 287, 306–7
Corbett, Jim, 41, 126, 137–38, 265, 270–71, 276
Corbett National Park, 41, 140, 209
Corcoran, Rose, 217, 248–59
counting tigers, 94–97, 114–116
    see also populations, tiger; tracking
courtship and mating, 29, 66, 145–49
crocodiles, 64, 142–43
cubs, 39, 42, 45, 49–51, 59–60, 79, 82–83, 90, 100, 103, 105, 111–12, 116
    care and feeding of, 47, 63–64, 127–29, 132, 142–43, 149
    hunting with, 49, 63–64, 69–70
    skills learned by, 63–73
cults, 151–67, 242

Dali, Salvador, 258

Darwin, Charles, 9–16
Delacroix, Eugène, 251–52, 267
dewclaws, 26
diet, 60–64, 69, 73, 132–44
Dionysus myth, 219–22
documentaries and films, 141, 206–13, 296
dry forest populations, 85–86
Dudhwa National Park, 141, 277, 288, 290
Durga, 152, 154, 166, 239

Eardley-Wilmot, Sainthill, 55
ears, 32–33, 122
Egyptian civilization, 170, 173, 176, 186
elephants, 126, 140, 155, 170, 179, 186, 193, 194
entertainments, 183–86, 206–7
    see also circuses
evolution, 12, 24
    see also Darwin, Charles
extinction, 20–21, 199–201, 310
    see also conservation
eyes, 31–32, 127

family life, 52–59, 74–76, 112
feeding, 47, 63–64, 100, 111–12, 122–25, 127–29, 132–35, 137, 142–43
    see also diet; prey
flehmen, 36, 103, 109
Forest Conservation Act (1980), 282
formants, 34
Forsyth, James, 99–100
fossils, 2–7, 15
fur, 27–29, 120
future for survival, 297–314

Gandhi, Indira, 42, 80, 280–83, 298, 303
Gandhi, Rajiv, 42, 282–283
Genghis, 90, 93, 99, 105–6, 130, 141, 209
Gérôme, Jean-Léon, 251–52
glands, scent, 39, 105
Goodrich, John, 106–9, 138, 292–95, 297
grooming, 27, 39, 47, 51, 116
Grzimek, Bernhard, 80
Gruisen, Joanna Van, 83–86
Gupta and Chola civilizations, 164

habitats, 17, 18, 19, 27, 85–86, 93, 94, 114–15, 130, 149, 277–83, 285, 296
    see also territories
Hailey National Park, see Corbett National Park
hair, see fur
Hamzanama, 230–31
Hanley, Patrick, 45, 135, 145
Harappa, 7, 155–57, 167
hearing, sense of, 32–33, 35, 102, 122

Hellenistic civilization, 170–71, 173
hierarchy, 64, 74, 81, 89, 90, 92–93
Himalayas, 17, 41
Homo erectus, 3–5
Homo habilis, 3
Homo sapiens, 5
human threat, 7, 68, 79, 85–86, 89, 93, 96, 114, 137, 165–66, 273–80, 296–97
    see also conservation; hunting
Humboldt, Alexander von, 11, 13
hunting, 9, 41, 42, 90, 92, 116–44, 235–38, 273–80, 284–90
    early, 186–88
    in eighteenth century, 188–90
    in nineteenth century, 190–95
    represented in art, 222–27, 235–38
    tiger skills and techniques for, 23–39, 49, 63–64, 69–70, 73–76, 122, 127–30
    in twentieth century, 193–201
Hyrcanian tigers, see Caspian tigers

ice ages, 3, 5, 6, 7, 19
incisors, 25
India, 5, 6, 7, 13, 17, 18, 29, 41–42, 83, 85
    ancient, 170, 173, 176
    conservation and protection programs in, 276–83, 297, 310
    cultural symbolism of tigers in, 153–67
    hunting in 186–201
Indo-Chinese tigers (Panthera tigris corbetti), 20, 81
Indonesia, 6, 21, 152
infrasound, 33
inspiration, tigers as, 248–58

Jacobson's organ, 36
Javan tigers, 5, 18–19, 21
    see also Sunda Island tigers
Journal of the Bombay Natural History Society, 55, 64, 93, 100, 136

Kanha National Park, 140
Karanth, Ullas, 94, 114–116, 141, 144, 211, 288, 297
Khan, M. Monirul H., 93–97
Kipling, Rudyard, 265
Kitchner, Andrew, 17–19
Kublai, 55–56, 90, 106, 146
Kublai Khan, 179–80

Landseer, Edwin, 181, 250–52, 254
langurs, 138–39
Laxmi, 52–59, 69–73, 90, 111–12, 133
leopards, 140–41
leucocystic, 28–29
lions, 4, 7, 171, 193, 261
literature, 171–73, 179–80, 261–71

McDougal, Charles, 111, 125, 140–41, 297
Machli, 66–68, 74, 76, 101, 209–11
Mahabharata, 158–62, 247
Manfredi, Paola, 170–78, 217, 219–27
mangroves, 17, 94
mating, *see* courtship and mating
Mauryan civilization, 162–63
menageries and captivity, 169, 173, 180–81, 214–15, 262, 267–68
miacids, 2–3
migration patterns, 20–21
Milne, A. A., 265
miniature paintings, 229–47
Miquelle, Dale, 83, 88–89, 291–97
mobility and range, 90–93
Mohenjo Daro, 7, 155
Mongol empire, 179–80
Morris, R. C., 64, 100
mosaics, 219–27
    see also art
Mughal civilization, 167, 181, 217, 229–38

Nagarahole National Park, 116, 141, 144
Nepal, 45, 82, 94, 140–41, 148, 281, 297, 312
Nick Ear, 90, 112, 120, 210
night vision, 31–32
Noon, 63–64, 127–29, 138–39, 146, 209–10, 284

Old Crooked Foot, 80–81
On the Origin of the Species (Darwin), 9–16

Padel, Ruth, 9, 10–16, 261–71
Padmini, 64, 69, 90, 111–12
pads, 26, 29
Pancatantra, 238, 242–247
pangolins, 133–34
Panna National Park, 68, 82, 85–86
Panthera, 1, 3, 12
    P. leo, 1
    P. onca, 1
    P. pardus, 1
    P. tigris, 1
    P. tigris altaica, 18, 20, 21, 88–89, 204, 296–97
    P. tigris amoyensis, 20
    P. tigris corbetti, 20, 81
    P. tigris sondaica, 18–19, 20, 21, 31
    P. tigris sumatrae, 20, 21, 281
    P. tigris tigris, 18–19, 20, 21, 88
    P. tigris vigata, 7, 18–19, 21
papillae, 39
parenting behaviors, 52–74
paws, 26, 120, 126
pelage, *see* fur
pets, tigers as, 214–15

pinnae, 33
poaching, 149, 162, 209, 284–88, 296–300, 303, 305–7, 310–11
    see also hunting
populations, tiger, 7, 9, 17–21, 68, 79, 82, 83, 85–86, 88–89, 93, 136
    see also territories; *specific populations*
porcupines, 137–38
Portier, Thierry Le, 206–7
portrait painting, 230–32
power, tigers as symbol of, 242–47
pregnancy, *see* birth
prey, 94–95, 102, 115, 133–44
    see also diet; hunting
Primorski Krai, Tiger Response Team of, 292–95
Proailurus, 3
Project Tiger, 279–81, 285–87, 309
protection, *see* conservation and protection
prusten, 35
Pseudaelurines, 3
pupils, 31
purring, *see* communications; sounds

Ramayana, 158–62
range *see* mobility and range
Ranthambhore National Park, 42–45, 49–79, 82–83, 90–93, 99–106, 111–13, 116–34, 137–43, 145–48, 208–12, 284–90, 298
Rapjut civilization, 238–47
Rathore, Fateh Singh, 76, 79, 141–43, 145–46, 209–11, 284, 288–89
religious symbolism, 166–67, 239
    see also cults
retina, 31
Rilke, Rainier Maria, 267
roaring, *see* communications; sounds
Rodin, Auguste, 267
Roman Empire, 7, 173–79
Roman Colosseum, 176, 178
Romanes, George, 10
Rousseau, Henri, 256–58, 267
royalty in art, 229–38
Russia, Russian Far East, 5, 6, 17, 18, 21, 45, 82, 88, 89, 108–9, 130, 307, 312–14
    see also Siberian Tiger Project; Siberian tigers

Salten, Felix, 265
sambar deer, 52, 58–59, 63–64, 119–120, 125, 126, 127–29, 130, 194
scent marking, 36–39, 102–9, 145
Schaller, George, 27, 41–42, 69–70, 92, 116, 126, 133, 311–14
Seidensticker, John, 94
self-medication, animals and, 27
Sellar, John M., 304–7
Sewall, Anna, 265
sexuality, tigers as symbol of, 265–67
Siberian Tiger Project, 106, 108–9, 138, 292–97
Siberian tigers, 17, 21, 82, 85, 108–9, 287, 292–97, 310

Singh, Billy Arjan, 76, 80–81, 92, 285, 288, 290
Singh, Kesri, 136–37
skeletal structure, 23–25, 121
skull, 24
smell, sense of, 24, 36–39, 102–6
social and communal behaviors, 34–35, 111–13, 122–25, 209–11
sounds, 1, 34–35, 99–102, 122, 145–48
    see also communications
South America, 7, 10–11
South China tigers (*Panthera tigris amoyensis*), 20, 310
spraying, 37–39, 102–9, 145
stalking, 122, 126
Stevens, Wallace, 268
stomach, 27
Stubbs, George, 67, 181, 248, 262–63, 267
subspecies, 17–21, 28–29, 81, 198, 280
Sumatra, 5, 17, 18–19, 21
Sumatran tigers (*Panthera tigris sumatrae*), 20, 21, 281
Sunda Island tigers (*Panthera tigris sondaica*), 18–19, 20, 21, 31
Sundarban tigers, 17, 93, 94–97
Sundarban East Wildlife Sanctuary, 94–97
Sunquist, Mel, 94, 116, 125
swimming, 93–95, 120–21, 129
symbolic uses of tigers, *see* art; literature; religious symbolism

tail, 29
"tangle," 11, 14, 15
tapetum lucidum ("bright carpet"), 31–32
taste, sense of, 39
teeth, 23, 24, 25, 39, 121–22
Temminck, Coenraad, 18
territories, 36–39, 76–97, 82–83, 102–9
Thapar, Romila, 153–67
Thapar, Valmik, 208–13, 284–85, 288–89
Tiger Haven, 80–81, 290
tigers
    anatomy of, 23–39
    climbing abilities of, 26, 65–66
    in Darwin's theory of evolution, 9–16
    family life of, 52–59, 69
    humans attacked by, 96, 273–77
    hunting of, *see* hunting
    and illness, 27
    infanticide among, 55
    life of, 41–149
    male, 55–59, 66, 85, 90, 92
    mating of, 29, 66, 145–49
    origins of, 1–22
    parenting behaviors of, 52–74
    as pets, 214–15
    populations of, 7, 9, 17–21, 82, 83, 85–86
    senses of, 31–39
    sounds made by, 1, 34–35, 99–102, 122, 145–48

stripes of, 3, 29
studies of, 1, 18, 19, 41–42, 297–98
subspecies of, 17–21
training of, 202–207, 250–51
    in zoos, 13, 45, 80, 149, 262
    see also specific species
tiger sticking, 183–186
tongue, 39
touch, sense of, 29–31
tracking, 46, 108, 114–15, 138, 144, 280–81
training, 202–207, 250–51
Turan tigers, *see* Caspian tigers
tylotrichs, *see* whiskers

Uncia, 1
urine spray, 36–37, 102–9, 145

Van Amburgh, Issac, 181, 250–51
Vedic corpus, 157–58
Verma, Archana, 229–47
vibrissae, *see* whiskers
vision, 31–32, 45
vocalization, *see* communications; sounds

Walsh, Edward J., 33, 34–35
Ward, Geoffrey C., 284–91
water, 17, 52, 55–56, 130, 312
Waugh, Evelyn, 265
West Asian tiger, *see* Caspian tigers
Western art, 248–58
whiskers, 29–31, 119–20, 127
white tigers, 28–29, 151–52, 186–87, 205
Wild Animals and Birds Protection Act (1951), 280
Wildlife Protection Act (1972), 280, 282
Wildlife Protection Society of India, 300–303
Williamson, Thomas, 125
World Conservation Union (IUCN), 94, 280
World Wildlife Fund, 289
Wright, Belinda, 300–303

Zolotaya Polyana, 292–95

Book designed by Jeremy Eberts

Cover designed by Anthony Hobbs

Two Brothers Press colophon designed by Alexi Hobbs

Type tuned by Richard Weston

The main text typeface is Minion, designed by Robert Slimbach.
The contributors' text typeface is MetaPlus, designed by Erik Spiekermann.

Production consultant: Katherine Rosenbloom

Scanning and pre-press: Professional Graphics Inc., Rockford, Illinois

Printed on acid-free Somerset paper by R. R. Donnelley & Sons, Roanoke, Virginia